Mob
Culture

Mob Culture

Hidden Histories of the American Gangster Film

Edited by Lee Grieveson,
Esther Sonnet, and Peter Stanfield

RUTGERS UNIVERSITY PRESS
NEW BRUNSWICK, NEW JERSEY

Library of Congress Cataloging-in-Publication Data

Mob culture : hidden histories of American gangster film / Edited by Lee Grieveson,
Esther Sonnet, and Peter Stanfield.
    p. cm.
    Includes bibliographical references and index.
    ISBN 0–8135–3556–5 (hardcover : alk. paper) — ISBN 0–8135–3557–3 (pbk. : alk. paper)
1. Gangster films—United States—History and criticism.   2. Sex role in motion pictures.
3. Race in motion pictures.   I. Grieveson, Lee, 1969–   II. Sonnet, Esther, 1961–   III. Stanfield,
Peter, 1958–
    PN1995.9.G3M63 2005
    791.43′6556—dc22

                                                                        2004011757

"Waddaya Lookin' At? Rereading the Gangster Film through *The Sopranos*," by Martha
Nochimson, was previously published in slightly different form in *Film Quarterly* 56, no. 2
(winter 2002–2003): 2–13.

Manufactured in the United States of America

Design by Karolina Harris

This book is dedicated to Agnes Rae, Frances,
Lauren, and Riley

Contents

CONTENTS

Acknowledgments

We wish to acknowledge the work of the staff at Rutgers University Press involved in the production of this book. We want to offer special thanks to our editor, Leslie Mitchner, for her consistently intelligent insights and vigorous support for this project, and to Joe Abbott for the superb job of copyediting. We'd also like to mark our appreciation of Vanessa Martin and Joan and Ron Sonnet for looking after our children while we worked on the introduction in Southsea during the summer of 2003.

Mob
Culture

Introduction

THE AMERICAN GANGSTER FILM has provided audiences with a rich narrative space for the articulation of shifting cultural desires and anxieties, yet academic and popular studies of the gangster film have consistently focused on a small number of well-known films, rarely moving far beyond *Little Caesar* (1931), *The Public Enemy* (1931), *Scarface: The Shame of a Nation* (1932), or *The Godfather* trilogy (1972, 1974, and 1990). This collection of new essays aims to restore complexity and vitality to the etiolated history of the Hollywood gangster film. Taking full account of the contemporary resurgence of interest in genre study, the collection places the cyclic production of gangster films both within the broad social, political, and cultural contexts that have, until now, been largely absent from ahistorical and archetypal accounts of the genre and within the discourses and practices of the American film industry.[1] The aim of this collection is to reinstate Hollywood gangster films within the material complexity of their production in order to illustrate how the gangster film has provided audiences with a rich narrative space for the articulation of shifting cultural desires and anxieties and to show how the gangster figure is produced differently within historical intersections of cultural identity and the shifting cultural figurations of criminality.

At midcentury, writing about the early 1930s, Robert Warshow argued that the "gangster movie is a story of enterprise and success ending in precipitate failure. Success is conceived as an increasing power to work injury, it belongs to the city, and it is of course a form of evil (though the gangster's death, presented usually as 'punishment,' is perceived simply as defeat)."[2] Working from two primary examples, *Little Caesar* and *Scarface*, Warshow identified a series of narrative, iconographical, and topographic features that would largely come to define the way the "classic" gangster film has subsequently been conceived. A "rise and fall" narrative of a disenfranchised

1

male, located in the city, whose modernity is signified through consumption of clothes, cars, apartments, and nightclubs, the gangster's illegitimate pursuit of wealth and success through violence parallels the goals of the American dream but subverts the normal avenues of its achievement. Lonely, melancholic, tragic, the gangster, Warshow argued, was the "man of the city" and embodied what he described as "the 'no' to that great American 'yes,'" challenging the optimism of "official" American culture: "In ways that we do not easily or willingly define, the gangster speaks for us, expressing that part of the American psyche which rejects the qualities and the demands of modern life, which rejects 'Americanism' itself."[3]

Warshow's provocative and important analysis has been enormously influential on subsequent scholarship on the gangster film. His coupling of the gangster film to a political agenda of popular resistance connected in particular with later work on the politics of the gangster film, emerging from the politicized context of post-1968 scholarship on cinema and continuing to the present day (for example, Jonathan Munby's recent characterization of gangster films as "a socially antagonistic cinematic tradition allied to lower-class and ethnically marginalized American interests in the 1930s").[4] Yet the weaknesses of Warshow's arguments have received less attention. The most immediate problem is the attempt to construct a generic archetype from an extremely limited set of examples and the concomitant formulation of a set of formal features that gangster films, to qualify *as* gangster films, must follow: "fixed dramatic patterns," associated with a rise-and-fall narrative that lays open the false promises of the work and success ethic underpinning the American Dream in the circular journey of the disenfranchised from the gutter and back again. The identification of the gangster film with the articulation of anxieties over the fate of the individual in the urban spaces of modernity, and in relation to economic instabilities, produces a highly restrictive definition. It reifies a particular cycle of films that were clearly closely connected to the particular socioeconomic context of the early 1930s; the articulation of a generic identity from a very small number of examples—two in Warshow's analysis, extended in others to include *The Public Enemy* (1931)—ignores the production of a vast number of other films about crime, gangs, and gangsters that do not fit with the restrictive definitions abstracted on the basis of the fact that those films fulfill preconceived ideas about the genre.[5] Jack Shadoian makes this problematic logic clear, beginning his analysis of the gangster genre with *Little Caesar, The Public Enemy,* and *Scarface* and observing simply that the gangster film "may be defined by what its succession of films continuously expresses, and films may be generically aligned by determining whether their structures contain the possibility of that expression."[6]

Yet the selection of two or three films from the early 1930s to stand in for the gangster film as a whole leads inevitably to a distortion of the history of the production of films about gangsters. One of the consequences of this critical practice is the effacement both of a diverse history that preceded the 1930s and the varied production in the early 1930s itself. As evidence of the kind of critical distortion this concentration on the early 1930s has effected, Shadoian's history of the gangster film admits only one example prior to the period. "The gangster/crime film," he writes, "took root as long ago as Griffith's *The Musketeers of Pig Alley* (1912) and then struggled in unfertilized soil through to the end of the twenties. It took a combination of the sound film, Capone's Chicago, Prohibition, and the mood of the depression to inaugurate the first distinct phase of the genre. It begins with *Little Caesar* (1930) and ends with *Scarface* (1932), and it is the source and example of all the phases that follow."[7] Likewise, Thomas Schatz in *Hollywood Genres* perpetuates the view that gangster films were an identifiable genre whose "narrative formula seemed to spring from nowhere in the 1930s."[8] Lee Grieveson's, Giorgio Bertellini's, and Peter Stanfield's essays in this collection belie this claim, recovering a number of films and cycles that articulate stories about gangsters existing in the silent era and showing both the longer history of gangster films and how the so-called classic paradigm was a variation on already common formulae. Even in histories with a much shorter reach, the idea of a stable origin for a generic model, typically the first two *Godfather* movies, is often propounded. These acts of forgetting or elision serve the need of the critic at the cost of the historical record.

In the formulation of an idea of genre based on exclusionary principles, work on the gangster film falsifies the realities of Hollywood's production practices and the contexts in which films were received. A typical example would be Tom Milne, who, writing about Rouben Mamoulian's *City Streets* (1931), which starred Gary Cooper and Sylvia Sidney as underworld lovers, states: "Although *City Streets* tells a typical gangster tale of bootlegging, hijacking and mob rule, it is not, strictly speaking, a gangster film. . . . The conventions of the gangster films, with their defiant heroes taking on the whole world . . . were yet to be defined, on the basis of *Little Caesar* (1930), by *Public Enemy* (1931) and *Scarface* (1932)."[9] Yet Milne's representative account simply ignores the films' connection to the production cycles of 1930/1931, which included *Doorway to Hell* (1930), *The Finger Points* (1931), *The Last Parade* (1931), *Quick Millions* (1931), and *The Secret Six* (1931), as well as *Little Caesar* and *The Public Enemy*. Milne's account evacuates the context in which *City Streets* was made and received: in place of the production and consumption context a canonical conception of film studies based on a select and limited number of films and evaluated on the basis of a few shared features of subject and structure is formulated.

Much of the critical work on the gangster genre simply ignores the great mass of films engaged with gangster narratives. "The theoretical clarity of film genre criticism," Rick Altman has observed, "is quite obviously challenged at every turn by the historical dimensions of film production and reception."[10] To overcome these critical limitations, recent work on genre and Hollywood has found it necessary to retrieve the specificity of production cycles and trends to better delineate the institutional and cultural contexts of production. Cycles are small, nuanced groupings of films that are not transhistorical and often only operate within one or two seasons of production, whereas trends are broad and inclusive categories made up of inter-connected cycles.

We have taken this distinction as a starting point for this collection of essays, which reexamines the gangster film beyond the restrictive focus on generic arche-types initiated by Warshow and followed by subsequent scholars. A number of the essays that follow focus on a short time span, sometimes a single production cycle. To give one example: in the same season that produced *Little Caesar* and *The Pub-lic Enemy*, five films identified by Esther Sonnet—*The Racketeer, Ladies Love Brutes, A Free Soul, Dance, Fools, Dance*, and *Corsair*—share little of the thematic concerns of the so-called classic gangster film. Sonnet shows that this cycle of films focuses on female sexual and class transgression and thus is considerably different from the thematic concerns identified by Warshow and others. In this cycle, Sonnet observes, films pivot on the capacity for female sexual desire to disrupt and destabilize class and ethnic boundaries. Within the restrictive definitions outlined by previous scholarship this cycle would have remained invisible, as, indeed, would have the centrality of women protagonists and the hitherto unacknowledged female address of a much larger range of gangster films.

Linked to the particular economic configuration of mainstream American film-making, the cycle that Sonnet identifies and examines is clearly marked by a hy-bridity that was characteristic of Hollywood production and its goals to maximize audience reach. Equally important for Sonnet are the connections of the films to social and political contexts, in this case around gender, sexuality, and class. Most of the essays in this collection also tie particular production cycles with broader pub-lic discourses. Together, the essays illustrate how discourses about crime, inflected in specific ways in relation to class, gender, and race, inform the history of the gang-ster film. In this sense the collection as a whole repositions gangster films as institu-tional and cultural history in precise relation to production cycles, situating films against transhistorical generic archetypes as rearticulations of public discourses.

The essays have been grouped into three thematic sections: "Producing Crime: Gangs and the Gangster Film" demonstrates that Hollywood gangster films are in-extricable from their contemporary contexts by examining their position with regard to discourses defining public criminality. The essays illustrate how different dis-courses have been used at various historical junctures to contain gangsters within explanatory models of criminality derived from schools of thought such as eugenics, sociology, and psychology. The second section, "Gangster Transgressions: Gender and Sexuality," retains the methodological emphasis on locating gangster films within social discourse but addresses their ideological importance as narratives that dramatize the boundaries of gender and sexuality. Through the destabilizing limi-nality of the gangster figure, the cycles explored in this section illustrate the promi-nence of discourses of masculinity and femininity and of homosexuality and hetero-sexuality in gangster films. The third section, "'Other' Gangsters: Race, Politics, and the Gangster Film," also examines issues of cultural identity by exploring film cycles that have explicitly articulated gangster criminality with notions of racial identity. Again, the gangster is shown to be a potent symbol open to various inflections of "otherness," which has historically been used as a racist tool but also as equivocal expression of racialized opposition.

Warshow contended that the gangster film created "its own field of reference" divorced from any basis in reality and, notably, he suggested from "the problem of crime."[11] Contra this claim, the essays in the first section examine the way in which the gangster film functioned at various moments as extensions of contemporary public discourses on crime. Lee Grieveson's essay reconsiders the silent era, so frequently dismissed in scholarship on the gangster film in the insistent focus on the early 1930s. He examines a number of cycles in the period between 1906 and 1929 in conjunction with public discourses about crime, in particular the nascent disciplines of criminology and sociology, positioning the films as complex meditations on, and social articulations of, the problem of crime, cities, and governance in early twentieth-century America. In doing so, he discerns two broad patterns: first, a cycle of films focusing on criminal underworlds and the necessity of surveillance and policing; second, a cycle, developing slightly later, focusing more clearly on the reformation of gangsters in connection with psychological, sociological, and environmentalist discourses about crime and city space.

Similarly, Richard Maltby's analysis of *The Public Enemy* precisely delineates the complex positioning of the film with relation to sociological discourses on the environmental causes of criminality associated principally with the so-called Chicago school, the work emanating from the Department of Sociology at the University of Chicago that was widely disseminated in public discourse in the 1930s. Maltby examines the relationship between social and cinematic discourses on delinquency and criminality, showing how the self-regulatory practices of the film industry intervened in the filmic articulation of stories about crime, gangs, and gangsters to counter the widely articulated criticism that movies contributed to criminal behavior. *The Public Enemy* was complexly positioned by the film industry, presented as a significant contribution to public debates but also as a form of harmless entertainment. A subsequent cycle of films about delinquent gangs, Maltby shows, was pushed more clearly toward the presentation of harmless entertainment, shifting the films' arguments away from environmentalist ones — connecting criminality or poor environmental conditions to bad individuals — and toward the solipsistic world prescribed by the Production Code.

One of the most overt examples of the connection between Hollywood and broader public discourses on crime is the cycles produced in direct response to senate inquiries on organized crime in 1950 and 1951, popularly known as the Kefauver hearings. In his essay Ronald Wilson invokes a historical conjuncture where the production of film cycles based on the hearings were shaped by the consolidation of a post–World War II liberal consensus, in part defined by anticommunism, and by major changes in the organization of the film industry.

The Paramount decrees of 1948—which challenged studio control of the industry by forcing the divorce of film production from exhibition—resulted in the rise of independent production companies more readily able to provide the topical and "adult" fare required to counteract the increasing threat to cinema attendance from family-oriented television experienced in this period. Wilson demonstrates how these independent companies exploited the Kefauver hearings for material on organized crime and its "invisible" control of American life to project the conception of the nation as an "imagined community" defined by enforced "consensus" around normative liberalism.

The essays in the following section point toward the unacknowledged centrality of gender and sexuality to the ideological provenance of the gangster film, marking a shift in emphasis from the gangster film's invocation of public discourses of criminality to the deployment of the gangster in the "private" domains of gender, sexuality, and the boundaries of normative heterosexuality. In an essay on the "retro" pastiche gangster film cycle of the 1990s, Sonnet and Stanfield suggest that the "replaying" of the 1930s gangster films operates on the covert terrain of sexual politics, where nostalgic invocation of period setting is ideally placed to articulate fears and pleasures in the recuperation of "lost" gender certainties. A vehicle for retrogressive, antifeminist, and hypermasculinized ideologies, the retro gangster cycle constructs social worlds predicated on the absence of women and made meaningful only by the homosocial bonds formed by men. Demonstrating fears over the loss of masculine control, the retro cycle offers representations of hegemonic masculinity overly marked as "hysterical" in which meaningful distinctions between homosocial, homosexual, and violent impulses are collapsed.

The process by which recent male gangster protagonists come to be characterized by a "profound psychologization" and even "pathologization" is indeed a properly historical one. Gaylyn Studlar's examination of three key films from 1941 and 1942 and the regulatory discourses surrounding them reveals the intricacies of Hollywood's negotiation of homoeroticism within gangster-derived depictions of masculinity as America entered World War II. Drawing on literary "hard-boiled" source texts and performing close readings of the specific filmic/textual patterns within *The Maltese Falcon* (1941), *Johnny Eager* (1941), and *The Glass Key* (1942), Studlar argues that these films were partly framed by homophobic psychoanalytic discourse but went beyond that to explore the sexual complexity of the bond forged by men within a homosocial underworld associated with gangsterism. The gangster's overt masculinity and proximity to violence, she contends, imports an erotic dimension to male-to-male relationships that undermines conventional boundaries held to separate homosocial friendships from homosexual desires within patriarchal masculinity and destabilizes the fragile boundaries between the normative and perverse.

In her essay on the HBO cable television series *The Sopranos*, Martha Nochimson demonstrates how crucial the gangster film's historical trajectory toward "pathologization" is for understanding contemporary registrations of the gangster figure. In her reading of the series, Nochimson identifies *The Sopranos'* reliance on dense intertextual references to cinema's gangster precursors as symptomatic of the series' mediation on the gangster film's ideological engagement with gender and identity. Perceiving the gangster film as "muscularized melodrama," Nochimson illustrates how the contemporary gangster figure makes explicit the genre's previously subtextual displacement of masculinity onto the terrain of violence. Consciously undermining the psychical self-sufficiency of heterosexual masculinity putatively represented in the gangster film by its foregrounding of therapeutic psychoanalysis, the series illustrates the continued utility of the gangster figure for registering profound social, sexual, and psychical uncertainties around the meaning and operation of a masculine adult self. In this sense the figure of Tony Soprano illustrates fin de siècle anxieties in constructing a male self within contradictory discourses of self, family, sexuality, emotion, and social connectedness, one in which violence, virility, and social agency are countermanded by personal vulnerability.

If the gangster figure is generally marked by a protean capacity for perverting psychosexual normalcy, this perversion is rendered even more "monstrous" when the outlaw figure is female (as the example of Tony Soprano's murderous mother would suggest). Mary Strunk explores this subject in her study of the cinematic incarnations of the Ma Barker figure. Strunk examines four versions of the legend surrounding the figure of Ma Barker, allegedly leader of a family gang, to assess its allegorical utility for reflecting changing discourses on motherhood, female sexuality, and domestic responsibility. For Strunk, *Queen of the Mob* (1940), *Guns Don't Argue* (1957), *Ma Barker's Killer Brood* (1960), and *Bloody Mama* (1970) articulate various prevailing conceptions of "unnatural" female behavior and encapsulate wider concerns for the weakening of patriarchal families that are expressed through the "grotesque" figure of the sexualized older woman as head of the family unit. She suggests that these variations on the story of Ma Barker and her gangster sons serve as negative social barometers by which women's deviant behavior is historically defined and normative behavior reinscribed.

Esther Sonnet's essay on the early 1930s similarly engages with the ways in which the public discourses of criminality are profoundly gendered by examining how, for women, criminality as a violation of the formal apparatus of law enforcement is transposed to violations of the symbolic laws of patriarchal heterosexuality. As an emblem of overwhelming, dangerous, and seductive male power, the cinematic gangster was utilized to examine the boundaries between illicit sexual desire and social acceptability during a period of major social change for women. Retrieving a "lost" history of Hollywood films that positioned the gangster as object of female desire, she argues that the plot structures of romance and melodrama offered vicarious spectatorial pleasures for female audiences through their identification with women in close proximity to the criminal male. Sonnet contends that the female-addressed early 1930s cycles—in which an upper-class woman is drawn into an erotic relationship with a low-class gangster male—provided imaginative scenarios in which women actively participated in dramas of illicitness and, despite conventionally moral plot closures, staged pleasurable transgressions of conventional heterosexual decorum.

Overall, the essays by Sonnet, Studlar, Nochimson, Strunk, and Sonnet and Stanfield demonstrate that gangster films have articulated criminality in conjunction with ideas about gender and sexuality, insistently connecting individual gender and sexual transgressions to public criminality. In a similar vein essays by Bertellini, Stanfield, and Munby show how crucial the articulation of discourses of criminality in relation to race have been in America and how this discourse has played into critical debates about national self-image. In his essay Bertellini explores turn-of-the-twentieth-century U.S. racial culture, showing how Italians were racialized subjects and how this racialization was frequently connected to ideas about law, crime, and dissonance. Bertellini observes that early gangster narratives positioned Italians as "othered" racial types who threatened social order. However, by the teens and 1920s racial discourse became more insistently focused on African Americans, and gangster narratives began to position the central Italian character as a figure of emotional allegiance in his challenge to the native capitalist and moral ethos. As Bertellini makes clear, the history of the gangster film is inseparable from the larger cultural dynamic germane to American racial culture.

In Stanfield's first essay in this section, "'American as Chop Suey,'" he considers the articulation of the "tongs" and Chinatown as a symbolic space where issues of American identity can be dramatized. He shows how criminality was frequently connected to racial "otherness," positioning Chinatown in particular as an alien criminal culture infecting the host culture, displacing concerns about law and order onto the symbolic space of racial difference and identity. In America's racially polyglot cities Chinatown functions in a wide body of films as an imaginary space where racial and ethnic difference can be policed, containing the mongrel gangland within the alien yet, paradoxically, domestic borders of Chinatown. Although Chinatown and the tongs may appear marginal to the concerns of the majority of the films within any given cycle, their recurrence within and across cycles from the beginnings of American film history to contemporary filmmaking suggests their importance to the production of fictional American ganglands.

In contrast, the presence of black gangsters in American cinema history is characterized by discrete moments of visibility rather than recurrence. Jonathan Munby examines the first cycle of films to deal exclusively with the figure of the black gangster, in particular the films made by black filmmakers Oscar Micheaux and Ralph Cooper in the 1930s. He examines the economic conditions of production and argues that the films are typified by their reliance on formulaic fictional strategies, again connecting race to criminality but also, at least partially, reworking these strategies to offer counterhegemonic and antiessentialist black self-representation and a black view on American possibility. Munby considers this cycle of films seminal in defining a black American cinematic experience as both oppressive and enfranchising.

In his essay "Walking the Streets" Stanfield turns to the second moment when black filmmakers produced a significant number of films, the 1970s cycle often labeled "blaxploitation," arguing that the counterhegemonic strategy is dramatized in the fictional confrontation between black urban gangsters and their rivals for control of the streets, the Mafia. This essay is framed by a concern both for the historical specificity of discourses about urban space and demographic changes in the audience for Hollywood's productions, in particular the identification of a newly constituted black urban audience. Blaxploitation films, while they register black experience and values, are limited to a world exclusively defined by the gangster film. Resisting the tendency to attribute authenticity to these films' representation of black urban experience, Stanfield contends that these tales of the city are not a kind of documentary on the social realities of the time. Rather, they are melodramatic excursions into a world that offers an extended play on escape and confinement. Blaxploitation's urban crime films share certain thematic, narratological, and formal properties with the cycle identified by Munby and the post-1980s "'hood" and "gangsta" cycles, yet they are also uniquely bound to their moment of production.

Collectively, the essays in this book confirm that gangster films are not simply narratives for telling the stories of ahistorical unidimensional criminal figures or gangs but sites of instability of wider cultural resonance in which the cultural figuration of crime is inseparable from the articulation of ideas about ethnicity, sexuality, gender, class, and race. Clearly this book does not, and could not, represent a comprehensive view of American gangster films. We have attempted to engage with gangster films in the immediacy of their various production and consumption contexts and to offer a contribution to the cultural analysis of discourses on crime and criminality. In doing so we hope to provoke further research about the history of gangster films and the continued vitality of the mediated gangster.

Notes

1. For example, Nick Browne, ed., *Reconfiguring Film Genres* (Berkeley: University of California Press, 1998); Rick Altman, *Film/Genre* (London: British Film Institute, 1999); Steve Neale, *Genre and Hollywood* (London: Routledge 2000); Peter Stanfield, *Hollywood, Westerns, and the 1930s: The Lost Trail* (Exeter: University of Exeter Press, 2001).

2. Robert Warshow, "Movie Chronicle: The Westerner" (1954), in *The Immediate Experience: Movies, Comics, Theatre, and Other Aspects of Popular Culture* (Cambridge, Mass.: Harvard University Press, 2001), 105–106.

3. Robert Warshow, "The Gangster as Tragic Hero" (1948), in *The Immediate Experience: Movies, Comics, Theatre, and Other Aspects of Popular Culture* (Cambridge, Mass.: Harvard University Press, 2001), 100.

4. Jonathan Munby, *Public Enemies, Public Heroes: Screening the Gangster from "Little Caesar" to "Touch of Evil"* (Chicago: University of Chicago Press, 1999), 10. For other work located in this intellectual context see, in particular, Colin McArthur, *Underworld U.S.A.* (London: Secker and Warburg, 1972); Jack Shadoian, *Dreams and Dead Ends: The American Gangster/Crime Film* (Cambridge, Mass.: MIT Press, 1977); Eugene Rosow, *Born to Lose: The Gangster Film in America* (New York: Oxford University Press, 1978). Warshow's connection to a postwar liberal consensus clearly shaped his work on the gangster film and popular culture, as Michael Denning has argued; the reuse of his work for those

seeking to articulate the political potential of popular genre cinema emerging in the post-1968 consolidation of academic film studies is intriguing. Michael Denning, *The Cultural Front: The Laboring of American Culture in the Twentieth Century* (London: Verso, 1996), 107, 111–116.

5. Warshow did not include *The Public Enemy* in his analysis, no doubt because it does not fit the narrative pattern of "rise and fall" that defines the quintessential gangster. Richard Maltby's essay in this collection notes how the identification of *The Public Enemy* with *Little Caesar* and *Scarface* has encouraged a reading of its plot as if it portrayed the rise and fall of a commercialized gangster, as opposed to the relatively mundane criminal activities of the central characters.

6. Shadoian, *Dreams and Dead Ends*, 3.

7. Ibid., 15.

8. Thomas Schatz, *Hollywood Genres* (New York: Random House, 1981), 81.

9. Tom Milne, *Rouben Mamoulian* (London: Thames and Hudson, 1969), 29.

10. Altman, *Film/Genre*, 16.

11. Warshow, "The Gangster as Tragic Hero," 100.

One
Producing Crime

Gangs and the Gangster Film

Gangsters and Governance in the Silent Era

Lee Grieveson

TWO FILMS RELEASED ONE AFTER THE OTHER by American Mutoscope and Biograph in early 1906 claimed to tell stories that were based on real-life confrontations between police and criminal gangs. Publicity for *The Silver Wedding* (1906) asserted that it was "based on a recent New York police round up."[1] In the film a gathering of "members of the under world" precedes a burglary of "costly gifts" from a silver wedding anniversary party and the subsequent pursuit of "the gang of thieves" by the police. The final scene continues the pursuit in "one of the huge trunk-line sewers of the big city," figuratively associating criminality with a subterranean network operating below the surfaces of civil society.[2] Threatening private property in the wealthy upper world, the gang transgresses spatial and class boundaries and "contaminates" the private sphere via the sewer as conduit between inside and outside. Yet the underworld gang is caught and "dragged away" at the close by the police, as the film ends appropriately enough with the gangsters being expelled from the sewer and the body politic and with the reestablishment of a social and governmental order figured as a cleansing or sanitizing of the city.

Later the same month American Mutoscope and Biograph released *The Black Hand* (1906), telling another story about "underworld" criminal gangs that (implicitly at least) connected the contamination of the social body to immigration and racial difference.[3] A title proclaims at the outset that the film was "a true story of a recent occurrence in the Italian quarter of New York City." Following this, a drunken criminal gang sends a "typical 'black hand'" ransom note to a butcher ("Beware! We are desperut!") before kidnapping his daughter in broad daylight on a snowy street in what the bulletin advertising the film describes as "the Italian quarter, with all the typical surroundings of the actual occurrence."[4] While the gang members gamble and drink, the parents contact the police, who set a trap

13

preceded in the film with the title: "A clever arrest actually as made by New York detectives." Hiding in the cold storage at the butcher's, the police emerge and capture one of the gang members as he seeks to collect the ransom. At the end the police raid the gang's hideout, and the daughter is reunited with her parents. As in *The Silver Wedding*, narrative order and the conversion of document into diegesis are connected to the reestablishment of a moral order carried through the policing of criminality. Together the films articulate a threat to a sociality figured in terms of domesticity, property, and, in the case of *The Black Hand*, respectable whiteness that is ultimately negated by the police's ability to decipher the networks of the city and embody the power of the state.

Linked simply in the production and release schedules of American Mutoscope and Biograph, these two films about urban criminality were also connected by the claims that they were "based on" real-life criminal events that were carried through a corresponding realist aesthetic visible in the selective use of location shooting ("a true story," "typical surroundings of the actual occurrence," "the interior of the sewer"). Ostensibly re-presenting pages from police records or from newspapers, the two films make particularly clear the permeable border between realist images and stories about crime, gangs and gangsters, and the wider discourses circulating about urban crime around the turn of the century. Visible most clearly in sensational newspaper and popular magazine accounts of "crime waves" and in disciplinary developments within the social sciences — notably the emergence of variants of criminology and sociology around the turn of the century — these discourses positioned criminals and criminal gangs as central to the urban gesellschaft seemingly characteristic of the new social and economic forces of capitalist modernity. Typically, the city as a space for the concentration of diverse transient and anonymous populations, the housing of what came to be called "the dangerous classes," and of class, religious, and racial heterogeneity and division was regarded as productive of the breakdown of inherited cultures and so of a social disorder and moral decay commonly figured in terms of an organized criminality shadowing civil society.[5] The "social problem is fundamentally a city problem," wrote sociologist Robert Ezra Park, having previously defined social problems as ultimately always "problems of social control," that is, of controlling conduct in accord with the needs of society.[6] Widespread rhetoric on the city as "tainted spots in the body politic" and the social dangers of criminality in what historians have called the "Progressive Era" in the early years of the twentieth century explicitly aimed to shape, manage and regulate the conduct of persons and of an urban mass;[7] these reflections were "governmental," rather than simply theoretical, because of their connection to practical goals, procedures, and institutions for the management of "anti-social practices," for the production of sociality, and for the establishment of modern state practices.[8]

Located in the context of governmental reflections on the social problems of cities and the social dangers of criminality, *The Silver Wedding*, *The Black Hand*, and many other films across the silent era can be taken to mark an extension of public discourse on criminality and the city and to figure as complex meditations on, and social articulations of, the problems of crime, cities, sociality, and governance as central problems of modernity in early twentieth-century America. In what follows, then, I focus on a series of films about crime and urban gangs from 1906 to the late 1920s that have not been subjected to the detailed critical attention hitherto reserved for a small number of early 1930s films to essay one aspect of the cultural articulation of modern experience.[9] I am particularly interested in situating the representational strategies and cultural work of these films in relation to other public discourses on crime and the city, examining the points of intersection within a body of knowledge, and thus considering in particular the positioning of the films in relation to the wider circuits of knowledge and power and the pervasive culture of social discipline in early twentieth-century America.[10] Two broad trends are important here: first, a cycle of films focusing on criminal underworlds and the necessity of surveillance and policing (as in the examples of *The Silver Wedding* and *The Black Hand*, alongside others); second, a cycle developing slightly later and focusing more clearly on the reformation of gangsters in connection with psychological, sociological, and environmentalist discourses about crime and city space. What follows begins to sketch out this material, offering a preliminary overview of the diversity of films about crime, gangs, and gangsters and concomitant discourses about crime and the city from 1906 until the late 1920s. Overall, the essay seeks to reconsider and recast the history of the gangster film beyond the restrictive context of Prohibition and the early 1930s economic depression, tracing out the beginnings of anxieties about criminal gangs in the turn-of-the-century period and the cultural refraction of that anxiety as episodes in the imagination of the governance of a mass public that predates — and indeed prepares the ground for — Prohibition and other practices of discipline and social control.[11]

Late nineteenth-century accounts of city life in urban guides, muckraking journalism, visual culture, and realist literature frequently articulated a sense of a criminal underworld threatening civil society, in the process mapping out a moral topography of urban spaces and a will to knowledge through the encounter with and mastery of the disorderly, the dark, and the hidden.[12] In *Underground, or Life Below the Surface; Incidents and Accidents beyond the Light of Day*, for example, journalist Thomas Knox delineated the labyrinthine underground of cities in various senses, covering literal spaces — sewers, mines, railroads, dive bars — alongside a metaphoric sense of how underground spaces in large cities were inhabited by criminals like "rats" who threaten moral order in "undermining the works and lives of others."[13] Knox's sense of a threatening criminal underground was connected to racial difference in descriptions of dive bars with "colored servants," with women wearing "oriental costume," and of a palpably disconcerting visit to a tenement in San Francisco's Chinatown as a manifestation of modernity's dark underbelly: "we could see nothing round us for the moment, but the stench was almost overpowering, and the chattering, which was going on in all directions, convinced us that we

were in a locality literally swarming with the lowest class of the Mongolian populations."[14] Outside or "pathological spaces," in architectural theorist Anthony Vidler's
term, mark out the limits of social order.[15] Linking class and racial difference,
Knox's account of the threatening underworld articulated a social Darwinist sense
of species difference in framing the subterranean criminality undermining the
modern metropolis.[16]

Likewise, in the later influential *Darkness and Daylight, or Lights and Shadows
of New York Life*, Knox, together with reformer Helen Campbell and former police
chief Thomas Byrnes, invoked Dante in presenting a voyeuristic account of the
"dark" regions of the criminal underworld city that connected these to specific
locations—Hell's Kitchen, the Bowery, boardinghouse regions—and again to
racially coded spaces in accounts of Chinatown and of the Italian quarter of the
city.[17] Transient populations in anonymous cities presented problems of moral and
civil order, the authors suggested, noting that the figures for how many people
lodged nightly "show what a vast army of idle, vicious, and impecunious people
maintain an existence in the great city." [18] Tenements, in particular, were widely regarded as "training schools of vice and crime," leading to the formation of criminal
gangs:[19] "The various 'gangs' that have infested the city and given the police force
no end of trouble for many years are found in the densely populated districts. The
tenement-houses afford them excellent hiding places and from them gangs are
recruited. . . . It is deemed commendable by these gangs to assault the police, to mo-
lest and rob citizens, to fight, steal and murder." [20] Tenements and gangs, connected
to the massing of "dangerous classes," undermine social order. Together, the two
books, alongside myriad other accounts of the city and criminality, imagined a fearful subterranean space threatening a social order constituted in class and racial
terms.[21] It was in this context that the very term *underworld* emerged and entered
common currency around the turn of the century,[22] associated with this sense of a
threatening uncivil space pulsing beneath the surface of the city as the precise "negative" of "the dream of transparency" and "visibility" characteristic of modernity.[23]

Visual culture was particularly important in delineating this dark and threatening space, initially via the proliferation of photographically based visual culture in
the mass press and in other factual accounts of the city like *How the Other Half
Lives* and, indeed, *Darkness and Daylight*.[24] Photographers like Jacob Riis had
explored the city, the preface to *Darkness and Daylight* claimed, seeking "living
material . . . in underground resorts and stale beer dives, in haunts of criminals and
training schools of crimes and nooks and corners known only to the police." [25] Once
again realism was crucial. "Nothing is lacking," the authors claimed, "but the actual
movement of the persons presented." [26] Later, *The Silver Wedding, The Black Hand*,
and other films labeled by *Variety* as simply "underworld" would remedy this, presenting, in *The Silver Wedding*, "under world" gangs threatening property, wealth,
and the family as a symbol of class affiliation and differentiation and, in *The Black
Hand*, connecting this threat to the racially coded space of the Italian quarter.[27]

The Musketeers of Pig Alley (Biograph, 1912), telling a story about criminal gangs in the Lower East Side of Manhattan, begins with a subtitle reading "New York's Other Side," so clearly alluding to Riis's well-known book.

Voyeurism aside, the crucial impetus behind the countless investigations of the city's underworld in the turn-of-the-century period was principally about reformation and governance. "Let us know the modern city in its weakness and wickedness," wrote settlement house worker Jane Addams, "and then seek to rectify and purify it."[28] Vice surveys, tenement house commissions, and the establishment of settlement houses to ameliorate urban conditions were important here.[29] Rational planning of city space was crucial also, establishing what Vidler calls "hygienic space" through the opening of cities to circulation to establish what Jeremy Bentham termed "universal transparency."[30]

Criminal gangs infested this space, negating transparency, as they do by inhabiting the sewer in *The Silver Wedding*. Indeed, this image is an important one, obliquely reflecting on the proliferation of discourses on sewers in the period that commented on the establishment of an underground space and world and that positioned them as "elemental" to the infrastructure of the modern city, crucial to the circulation of matter that underpinned the city and that guaranteed health.[31] Planning and building sewer systems in large cities in the latter part of the nineteenth century was an important part of the enactment of an expanding urban police power and governmental rationality in a merging of public and private interest predicated on the establishment of the physical and, it was thus imagined, moral health of the urban populace.[32] In this, Thomas Osborne has argued, drains and sewers functioned "as the material embodiments of an essentially political division between public and private spheres," manifesting a "strategy of indirect government; that is, of inducing cleanliness and hence good moral habits."[33] For many the correct circulation of social waste was critical to the management of urban space and populations. Indeed, if we conceive modernity more generally as defined by "techniques of circulation," as Vidler, Wolfgang Schivelbusch, and Tom Gunning, for example, do, then the sewer and the treatment of refuse was a critical, indeed, elemental aspect of this.[34]

Yet in *The Silver Wedding* this circulation is challenged, as the sewer is initially blocked by the criminal gang, connected now to the waste products of social order and to the parasitical vermin who inhabit the sewers.[35] Rather than being an effective meshing of public and private order, the sewer is transformed by the gang into a structure that directly threatens property and contaminates domesticity (the silver wedding party as the very celebration of domesticity, the space of morality and spiritual culture). The sewer connects the criminality of the city to the home as an example of the threatening "webbed social life" characteristic for many of city life.[36] A criminal underclass and underworld erupts into middle-class society in an image that encapsulates what muckraking journalist George Kibbe Turner described the following year as "the irruption of the low-class criminal from the territory of cheap dissipation."[37] Turner's fear about the connectedness of "low-class" criminality with middle-class existence in the city was widespread. Furthermore, in temporarily blocking the sewer as a space of moral and public order, the gang threatens the circulatory system of modernity. The conclusion of the film, the expulsion of the gang from the sewer and the body politic, rectifies this, though, in the process literally transcribing the image of criminals and criminal gangs as what G. Frank Lydston described in his 1904 book *The Diseases of Society* as "simply excrementitious matter" that should "be placed beyond the possibility of its contaminating the social body."[38]

Lydston's arguments in *The Diseases of Society* were predicated on the connection of criminality to disease and to social pathology, so effectively correlating bodily health to social "health" in a way that was consistent with widespread ideas about "degeneration."[39] His fairly typical account of criminality as a social pathology was informed in particular by criminal anthropology, the dominant conception of criminality current in the United States around the turn of the century. Taking a lead in part from the Italian scholar Cesar Lombroso's influential work in the late nineteenth century, criminal anthropologists believed that criminality had a biological basis and was literally marked on the body of criminals via pathological stigmata (for example, particular skull, jaw, or ear shapes).[40] Lombroso had argued that most crime resulted from atavism. The criminal, he wrote, was "an atavistic being who reproduces in his person the ferocious instincts of primitive humanity and the inferior animals."[41]

Turn-of-the-century criminology in the United States reformulated this notion of atavism slightly in hereditarian terms, arguing that criminality was connected to "racial stock." In this, criminology merged with the doctrine of eugenics, the "science" of improving stock, which was widely articulated in the United States in the early years of the twentieth century in conjunction with anxieties about immigration and the maintenance of racial hierarchies.[42] What has been called "eugenic criminology" thus argued that a subterranean criminal class was connected to "inferior racial stock" that presented a threat to white social order.[43] W. Duncan McKim, in *Heredity and Human Progress*, for example, began by referencing Francis Galton's influential work on eugenics in arguing that criminality had a hereditary basis and that the criminal is a "'gangrenous member to be cut away forever from the social body.'"[44] In so arguing, McKim, and other American criminal anthropologists like Arthur MacDonald and August Drahms, invoked notions of eugenic atavism to argue that criminality was inextricably linked to racial identities.[45]

To take one prominent example: Italians were regarded as a racial other, characterized by a hyperemotionality and a propensity to violence that placed them outside the realm of the American polity, as ostensibly "unfit," from a racial standpoint, to adapt to and assimilate within mainstream American society. Leading American eugenicist Charles P. Davenport, in his 1911 book *Heredity in Relation to Eugenics*, argued that immigrants from southeastern Europe would make the country's population "darker in pigmentation, smaller in stature, more mercurial . . . more given to crimes of larceny, kidnapping, assault, murder, rape, and sex-immorality."[46] Italian communities in cities were widely regarded as presenting a racial and civic dissonance within American society. Academic discourse spread outward, informing government reports—a 1911 report on immigration described Sicilians as "excitable, superstitious, and revengeful"—and popular journalistic accounts of Italians as manifesting a "highly excitable and emotional disposition" and as excelling at kidnapping, blackmailing, and crimes of violence.[47]

In this context the focus on so-called black-hand gangs, that is, Italian criminal gangs, which emerged in the early years of the twentieth century, was inevitably articulated in conjunction with nativist rhetoric. Kidnapping was central here. Rhetoric on black-hand gangs as kidnappers presented a frightening image of urban gangs threatening the sanctity of the family and the ideals of domesticity that were frequently articulated as central to the white middle-class mainstream in contradistinction to other class and racial groups.[48] Urban criminality threatened the destruction of the family and of class and racial hierarchies. Likewise, black-hand gangs threatened to control city space, commentators argued, rendering the inner city a dangerous and foreign zone. In a cartoon originally published in the *Chicago Herald* in 1915, for example, Chicago's "Little Italy" is literally in the grip of a black hand.[49] Widely articulated anxieties about the criminal activities of black-hand gangs thus crystallized many of the concerns about criminality, racial difference, and the control of urban space central to the proliferation of accounts of crime and the city. Later accounts of the Mafia would develop this.[50]

To return to the film *The Black Hand* in this context is instructive, for the cultural figuration of Italian criminality in the film was consistent with eugenic criminology and the public rhetoric on black-hand gangs. Linguistically incompetent ("Beware! We are desperut!"), the gang presents the menace of racial dissonance marked by an emotional excess and "ill-regulated desires" characterized by drunkenness and a brutality that nearly results in the beating of the kidnapped daughter.[51] Racially coded criminality poses a direct threat to domesticity. Overt claims to realism in the film and in the surrounding publicity discourse call attention to the location of "the Italian quarter," positioned as a space of racial dissonance as it is in other guides to the urban underworld and in rhetoric on the city. In this sense the film is consistent with the voyeuristic and disciplinary imperatives of other efforts to shine light on the moral darkness of criminality in the city with the aim ultimately of representing the successful policing of domesticity and city space via the expulsion of the racialized criminal gang.

Late in 1906 the *New York Times*, in fact, called for a special police force to combat Italian delinquency, and in 1908 Italian-born Lieutenant Joseph Petrosino was nominated head of the special squad.[52] In January 1909 Kalem released *The Detectives of the Italian Bureau*. In the film the black-hand gang kidnaps a young girl, although she manages to escape and alert the detectives of the Italian bureau, who arrest the gang. Later *The Adventure of Lieutenant Petrosino* (Feature Photoplay Co., 1912) made, trade journal *Moving Picture World* noted, "the alleged machinations of the so-called Black Hand Society its most prominent feature and there are many blood-curdling scenes in showing the workings of that mysterious band of the underworld."[53] A cycle of black-hand films followed, including *The Black Hand* (Éclair, 1912), *The Black Hand* (Kalem, 1913), *Black Hand Conspiracy* (Appollo, 1914), *The Black Hand* (Royal, 1914), and *The Last of the Mafia* (Neutral, 1915), telling a thinly veiled account of Petrosino's work and his murder by a criminal gang.[54] Later, *Poor Little Peppina* (Famous Players–Mary Pickford Co., 1916) begins with a backstory of how Peppina was kidnapped by the Black Hand and reared in Italy before returning to America and finding her real parents. Most impressive in the film, *Moving Picture World* observed, was the "selection of types," notably those of Italians.[55] Typology connects to eugenics in this sense, leading to the selection of actors for criminal roles that was informed by eugenic ideas about physical appearance.

Lydston's account in *The Diseases of Society*, and eugenic criminology more generally, was consistent with a belief in the necessity of strengthening state response to crime. The rhetoric of criminal anthropologists legitimized a wide variety of technologies of repression and control, evidenced by the creation of the special police force led by Petrosino and by new police methods of identification associated with anthropometric measurements, photographing criminals, and, later, with fingerprinting and the beginning of a national crime files system as what the *National Police Magazine* called a "library of crime."[56] The efforts to establish an elaborate social machinery to identify and manage criminals stands as a concrete example of the new forms of surveillance characteristic of modernity that formed a capillary network through which power was distributed throughout society, rendering its domains constantly visible to the gaze of government.[57]

To identify criminals was, sociologist Edward Ross wrote, "a sanitary measure demanded in the interest of public health."[58] Once identified, the criminal should be eliminated from the social body via death or incarceration.[59] W. Duncan McKim argued that "the ineradicability of inborn tendenc[ies]" meant that "[w]e may in some measure restrain, but we can never reform" the criminal.[60] McKim and other criminal anthropologists argued that the correct treatment of those archaic groups who were unable to keep up with the proper pace of evolution and who threatened social order was not reform but elimination. For many, this process of elimination and social defense could be strengthened by practices of sterilization among those "unfit" for citizenship. Once again, discourse about race, criminality, and citizenship had material effects when legislation was passed in sixteen states between 1907 and 1917 giving states the power to compel the sterilization of habitual or confirmed criminals.[61]

Legislation dealing with so-called white slave gangs is instructive in relation to the elaboration of an intensified surveillance of racial others and urban space. Indeed, the white slavery scare marks one of the central conceptions of organized criminal activity in the early years of the twentieth century aside from that of the Black Hand or tongs (on tongs see Peter Stanfield in this volume). Rhetoric on the forced abduction of white women into prostitution by criminal gangs proliferated widely in the United States from around 1907.[62] Various commentators suggested that white slave gangs ran elaborate networks beneath the surface of society, isolating and abducting vulnerable women and frequently transferring them from city to city. Indeed, the city, as what George Kibbe Turner called "the marketplace of dissipation," was frequently singled out for commentary in the proliferation of discourse on white slavery, rendered as a dangerous space characterized by criminal activity and sexual perversity.[63] Women were warned to avoid coming to the big city.[64] White slave gangs were also consistently linked to particular immigrant groups. Accounts of white slave gangs frequently associated them with southern European immigrants and Jewish groups, tying in with the nativist and anti-Semitic rhetoric that informed eugenics and eugenic criminology. It was, declared Turner, "the Jewish dealer in women . . . who has vitiated, more than any other single agency, the moral life of the great cities of America in the past ten years."[65] Jean Turner Zimmerman argued similarly, in *America's Black Traffic in White Girls*, that white slavery is "carried on and exploited by a foaming pack of foreign hellhounds . . . the moral and civic degenerates of the French, Italian, Syrian, Jewish or Chinese races. . . . [A]n American or Englishman conducting such a business is almost entirely unknown."[66] Together, accounts of black-hand and white slave gangs connected criminality directly to immigration and racial difference and articulated a growing sense of organized crime in cities shadowing civil society.

Local, national, and international concerns about white slavery led to an international conference in 1902 and to the subsequent formulation of a treaty in 1904 calling for the "supervision . . . [of] stations, ports of embarkation," and international journeys to act against "the traffic in women" and to set in place an international policing of space and mobility.[67] The United States was not able to fully ratify the treaty with the other nations because of a lack of a national police force but signed in principle in 1905. Shortly thereafter, a national policing force was established after President Theodore Roosevelt and Attorney General Charles Bonaparte defied the wishes of Congress and their concerns about the expansion of national police power to create the Bureau of Investigation in June 1908.[68] Later the same month, Roosevelt proclaimed the 1904 treaty in effect, to be policed by the Bureau of Investigation.[69] The transnational surveillance of borders set in play by the 1902 conference and 1904 treaty was central to the establishment of a national policing institution, then, as the regulation of gang-related criminality and racial hierarchies fed directly into the construction of a state-controlled agency of surveillance that would fix, arrest, or regulate movement and bring order to society in part through an ordered knowledge of its component populations and population movement. In this respect the Bureau of Investigation emerged as a central component of the new technologies of governance and social control important to the managing of modernity. Later, the Bureau of Investigation and the Federal Bureau of Investigation, as it was renamed in 1935, would play a well-publicized role in combating criminal gangs.

Traffic in Souls (Universal, 1913), a film about white slavery, offers a remarkable articulation of the stance on criminality, urban gangs, urban space, and social control visible in nascent form in *The Silver Wedding* and *The Black Hand*. The film tells the story of a white slave gang abducting women in New York City to a life of forced prostitution and the subsequent rescue of the women from the white slavers by the police and the family of one of the victims. The white slave gang is led by a hypocritical social reformer called William Trubus, "the man higher up," who directs the gang members to abduct immigrants from the Battery in Lower Manhattan (the disembarkation point for Ellis Island), a rural migrant arriving at Penn Station, and a young woman named Lorna Barton from the candy store where she works. White slavers thus monitor city space, preying on women who cannot manage the city — notably those new to the city — disrupting families and controlling movement and traffic. Trubus listens to the conversations of the gang directly below his office via a Dictaphone and communicates with one of the gang members with an electronic writing pad. In doing so he directs the gang at one remove, remaining invisible, Tom Gunning observes, because "shielded by the sort of concealed conduits of communication that constitutes the circulatory substratum of the new technological city."[70] In this sense one can discern a congruence between the sewers in *The Silver Wedding* and the telecommunications system in *Traffic in Souls*: both make the world "modern" (clean and disease-free in the case of the sewers, abstract and fetishistic with a connection to the rules of capitalism in the case of the communications system); but, on the other hand, they point out that private space is not impenetrable, as the criminals' usage of them drives home. The connection of spaces that should be kept separate is central to anxieties about crime and the city.

White slave gangs thus utilize disembodied communication to subvert the proper circulation of bodies in the city, taking women from the home and placing them in its opposite, the brothel;[71] the criminal traffic pulsing beneath the surface of the perverse city converts women into a commodity and in so doing directly threatens moral order. Yet the criminal control of urban space is challenged by various forces, including the police and the agency of Lorna's intrepid sister, Mary, and their father. Police officer Burke, the fiancé of Mary, chances on the brothel where the immigrants abducted from the Battery were held. After a fight with the white slavers he rescues the immigrants. He returns to the station and is quickly assigned the task of finding Lorna. The rescue works like this: Mary is sacked the day after Lorna's abduction from the candy store where she and Mary worked because of the bad publicity the abduction brought to the store but is immediately re-employed by Trubus's wife as Trubus's secretary. On her first day at work Mary is asked to clean up the Dictaphone that Trubus uses to talk to his "go-between" in the vice traffic. She immediately recognizes the voice of the white slaver who had abducted Lorna and traces the wire of the Dictaphone down to the office below (the sequence offers a remarkable visual account of the widely articulated belief in the imbrications of a seemingly legitimate "upper world" in underworld criminality).[72] Mary alerts Officer Burke, and together they hatch a plan to record Trubus's conversations with the help of Mary's father's invention of a device "for intensifying sound waves and recording dictagraph sounds on a phonographic record." Leaving Trubus's office with the rolls of recorded conversation, Mary arrives at the police station just after Burke has discovered the location of the brothel in which Lorna is held, and together they drive there. Lorna is rescued by the police just before being whipped into submission. Technology recuperates the dangers it unleashes, notably by effectively establishing identification. The film concludes with a shot of an impersonal urban scene showing a garbage can with a newspaper telling of Trubus's suicide, again visually connecting criminality to waste that should be placed outside the social body.

Together, the ears of the father, the agency of the sister, and the active watching of the police in *Traffic in Souls* extend through urban space, secretly recording and surveying the dark recesses of criminality and the city. Read as the imagining of a governance of urban space, the film represents the superseding of private reform agencies — the corruption of Trubus's "International Purity and Reform League" — first by the agency of the state, figured as the police, and ultimately by the internalization of this policing function within the family itself. Lorna's family help enact a policing of city space and sexuality hitherto reserved solely for the state. In this sense the film marks a transitional moment in the articulation of ideas about cities, gangs, and governance, connected to the interweaving of narrative and policing in *The Silver Wedding* and *The Black Hand* but also to the later representation of the self-discipline of gangsters who reform themselves in conjunction with the ideals of domesticity.

Within *Traffic in Souls* the thematization of the necessity of urban surveillance to combat the ever present social danger of criminality finds a different level of articulation in the elaboration of an omniscient or, indeed, panoptic narration that mimics the combined surveillance of the police and the father and offers a mapping of urban space similar to previous accounts of crime and the city. Indeed, the subtitle of the film, *While New York Sleeps*, makes this connection clearer, showing the continuity of interests in delineating the underworld of urban spaces.[73] *Traffic in Souls* effectively internalized the configuration of surveillance of urban spaces largely ushered in by accounts of crime and the city and, as we have seen, in particular, by the discourses and practices associated with the regulation of white slavery, offering the fantasy of a "totalitarian aspiration towards a transparent society" characteristic of the detective story that itself emerged with the growth of the modern city and concomitant governmental discourses and practices.[74] A subsequent cycle of white slave films, including *The Inside of the White Slave Traffic* (Moral Feature Film Company, 1913), *The House of Bondage* (Photo Drama Motion Picture

Co., 1914), *Is Any Girl Safe?* (Anti-Vice Motion Picture Company, 1916), and others offered similar articulations of the social threat of urban criminality and the necessity of a precise urban surveillance.

While New York Sleeps, the subtitle for *Traffic in Souls*, in fact became the title of a 1921 omnibus film that presented three stories of New York City life at nighttime, offering what the prefatory title described as a "chronicle of the metropolis" and what *Moving Picture World* called a "thrilling story of the upper and under worlds of the great city of New York."[75] One of the segments tells a story about a gang called "the River Rats" in New York's "Eastside," a space where, the title observes, "civilization's veneer is thinnest." The gang congregates at "Hop Ling's" basement dive bar near the docks "to talk business." Later they steal from the docks and escape in a boat; the watchman, Ned, calls the police, who chase the gangsters down the river and after a shoot-out catch all but one of the gang. The central gangster escapes from the boat, crawling up a sewer that leads into the house that Ned shares with his wife and paralyzed and mute father. Arriving in the house, the gangster implores Ned's wife, Nina, to hide him. She agrees, hiding him in the attic of the house; gradually the gangster and Nina develop a relationship witnessed by the mute father, who is unable to inform Ned but whose gestures to the attic eventually alert Ned to the presence of the gangster. After a fight, Ned is killed, and the gangster and Nina put his body down the hatch leading to the sewer the gangster had ascended, watched by the helpless father. Later, the police arrive, searching for the gangster, and the father is able to signal to them by looking at Nina and the attic; after a shoot-out Nina and the gangster are killed. The film ends with a close-up of the father's eyes.

While New York Sleeps conforms in many respects to the representational strategies of the films about crime, urban gangs, and gangsters considered thus far. Like *The Silver Wedding* and *Traffic in Souls*, *While New York Sleeps* depicts a gang visibly connected to waste and to rats, a prevalent trope, as we have seen, in rhetoric about gangsters (also overtly visible in the earlier film *The Water Rats* [Lubin, 1912], another film about gangs congregated around the docks of a large city). Once again, the sewer functions as a conduit between underworld criminality and domestic space, making the connection between underworld and civil society frighteningly easy. Visiting Hop Ling's, the River Rats are also connected to the racially coded underworld glimpsed in *The Black Hand* and particularly visible in the cycle of films about Chinatown like *Chinatown Villains* (Vogue Motion Picture Company, 1916), *The Tong Man* (Haworth Pictures Corporation, 1919), and others discussed at length in this volume by Peter Stanfield. And like *Traffic in the Souls*, the disabled patriarch ultimately defeats the gang; the ears and eyes of the father patrol criminality as patriarchal and state forces are intertwined to uphold social order. Together, the films I have discussed thus far connect the narrative about crime and urban gangs together with a focus on the surveillance and policing of criminality as critical to the establishment and maintenance of social order.

Two films released in 1915 mark an important transformation in this representational strategy, shifting away from a narrative about policing to a story about the reformation of the gangster in accord with norms of social order that is connected to a different conception of criminality and its causes.[76] In *Alias Jimmy Valentine* (World Film, 1915), based on a short story by O. Henry and subsequent play, the central gangster is a "respectable citizen" by day but "by night he is Jimmy Valentine — enemy to society."[77] Valentine leads a gang of bank robbers. After a successful robbery Valentine fights with one of his gang's members who was harassing a woman, and the gangster talks to the police. Valentine is jailed for ten years (and scenes were actually shot within Sing Sing prison and included footage of the reforming governor of the prison).[78] The young woman he saved, named Rose, happens to visit the prison alongside her father, and she recognizes Valentine. Rose and her father work for his release. Once outside prison, Valentine goes to visit Rose and her father to thank them, and he accepts a job working for the father in a bank. Two years pass and Valentine has "buried his past life and alias" and is "[n]ow a trusted cashier." When a former gang member visits and reminds Valentine of "the old thrills of the past," there is a flashback to various crimes, and Valentine becomes increasingly animated. He makes as if he will go with the gang member, but just then Rose enters with her younger brother and sister, and he tells his former accomplice: "I swore to go straight and I'll keep my word." However, the detective who originally arrested him has tracked him down because he is investigating an old case and suspects Valentine. Valentine denies being involved and produces a faked photograph to show he was giving a speech at the time of the crime (unlike in *Traffic in Souls*, technology is used to subvert identification). Circumstances conspire, though, to reveal his identity. At the bank where he works Rose's young sibling is accidentally locked into a new safe that is seemingly impregnable. Valentine, watched by the detective and by Rose, is able to use his criminal skills to open the safe and rescue the child. At the end, as Rose pleads for Valentine, the detective agrees to let him go, convinced of his genuine reform.

Later the same year, *Regeneration* (Fox, 1915), based on a memoir by former gang member Owen Kildare, told another story about the determined reformation of a gangster.[79] In this case the story starts with the death of Owen's mother, leaving him alone in a threadbare tenement in what *Moving Picture World* described as an "accurate" presentation of "the depressing squalor of tenement life on the East Side of New York."[80] He watches as her coffin is taken away and is then taken in by the neighbors, although the man in the house is a violent drunkard who beats Owen. "And so the days pass," a title observes, "in the only environment he knows." Location shooting in the city emphasizes the crowded and squalid nature of that environment. Later Owen becomes the leader of a criminal gang, "by virtue of a complete assortment of the virtues the gangsters most admire," and organizes a robbery in a saloon. Owen's gang is opposed by a district attorney who has resolved "to sweep the city clean." Together with his friend Marie Deering, the district attorney visits a nightclub known to be a gangster hangout to satisfy Marie's curiosity about gangsters. Recognized by the gangsters, the district attorney is surrounded and threatened, but after an exchange of looks between Owen and Marie, Owen rescues him. Following this, and after listening to a speech about the need for charity in the local neighborhood, Marie sets up a settlement house, and a relationship between her and Owen begins. Owen helps at the settlement house. He buys Marie flowers. Later, after old loyalties had forced Owen to shelter a gangster, Marie searches for Owen and is trapped and threatened by one of Owen's former gang members. Owen and the police rush to the rescue—but too late; she is shot and killed. Owen returns to the gang hideout to kill the gangster responsible, but the apparition of Marie stops him. Trapped, the gangster looks down to see a rat in a hole (a consistent trope, as we have seen, connecting gangsters to vermin and social waste); he is killed by Owen and Marie's friend as he tries to escape across washing lines threaded in front of a tenement skyline. At the close Owen and the friend visit the grave of Marie and place flowers there; the flowers consistently associated with Marie connect her to a nature uncontaminated by the city.

Together, *Alias Jimmy Valentine* and *Regeneration* shift in some respects away from the articulation of criminality in *The Black Hand, The Silver Wedding, Traffic in Souls*, and other films previously considered. One way they do so is simply by articulating the possibility of reformation. Valentine reforms because of his love for Rose, and his reformation is directly connected to the protection of children and, by extension, domestic social order. A scene shortly after Valentine leaves prison is important here. He goes to a saloon to discuss a potential robbery with one of his gang members, and this meeting is crosscut with Rose reading a story to her younger siblings. Valentine and gang-related criminality are connected to the space of the saloon, commonly regarded, and here literally presented, as diametrically opposed to that of the home. *The Gangsters of New York* (Reliance, 1914), a film of the previous year, had made this connection clear also, showing how "the existence of gangsters is made possible by the saloon," depicted in the film "exactly as it is, a nuisance, the caterer to all that is low in man's nature, blunting his moral sense and perpetuating organized crime."[81] Valentine's reformation in "going straight" is connected to a movement away from the space of the saloon and toward that of the domestic space inhabited by Rose and by her young siblings; the detective is accordingly convinced of his genuine reformation when he saves the child at the end.[82] Reformation is thus directly supportive of ideals of domesticity that were, historians have shown, closely linked to the constitution and self-definition of the middle class.[83] Indeed, Richard Ohmann's analysis of fiction in magazines in the turn-of-the-century period, including a brief analysis of the O. Henry short story on which *Alias Jimmy Valentine* is based, suggests that the insistent theme of reformation eased the contradiction between urban, corporate order and ideals of individual action and character that was particularly pressing for members of the middle class.[84]

Valentine's reformation is important also for what it suggests about the model of criminality implicitly articulated and thus the shifting ground of discourses about crime. Criminal anthropologists and eugenic criminologists argued that reformation for the criminal was unlikely if not impossible. W. Duncan McKim, for example, had explicitly stated that "[w]e may in some measure restrain, but can never reform" the criminal, and "reformation is *not* the true thing, not a change of heart, but a mere change of conduct based upon an enlightening of selfish motive."[85] Yet this is clearly not true of Valentine, whose genuine reform is connected, I believe, to a different model of criminology, one informed more by psychology and sociology than by biology and beliefs about hereditary influence and that accordingly articulated a different conception of the causes of crime and its possible treatment.

Work on the shaping effects of psychology and social organization on the behavior of individuals and groups had coalesced into the academic disciplines of psychology, sociology, and social psychology in the late nineteenth century.[86] The disciplines of sociology and social psychology in particular were concerned with the forces that bound individuals to society, notably through the concept of "social control," understood as the way in which democratic society organizes what was widely called "good citizenship" and so establishes the governance of a diverse mass public. Articulated first by Edward Alsworth Ross in a series of articles in the newly formed *American Journal of Sociology* and gathered together as the book *Social Control: A Survey of the Foundations of Order* in 1901, the question of how society organizes social order by modifying individual feelings, ideas, and behaviors was widely debated.[87] In the influential textbook *Introduction to the Science of Sociology* Robert Park and Ernest Burgess could simply state that "[a]ll social problems turn out, finally, to be problems of social control" and thus that social control should be "the central fact and problem of sociology."[88] For Ross, Park, Burgess, and others, the question of social control was intimately connected to the space of the city and the management of its diverse populations.

To deal with the criminal and the gang was consequently a subset of the pressing imperative to convert an urban mass public into a rational citizenry. It was within this intellectual and governmental context that the American Institute of Criminal Law and Criminology and corresponding *Journal of the American Institute of Criminal Law and Criminology* were established in 1909.[89] Various arguments doubting the veracity of Lombroso were articulated in the organization and in the pages of its journal, as criminologists came to focus more clearly on the psychological and sociological factors that pushed individuals and groups toward crime. William Healy's important book *The Individual Delinquent*, for example, published in the same year that *Alias Jimmy Valentine* and *Regeneration* were released, utilized psychology and, to a lesser extent, sociology to delineate case studies and to argue that theorizing about criminals as a unified type or simply as a "dangerous class" was useless.[90] Healy instead argued that the causative factors of crime were simply too complex and interdependent for one to draw generalizations.

Likewise, reformers, sociologists, and sociologically oriented criminologists focused increasingly on the effects of environment on the development of criminality, delinquency, and, in particular, the formation of criminal gangs. The shaping effects of environment were recognized by many progressive reformers, and this motivated, for example, the establishment of settlement houses in immigrant sections in cities and the corresponding emphasis on the role of environmental factors in shaping the lives of the immigrant masses. Academic sociology and criminology took a lead from this environmental perspective;[91] support for eugenic criminology waned after 1915 as academic support intensified for environmentalist stances.[92] "The gangster," John Landesco wrote in *Organized Crime in Chicago*, "is a product of his surroundings."[93] Other work in the 1920s articulated similar perspectives on the shaping effects of environment, including Louis Wirth's *The Ghetto*, Harvey W. Zorbaugh's *The Gold Coast and the Slum*, Frederic M. Thrasher's *The Gang: A Study of 1,313 Gangs in Chicago*, and Clifford Shaw's *Delinquency Areas: A Study of the Geographical Distribution of School Truants, Juvenile Delinquents, and Adult Offenders in Chicago*.[94]

Looking to delineate the social disorganization of urban life, and to explain the distribution and social relations of criminal behavior, these scholars, like earlier reformers, inevitably focused considerable attention on the city in general as well as on specific locations within the city. Together, work within criminology and what came to be called urban sociology was informed by the widespread belief that the city inaugurated a critical shift in social order, often understood along European models as a shift from *Gemeinschaft* to *Gesellschaft*, that is, from the moral order of rural spaces and social organizations like the family and community to the moral disorder of the city. In his influential essay of 1915, "The City: Suggestions for the Investigation of Human Behavior in the Urban Environment," Robert Ezra Park described the city as a "laboratory for the investigation of collective life . . . [a] clinic in which human nature and social processes may be conveniently and profitably studied."[95] Park concluded in later work on the city that the "social problem is fundamentally a city problem," that is, "the problem of achieving in the freedom of the city a social order and a social control equivalent to that which grew up naturally in the family, the clan, and the tribe."[96] Weakening moral bonds, cities led to the enactment of "suppressed desires" and to "man" thus becoming "a problem to himself and to society in a way and to an extent that he never was before."[97]

Urban sociologists conceived of the city as an ecological system, suggesting that urban communities developed into "natural areas" with particular characteristics under the effect of the environment.[98] Variously shaped by ecological influences, some "natural areas" would assume the character of a "moral region," in which a distinctive moral code diverging from the city's norm operated. Ernest W. Burgess formalized this notion with his famous diagram that outlined the five concentric zones that formed any urban ecology, radiating outward from Zone 1—the central business district—and including the zone of transition near the central zone that was characterized by the rapid turnover of immigrant and lower-class populations. Within this zone there developed what Burgess called "gangland," where gangs, Park observed, "grow like weeds."[99] Later, Clifford Shaw's work on delinquency pursued this concept of moral regions, showing how social disorganization contributed to delinquent and criminal behavior and how this behavior was "transmitted socially just as any other cultural and social pattern is transmitted."[100] For urban sociologists and criminologists, then, the environment, and, in particular, the configuration of modern cities, was an important contributing factor to criminal behavior; the shift away from a biological to an environmental model was a critical one in the history of discourses about crime.

Regeneration is informed principally (but not wholly) by a sense of the environmental causes of gang-related criminality.[101] Location shooting establishes the importance of the city. The opening of the film in the threadbare and violent tenement emphasizes the environmental factors that push Owen toward crime, showing, *Moving Picture World* observed, how the gangster "is the natural product of an unfavorable environment."[102] Owen is connected to a saloon culture that dominates the tenement region, at one point near the beginning moving through crowded streets of the neighborhood to collect a pail of beer for his violent surrogate father and later visiting a saloon and drinking in a nightclub. Counterpoised to the space of the tenement, saloon, and nightclub is the redemptive space of the settlement house. Here the film draws directly on the environmental discourses that sustained the settlement house movement. Jane Addams, founder of Hull House settlement house in Chicago and influential progressive reformer, had written widely of the transformative effects of settlement houses in immigrant communities in the early years of the twentieth century.[103] Informed by this rhetoric, the film has the settlement worker Marie—who in the original book was actually a teacher—help reform Owen, drawing him away from the gang and corresponding underworld spaces toward a role as upstanding citizen.

Once again, this reformation is conceived in terms of a realignment with domestic space. Underworld spaces can be transformed, overwritten by the space of domesticity. The breakdown of domesticity—the death of Owen's mother, the violence of the father surrogate—is seen to lead directly to crime, but, the film argues, this can be counteracted by the reestablishment of domestic space, now writ large as the settlement house. Owen's reformation is complete when he helps Marie rescue a baby from a violent father and restore it to its mother. In effect, the expanded domestic space counteracts crime and the gang; the film thus takes the logic of *Traffic in Souls* one step further: the community as family negates criminality, now without the force of the state personified as the police.

In doing so *Regeneration*, like *Alias Jimmy Valentine*, presents reformation also as a self-disciplining, a process that Michel Foucault would call a technique of the self—that is, as an internalization of ideals of responsibility and good citizenship closely linked to the expanding technologies for the discipline and control of

1. *Regeneration* (1915). Photo courtesy of the Library of Congress Motion Picture, Broadcasting, and Recorded Sound Division.

bodies, populations, and society itself.[104] Techniques of discipline — the police detective in *Alias Jimmy Valentine*, for example — interact now with technologies of the self, the determined self-reformation of the gangster and the internalization of ideals of social control. In both films these ideals are connected to a feminized configuration of domesticity and, thus, class alignment. Acting on the self like this requires work, the films show. Valentine in *Alias Jimmy Valentine* is twice tempted to return to his gang and a life of crime but decides against it, the first time after his meeting in the saloon is crosscut with Rose at home and the second time after Rose and her younger siblings enter the room. In *Regeneration* the work of internalizing a gendered configuration of respectability is most apparent when Owen seeks revenge for Marie's death at the hands of the gangster but is stopped by the apparition of Marie, a ghostly and now internal presence guiding the morality of the reformed gangster.

Yet there are, it is worth noting, limits to the imagination of this self-disciplining. In both *Regeneration* and *Alias Jimmy Valentine* the reformable gangster is white and not connected to particular racial groups, as in the black-hand or Chinatown cycles. One scene in a nightclub in *Regeneration* is particularly pertinent here. The scene opens with a close-up of a black musician singing, pulling out to reveal three black musicians playing against a painted backdrop of the city. In figuratively associating blackness with the city, the film extends a trope visible throughout of connecting somehow physically "deformed" bodies with the city. We see, for example, a close-up, for no narrative purposes, of a man whose nose is disfigured as a conse-

2. *Regeneration.* Photo courtesy of the Library of Congress Motion Picture, Broadcasting, and Recorded Sound Division.

quence, it seems, of syphilis and alcohol, and we also see obese and disabled inhabitants of the tenement regions of the city. Representing what *Moving Picture World* called a "selection of types that are in no way an exaggeration of those to be found in the streets of the East Side and in the dives frequented by Owen," this vaguely eugenic presentation sits uneasily with the overall environmental perspective articulated in the film and clearly suggests the limits to that perspective and the continued commingling of different discourses about crime and the city.[105] Films with a Chinatown setting further developed this sense of the city. Later in the scene in the nightclub, Owen and Marie exchange looks, leading to Owen's saving the district attorney and leaving the club with them — moving from the space of blackness associated with crime and the city to that of the whiteness associated with Marie and the settlement house.

A commingling of environmental and eugenic discourses was visible in other films. A series of films in the 1920s starring Lon Chaney pictured an underworld populated by deformed bodies, thus connecting criminality to physical disability or otherness in accord with well-established eugenic principles. In these films Chaney functions as what Gaylyn Studlar describes as a "polluted object."[106] Yet some form of redemption is possible. In *The Penalty* (Eminent Authors Pictures, 1920), for example, Chaney plays Blizzard, a character whose legs have been unnecessarily amputated as a boy and who subsequently becomes a violent "lord and master of the underworld" who plans to rouse thousands of the city's disgruntled foreign laborers to revolt, during which Blizzard and his gang will loot the city's treasury. Yet in the end a doctor operates on Blizzard's brain, removing a "contusion at the base of the skull" that has driven him to criminality. In *Outside the Law* (Universal,

1920), Silent Madden and his daughter Molly are persuaded to reform by Confucian Chang Low (Chaney), who finally kills the gangster Black Mike (also played by Chaney).[107] Location shooting in San Francisco's Chinatown positioned that space not as the threatening space of many other films with a Chinatown locale but as a potentially redemptive space. In *The Shock* (Universal, 1923) Chinatown occupies the more familiar space of orientalized underworld. Chaney plays a cripple in the employ of the Queen of the San Francisco underworld. At the close the San Francisco earthquake destroys the "whirlpool of vice and intrigue" in Chinatown, in the process curing Chaney of his deformity and enabling him to pursue a relationship with the woman he loves. In *The Unholy Three* (MGM, 1925) Chaney plays a sideshow ventriloquist who forms a gang with a strongman and a midget but ultimately reforms and confesses in order to facilitate the relationship of the woman he loves with another man.

Likewise, the well-known *Underworld* (Paramount, 1927) develops this story of sacrifice connected to the imagination of the city's underworld. The film begins with a subtitle reading a "great city in the dead of night . . . streets lonely, moon flooded . . . buildings empty as the cave dwellings of a forgotten age" before the opening image of a skyscraper superimposed on a clock. Bull Weed emerges from the darkness at the bottom of the building, having robbed a bank. Here the modern city is haunted by an underworld, connected to the animal-like and destructive gangster—his very name connoting the power of destruction—and literally figured in the space of the film as a basement saloon called "Dreamland," where gangsters congregate and in a gangster's underground ball, "where the brutal din of cheap music—booze—hate—lust made a devil carnival."[108] Visualizing the modern uncanny as "the savagery that lurks in the midst of civilization," this representation of the primitivism of the underworld threatening modernity is apparent also in the early sound film *Broadway* (Universal, 1929), which begins its title sequence with a giant man in a loin cloth stumbling through the city that he towers over, spilling alcohol from his glass.[109] The threatening primitivism in *Underworld* is partly contained, though, as Bull Weed undergoes a kind of reformation after he realizes that his partner in crime and girlfriend were loyal to him despite their love for each other. He helps them escape and accepts his fate, to die at the hands of the police: even Bull Weed can be softened by love.

Various other films in the 1920s continued to develop the environmental and rehabilitation perspectives visible in nascent form in *Alias Jimmy Valentine* and *Regeneration*. *Alias Jimmy Valentine* and *Regeneration* were themselves in fact both remade in the early 1920s (*Regeneration* was entitled *Fool's Highway* [Universal, 1924], and in this version the gangster reforms and becomes a policeman!). Likewise, in *Environment* (Principal, 1922), "Chicago Sal" is sent to a country jail to be cleansed of the city. Although she relapses, and returns to the city to her old gang to commit a crime, she falls in love with one of the men she planned to rob. She is arrested and returns to the country jail, promising to reform to be worthy of the man she loves. In *Big Brother* (Famous Players Lasky, 1923) a tough gang leader is redeemed by his commitment to care for an orphaned boy. In *Boomerang Bill* (Cosmopolitan, 1922) a policeman talks to a young man about to take part in a robbery. The policeman tells him the story of a gangster who had vowed to go straight but who was framed by "Tony the Wop" for robbing a bank to help his girlfriend's mother, who was unwell. When he comes out from jail he finds his girlfriend has married but is happy, so he leaves the couple alone. Moved by the story of the reformed gangster, the young man listening to the story resists the temptation to steal and promises to seek honest employment. Again, the film mixes discourses about race and criminality — Tony the Wop — and reformation. Later in the 1920s a cycle of films that *Variety* came to label simply "underworld" continued this perspective on environment and rehabilitation.[110] For example, *Me, Gangster* (1928), based on the life story of another gangster turned writer, follows the central gangster from his upbringing in a tenement to armed robbery with a local gang. He is arrested, and while he is in prison, his mother dies, triggering a moral reformation.

Almost all of the films I have considered in detail here are in some way initially based on factual discourses in newspaper accounts, social reform documents, autobiographies — before establishing fictional paths from this factual basis through highly charged ideological territories, notably pressing questions of social control and governance inaugurated by a modernity symbolized for many by the city.[111] Urban underworlds threatened social order and, indeed, modernity as the promise of progress and rationality, incisively shown at the beginning of *Underworld* when Bull Weed emerges from the darkness at the base of a skyscraper. Two ways of conceiving the causes of crime and thus the correct ways of managing criminal groups dominated contemporary discourse: a biological and eugenic model proposing incarceration, sterilization, or execution; and an environmental model consistent both with progressive reform and with the discipline of sociology that proposed interventions tailored to individual psychology and to the regeneration of urban space. Taken together, the various cycles of films surveyed here offer different ways of imagining the threat of criminal underworlds and of the reestablishment of social control. This reestablishment is figured as a consequence of direct state intervention in *The Silver Wedding*, *The Black Hand*, and subsequent cycle; of the commingling of state and family forces in *Traffic in Souls* and *While New York Sleeps*; and of the internalization of domestic ideals and self-discipline in *Alias Jimmy Valentine*, *Regeneration*, and subsequent films about the rehabilitation of gangsters. Yet the fundamental motivating question informing different configurations of criminology and film production was about how to manage criminal underworlds and establish governmental control over an urban mass public. Telling stories about criminal gangs in the silent era reflected and refracted the widespread anxieties about urbanization, criminality, and governance that characterized the early years of the twentieth century.

Notes

A grant for Humanities Research from the School of Humanities, King's College London, supported the research for this chapter. My thanks also to Peter Kramer, Peter Stanfield, and Kay Dickinson for comments that substantially improved the essay.

1. *The Silver Wedding, Biograph Bulletin* no. 65, March 17, 1906, in *Biograph Bulletins, 1908–1912*, ed. Eileen Bowser (New York: Farrar, Straus, and Giroux, 1973), 240.

2. Ibid. The bulletin accompanying the film includes a picture of this scene, offered as the central attraction of the film.

3. I am using the term *race* as it figured in the politics of industrializing America, as a multifaceted concept that purported to identify differences in culture, religion, biological makeup, national language, civic attitude, and skin color. See Mathew Frye Jacobson, *Whiteness of a Different Color: European Immigrants and the Alchemy of Race* (Cambridge, Mass.: Harvard University Press, 1998); and Mathew Pratt Guterl, *The Color of Race in America, 1900–1940* (Cambridge, Mass.: Harvard University Press, 2001).

4. *The Black Hand, Biograph Bulletin* no. 66, March 29, 1906, in *Biograph Bulletins, 1908–1912*, ed. Eileen Bowser (New York: Farrar, Straus and Giroux, 1973), 241.

5. On widespread antiurban discourses in the nineteenth and early twentieth centuries see, e.g., Paul Boyer, *Urban Masses and Moral Order in America, 1820–1920* (Cambridge, Mass.: Harvard University Press, 1978). "What forces are there," asked muckraking journalist George Kibbe Turner in 1907, "hidden in American cities, which are dragging them, according to the record of their own press, into a state of semibarbarism?" (George Kibbe Turner, "The City of Chicago: A Study of the Great Immoralities," *McClure's*, April 1907; repr. in *The Muckrakers*, ed. Arthur and Lila Weinberg [New York: Capricorn Books, 1964], 389).

6. Robert Ezra Park, "The City as a Social Laboratory," in *Chicago: An Experiment in Social Science Research*, ed. T. V. Smith and Leonard D. White (Chicago: University of Chicago Press, 1929), 2; Robert E. Park and Ernest W. Burgess, *Introduction to the Science of Sociology* (1921; repr. Chicago: University of Chicago Press, 1969), 785.

7. Josiah Strong, *Our Country: Its Possible Future and Its Present Crisis* (New York: American Home Missionary Society, 1885), cited in Andrew Lees, *Cities Perceived: Urban Society in European and American Thought, 1820–1940* (Manchester: Manchester University Press, 1985), 166. The so-called Progressive Era witnessed a proliferation of social reform movements that allied with an increasingly activist judiciary and (temporarily) diminished tenets of localism and laissez-faire to produce a transformation in the traditional understanding of the scope of legislation and the locus of public power and a corresponding remarkable upsurge in governmental regulation and state definition. On this see, e.g., Robert H. Wiebe, *The Search for Order, 1877–1920* (New York: Hill and Wang, 1967); Boyer, *Urban Masses and Moral Order in America*, esp. 191–283; Arthur S. Link and Richard L. McCormick, *Progressivism* (Arlington Heights, Ill.: Harlan Davidson, 1983); and Morton Keller, *Regulating a New Society: Public Policy and Social Change in America, 1900–1933* (Cambridge, Mass.: Harvard University Press, 1994).

8. Edward Alsworth Ross, *Sin and Society: An Analysis of Latter-Day Iniquity* (1907; repr. Gloucester, Mass.: Peter Smith, 1965), 46. I draw here on Michel Foucault's work on "governmentality," defined broadly as "the conduct of conduct" and connected for Foucault to the establishment of various epistemological and institutional practices focused on the management of bodies and populations so as to shape, guide, correct, and modify the ways in which individuals and groups conduct themselves. On this see, in particular, Michel Foucault, "Governmentality," in *The Foucault Effect: Studies in Governmentality*, ed. Graham Burchell, Colin Gordon, and Peter Miller (London: Harvester Wheatsheaf, 1991). On the establishment, development, and expansion of three of the crucial institutions directed against crime in turn-of-the-century America — the police, the asylum, and the prison — see Robert M. Fogelson, *Big City Police* (Cambridge, Mass.: Harvard University Press, 1977); Sydney L. Harring, *Policing a Class Society: The Experience of American Cities, 1865–1915* (New Brunswick, N.J.: Rutgers University Press, 1983); David J. Rothman, *Conscience and Convenience: The Asylum and Its Alternatives in Progressive America* (Boston: Little, Brown, 1980); and Alexander W. Pisciotta, *Benevolent Repression: Social Control and the American Reformatory-Prison Movement* (New York: New York University Press, 1994).

9. Little has been written about silent gangster films. Jack Shadoian's observation that "[t]he gangster/crime film took root as long ago as Griffith's *The Musketeers of Pig Alley* (1912) and then

struggled in unfertilized soil through to the end of the twenties" is symptomatic of this critical neglect and myopia. Jack Shadoian, *Dreams and Dead Ends: The American Gangster/Crime Film* (Cambridge, Mass.: MIT Press, 1977), 15. In singling out Griffith's film Shadoian and other authors pursue an auteurist focus, an outdated Griffith-centered account of silent cinema, and ignore the fact that the film participated in distinct generic trends. Even though other authors have considered the silent period in slightly more detail, the focus rarely gets beyond *Musketeers* before shifting to the early 1930s and, indeed, to the trilogy *Little Caesar, The Public Enemy,* and *Scarface*. This is true even of the best studies of the gangster film, Eugene Rosow, *Born to Lose: The Gangster Film in America* (New York: Oxford University Press, 1978); and Jonathan Munby, *Public Enemies, Public Heroes: Screening the Gangster from "Little Caesar" to "Touch of Evil"* (Chicago: University of Chicago Press, 1999). I agree here with Steve Neale, whose important recent work on genre has called for a reevaluation of silent gangster films. Steve Neale, *Genre and Hollywood* (London: Routledge, 2000), 79. Given the paucity of extant films in this period, my reevaluation inevitably stems from a small sample of surviving films but also from plot summaries and contemporary reviews.

10. I will not consider here the regulation of cinema itself as a problem of governance in the silent era and the impact of this on the production of films about criminal gangs. It is worth noting, though, that the articulation of criminality and policing in films like *The Silver Wedding, The Black Hand,* and others marked a shift from earlier representations like *How They Do Things on the Bowery* (Edison, 1902), which showed a country "rube" visiting the city, being drugged in a bar by a woman who steals from him, and being thrown out by a waiter. A gleeful account of urban criminality, alongside a world-weary cynicism about the corruption of the police, characterized a number of early films. Yet this representation changed after the emergence of nickelodeons from around 1906 had opened moving pictures to a lower-class and immigrant audience that had not previously attended theatrical entertainments, leading to a clearer articulation of morality and to the establishment of regulatory institutions that carefully guided the representation of criminality. For more on this see Lee Grieveson, *Policing Cinema: Movies and Censorship in Early-Twentieth-Century America* (Berkeley: University of California Press, 2004).

11. Anxieties about criminal gangs certainly predate Prohibition. For example, Herbert Asbury's popular history, *The Gangs of New York: An Informal History of the Underworld* (Garden City, N.Y.: Knopf, 1927), considers gang organization principally in the nineteenth century, concluding that criminal gangs were on the wane by the late 1920s (344–345). "Contrary to the assumptions of later commentators," David Ruth notes, "the modern gangster predated his bootlegger incarnation" (David E. Ruth, *Inventing the Public Enemy: The Gangster in American Culture, 1918–1934* [Chicago: University of Chicago Press, 1996], 45). The mistaken connection of gang organization with bootlegging helps explain the critical neglect of films made prior to Prohibition. On Prohibition as an exercise in fading Protestant cultural hegemony see, e.g., Norman H. Clark, *Deliver Us from Evil: An Interpretation of American Prohibition* (New York: Norton, 1976).

12. Literary accounts of the "mysteries" of the city emerged from the mid-nineteenth century, both in pulp fiction and in a developing literary realism that in turn proliferated around the turn of the century. See Michael Denning, *Mechanic Accents: Dime Novels and Working-Class Culture in America* (London: Verso, 1987), esp. 85–117; and, on literary realism, David E. Shi, *Facing Facts: Realism in American Thought and Culture, 1850–1920* (New York: Oxford University Press, 1995), esp. 103–125.

13. Thomas Knox, *Underground, or Life Below the Surface; Incidents and Accidents beyond the Light of Day* (London: Sampson, Low, 1878), 269, 257.

14. Ibid., 643, 638, 257.

15. Anthony Vidler, *The Architectural Uncanny: Essays in the Modern Unhomely* (Cambridge, Mass.: MIT Press, 1992), 168.

16. On the racialization of the lower classes in late nineteenth-century explorations of the underworld of the city see Deborah Epstein Nord, "The Social Explorer as Anthropologist: Victorian Travelers among the Urban Poor," in *Visions of the Modern City: Essays in History, Art, and Literature,* ed. William Sharpe and Leonard Wallock (Baltimore: Johns Hopkins University Press, 1987).

17. Helen Campbell, Thomas Knox, Thomas Byrnes, *Darkness and Daylight, or Lights and Shadows of New York Life* (Hartford, Conn.: A. D. Worthington, 1892). "This underworld would appall even Dante," the authors wrote, "whose journey lay through hell and whose 'Inferno' holds no more terrible picture than those to be encountered" in the streets of the city at night (213–214).

18. Ibid., 433.

19. Ibid., 481. Jacob Riis, in the widely read *How the Other Half Lives: Studies among the Tenements of New York* (1890; repr. New York: Hill and Wang, 1957), had likewise earlier called tenements "nurseries of crime" (1).

20. Campbell, Knox, and Byrnes, *Darkness and Daylight*, 286.

21. For example, in *Lights and Shadows of New York Life; or, the Sights and Sensations of a Great City* (Philadelphia: National Publishing, 1872), the Reverend James D. McCabe presented "full and graphic" accounts of divisions within the city, mapping the city through "its splendors and wretchedness; its high and low life; its marble palaces and dark dens; its attractions and dangers" (2). Likewise, in *The Nether Side of New York; or the Vice, Crime, and Poverty of the Great Metropolis* (New York: Sheldon, 1872), Edward Crapsey delineated the world of professional criminals like gangs stealing from the docks, showing, the *New York Times* review commented, that underworld criminals were "as destructive" to respectable society "as are the earthquake and volcano to the fair face of the earth" (*New York Times*, June 24, 1872, 2, cited in Larry K. Hartsfield, *The American Response to Professional Crime, 1870–1917* [Westport, Conn.: Greenwood Press, 1985], 90).

22. The term was popularized in particular by Josiah Flynt, who reported firsthand on his experiences with tramps and professional criminals in his books *Tramping with Tramps* (New York: Century, 1899); *Notes of an Itinerant Policeman* (1900; repr. Freeport, N.Y.: Books for Libraries Press, 1972); and *The World of Graft* (London: McClure, Philips, 1901).

23. Michel Foucault, "The Eye of Power," in *Power/Knowledge: Selected Interviews and Other Writings, 1972–1977*, ed. Colin Gordon (New York: Pantheon, 1980), 153, 154.

24. Maren Strange, *Symbols of Ideal Life: Social Documentary Photography in America, 1890–1950* (Cambridge, U.K.: Cambridge University Press, 1989), esp. 1–46.

25. Campbell, Knox, and Byrnes, *Darkness and Daylight*, ix.

26. Ibid, xi (emphasis in original).

27. *Variety*, July 11, 1928. Other films also presented images of the underworld of cities, including "actualities" like *Bowery Waltz* (Edison, 1897) and *A "Tough" Dance* (Edison, 1901); actuality/fiction hybrids like *The Haymarket* (American Mutoscope and Biograph, 1903); a cycle of films about "rubes" visiting the city and encountering various difficulties there such as *How They Do Things on the Bowery* (Edison, 1902), *How They Rob Men in Chicago* (American Mutoscope and Biograph, 1902), *Rube Brown in Town* (American Mutoscope and Biograph, 1905), *A Rube in the Subway* (American Mutoscope and Biograph, 1905); and a cycle of "slumming" comedies showing out-of-towners being duped by sophisticated city folk in dangerous areas of the city, including in particular Chinatown in *Lifting the Lid* (American Mutoscope and Biograph, 1905) and *The Deceived Slumming Party* (Biograph, 1908).

28. Jane Addams, *The Spirit of Youth and the City Streets* (1909; repr. Urbana: University of Illinois Press, 1972), 14.

29. Boyer, *Urban Masses and Moral Order*, esp. 162–174, 233–251.

30. Vidler, *The Architectural Uncanny*, 168. On city planning see M. Christine Boyer, *Dreaming the Rational City: The Myth of American City Planning* (Cambridge, Mass.: MIT Press, 1983).

31. Frederick Howe, *The City: The Hope of Democracy* (London: T. Fisher Unwin, 1905), 47. On the discourses about sewers as the imagination of an underground world see Rosalind Williams, *Notes on the Underground: An Essay on Technology, Society, and the Imagination* (Cambridge, Mass.: MIT Press, 1990), 52–53, 70–73. And on the role of sewers as part of what he calls "moral environmentalism" see Stanley K. Schultz, *Constructing Urban Culture: American Cities and City Planning, 1800–1920* (Philadelphia: Temple University Press, 1989), 111–119.

32. Maureen Ogle, "Water Supply, Waste Disposal, and the Culture of Privatism in the Mid-Nineteenth-Century American City," *Journal of Urban History* 25, no. 3 (March 1999): 321–347; Schultz, *Constructing Urban Culture*, 167–175. The "police power" assigned to states in the Constitution, defined as the right (and duty) of the states to protect the health, morals, and safety of their citizens, was implemented with special vigor when public health and morals appeared to be at stake. See Morton Keller, *Affairs of State: Public Life in Late Nineteenth Century America* (Cambridge, Mass.: Harvard University Press, 1977), 409–438.

33. Thomas Osborne, "Security and Vitality: Drains, Liberalism, and Power in the Nineteenth Century," in *Foucault and Political Reason: Liberalism, Neo-Liberalism, and Rationalities of Government*, ed. Andrew Barry, Thomas Osborne, and Nikolas Rose (London: University College London Press, 1996), 114–115.

34. Vidler, *The Architectural Uncanny*; Wolfgang Schivelbusch, *The Railway Journey: Trains and Travel in the Nineteenth Century* (New York: Urizen Books, 1979); Tom Gunning, "Tracing the

Individual Body: Photography, Detectives, and Early Cinema," in *Cinema and the Invention of Modern Life*, ed. Leo Charney and Vanessa R. Schwartz (Berkeley: University of California Press, 1995), 15. At the same time he was reconstructing the surface of Paris, opening the city to the flow of traffic, Baron Georges-Eugéne Haussmann also regularized subterranean Paris. A comprehensive and rational system of sewers was built, celebrated by Victor Hugo in *Les Misérables* (Williams, *Notes on the Underground*, 70–72).

35. In this the film differs from a number of earlier actuality films that portrayed the correct management and circulation of urban waste, implicitly connecting this process to the proper governance of city space. See, e.g., *Sorting Refuse at Incinerating Plant, New York City* (Edison, 1903), *Panorama of Riker's Island, New York* (Edison, 1903), *New York City Dumping Wharf* (Edison, 1903), and *White Wings on Review* (Edison, 1903), showing rows of men wearing the white uniforms of New York street sweepers.

36. Ross, *Sin and Society*, 6.

37. Turner, "The City of Chicago," 404.

38. G. Frank Lydston, *The Diseases of Society. The Vice and Crime Problem* (Philadelphia: Lippincott, 1904), 566.

39. Articulated within the prevailing language of biological materialism, ideas about degeneration posited the specter of the physical and intellectual decline of the population closely connected to anxieties about class and racial difference. For a survey of materials on degeneration see Daniel Pick, *Faces of Degeneration: A European Disorder, 1848–1918* (Cambridge, U.K.: Cambridge University Press, 1988). On the connection of immigrants and immigration with disease in the United States see Alan M. Kraut, *Silent Travelers: Germs, Genes, and the "Immigrant Menace"* (Baltimore: Johns Hopkins University Press, 1994).

40. On Lombroso and criminal anthropology see, e.g., Marie-Christine Leps, *Apprehending the Criminal: The Production of Deviance in Nineteenth Century Discourse* (Durham, N.C.: Duke University Press, 1992), esp. 32–41. Criminal anthropologists, Pasquale Pasquino observes, regarded the "criminal as an excrement of the social body, at once a residue of archaic stages in the evolution of the species and a waste-product of social organization" (Pasquale Pasquino, "Criminology: The Birth of a Special Knowledge," in Burchell, Gordon, and Miller, *The Foucault Effect*, 238).

41. Lombroso, cited in Piers Bierne, *Inventing Criminology: Essays on the Rise of Homo Criminalis* (Albany: State University of New York Press, 1993), 29.

42. On eugenics more generally see Marouf Arif Hasian Jr., *The Rhetoric of Eugenics in Anglo-American Thought* (Athens: University of Georgia Press, 1996).

43. Nicole Hahn Rafter, *Creating Born Criminals* (Urbana: University of Illinois Press, 1997), esp. 6–10.

44. W. Duncan McKim, *Heredity and Human Progress* (New York: Putnam's Sons, 1900), 2, 13. McKim is citing E. Laurent, *Les Habitudes des Prisons de Paris* (Paris, 1890).

45. Arthur MacDonald, *Criminology* (New York: Funk and Wagnalls, 1893); August Drahms, *The Criminal: His Personnel and Environment* (1900; repr. Montclair, N.J.: Patterson Smith, 1971). See also the discussion of turn-of-the-century criminology in the United States in Hartsfield, *American Response to Professional Crime*, 149–188.

46. Charles P. Davenport, *Heredity in Relation to Eugenics* (New York: Henry Holt, 1911), 221–222.

47. 61st Cong., 3rd sess., Doc. 662, *Reports of the Immigration Commission, Dictionary of Races or Peoples* (Washington: Government Printing Office, 1911), cited in Jacobson, *Whiteness of a Different Color*, 117; Edward Grant Conklin, "Some Biological Aspects of Immigration," *Scribner's*, March 1921, 356, cited in Ruth, *Inventing the Public Enemy*, 13.

48. For a brief account of black-hand activity see Asbury, *The Gangs of New York*, 268. On ideals of domesticity and their connection to class formation see Mary P. Ryan, *Cradle of the Middle Class: The Family in Oneida County, New York, 1790–1865* (Cambridge, U.K.: Cambridge University Press, 1981); and Stuart M. Blumin, *The Emergence of the Middle Class: Social Experience in the American City, 1760–1900* (Cambridge, U.K.: Cambridge University Press, 1989).

49. *Literary Digest*, June 19, 1915; and in Ruth, *Inventing the Public Enemy*.

50. Luc Sante, *Low Life* (New York: Vintage, 1992), 231–233.

51. McKim, *Heredity and Human Progress*, 2.

52. See Giorgio Bertellini, "Black Hands and White Hearts: Southern Italian Immigrants, Crime, and Race in Early American Cinema," in this volume.

53. *Moving Picture World*, Nov. 16, 1912, 668.

54. *Moving Picture World*, June 7, 1913, 1031; *Moving Picture World*, Feb. 28, 1914, 1089; *Moving Picture World*, Oct. 31, 1914, 641; *Moving Picture World*, March 20, 1915, 1784. A later film, *Black Hand* (MGM, 1950), also dealt with Petrosino and the black-hand gang. A cycle of films, Bertellini notes, equated hotheaded gangsters with political radicals, thus, it seems, merging anxieties about criminality and political instability. See, e.g., *A Bum and a Bomb* (Champion, 1912), *Giovanni's Gratitude* (Mutual, 1913), and *The Bomb Throwers* (Pathe-Freres, 1915).

55. *Moving Picture World*, March 4, 1916, 1491.

56. *National Police Magazine*, Sep. 1912, 12.

57. Michel Foucault, *Discipline and Punish: The Birth of the Prison*, trans. Alan Sheridan (New York: Vintage Books, 1979); Alan Sekula, "The Body and the Archive," *October* 39 (winter 1986): 3–64; John Tagg, "Power and Photography: Part One, A Means of Surveillance: The Photograph as Evidence in Law," *Screen Education* 36 (autumn 1980): 17–55.

58. Ross, *Sin and Society*, 50.

59. Michel Foucault, "The Dangerous Individual," in *Michel Foucault: Politics, Philosophy, Culture. Interviews and Other Writings, 1977–1984*, ed. Lawrence D. Kritzman (New York: Routledge, 1988), 144; Leps, *Apprehending the Criminal*, 59.

60. McKim, *Heredity and Human Progress*, 13, 21.

61. Daniel J. Kevles, *In the Name of Eugenics: Genetics and the Uses of Human Heredity* (New York: Knopf, 1995), 100.

62. Mark Thomas Connelly, *The Response to Prostitution in the Progressive Era* (Chapel Hill: University of North Carolina Press, 1980); Ruth Rosen, *The Lost Sisterhood: Prostitution in America, 1900–1918* (Baltimore: Johns Hopkins University Press, 1982); Frederick K. Grittner, *White Slavery: Myth, Ideology, and American Law* (New York: Garland, 1990).

63. Turner, "The City of Chicago," 390. See also, e.g., George Kibbe Turner, "The Daughters of the Poor," *McClure's*, Nov. 1909; and Vice Commission of Chicago, *The Social Evil in Chicago: A Study of Existing Conditions* (Chicago: Chicago Vice Commission, 1911).

64. See, e.g., Ernest A. Bell, *Fighting the Traffic; or, War on the White Slave Trade* (Chicago: L. S. Ball, 1910), 25–26.

65. Turner, "The Daughters of the Poor," 57–58. Anti-Semitic rhetoric informed policing practices. Theodore Bingham, New York City police commissioner, published an article titled "Foreign Criminals in New York" in *North American Review*, Sep. 1908. In it he alleged that 85 percent of New York's criminals were foreign born, with half of the total being Jews.

66. Jean Turner Zimmerman, *America's Black Traffic in White Girls*, 1912, cited in Connelly, *The Response to Prostitution*, 118.

67. A copy of this treaty was reproduced in Edward Seligman, ed., *The Social Evil, with Special Reference to Conditions Existing in New York City* (New York: Putnam's Sons, 1912), 202–203; and more recently in Francesco Cordasco and Thomas Monroe Pitkin, *The White Slave Trade and the Immigrants: A Chapter in American Social History* (Detroit: Blaine-Ethridge Books, 1981), 85–86.

68. Don Whitehead, *The FBI Story: A Report to the People* (New York: Random House, 1956), 20–21; Fred J. Cook, *The FBI Nobody Knows* (New York: Macmillan, 1964), 49–70.

69. David J. Langum, *Crossing over the Line: Legislating Morality and the Mann Act* (Chicago: University of Chicago Press, 1994), 49.

70. Tom Gunning, "From the Kaleidoscope to the X-Ray: Urban Spectatorship, Poe, Benjamin, and *Traffic in Souls* (1913)," *Wide Angle* 19, no. 4 (Oct. 1997): 49.

71. Kristen Whissel, "Regulating Mobility: Technology, Modernity, and Feature-Length Narrativity in *Traffic in Souls*," *Camera Obscura* 49, 17, no. 1 (2002): 12.

72. On the intertwining of a legitimate "upper world" in underworld criminality see the accounts of Josiah Flynt in *The World of Graft*; for a "muckraking" account of municipal corruption see, e.g., Lincoln Steffens, *The Shame of the Cities* (London: William Heinemann, 1904).

73. George Loane Tucker and Walter Macnamara *"Traffic in Souls* or *While New York Sleeps,"* Box 107, National Board of Review of Motion Pictures Collections, Rare Books and Manuscripts Division, New York Public Library.

74. Franco Moretti, *Signs Taken for Wonders: Essays in the Sociology of Literary Forms* (London: Verso, 1983), 136.

75. *Moving Picture World*, Aug. 7, 1920, 719.

76. Let me emphasize that this transformation was not complete, as the previous examples of the 1921 film *While New York Sleeps* makes clear. Instead, I seek here to map dominant trends; the shift to

stories about rehabilitation, connected in many cases to arguments about the environmental causes of crime and criminal gangs, becomes increasingly prevalent from 1915 on. I consider the intertwining of different discourses about criminality further below.

77. O. Henry, "A Retrieved Reformation," in *The Complete Works of O. Henry* (New York: Garden City Publishing, 1938), 428–434; Paul Armstrong, *Alias Jimmy Valentine* (1910).

78. *Moving Picture World*, March 6, 1915, 1459.

79. Owen Frawley Kildare, *My Mamie Rose; the Story of My Regeneration* (New York: Baker and Taylor, 1903). Kildare's book was turned into a play by Kildare and Walter Hackett and became a Broadway success. See Kevin Brownlow, *Behind the Mask of Innocence* (New York: Knopf, 1990), 180–195, esp. 190.

80. *Moving Picture World*, Oct. 2, 1915, 94.

81. *Moving Picture World*, Feb. 21, 1914, 932. The film tells the story of a gangster who reforms and leaves the city to live the life of a farmer with his wife and "plainly indicates," *Moving Picture World* noted, "that present punitive methods, failing to attain the desired end, are short-sighted if not mistaken, because they fail to show progress. The root of such evil lies in an abnormal social existence, best remedied, as in this case, by a total change that will enable the embryonic criminal to reorganize himself on a better plane."

82. In this the film follows what I take to be a dominant trend in American cinema from around 1909: the story of male reformation. Often this is connected to gendered ideals of respectability, as in a cycle of temperance dramas from 1909/1910, although it is also visible, for example, in the western. On this trend of reformation see Grieveson, *Policing Cinema*, 78–120.

83. Ryan, *Cradle of the Middle Class*; Blumin, *Emergence of the Middle Class.*

84. Richard Ohmann, *Selling Culture: Magazines, Markets, and Class at the Turn of the Century* (London: Verso, 1996), 329–337.

85. McKim, *Heredity and Human Progress*, 21, 20.

86. Dorothy Ross, *The Origins of American Social Science* (Cambridge, U.K.: Cambridge University Press, 1991), esp. 143–171, 219–256, 303–329.

87. Edward Alsworth Ross, *Social Control: A Survey of the Foundations of Order* (1901; repr. New York: Macmillan, 1932). On the influence of Ross see Dorothy Ross, *Origins of American Social Science*, 236. Significantly, Edward Ross began his book with a description of life in the city: "A condition of order at the junction of crowded city thoroughfares implies primarily an absence of collisions between men or vehicles that interfere one with another. Order cannot be said to prevail among people going in the same direction at the same pace, because there is no interference. . . . It does not exist when persons are constantly colliding one with another. But when all who meet or overtake one another in crowded ways take the time and pains needed to avoid collision, the throng is *orderly.* Now, at the bottom of the notion of social order lies the same idea" (1; emphasis in original). For Ross, and others, the city inaugurated anxieties about the maintenance of social order.

88. Park and Burgess, *Science of Sociology*, 785, 42.

89. Hartsfield, *American Response to Professional Crime*, 184–185. "[I]t was the establishment of the first-ever American sociology department at the new University of Chicago in 1892," Stephen Jones observes, "which provided the immediate direction for American criminology" (Stephen Jones, *Criminology* [London: Butterworths, 1998], 5).

90. William Healy, *The Individual Delinquent* (Boston: Little, Brown, 1915).

91. On this connection see Park, "The City as Social Laboratory," 5–6; and Ross, *Origins of American Social Science*, 226–227.

92. Lynn McDonald, *The Sociology of Law and Order* (London: Faber and Faber, 1976), 100–103; Hartsfield, *American Response to Professional Crime*, 179–188; Jones, *Criminology*, 109–114.

93. John Landesco, *Organized Crime in Chicago* (1929; repr. Chicago: University of Chicago Press, 1968), 221.

94. Louis Wirth, *The Ghetto* (Chicago: University of Chicago Press, 1928); Harvey W. Zorbaugh, *The Gold Coast and the Slum* (Chicago: University of Chicago Press, 1929); Frederic M. Thrasher, *The Gang: A Study of 1,313 Gangs in Chicago* (Chicago: University of Chicago Press, 1927); and Clifford Shaw, *Delinquency Areas: A Study of the Geographical Distribution of School Truants, Juvenile Delinquents, and Adult Offenders in Chicago* (Chicago: University of Chicago Press, 1929).

95. Robert E. Park, "The City: Suggestions for the Investigation of Human Behavior in the Urban Environment," in *The City*, ed. Robert E. Park and Ernest W. Burgess (1925; repr. Chicago: University of Chicago Press, 1967), 22.

96. Park, "The City as Social Laboratory," 2.

97. Ibid.

98. Sudhir Venkatesh, "Chicago's Pragmatic Planners: American Sociology and the Myth of Community," *Social Science History* 25, no. 2 (summer 2001): 275–317.

99. Ernest W. Burgess, "The Growth of a City: An Introduction to a Research Project," in *The City*, ed. Robert E. Park and Ernest W. Burgess (1925; repr. Chicago: University of Chicago Press, 1967), 24; Robert Park, Preface to Thrasher, *The Gang*, viii.

100. Shaw, *Delinquency Areas*, 205.

101. *Are They Born or Made?* (Humanology Film Producing Company, 1915) also advocated an environmentalist approach to the question of the creation of criminals and criminal gangs. In the film the central gangster tells his wife how his father's death and the forfeiture of their home in the country led him to move to the city slum and become caught up in gang activity. At the close they move away from the city and begin a new life on a farm. *Moving Picture World*, Jan. 2, 1915, 83. Humanology was founded by former gangster and gambler Jack Rose. Rose had informed on a number of gangsters involved in the gangland killing of Herman Rosenthal in July 1912. He left prison and became a stalwart on the church lecture circuit. *The Musketeers of Pig Alley* was made after the Rosenthal affair to capitalize on the publicity surrounding it.

102. *Moving Picture World*, Oct. 2, 1915, 94.

103. See, e.g., Jane Addams, *Democracy and Social Ethics* (New York: Macmillan, 1902); Addams, *Spirit of Youth*.

104. See, e.g., Michel Foucault, "The Political Technology of Individuals," in *Technologies of the Self: A Seminar with Michel Foucault*, ed. Luther H. Martin, Huck Gutman, and Patrick H. Hutton (London: Tavistock, 1988).

105. *Moving Picture World*, Oct. 2, 1915, 94.

106. Gaylyn Studlar, *This Mad Masquerade: Stardom and Masculinity in the Jazz Age* (New York: Columbia University Press, 1996), 213, and, on Chaney more generally, 199–248. See also John McCarty, *Hollywood Gangland: The Movies' Love Affair with the Mob* (New York: St. Martin's, 1993), 12–29.

107. *Moving Picture World*, Jan. 22, 1921, 465.

108. *Tenderloin* (Warner Bros., 1928), the early sound film, continued this sense of the dingy and threatening underworld of the city visible thus far. Likewise, in *Thunderbolt* (Paramount, 1929) the gangster arranges a meeting with his girlfriend in an all-black nightclub. Yet other films from this moment on would increasingly reimagine the space of the underworld, effectively disconnecting it from particular locations within the city and reconfiguring criminal space as more pervasive throughout the city and frequently as linked to glamorous spaces like the nightclubs in, for example, *Broadway* (Universal, 1929) and *Scarface*. "Criminals of nowadays do not haunt particular sections of New York," *Atlantic* writer Morris Markey noted in 1928. "In the old days there were 'honky-tonks,' those fantastic embellishments of city life which were recognized haunts for all types of backgrounds. . . . They were the ganglia, as it were, of Manhattan's criminal life. . . . The underworld no longer has a habitat—it is everywhere" (Morris Markey, "Gangs," *Atlantic*, March 1928, 305, cited in Ruth, *Inventing the Public Enemy*, 28).

109. James Donald, *Imagining the Modern City* (Minneapolis: University of Minnesota Press, 1999), 89.

110. Reviewing *Lights of New York* (Warner Bros., 1928), *Variety* observed simply: "It's underworld" (*Variety*, July 11, 1928). Likewise, the journal described *The Racket* (Paramount, 1928) as "[a]nother great underworld picture" (ibid.).

111. *The Silver Wedding* and *The Black Hand* were both based on newspaper accounts of recent crimes. *Underworld* was written by former journalist Ben Hecht. *Traffic in Souls* was claimed by Universal to have been based on a social reform report; see George Kneeland, *Commercialized Prostitution in New York City* (New York: Bureau of Social Hygiene, 1913). *Regeneration* and *Me, Gangster* were based on memoirs by former gang members; O. Henry stated he wrote *A Retrieved Reformation*, on which *Alias Jimmy Valentine* was based, after spending time in prison with a criminal he claimed was the real Jimmy Valentine. *The Musketeers of Pig Alley* was made to capitalize on the ongoing headlines about the recent gangland slaying of Herman Rosenthal. *Moving Picture World* described the film as "an underworld story which will remind many who see it of some recent happenings in New York City" (*Moving Picture World*, Nov. 16, 1912, 658). See also Russell Merritt's insightful discussion of the film in *The Griffith Project*, vol. 6, ed. Paolo Cherchi Usai (London: British Film Institute, 2002), 158–165. The connection with real-life events is a consistent feature of the gangster film, as many of the essays in this volume show.

Why Boys Go Wrong

Gangsters, Hoodlums, and the Natural History of Delinquent Careers

Richard Maltby

The street, the sidewalks swarm with people. Pushcarts range along the curb; the proprietors hawking their wares to all passersby. In the store windows bordering the street is a bizarre assortment of dry goods, cheeses, condiments and liquors, and from opened doorways and cellars issue a host of smells even more provocative. People elbow each other for passage along the sidewalk while others pause to bargain loudly with the pushcart peddlers. The shrill notes of a hurdy-gurdy are heard down the street and from somewhere overhead in the solid block of dingy six floor tenements comes the strident noise of a radio out of control. A street car clangs its way along among the pushcart peddlers and their customers. . . . [F]rom another direction a heavy truck lumbers along spreading the dust and dirt of the street in its wake. The boys in the side street at their game of ball give way before it, but in the ensuing traffic are able in some way to continue their play.[1]

THIS DESCRIPTION OF AN INNER-CITY STREET SCENE might have come from the screenplay of *The Public Enemy* (1931), *Dead End* (1937), or *Angels with Dirty Faces* (1938), all of which open with a scene establishing their environment of urban poverty. It is instead the beginning of a manuscript entitled "The Community—A Social Setting for the Motion Picture," written in December 1932 by Paul G. Cressey as a draft of *Boys, Movies, and City Streets*, a projected but eventually unpublished volume in the Payne Fund investigations into "Motion Pictures and Youth."[2] Like many of the other scholars in the Payne Fund project, Cressey was a product of the University of Chicago's school of urban sociology, the dominant academic institution developing sociological inquiry in the United States in the 1920s.[3] His book, which was to be jointly authored by Frederic Thrasher, aimed to extend his previous work on commercialized recreation, *The*

41

Taxi-Dance Hall, by constructing a "natural history" of the neighborhood movie theaters in a section of Manhattan from which had come "many of New York's youthful gunmen and desperados of recent years," including some notorious from coast to coast for their association "with organized crime of the worst forms."[4] Cressey's study aimed to place movies and their effects in the context of "the social backgrounds, the personal dynamics," and "the characteristic conditions of life" of the boys in this urban environment.[5] Pursuing an elliptical course through the gang history of Chicago and the influence of James Cagney's hoodlum heroics, this essay follows Cressey's project in examining the relationship between cinematic and sociological discourses on delinquency and criminality in the 1930s.

Like many 1930s crime movies, *The Public Enemy* begins with an explicit statement of authorial intent: "It is the intention of the authors of *The Public Enemy* to honestly depict an environment that exists today in a certain strata [*sic*] of American life, rather than to glorify the hoodlum or the criminal." It is frequently argued that this "rhetoric of civic responsibility" was an empty and largely cynical gesture intended to appease critics concerned about the movies' socially destabilizing effects.[6] This interpretation, however, places an ahistorical emphasis on the often claimed but seldom demonstrated "subversive" effects of these movies and simplifies their complex and contradictory position within the discourses on criminality circulating at the time of their release. Contemporary reviews treated *The Public Enemy*'s claim to provide "a picture of gangland as it really is . . . a sociological study of the entire situation as it exists in Chicago" more seriously.[7] Reviewer André Sennwald's description of Warner Bros.' motive in making *The Public Enemy* as "laudable" may have been ironic, but his assessment of its central performances as "remarkably lifelike portraits of young hoodlums . . . a hard and true picture of the unheroic gangster" was typical of reviewers' endorsements of the movie's claims to realism.[8] In the *National Board of Review Magazine* James Shelley Hamilton took the movie's claim to be "something of a sociological document, presenting . . . its story and characters as a problem which the country must . . . solve," seriously enough to debate the value of its contribution to the public discourse on the causes of criminality.[9]

The studio was not, of course, primarily seeking to produce a sociological treatise, any more than it intended to produce a "subversive" movie. Its aim was to produce the "roughest, toughest, and best of the gang films to date," avoiding any sentimentality in the representation of its amoral characters.[10] The editorial position expressed in the movie's opening and closing titles provided a plausible defense for its "vigorous and brutal assault upon the nerves"; without such a defense the picture could not have been widely exhibited.[11] The motion picture industry was well aware that it needed to address the persistent criticism that movies were a source of inspiration for criminal behavior and knowledge of criminal technique, in both its general statements of intent and its justification of individual pictures. As I have detailed elsewhere, industry leaders had on previous occasions countered allegations that movies were "the basic cause of the crime waves of today" and recognized the economic and political necessity of justifying the content of their products as simultaneously harmless and socially responsible.[12] The requirement to present *The Public Enemy* as a contribution to social debate was not something tacked on to the end of the project to fool the censorious but an integral part of the movie's process of construction.

On January 6, 1931, Darryl F. Zanuck, head of production at Warner Bros., sent Col. Jason S. Joy, director of the Studio Relations Committee (SRC) of the Motion Picture Producers and Distributors of America, Inc. (MPPDA), a draft copy of the script of *The Public Enemy*. Anticipating the likely censorship difficulties that its subject matter would present, Zanuck sought to justify the movie's "biography of a couple of young gentlemen from Chicago" as a contribution to public debate. In addition to its insistence on "the futility of crime as a business or as a profit," he argued that *The Public Enemy* carried "a secondary theme, that

> PROHIBITION is not the cause of the present crime wave—mobs and gangs have existed for years and years BECAUSE of *environment* and the only thing that PROHIBITION has done is to bring these unlawful organizations more noticeably before the eye of the public. REPEAL of the Eighteenth Amendment could not possibly stop CRIME and WARFARE. The only thing that can STOP same is the betterment of ENVIRONMENT and living conditions in the lower reasons [*sic*]. In other words, "The Public Enemy" is the story of two boys who know nothing but CRIME, STEALING, CHEATING AND KILLING, and they both come to their death in the picture because of their activities. . . . Our picture is going to be a biography more than a plot. . . . I feel that if we can sell the idea that . . . ONLY BY THE BETTERMENT OF ENVIRONMENT AND EDUCATION for the masses can we overcome the widespread tendency toward *lawbreaking*—we have then punched over a moral that should do a lot toward protecting us.[13]

To promote the movie in a way that would disarm its potential critics, or else ensure that protests would enhance its box office performance rather than damage it, Zanuck's argument had to be plausible enough to earn the endorsement of at least some reviewers and other contributors to public debate, such as educators, criminologists, and sociologists. It also had to be integral to both the structure of the movie and its publicity. The movie's self-justification lay in the combination of its claim to historical and factual accuracy, its rejection of the "sentimental, preachy type" of plot "in which a 'moll' saves the day for justice and humanity," its substitution of "handsome youths whose looks belie their evil deeds" for the "outmoded" caricatures of crooks as "blue-jowled monsters with cauliflower ears and flattened noses," and its representation of an environmental account of the causes of criminality, which echoed both the conclusions and the method of the most recent sociological research in its presentation of "an intense biographical document."[14]

During the late 1920s the University of Chicago Press published several major works on the role played by environment and personality in the development of criminal behavior, particularly among the young. Led by Robert E. Park and Ernest W. Burgess, and explicitly deriving its terminology from the study of natural history, the Chicago school of sociology conceived the city as an ecological system, subject to "the selective, distributive, and accommodative forces of the environment" that distributed and segregated a city's population, encouraging the evolution of what Park termed "natural areas," each with their own "peculiar selective and cultural characteristics."[15] Under these ecological influences some "natural areas" would assume the character of a "moral region," in which a distinctive moral code diverging from the city's norm operated.[16] The Darwinism underlying this analysis was encapsulated by Harvey Zorbaugh in *The Gold Coast and the Slum* in 1929: "The slum gradually acquires a character distinctly different from that of other areas of the city through a cumulative process of natural selection that is continually going on as the more ambitious and energetic keep moving out and the unadjusted, the dregs, and the outlaws accumulate."[17] The most fully elaborated application of the concept of the "moral region" occurred in Clifford Shaw's studies of "delinquency areas." Shaw demonstrated that rates of truancy, juvenile delinquency, and adult felony were subject to high geographical variation in different areas of Chicago, with the highest rates found in "interstitial" areas in transition from residential to business or industrial use and in areas "characterized by physical deterioration, decreasing population, and the disintegration of the conventional neighborhood culture and organization." He maintained that the intrusion of business and industry into residential areas caused "a disintegration of the community as a unit of social control," which was intensified by "the influx of foreign national and racial groups whose old cultural and social controls break down in the new cultural and racial situation of the city."[18]

In his 1942 book on the ecology of delinquency and crime Shaw argued that in these interstitial areas, where there existed "the greatest disparity between the social values to which the people aspire and the availability of facilities for acquiring these values in conventional ways," crime might become "an organized way of life," the means by which people attempted to acquire "the economic and social values generally idealized in our culture." Adolescent boys in such areas knew that many criminals became rich and powerful: "their clothes, cars, and other possessions are the unmistakable evidence of this fact." For such boys the gangster represented the only available model of American success, and this knowledge helped determine "the character of their ideals."[19] This was particularly true, the Chicago sociologists argued, for the children of immigrants, who experienced an increasing amount of personal disorganization as a result of trying to live in two social worlds with conflicting values:

> The child cannot live and conform in both social worlds at the same time. The family and colony are defined for him in his American contacts by such epithets as "dago," "wop," "foreign," and the like. He feels the loss of status attached to his connection with the colony. . . . In his effort to achieve status in the American city he loses his rapport with family and community. Conflicts arise between the child and his family. Yet by virtue of his race, his manner of speech, the necessity of living in the colony, and these same definitive epithets, he is excluded from status and intimate participation in American life. Out of this situation . . . arises the gang, affording the boy a social world in which he finds his only status and recognition.[20]

For the most part the Chicago sociologists were more concerned with the gang than with the gangster. In his 1927 book *The Gang*, which for decades remained "the basic work concerning the gang as a form of social organization," Frederic Thrasher used the term *gangster* only once to refer to Capone-like criminals "at the top" of organized crime. Thrasher's central concern was with the gang as an adolescent phenomenon. Occupying a period "between childhood, when he is usually incorporated in a family structure, and marriage, when he is reincorporated into a family and other orderly relations of work, religion, and pleasure . . . the gang appears to be an interstitial group, a manifestation of the period of readjustment between childhood and maturity."[21] While gangland included "most of the underworld districts" within its borders, it was inhabited by adolescent gangs rather than by adult criminals, and Thrasher argued that there was "no hard and fast dividing line between predatory gangs of boys and criminal groups of younger and older adults." In gangland, argued Thrasher, boys learned demoralizing personal habits, familiarity with criminal techniques, and a philosophy of life that facilitated further delinquency, merging imperceptibly into a life of hardened criminality for some gang members. Chicago's crime was rooted in the adolescent gang "as its basic organized unit, no matter how it may have become elaborated into rings and syndicates," and almost all of Chicago's supposed ten thousand professional criminals had received gang training.[22]

Members of the Chicago school frequently suggested that social phenomena had a "natural history," in order to give temporal shape to the proposition that the ecological forces of the city exercised a determining influence on the lives of its inhabitants.[23] When applied to an individual presented as a representative case history, as Shaw did in his studies of *The Jack-Roller* (1930), *The Natural History of a Delinquent Career* (1931), and *Brothers in Crime* (1938), the conception of a "natural history" served as a determining condition of the biography under consideration.[24] In Shaw's analysis criminal behavior was not the result of individual depravity, mental deficiency, or psychopathology but a response to "the cultural disintegration which has resulted from the natural processes involved in the growth and expansion of the city."[25] Shaw identified delinquency as an effect of the mutual alienation of adolescent males and conventional social organization, a symptom of "the gulf between residents of slum communities and the larger society." Criminal careers resulted from the combined effect of boys drifting into delinquency as a way of life and the rejection of the convicted delinquent by conventional society. Alienation was a consequence of powerlessness, and crime, delinquency, and social disorganization were in turn "complex products of alienation and the forces related to it."[26]

Although Shaw and Thrasher made extensive use of first-person accounts to dramatize the sociological phenomena they examined, they viewed the delinquents they studied as constructs of the city and ascribed them very little individual agency in the process of their own social construction. Their proposition that the gang culture of juvenile delinquency bred the adult gangster through a continuum of demoralization from truancy, vulgarity, smoking, and crap shooting to jack-rolling (mugging), bootlegging, and murder became common sociological wisdom in the second quarter of the century. When Thrasher suggested that the hoodlum might develop into either "a seasoned gangster *or* a professional criminal," however, he was making a semantic distinction in keeping with its generally accepted meaning of the term prior to 1925.[27]

During the 1920s, however, the meaning of the term *gangster* was shifting significantly as the organizational, discursive, and social structures of criminality changed. The word was of late nineteenth-century American coinage (the *Oxford English Dictionary's* earliest etymological reference is in 1896) and referred most commonly to the imbrication of criminality and machine politics in low-income areas of major cities.[28] In his 1927 book *The Gangs of New York* Herbert Asbury proclaimed that the gangster "has now passed from the metropolitan scene," having existed for the previous decade "mainly in the lively imaginations of industrious journalists."[29] "There are now no gangs in New York," Asbury declared, "and no gangsters in the sense that the word has come into common use." The "gangs" described by newspapers in the 1920s bore little resemblance to the "great brawling, thieving gangs" of the late nineteenth century: "They are gunmen and burglars, but none of their killings and stealings have anything to do with gang rivalry or questions of gang jurisdiction. . . . Their operations lack the spectacularity of the deeds of the old timers, and probably will continue to lack it until they have been touched by the magic finger of legend."[30] Legend was, however, actively constructing a revised mythology of the gangster as businessman around the figure of Al Capone, "the Horatio Alger lad of Prohibition," principally through a style of press reporting "not shy about printing higher truths which transcended mere fact."[31] As David Ruth notes, the inventors of the post-1925 gangster's public image were journalists "who moved easily from medium to medium": "'Factual' journalistic accounts relied on imaginative conjecture and regularly included material, from the dialogue at ultra-secret meetings to the unuttered thoughts of dying men, beyond the range of even the most capable reporter. 'Fictional' accounts . . . invariably claimed authenticity, asserting the author's intimate knowledge of gangland, highlighting the use of shady underworld consultants, or incorporating well-known real settings and events."[32] The shift in the meaning of *gangster* to embrace the Prohibition-inspired model represented by Capone was both gradual and contradictory. While eulogizing Capone as "the greatest and most successful gangster who ever lived," the anonymous author of 1930's *X Marks the Spot* maintained that "what is significant is that *he really is a gangster,* as much so as the celebrated Monk Eastman and Big Jack Zelig of New York. As a youth he was himself a member of their notorious Five Points gang, and the difference between him and all other gangsters is that he is possessed of a genius for organization and a profound business sense."[33]

Academic accounts of "the empire of gangland" also emphasized its historical continuities with the neighborhood criminal gangs of the 1890s as strongly as they dwelt on the changes in gang activity brought about by Prohibition. In his 1929 study, *Organized Crime in Chicago,* undertaken under the auspices of the Chicago school and published as part of the Illinois Crime Survey, John Landesco argued that organized crime had not originated with prohibition and that the underworld providing Chicagoans with alcohol displayed crucial continuities in gang leadership and gang activity, and above all in the "unholy alliance between organized crime and politics," that had existed thirty years earlier.[34]

Thrasher described municipal politics as a complex of personal relationships and mutual personal obligations "which make service in the interest of an impersonal public and an abstract justice very difficult."[35] In the slum districts of gangland, wrote Harvey Zorbaugh, the immigrant vote was "a commodity upon the market . . . controlled by the bosses and kings of the colony, marshalled, if need be, with the aid of gangs and automatics, and traded to the higher-ups for petty political favors."[36] Local politicians actively cultivated gangs, providing some of them with clubrooms and protection from prosecution, so that when they came of age they would become loyal members of the local political machine. As an example of the way that gang influence was enlisted in the support of political machines, Thrasher cited the history of Ragen's Colts, an "athletic club" sponsored by a district politician, operating for twenty-five years as both a political organization that bred "aldermen, police captains, county treasurers, sheriffs . . . some of whom have made good records in public service," and an effectively lawless gang so well protected from punishment that its members "succeeded pretty well in terrorizing their immediate community."[37] This protection, in turn, reinforced the gang's political power: most visibly, a gang leader's ability to influence a district election result was rewarded with immunity from effective punishment for the most serious of crimes, including rioting and murder. "It has become customary in Chicago to refer to these gangsters as 'immune criminals,'" declared Thrasher. "The immunity which the politician confers is not without its effect upon gang boys, who are prospective gangsters."[38] Such immunity, indeed, was most frequently exercised in excusing the day-to-day criminal activities of adolescent gang members.[39]

The pattern of mutual obligation between politicians, municipal officials, and criminal gangs had long constituted a significant part of the history of gangs as both Asbury and the Chicago sociologists understood them. Thrasher and Landesco, however, recognized that as well as augmenting the power of criminal gangs to corrupt public officials, the vast profits to be made from bootlegging had introduced "a different and more sinister form of relation between the gangster and the politician," creating "the commercialized gang of today": "Neighborliness and friendly relations recede to the background. Operations in crime and political protection from its consequences are no longer local but city-wide. Immunity is no longer obtained by friendship, but from graft. Organized crime and organized political corruption have formed a partnership to exploit for profit the enormous revenues to be derived from law-breaking. . . . [W]hile neighborhood criminal gangs can rely only on the influence of the local politician, mercenary criminal gangs have understandings with the highest sources of protection in the county, the city, and certain of the nearby towns and villages."[40] The "commercialized gang" was ceasing to be a neighborhood group and becoming instead "a feudal group of professional gunmen formed to exploit the business of crime . . . a retinue of mercenaries held together by need of protection and expectation of profits."[41]

In his discussion "The Gang and Organized Crime" Thrasher distinguished three types of criminal gangs, identifying the most "successful and permanent type" as the "Master Gang." The principal business of these gangs was bootlegging, but many were also involved in robbery or the promotion of gambling or prostitution. The names of the "ten to twenty" such gangs operating in Chicago "are sufficient to strike terror into the hearts of the peaceful residents of the districts where they hold sway."[42] Typical of such groups was the Valley Gang, which had been in existence for over fifty years. From the 1870s it had controlled the Fifteenth Street district politically and socially, maintaining Irish hegemony in the district in the face of German, Jewish, and southern Italian immigration and having "an element of genuine leadership and loyal following" in the neighborhood.[43] From the mid-1890s to 1920 the gang was led by "the feared and fearless dictator of the district," Patrick "Paddy the Bear" Ryan, who added "labor slugging" to the gang's mixture of criminal and political activities.[44] When Ryan was assassinated in June 1920 by another member of the gang, leadership passed to his protégés Terry Druggan and Frankie Lake, who moved into beer trafficking, eventually controlling half a dozen breweries in partnership with brewing magnate Joseph Stenson, and providing Capone's mentor John Torrio with a model of successful collaboration between bootleggers and respectable business. The "wizened and dwarfish" Druggan and "big and bull-like" Lake were boyhood friends who dressed alike and became known to the tabloid press as "the Damon and Pythias of gangland"; they were less flatteringly described by John Kobler as "the comic turn of Chicago gangland, a vaudeville brother act about to break into a song-and-dance routine."[45]

Although Druggan and Lake feature in recent histories of organized crime only as minor characters, they were the first gangsters to distribute beer on a large scale in Chicago after Prohibition and the first gangsters to be pursued by the federal government for unpaid taxes, and their exploits were prominently reported in the Chicago press.[46] Before Torrio established his cartel, the Valley Gang continued its criminal activities, and both Druggan and Lake were arrested for robbery and hijacking in the early 1920s, although their political connections ensured they were never brought to trial. By 1924, however, bootlegging had made them millionaires, and Druggan boasted to the press that even the lowliest member of his gang wore silk shirts and rode in chauffeur-driven Rolls Royces. They were both imprisoned for contempt of court in July 1924 but served their year's sentence in considerable comfort after "the usual considerations and conveniences" had been afforded to the local authorities, coming and going from Cook County jail "almost as freely as though they were living at a hotel."[47] During Chicago's "beer wars" of the mid-1920s Druggan and Lake largely succeeded in maintaining a profitable neutrality, but they were indicted on federal tax charges in 1928 and eventually sentenced in 1932.[48]

According to August Vollmer, the foremost police reformer of the period, *The Public Enemy* was "more or less a correct depiction of events which transpired in Chicago recently, and may be said to follow very carefully one of the notorious characters of that city from his infancy to his last hour on earth."[49] It was based on an unpublished novel, "Beer and Blood," written by Kubec Glasmon and John Bright.[50] Glasmon was a pharmacist, drugstore owner, and minor bootlegger in Chicago in the 1920s. Bright worked for him and with Glasmon's encouragement wrote "Beer and Blood" out of their experiences. In later interviews Bright described the original story as including "every aspect of the Chicago underworld, Italians, Irish, Jewish, Polish, with no group's particular methods and interests specified."[51] Zanuck chose to focus the movie on the single story of "'The Public Enemy' and his friend," which he thought was "the most commercial and easiest to adapt" of the book's several plotlines.[52] Warner Bros. bought the rights to "Beer and Blood" but never published it, instead producing a tie-in novelization of the movie plot rewritten by an anonymous studio writer.[53] "Beer and Blood" was a light fictionalization of the newspaper history of the beer wars, and the screenplay adapted incidents from that history into the lives of its two protagonists. Bright claimed that the character of Tommy Powers was based on "an Irish hoodlum of our acquaintance," and the movie's press book explicitly identified the two protagonists as "the Damon and Pythias of gangland":[54] "Those who know their post-Volstead Chicago history will immediately recognize in the characters of Tom Powers and Matt Doyle the well known Chicago underworld figures of Frankie Lake and Terry Druggan, who operated the first breweries and beer trucks after prohibition."[55]

The first half of *The Public Enemy* presented a plausible "natural history" of characters resembling Druggan and Lake, particularly in their relationship with

Paddy Ryan. Tommy and Matt's delinquent careers, however, bore a generic resemblance to those of most of Chicago's "commercialized gangsters" of the 1920s and traced the gangster's evolution described by Landesco in the individualized terms of what amounted to a composite biography, entirely consonant with the Chicago school's analysis and hardly less factual than those of the Chicago press. The commercialized gangsters of the 1920s were almost all born between 1892 and 1899, achieving their brief media celebrity in their mid-twenties.[56] Dion O'Banion, for instance, was born in 1892 and at the age of nine moved to Chicago to live with his grandparents after the death of his mother. Living in a North Side district known at different times as Kilgubbin or Little Hell, he became an altar boy at Holy Name Cathedral and joined the juvenile division of the Market Street gang, where he acquired his education in petty thievery and mayhem and made the acquaintance of Vincent "Schemer" Drucci, George "Bugs" Moran, and Earl J. Wajciechowski, a.k.a. Hymie Weiss. At seventeen he was imprisoned in the Chicago House of Correction for theft and two years later for assault and possession of a deadly weapon. Subsequently, he became a "slugger" in Chicago's newspaper circulation wars, took control of the forty-second and forty-third wards and entered the bootlegging business, while continuing to pursue his career as a burglar and safecracker. O'Banion's delinquent career matches that of Tommy Powers quite closely, although according to the movie's chronology Tommy would be much closer in age to Wajciechowski, who was born in 1898.

The second half of Tommy's biography borrows freely from the "factual" accounts of the O'Banion gang's exploits, incorporating several identifiable incidents from newspaper reports of the lives of O'Banion, Weiss, and Louis "Two-Gun" (or occasionally "Three-Gun") Alterie.[57] Most famous of these was the 1923 death of Samuel "Nails" Morton in a riding accident and the subsequent execution of the horse by either O'Banion or Alterie.[58] After O'Banion's assassination in November 1924, Alterie vowed revenge by proposing a publicly staged shoot-out with O'Banion's killers, akin to Tommy's attack on Schemer Burns's headquarters, declaring that he would "get two or three of them before they get me."[59] Weiss, Moran, and Drucci made several spectacular but unsuccessful attempts on the lives of Torrio and Capone, demonstrating their public reputation as "rowdy Irish in temperament if not in fact."[60] Weiss was notorious for his evil temper and impulsiveness, and reports that he once pushed an omelet into a girlfriend's face were cited as the source of *The Public Enemy*'s infamous grapefruit incident. His assassination in the first "machine-gun nest" murder in October 1926 was recreated in the killing of Matt Doyle (Edward Woods). *The Public Enemy*'s other references to "actual" events involved the activities of other gangs: the robbery of the bond warehouse copied an unsuccessful attempted robbery of the Morand government warehouse by members of the South Side O'Donnell gang in 1926, and Tommy's kidnapping from hospital invoked one of the many unsuccessful assassination attempts on New York gangster Jack "Legs" Diamond.

The well-read viewer would, therefore, have recognized the movie's references to several notorious underworld characters, whose names and deeds were, as the press book declared, only "thinly disguised in the cast of characters." There are, however, two more substantial points to be made from these references. First, the adaptation omitted any discussion of the mutually dependent relationship between organized criminality and municipal politics, which occupied a central place not only in the Chicago sociologists' analysis but also in Bright and Glasmon's source novel. Gangster movies consistently avoided any substantial or detailed representation of what the sociologists regarded as the core element enabling gangster activity, local political protection, in favor of their representation of the spectacle and melodrama of criminal performance. To that extent, criticisms, such as James Shelley Hamilton's, that gangster pictures were "merely entertainment . . . a sensational pastime" providing "nothing but thrills and horrors, and some amusement," were unarguable.[61]

Second, all the "actual" events alluded to in the movie—however invented those events might originally have been—refer to criminal groupings other than the Capone-Torrio gang, which is conventionally credited with the organization of Chicago's bootlegging into a business. Rather, they refer to gangsters belonging to an earlier mode of criminal behavior rooted much more in the neighborhood and the criminal traditions of the gangs described by Thrasher and Asbury. Although contemporary reports represented O'Banion and his followers as offering Torrio and Capone "their only challenge for domination of the city," they were depicted in the public discourse of criminality as figures of local color rather than as businessmen. The anonymous 1930 publication X Marks the Spot described O'Banion as the underworld's "most fantastic and picturesque personality," a "paradoxical mixture of ferocity and sentimentality . . . a typical neighborhood gangster from boyhood," whose "power resulted from the application of methods quite unlike those of Johnny Torrio and Capone. . . . Torrio was a businessman first and a gangster second. O'Banion was a gangster. . . . One didn't want trouble; the other was always looking for it." Unlike the commercialized gang that Capone inherited from Torrio, O'Banion's gang "was built on friendship, with pecuniary considerations secondary. O'Banion depended upon his pals, and his pals depended upon him."[62] "To his way of thinking, humanity was divided into two classes—'right guys' and 'wrong guys.'"[63] To Landesco, O'Banion's propensity for uncalculated random acts of violence was childishly irresponsible, and O'Banion himself was "just a superior sort of 'plug-ugly.'"[64] Summarizing these accounts, David Ruth suggests that the conflict between Capone and the North Side gang was represented as "one between two systems, the former mercenary and businesslike, the latter based on 'friendship, loyalty and affection.'"[65] The gangster philosophy articulated in The Public Enemy was closely aligned to the personal and neighborhood loyalties of Druggan, O'Banion, or Weiss rather than to Torrio or Capone's expediency. Although the movie's biographical subject shifted from the comparatively inconspicuous Valley

1. In *The Public Enemy* (1931) James Cagney and Edward Woods progress from delinquents to hoodlums, whose "heroism," according to Frederic Thrasher, might be extolled in "unsupervised gangs of younger adolescents" (273). Courtesy of the British Film Institute.

Gang to the more flamboyant North Siders, it was a quite precise depiction of a particular type of gangster, progressing in his delinquent career through the several levels of a neighborhood gang culture before joining a "Master Gang." Tommy inherited his "passionless savagery," his "sunny brutality," and his impulsiveness and lack of organizational prowess from press accounts of O'Banion and Weiss and the declining tradition of gangster practice they represented.

In the authorial discourse of its opening and closing titles, *The Public Enemy* identified its protagonist as a "hoodlum" rather than a "gangster." Indeed, for a movie invariably considered an urtext of the genre, it is remarkable that the term *gangster* occurs only once in the movie, in a newspaper headline describing the funeral of "noted gangster 'Nails' Nathan." According to the *OED* the word *hoodlum* dates from the 1870s and is most likely of Californian origin, meaning "a youthful street rowdy; 'a loafing youth of mischievous proclivities'; a dangerous rough." More exactly, Frederic Thrasher suggested that the hoodlum was a protocriminal, not yet the fully formed entity: "If the younger undirected gangs and clubs of the gang type, which serve as training schools for delinquency, do not succeed in turning out the finished criminal, they often develop a type of personality which may well foreshadow the gangster and the gunman. A boy of this type may best be described as a hoodlum, the sort of 'hero' who is extolled in most unsupervised gangs of younger adolescents."[66] *The Public Enemy*'s identification with *Little Caesar* and *Scarface* as the trilogy of "classic" early 1930s gangster movies has encouraged a reading of its plot as if it portrayed the rise and fall of a commercialized gangster. Unlike *Little Caesar* or *Scarface*, however, *The Public Enemy* does not depict the acquisition, exercise, or loss of power, and Tommy remains "a classically ordinary criminal," untroubled by either ambition or any desire to escape the neighborhood.[67] Instead, *The Public Enemy* traces Tommy's hoodlum career. Throughout the movie Tommy and Matt's criminal activities remain at a mundane level. Their earliest attempt at adult criminality is a semicomic disaster, when Tommy's panicking at seeing a stuffed bear in a fur shop results in the deaths of a friend and a cop. We see them stage a successful warehouse robbery and threaten a bartender in their work as Nails Nathan's "trouble squad," but their more extreme acts of violence are both instances of personal revenge enacted against defenseless victims: Rajah the horse and Putty Nose. They occupy a subordinate role in the bootlegging business, not an organizational one, obeying instructions rather than giving them. Despite Tommy's apparent status as Nails's and Paddy's favored son, he can do nothing to hold the gang together on his own after Nails's death, and their business operation collapses, leaving Ryan at the mercy of Schemer Burns and willing to quit the racket.

Tommy does become a member of the nouveau riche, dressing and driving in the style to which Terry Druggan's gang became accustomed and visiting as ritzy a nightclub as Warner's set budget would allow, but his wardrobe and money bring him little evident satisfaction, either with women or in his attempts at family reconciliation. Apparently incapable of domesticity—Matt says he is "not the marrying kind"—Tommy seeks to treat women as a form of property, a means to display his new affluence, along with clothes and cars. Unlike cars, however, women disrupt his homosocial relationships. Tom twice disturbs the development of Matt and Maisie's romance: in the Washington Arms hotel, when he interrupts their noisy lovemaking in the room next door, and at the night club, when he drags Matt away from his marriage celebration to kill Putty Nose. When Kitty's attempts at domesticity start "getting on my nerves," he trades up for a more luxurious model, but while Gwen "ain't no Ford," he seems to have trouble with her gears:

> Tommy: All my friends think that things are different between us than they are. They think they know me pretty well, and they don't think I'd go for a merry-go-round.
> Gwen: . . . Do you want things to be different, to please your boyfriends?
> Tommy: No, but how long can a guy hold out? I'd go screwy.

Later in this scene—the most awkward in the movie—Gwen describes the character she is attracted to: ". . . you're so strong. You don't give, you take. Oh, Tommy, I could love you to death." Her description matches that paraded in the movie's advertisements, of "men who take whatever they desire from life . . . expensive cars . . . expensive women . . . all theirs for the commanding!" Such an account hardly fits Tommy's conduct in the movie, however. Always subordinate to Tommy's need for revenge and his obedience to Ryan, Gwen herself disappears from the screen after Nails's death and, significantly, is not part of the family reunion at the hospital.[68]

The contradictions in their relationship—she smothers him in her breast while telling him how dominant and aggressive he is—are never resolved, and their relationship is never consummated, since Matt interrupts them with the news of Nathan's death, and Tommy is deprived of the social and sexual opportunity Gwen presents because he has to go and shoot a horse. Tommy and Matt remain "boys" throughout the movie, and Tommy's psychological immaturity is most vividly demonstrated in his relationships with women: he is "Tommy boy" and "my baby" to his mother, "big boy" to Kitty, a "spoiled boy" and a "bashful boy" unable to articulate his desire to Gwen, and a "fine boy" to Jane, the older woman who "takes care" of Paddy's "boys" when they are hiding out.

In several respects *The Public Enemy* gestures toward an Oedipal drama. Tommy's father makes only one appearance in the movie, when he emerges from the house in police helmet and suspenders, to beat Tommy for stealing some roller skates. His silence intensifies the symbolic identity as both Father and the Law bestowed on him by his improbable costume. He is subsequently absent from the movie, an absence explained in the 1917 scene ("If your pa was alive I wouldn't care so much") but that is perhaps better accounted for by the 1915 robbery, in which Tommy shoots the cop who is chasing them.[69] For the remainder of the movie the law is present only through the appearance of the garrulous Officer Patrick Burke, who tells Mike that "the worst part" of Tommy's delinquency "is that he's been lying to his mother." The absent figure of the Law is thus combined with the absent figure of the Father, who might complete and secure the family unit. Without him the family is self-destructive. Tommy and his elder brother, Mike, fight in every scene they share until Tommy is in the hospital, and Mike disrupts every opportunity for family harmony, hitting Tommy three times and breaking the furniture on two occasions.[70] For all his moral rectitude, Mike is afforded no authority in the movie, and Tommy's dysfunctional family embodies the relationship between delinquency and the absence of "normal" family conditions indicated in all the contemporary sociological studies.[71]

The Public Enemy's family melodrama stages a conflict between the two social worlds of the second generation immigrant. The movie's Oedipal narrative dramatizes the family conflicts generated by the process of Americanization, in which traditional structures of family and community authority disintegrated under the pressure of what Harvey Zorbaugh called the "cosmopolitanism of the slum."[72] That the drama of the second-generation immigrant child was enacted as an Irish American story conformed to a pattern of cultural succession, hybrid identity, and ethnic disguise common to moviemakers, gangsters, and the subjects of Clifford Shaw's "natural histories," whose Polish and Jewish immigrant identities were concealed behind their Anglicized names.[73] Just as the Anglicized immigrant Jews Emmanuel Goldenberg and Friedrich Muni Meyer Weisenfreund established their Hollywood careers by playing Rico Bandello and Tony Camonte, many gangsters themselves practiced a form of transposable ethnic disguise in their choice of alternate identities, in which Anglicization was only one element. For part of the 1920s Al Capone was better known by his alias, Al Brown.[74] More intricately, Polish Catholic Earl Wajciechowski acquired the apparently Jewish nom de guerre Hymie Weiss, and Louis Alterie was born Leland Varain and had a brief professional boxing career under the name "Kid Haynes." "Machine Gun" Jack McGurn, a prime suspect in the St. Valentine's Day Massacre, was born Vincenzo Gebardi and also traveled as James DeMora; and James Clark, one of the massacre victims, was born Albert Kashellek and was allegedly a full-blooded Sioux. In "Beer and Blood," when Tommy asks "Where does the Polak get the Burns moniker?" his companion responds, "Hell, a name ain't no indication o' what a guy is."[75]

In the movies this ethnically fluid form of Americanization enabled actors to perform ethnicities other than their own but also facilitated the creation of more generalized signifiers of a nonspecific ethnicity in performance, encapsulated by *Variety*'s description of Cagney as "a deese, dose and dem, chip-on-the-shoulder, on-the-make example of young America."[76] Mediating mass commercial culture through their peer groups, young second-generation immigrants adapted these signifiers to specify their own hybrid ethnicity and reconcile their foreign origins with American identities, using shared strategies of participation, identification, and interpretation of the movies in their neighborhood.[77]

In its plot and character delineation *The Public Enemy* attempted to render its protagonist unattractive, but the picture's most problematic element was also its most significant commercial achievement: the creation of a new star in James Cagney. To an even greater extent than was true of Edward G. Robinson's performance in *Little Caesar*, Cagney's screen persona was defined by his first starring performance, and both Cagney and his studio were occupied in negotiating its limitations for much of the 1930s.[78] The actor remained ostentatiously uncomfortable with the extent to which his audience appeal restricted his roles, and he fought his typecasting more or less unsuccessfully throughout his career. The studio, however, was faced with the related issue of containing the specific commercial appeal of his rebellious, iconoclastic behavior—what *Variety* called his "you-be-damned personality" and "roughneck character work"—within an acceptable narrative framework.[79]

Almost alone among the major stars of Classical Hollywood, Cagney's appeal was almost exclusively to "the boys who go for the gangster stuff," an urban male audience identified by Lincoln Kirstein as "the American majority . . . the semi-literate lower middle class," who apparently found no anxiety in recognizing themselves in Cagney.[80] Reviewing *Taxi!*, his fourth starring picture, *Variety* noted that "Cagney so closely approaches the way the average citizen in moments of everyday stress would like to act that it seems to be one of the strongest bonds between the actor and the witnessing men."[81] Cagney's appeal to the semidelinquent rapidly became trade press folklore. Certainly, some of his most disreputable fans accepted the authenticity of his performance. The boys Paul Cressey interviewed believed that both Cagney and Robinson were slum boys who had "made good in a big way in the movies." Cagney was rumored to have "used his 'dukies' (fists) to scare Jewish movie magnates into giving him a chance," and the gang boys' "conviction that these two actors are products of the local community is abetted by the feeling that their acting is a perfect depiction of styles of conduct approved among the street boys of the community."[82]

After his first starring role Cagney did not play a gangster—that is, a character making his living through organized criminal activity and in armed conflict with the police—until *Angels with Dirty Faces* in 1938. In the series of performances that followed *The Public Enemy*, however, he played characters who behaved very much as gangsters behaved—gamblers, con artists, ex-gangsters, and reformed criminals—establishing a close correlation between his own performative idiolect and that of the "gangster type."[83] In this sequence of early roles he became the mediated, heroic embodiment of the "social type" identified by Thrasher and Shaw as the hoodlum.[84] Like the men whom John Landesco described frequenting neighborhood gambling houses, Cagney appeared "good-natured, well-dressed, adorned and sophisticated, and above all, . . . American, in the eyes of the gang boy."[85] His mannered performance of ethnic urbanity provided a model of behavior that was both easily imitated and immediately recognizable precisely because it was codified as a set of reiterable gestures. The ease with which Cagney's hoodlum hero could be stylistically imitated exacerbated anxieties that such gestures were merely the most visible signs of the gangster's influence over a continuum of unsupervised adolescent behavior.

Within a year of *The Public Enemy*'s release, Cagney's influence on the movies' representation of juvenile delinquency was evident. Reviewing RKO's *Are These Our Children?* (1931), Richard Hanser described it as "a sort of adolescent *Public Enemy*," bringing "the well-known gangster theme down to the schoolboy level." Eric Linden's "gestures, his mannerisms, and even his speech continually bring to mind Cagney's potent performance in *The Public Enemy*."[86] Like *The Public Enemy, Are These Our Children?* told a quasi-Oedipal second-generation-immigrant story in which the protagonist, Eddie Brand (Linden), was already thoroughly Americanized, whereas the representation of immigrant ethnicity was displaced onto secondary characters, most notably Heinie Krantz, Eddie's adoptive father figure (William Orlamond), who preserves old-country values in the pickles and sausages he sells in his delicatessen. Eddie is a "good boy" led on a downward path fueled by alcohol, jazz dancing, and racketeering friends until he kills Heinie in a drunken rage and is sentenced to death. Promoted by the MPPDA among civic and women's groups as "a powerful preachment against liquor, loose living and the evil consequences of bad companions," the movie ran foul of several state censor boards and other representatives of the civically responsible audience, who complained that "its detailed portrayal of the wild life among high school students" and "suggestive love-making between intoxicated boys and girls" would "lower the moral values of those who see the picture."[87]

Are These Our Children? presented a psychological explanation for Eddie's precipitate descent into criminality rather than a sociological one. The burden of the

2. Eric Linden (left), played by Eddie Brand, on the downward path as good girlfriend Mary (Rochelle Hudson) looks on helplessly in *Are These Our Children?* (1931), which the MPPDA hoped would be "a powerful preachment against liquor, loose living and the evil consequences of bad companions." Courtesy of the Academy of Motion Picture Arts and Sciences.

movie's anxiety, however, was placed by its title on the typicality of Eddie's experience. However unrealistic the movie's suggestion that staying out late, drinking, and promiscuity led inexorably to patricide was as an account of actual delinquent behavior, it was symptomatic of a bourgeois parental concern that despite their upbringing, their own children could be easily led astray by bad companions or influences, including what E. W. Burgess called "the commercialization of stimulation" in the recreational life of the American city.[88] The fear that adolescence was in itself a cause of delinquency, and that bourgeois children, too, might become hoodlums by imitating the gestural practices of the urban proletariat, promoted the policing of adolescence in all social classes.[89] An environmentalist account of delinquency, by contrast, held some comfort for middle-class parents, since it located the problem as resulting from conditions unlike those in which they brought up their own children. The gradual ascendancy to sociological orthodoxy of an environmentalist explanation of delinquency based on the Chicago school's research was echoed in Hollywood's intermittent return to the subject throughout the 1930s, in movies that also made evident Cagney's definitive influence over the performance of delinquency.[90] In *The Mayor of Hell* (Warner Bros., 1933) Cagney reformed both his character and his performance to become "a big-fisted big brother of boys gone wrong" by playing a "cheap ward-heeler" who turns his sinecure at a reform school into a crusade to improve conditions. Although the movie's depiction of endemic corruption and racketeering in municipal politics was more explicit than in any of the movies of the gangster cycle (Cagney tells a politician, "I'm telling you what I want, and I'm gonna get it, or else I'll take my votes and peddle them elsewhere"), Cagney's character was accorded an implausible innocence of the conditions of juvenile detention. Despite what must have been his backstory education in juvenile gangs and adolescent athletic clubs, he appears to know nothing of what reform school teaches its inmates. More important, Cagney is absent from the mood-setting first third of the movie and from the prison riot at the end, when he is confined out of harm's way in an out-of-state hotel room, absolved of any responsibility for the plot's development. These contradictions in character and action detach Cagney from the movie's principal action, separating his performance of gangster manners from the activity of the gang.

The Mayor of Hell's advertising campaign invited audiences to see "the producers of I Am a Fugitive tear the taboo from another forbidden theme . . . a theme more terrific than The Public Enemy."[91] In justifying the movie to the SRC, Zanuck had used familiar arguments: "This is a story of reformation — reformation of young boys — reformation of terrible conditions existing in some reform schools today."[92] The MPPDA had qualms over the movie's title and some of its action, as well as what SRC director James Wingate identified as "the express purpose of the producer to make a picture that will attract public thought and criticism to the problem presented," an intention, Wingate noted, that "presages difficulties for us."[93] These difficulties were most succinctly explained by the MPPDA's Canadian representative, Colonel John Cooper, reporting on Canadian censors' criticisms of Are These Our Children? "They reasoned that if we say our pictures are intended for entertainment and not for education, we cannot depart from this argument on occasion to ask that a picture be passed for its educational value. In other words, they tell us that we cannot have our pie and eat it."[94]

The position that The Public Enemy's authorial intention had sought to occupy, of contributing to public debate, was denied to subsequent movies on the grounds that it transgressed the films' cultural function as entertainment. The industry's solution to this conundrum was to limit its commentary to the initial exposition of a social problem, which was then individualized and resolved through a fantastical act of benevolence. In The Mayor of Hell, for example, a benign judge forgives the inmates' rioting and manslaughter and hands the reform school back to Cagney, despite his criminal record. Above all, the administrators of the Production Code insisted that the conditions from which the problem emanated be not represented as endemic but as the result of the actions of bad individuals, and therefore remediable. At worst, this caused their products to be denounced as unrealistic, which was, after all, what they were supposed to be.

In 1937 Samuel Goldwyn's production of *Dead End* demonstrated the commercial viability of "ameliorative environmentalism," offering a utopian solution to urban crime in the architect hero's dreams of tearing down the tenements and building "a decent world where people could live decent and be decent."[95] Sidney Kingsley's play had been a Broadway success in 1935 but was not adapted for the movies for two years, in part because of anticipated censorship difficulties. When RKO was considering buying the play in 1935, Production Code Administration director Joseph Breen pointed to the conundrum the Canadian censors had mentioned three years previously: "Our experiences with political censor boards indicate that they are disposed definitely to oppose pictures showing children engaged in crime. . . . [I]n the present instance the social values of the play are so definitely dependent upon the showing of the criminal activities of the kids that there would be no play without showing these activities and, consequently, no important social document."[96] The Goldwyn adaptation was nevertheless strongly promoted on the basis of its social commentary, declaring in its press book that "*Dead End* cries aloud to America to suffocate its criminals in the cradle. It beseeches Society to do something to alleviate the disease-breeding tenements in which its future citizens are asked to grow strong."[97] Its advertising also featured endorsements from civic leaders, as well as journalists, and Senator Robert F. Wagner, who had strenuously propounded the environmentalist argument in seeking passage of housing legislation to initiate a major program of slum clearance, was a prominently displayed guest at *Dead End*'s New York premiere.

Dead End's principal attraction was "the six incomparable urchins imported from the stage production," who provided the closest representation of the gangs described by Thrasher that Hollywood had yet seen, in the most unambiguous representation of the Chicago school's explanation of the origins of criminality: "The Kingsley theme is that tenements breed gangsters, and no one does anything about it. The vicious cycle continues with each succeeding crop of children, thwarted in their growth of any sense of social responsibility by the pressure of vicious environment."[98] The Dead End Kids were promoted as authentic products of the inner city, "New York tenement kids" imported for the movie from "their slum homes."[99] Their early popularity, like their invented "slumdom to stardom" histories, echoed Cagney's. Reviewing the Kids' Warner Bros. movie *Crime School*, the *New York Journal-American* reported, "The same Strand audiences that used to tear down the theater doors in the days of the early Cagneys were out in full force yesterday . . . and practically drowned out the dialogue on the screen with their approving hoots and applause."[100] Having picked up the Kids' contracts from Goldwyn, Warners developed a project with the ingredients Goldwyn had originally wanted for *Dead End* itself, casting Cagney opposite the juveniles who imitated his delinquent performance style.[101]

Angels with Dirty Faces retains elements of Thrasher's depiction of gang life in the behavior of the Dead End Kids and the presentation of a gang tradition passed

3. Kept at a safe distance "from any actual scenes of crime," the Dead End Kids read about Rocky Sullivan's unheroic end in *Angels with Dirty Faces* (1938) in their basement boiler room. Courtesy of the Academy of Motion Picture Arts and Sciences.

on from one adolescent generation to another. Its representation of Rocky Sullivan's (Cagney) integration into the neighborhood, and his familiar and affectionate relationship with Father Jerry Connolly (Pat O'Brien), suggests what John Landesco described as "the genuine popularity of the gangster, home-grown in the neighborhood gang, idealized in the morality of the neighbourhood." [102] A reformist social agenda was, however, an integral element of this "junior gangster" cycle, evident not only in the movie's publicity but woven firmly and in detail into its structure. [103] Combined with the celebration of Cagney's performance style, this requirement committed the movie to an incoherent and contradictory representation of Cagney's character, in particular in his relationship with the Dead End Kids, for whom he is "both a pariah and a role model to aspire to." [104] The movie's press book seemed to revel in these contradictions, simultaneously editorializing its "strong social message" that "the children of the slums . . . be given the helping hand that will spell for them the difference between a good life and a life of crime" and advertising its unmatched depiction of the "glamour of gangsterism." [105]

The problems the industry faced in imitating *Dead End* were indicated by press reports in late 1937 that some New York schoolchildren had begun to copy one of the more violent incidents in the movie, scarring their classmates with "the mark of the squealer," which seemed to offer anecdotal confirmation of the most sensational hypotheses of the movies' bad influence.[106] Such reports gave substance to Breen's concerns that as "virtually every studio" set about acquiring a "boys gang" in early 1938, they would produce a cycle as dangerous to the industry's public relations as the gangster movies of 1930 and 1931.[107] The PCA introduced an amendment to the Production Code's regulations on crime, stipulating that "pictures dealing with criminal activities in which minors participate or to which minors are related, shall not be approved if they incite demoralizing imitation on the part of youth."[108] Although this resolution was not in force until after *Angels with Dirty Faces* was completed, the movie substantially accommodated its concerns by separating the gangster's performance from any recognizable form of criminal activity.

In negotiations over the script, the Production Code Administration insisted that the Kids "be kept as far as possible from any actual scenes of crime," presenting the studio with the task of representing the Kids' proximity to crime without showing them participating in any criminal activity themselves.[109] In conforming to this requirement, *Angels with Dirty Faces* develops two discrete plotlines. In one Rocky finds himself a gangster without a gang, excluded from the undefined criminal activities of Frazier (Humphrey Bogart) and Keefer (George Bancroft) and in conflict with the forces of organized crime throughout the movie. In the other he renews old neighborhood friendships and socializes with the Dead End Kids, who have no direct contact with Rocky's dealings with his ex-associates. Their only access to Rocky's criminal activities, indeed, is through the newspaper stories they read in their boiler-room basement. These reports seem to be about a third Rocky, very different from the charming, comic and sympathetic character with whom they eat lunch and play basketball.[110] The movie's montage sequences and newspaper headlines represent this third strand, not otherwise present in the movie's action, in which "Two-Gun Rocky Sullivan, well-known gangster and badman," is reported to rule the city through his mysterious, unspecified power over "corrupt officialdom." The movie remains set firmly inside the domain protected by Father Jerry's moral authority; and the "outside," where the Kids are "surrounded by the same rotten corruption and crime and criminals" for them "to look up to and revere and respect and admire and imitate," exists only in the mediated form of newspaper stories, which take place in a "real" world not inhabited by the movie's characters. Rather than "exposing the rackets," Jerry confronts and then manipulates the mediated image of the gangster, as personified by parts of Cagney's performance.

Angels with Dirty Faces internalizes the Production Code's discourse and enacts a drama of self-regulation in which the gangster conforms to the Code's requirement that he "turn yellow"—the most consistent demand of the SRC in the 1930–1931 cycle—because the moral reformer, constructed in the PCA's self-image, asks him to.[111] Jerry asks Rocky to "have the heart" to go to the electric chair screaming for mercy so that the Kids will "despise your memory." Rocky must renounce his public persona and unify and redeem his character through a final duplicitous act of heroic cowardice to ensure that the Kids will repudiate him and the values he represents. With the institutional force of both the Catholic Church and the PCA behind him, Jerry insists that Rocky has "been a hero to these kids and hundreds of others all through your life and now you're going to be a glorified hero in death, and I want to prevent that, Rocky. They've got to despise your memory. They've got to be ashamed of you." Rocky pleads for his dignity — "You're asking me to throw away the only thing I've got left, the only thing they haven't been able to take away from me" — but to no avail, for this debate is conducted to ensure the triumph of Father Jerry's moral narrative over the glamorous spectacle of Cagney's performance.

Angels with Dirty Faces thus contains the movies' influence on delinquency within itself, both in the sense that this is the subject of the movie and in the manner in which the anxiety of influence is resolved within the movie's morally victorious narrative. The movie's ending marks the final recuperation of Cagney's decade-long performance of glamorous criminality within the solipsistic world prescribed by the Production Code, where redemption was attainable only through the compensating moral values of suffering and punishment, and the appropriate moral lessons were absorbed by all those onscreen — whatever alternative conclusions actual audiences may have reached.

In accordance with the prohibition on criminal activities that might "incite demoralizing imitation on the part of youth," in *The Angels Wash Their Faces* (1939) the Kids themselves became agents of reform, fighting civic corruption. Within the year they were at military academy (*On Dress Parade*), a prelude to their meritorious wartime service fighting Axis spies in *Let's Get Tough* (1943) and the *Junior G-Men* series (1940–1943). In the long-running series and serials in which they appeared as the Little Tough Guys, the East Side Kids, and the Bowery Boys they turned the representation of delinquency into an interminable comedy of bad manners, ever more divorced from its sociological and cinematic origins. After more than a decade of generic dilution, the descendants of *The Public Enemy* were finally rendered harmlessly entertaining to the juvenile audiences to whom they appealed.[112]

Notes

1. Paul G. Cressey, "The Community — A Social Setting for the Motion Picture," in *Children and the Movies: Media Influence and the Payne Fund Controversy,* by Garth S. Jowett, Ian C. Jarvie, and Kathryn H. Fuller (Cambridge, U.K.: Cambridge University Press, 1996), 133. This passage is also quoted in Henry James Forman, *Our Movie-Made Children* (New York: Macmillan, 1933), 251.

2. The full text of "The Community — A Social Setting for the Motion Picture" is published in Jowett, Jarvie, and Fuller, *Children and the Movies,* along with a detailed account of the project's vicissitudes.

3. "For well over a decade after the end of the First World War Chicago sociology was, in effect, American sociology" (Dennis Smith, *The Chicago School: A Liberal Critique of Capitalism* [New York: St. Martin's, 1988], 2).

4. Cressey, "The Community," 133.

5. Ibid., 230.

6. Jonathan Munby, *Public Enemies, Public Heroes: Screening the Gangster from "Little Caesar" to "Touch of Evil"* (Chicago: University of Chicago Press, 1999), 51.

7. Warner Bros. press book for *The Public Enemy*.

8. André Sennwald, "Two Thugs," *New York Times*, April 24, 1931, 27.

9. James Shelley Hamilton, "Some Gangster Films," *National Board of Review Magazine*, May 1931; repr. in *From Quasimodo to Scarlett O'Hara: A National Board of Review Anthology, 1920–1940*, ed. Stanley Hochman (New York: Ungar, 1982), 144.

10. Review of *The Public Enemy*, *Variety*, April 29, 1931.

11. Ibid.

12. Roger W. Babson, "Crime Waves," *Babson's Reports Special Letter*, April 8, 1929. My extended discussion of this issue is in Richard Maltby, "The Spectacle of Criminality," in *Violence and American Cinema*, ed. J. David Slocum (New York: Routledge, 2001), 118–152.

13. Zanuck to Joy, Jan. 6, 1931, *The Public Enemy* PCA file, Margaret Herrick Library, Academy of Motion Picture Arts and Sciences (hereafter cited as MHL-AMPAS). Typography in original. Warner Bros. bought the story, "Beer and Blood," on Dec. 1, 1930. The final screenplay by Harvey Thew was dated Jan. 18, 1931, and shooting began in February.

14. Warner Bros. press book for *The Public Enemy*.

15. R. D. McKenzie, "The Ecological Approach to the Study of the Human Community," in *The City*, ed. Robert E. Park and Ernest W. Burgess (1925; repr. Chicago: University of Chicago Press, 1967), 63, 77.

16. Robert E. Park, "The City: Suggestions for the Investigation of Human Behavior in the Urban Environment," in *The City*, ed. Robert E. Park and Ernest W. Burgess (1925; repr. Chicago: University of Chicago Press, 1967), , 45.

17. Harvey Warren Zorbaugh, *The Gold Coast and the Slum: A Sociological Study of Chicago's Near North Side* (1929; repr. Chicago: University of Chicago Press, 1976), 128–129.

18. Clifford R. Shaw, with the collaboration of Frederick M. Zorbaugh, Henry D. McKay, and Leonard S. Cottrell, *Delinquency Areas: Study of the Geographic Distribution of School Truants, Juvenile Delinquents, and Adult Offenders in Chicago* (Chicago: University of Chicago Press, 1929), 204–206.

19. Clifford R. Shaw and Henry D. McKay, *Juvenile Delinquency and Urban Areas: A Study of Delinquency in Relation to Differential Characteristics of Local Communities in American Cities*, rev. ed. (Chicago: University of Chicago Press, 1969), 315–320.

20. Zorbaugh, *Gold Coast and the Slum*, 176–177.

21. James F. Short Jr., introduction to *The Gang: A Study of 1,313 Gangs in Chicago*, by Frederic M. Thrasher, abr. ed. (Chicago: University of Chicago Press, 1963), lii; Frederic M. Thrasher, *The Gang: A Study of 1,313 Gangs in Chicago*, abr. ed. (Chicago: University of Chicago Press, 1963), 32.

22. Thrasher, *The Gang*, 281, 267, 291.

23. Jon Snodgrass, "The Jack-Roller: A Fifty-Year Follow-Up," *Urban Life* 11, no. 4 (Jan. 1983): 440–441.

24. Clifford R. Shaw, *The Jack-Roller: A Delinquent Boy's Own Story* (Chicago: University of Chicago Press, 1930); Clifford R. Shaw, in collaboration with Maurice E. Moore, *The Natural History of a Delinquent Career* (Chicago: University of Chicago Press, 1931); Clifford R. Shaw, with the assistance of Henry D. McKay and James F. McDonald, *Brothers in Crime* (Chicago: University of Chicago Press, 1938).

25. Shaw, *Brothers in Crime*, 359.

26. James F. Short Jr., introduction to Shaw and McKay, *Juvenile Delinquency and Urban Areas*, xlvii–xlviii.

27. Thrasher, *The Gang*, 257 (my emphasis).

28. Derivative and competing terms proliferated in the early twentieth century: *gangland* dates from the 1910s; *racketeer, gangsterism*, and *gangsterdom* were creations of the 1920s press.

29. Herbert Asbury, *The Gangs of New York: An Informal History of the Underworld* (New York: Knopf, 1927; repr. London: Arrow, 2002), xiv (pagination refers to the 2002 edition). In 1940 Asbury published "An Informal History of the Chicago Underworld," primarily concerned with the pre-Prohibition period, under the title *Gem of the Prairie* (New York: Knopf), which was reprinted as *The Gangs of Chicago* (New York: Thunder's Mouth Press, 2002).

30. Asbury, *Gangs of New York*, xv–xvi.

31. Fred D. Pasley, *Al Capone: The Biography of a Self-Made Man* (1931; repr. London: Faber, 1966), 317; William Helmer with Rick Mattix, *Public Enemies: America's Criminal Past, 1919–1940* (New York: Checkmark, 1998), 82.

32. David E. Ruth, *Inventing the Public Enemy: The Gangster in American Culture, 1918–1934* (Chicago: University of Chicago Press, 1996), 5.

33. Anonymous [Hal Andrews], *X Marks the Spot: Chicago Gang Wars in Pictures* (Chicago: Spot Publishing, 1930); http://www.x-marksthespot.com (my emphasis).

34. John Landesco, *Organized Crime in Chicago: Part III of The Illinois Crime Survey 1929* (Chicago: University of Chicago Press, 1968), 277.

35. Thrasher, *The Gang*, 321.

36. Zorbaugh, *Gold Coast and the Slum*, 139.

37. Thrasher, *The Gang*, 318.

38. Ibid., 320–322, 326–327.

39. Ibid., 329.

40. Landesco, *Organized Crime in Chicago*, 189, 281.

41. Ibid., 181, 245.

42. Thrasher, *The Gang*, 298, 300.

43. Landesco, *Organized Crime in Chicago*, 169.

44. [Andrews], *X Marks the Spot*; Thrasher, *The Gang*, 299.

45. [Andrews], *X Marks the Spot*; John Kobler, *Capone: The Life and World of Al Capone* (London: Coronet, 1971), 89.

46. In the Chicago Crime Commission's first list of Public Enemies, which ran to twenty-eight names, Lake was listed at number twenty-two and Druggan at twenty-three.

47. Thrasher, *The Gang*, 298–300.

48. Druggan and Lake's partnership dissolved in the early 1930s, and the Valley Gang effectively ceased to exist after Prohibition. After their release Lake moved to Detroit and became president of a coal and ice company, dying in 1947. Druggan's health deteriorated, and he died in poverty in 1954.

49. August Vollmer to Will Hays, memorandum, April 20, 1931, *The Public Enemy* PCA file, MHL-AMPAS. Vollmer, chief of police in Berkeley, Calif., was the author of the Illinois State Crime Commission report on the Chicago police.

50. The typescript of the novel, "Beer and Blood: The Story of a Couple o' Wrong Guys," by Kubec Glasmon and John Bright (n.d., 348 pages), is held in the Warner Library of the Wisconsin Center for Film and Theater Research.

51. Lee Server, *Screenwriter: Words Become Pictures: Interviews with Twelve Screenwriters from the Golden Age of American Movies* (Pittstown, N.J.: Main Street Press, 1987), 74.

52. Patrick McGilligan and Paul Buhle, *Tender Comrades: The Backstory of the Hollywood Blacklist* (New York: St. Martin's, 1997), 131; Server, *Screenwriter*, 74.

53. Kubec Glasmon and John Bright, *The Public Enemy* (New York: Grosset and Dunlap, 1931). Warners sold the novelization rights to Grosset and Dunlap for $400 on March 2, 1931. The book was published on March 20, several weeks before the movie's release, and sold seventeen thousand copies. See Henry Cohen, introduction to *The Public Enemy*, ed. Henry Cohen (Madison: University of Wisconsin Press, 1981), 13.

54. Server, *Screenwriter*, 74; Warner Bros. press book for *The Public Enemy*. Terry Druggan features, along with Capone and several other actual Chicago criminals, as an incidental character in "Beer and Blood." Tom also emulates a notorious incident in Druggan's history when he assaults a journalist in jail.

55. "James Cagney and Distinguished Cast seen here in a thrilling melodrama of the Dark Powers" (Warner Bros. press book for *The Public Enemy*).

56. The one exception among the group of Chicago-based figures discussed here was John Torrio, who was born in 1882 and "retired" after a near-fatal shooting in 1925 at the age of forty-seven.

57. Extant photographs show that Robert O'Connor, the actor who played Paddy Ryan, bore a resemblance to Dion O'Banion.

58. William Helmer suggests that "the murder of the horse appears to be pure myth, possibly based on a passing comment by Charles Gregston in the *Chicago Daily News* for November 19, 1924" (Helmer, *Public Enemies*, 82).

59. The hostile public response to these comments allegedly led Weiss to tell Moran to order Alterie out of Chicago and back to his ranch in Colorado. A figure of no further consequence in crime history, Alterie was shot to death in Chicago in 1935.

60. Helmer, *Public Enemies*, 54.

61. Hamilton, "Some Gangster Films," 146.

62. [Andrews], *X Marks the Spot*.

63. Pasley, *Al Capone*, 41. In the movie Paddy Ryan explains to Tom and Matt, "So far as Paddy Ryan is concerned there's only two kinds of people . . . right and wrong."

64. Landesco, *Organized Crime in Chicago*, 93.

65. Quoted in Ruth, *Inventing the Public Enemy*, 131–132.

66. Thrasher, *The Gang*, 273.

67. Cohen, *The Public Enemy*, 19.

68. In the screenplay Tommy returns to Gwen's apartment after Matt is killed, only to discover that she has left him (in the source novel, she has left him for another woman). In the novel it is his own sexual betrayal of Paddy with Jane, Gwen's desertion, and the belief that "everything has slipped out from under him" that "impel him in rage and disgust on his final errand" (Cohen, *The Public Enemy*, 20, 164).

69. In the novel Tommy's father is killed by a criminal while on duty.

70. Both the source novel and the script explicitly identify Mike as a war hero; ironically, Tom and Matt are given jobs delivering legal alcohol to pharmacies because of their boss's admiration for Mike's war record. See Cohen, *The Public Enemy*, 96–98.

71. For a summary of these studies see John M. Gillette and James M. Reinhardt, *Current Social Problems* (New York: American Book, 1933), 675–677.

72. Zorbaugh, *Gold Coast and the Slum*, 151.

73. Shaw gave the five second-generation Polish immigrants in *Brothers in Crime* the names John, Edward, James, Michael, and Carl Martin.

74. In *The Roaring Twenties* (1939), the Irish-American actor Paul Kelly plays a spaghetti-eating gangster called Nick Brown. See Ruth Vasey, *The World according to Hollywood, 1918–1939* (Exeter: University of Exeter Press, 1997), 143–144.

75. Quoted in Cohen, *The Public Enemy*, 19.

76. Review of *Taxi! Variety*, Jan. 12, 1932.

77. Lizabeth Cohen, *Making a New Deal: Industrial Workers in Chicago, 1919–1931* (Cambridge, U.K.: Cambridge University Press, 1990), 144–147.

78. Anticipating protests against the movie and its cycle, *Variety* recognized that Cagney "won't find it easy to follow this performance" because it was likely to typecast him. Review of *The Public Enemy*, *Variety*, April 29, 1931.

79. Review of *Lady Killer, Variety*, Jan. 2, 1934.

80. Lincoln Kirstein, "James Cagney and the American Hero," *Hound and Horn* 5 (April–June 1932): 466–467, quoted in Robert Sklar, *City Boys: Cagney, Bogart, Garfield* (Princeton, N.J.: Princeton University Press, 1992), 12; Review of *Delicious, Variety*, Dec. 29, 1931. Cagney's lack of appeal to female audiences is evidenced by the dearth of stories on him in fan magazines, notably *Photoplay*.

81. Review of *Taxi! Variety*, Jan. 12, 1932.

82. Cressey, "The Community," 181.

83. Whether or not Bright and Glasmon were principally responsible for Cagney's casting as Tom Powers, as Bright persistently claimed, his star persona was formed in significant part by their work as the writers of his next four movies, *Smart Money, Blonde Crazy, Taxi!*, and *The Crowd Roars*.

84. Thrasher, *The Gang*, 273.

85. Landesco, *Organized Crime in Chicago*, 210.

86. Richard Hanser, review of *Are These Our Children?* (RKO), *Buffalo Times*, Nov. 13, 1931. Linden's second movie appearance was on loan to Warner Bros. in *The Crowd Roars*, in which he played James Cagney's younger brother.

87. Trotti to Joy, telegram, Oct. 28, 1931, *Are These Our Children?* PCA file, MHL-AMPAS; Joseph Breen to Samuel Briskin, RKO, Feb. 10, 1937, *Are These Our Children?* PCA file, MHL-AMPAS.

88. Burgess, introduction to Cressey, *The Taxi-Dance Hall*, n.p.

89. Joseph F. Kett, *Rites of Passage: Adolescence in America, 1790 to the Present* (New York: Basic Books, 1977), 256.

90. Cagney's influence is evident in the performances of Frankie Darro in *The Mayor of Hell* and *Wild Boys of the Road* (both 1933—Darro had played Matt Doyle as a child in *The Public Enemy*), Mickey Rooney in MGM's *The Devil Is a Sissy* (1936) and *Boys Town* (1938), and the Dead End Kids.

91. Warner Bros. press book for *The Mayor of Hell*.

92. Zanuck to Wingate, Jan. 26, 1933, *The Mayor of Hell* PCA file, MHL-AMPAS.

93. Wingate to Julia Kelly, March 18, 1933, *The Mayor of Hell* PCA file, MHL-AMPAS.

94. Col. John Cooper, head of the MPPDA office in Canada, to Col. Joy, June 24, 1932, *Are These Our Children?* PCA file, MHL-AMPAS.

95. Sklar, *City Boys*, 75.

96. Breen to Ben Kahane, RKO, Nov. 6, 1935, *Dead End* PCA file, MHL-AMPAS.

97. *Dead End* press book.

98. Review of *Dead End*, *Variety*, Aug. 3, 1937.

99. Donita Ferguson, "Movie of the Week: *Dead End*," *Literary Digest*, Sep. 4, 1937, 40. The actors in fact all came from upper- or middle-class New York families, and most of them had careers as child actors before *Dead End*. Kyle Crichton, "Made-to-Order Punks," *Collier's*, July 29, 1939, 13+. I am grateful to Kevin Esch for these references.

100. Quoted in Sklar, *City Boys*, 75.

101. Frankie Burke's playing of the boy Rocky mimics Cagney's performance mannerisms exactly.

102. Landesco, *Organized Crime in Chicago*, 169.

103. *Motion Picture Herald*, Oct. 29, 1938.

104. Fran Mason, *American Gangster Cinema: From "Little Caesar" to "Pulp Fiction"* (London: Palgrave, 2002), 45.

105. "Editorial," in *Angels with Dirty Faces* press book (1938).

106. "Just Like the Movies," *Literary Digest*, Dec. 11, 1937, 4.

107. A partial listing of *Dead End*'s immediate imitations, excluding those featuring the Dead End Kids themselves, would include *Boy of the Streets*, released in December 1937 and starring Jackie Cooper, which *Variety* described as Monogram's most ambitious production to date and which won *Parents* magazine's medal for the best movie of the month; *Reformatory* (Columbia, released June 1938), with Jack Holt and Frankie Darro; *Boys Town* (MGM, released September 1938), with Spencer Tracy and Mickey Rooney; and *Juvenile Court* (Columbia, released September 1938).

108. Breen and Harmon to Hays, Nov. 23, 1938, MPPDA Microfilm Archive; MPPDA interoffice memo, Dec. 20, 1938, re Crime in Motion Pictures, MPPDA Microfilm Archive.

109. Breen, memorandum, April 5, 1938, *Angels with Dirty Faces* PCA file, MHL-AMPAS.

110. I am indebted to Michael Meneghetti, "Angels of Self-Regulation: *Angels with Dirty Faces* and the PCA" (unpublished essay, University of Iowa, 2001), for this description of Rocky's character and, more generally, to Meneghetti's insightful analysis of *Angels* for several of the arguments in this section.

111. Pat O'Brien's more than passing physical resemblance to Joseph Breen as crusading Catholic Father Jerry may be as coincidental as Robert O'Connor's resemblance to Dion O'Banion.

112. After *Dead End* the Kids were signed to a two-year contract by Goldwyn, who then sold them to Warner Bros. They made six movies for Warners in 1938 and 1939, including *They Made Me a Criminal* and *Hell's Kitchen*. In 1938 Universal borrowed Bernard Punsley, Huntz Hall, Billy Halop and Gabriel Dell to make *Little Tough Guy*. In late 1939 Warners dropped their contracts after the release of *On Dress Parade*, and Universal picked up these four as the core of the *Little Tough Guys* series for eight further movies and three twelve-part serials made between 1939 and 1943. From 1940 to 1945 Sam Katzman produced the "East Side Kids" for Monogram, featuring some of the same actors and Leo Gorcey. In 1946 Gorcey revamped them as the "Bowery Boys" in a series of forty-eight movies running until 1958 and built around the comedy duo of Gorcey and Hall. David Hayes and Brent Walker, *The Films of the Bowery Boys* (New York: Citadel Press, 1984).

Gang Busters

The Kefauver Crime Committee and the
Syndicate Films of the 1950s

Ronald W. Wilson

I N A L E T T E R T O H I S F R I E N D James Sandoe, dated March 6, 1952, crime novelist Raymond Chandler wrote: "I don't know whether you have a television set or whether having one you could have seen films of the Kefauver committee hearings. I saw part of those held in Los Angeles and found them fascinating. Obviously nothing that a mystery writer could dream up could be more fantastic than what actually goes on in the hoodlum empire which infests this country."[1] The televised hearings of the Senate Special Committee to Investigate Organized Crime in Interstate Commerce, popularly known as the Kefauver Committee, were the focus of the nation's attention between 1950 and 1951, garnering larger newspaper headlines even than the trial of Ethel and Julius Rosenberg. Audiences who did not own television sets could go to the local movie theater and see the televised hearings projected on the big screen, and newsreels, newspapers, and radio also kept the public informed on the proceedings. *Life* magazine reported, "Never before had the attention of the nation been so completely riveted on a single matter. The Senate investigation into interstate crime was almost the sole subject of national conversation."[2]

Chandler noted that a mystery writer could never dream up more fantastic crime tales, yet Hollywood could—and did. Throughout the 1950s, Hollywood studios produced numerous crime films that either were directly or indirectly influenced by the events and proceedings of the Kefauver Committee crime hearings. Ranging from 1950, with the Columbia release *711 Ocean Drive*, which contained a foreword by Senator Alexander Wiley of Wisconsin (a member of the Senate crime committee) to Samuel Fuller's *Underworld U.S.A.* (1961), in which a criminal syndicate is represented as a corporate empire, "syndicate films" continually emphasized the threat of the "greatest menace"[3]—organized crime—and the extent of its supposed stranglehold on postwar America.

The cold war produced a culture in which anxieties concerning communism and the atomic bomb centered on the internal infiltration of "normal" life by alien "others": communists were indistinguishable from ordinary, "respectable" citizens; thus, the self-appointed role of the House Un-American Activities Committee (HUAC) was to ferret out communist activity in seemingly secure areas such as the army and Hollywood. Similarly, organized crime was believed to have infiltrated American society in such a fashion that it, too, was an invisible presence posing its primary threat from within. The Kefauver hearings often referred to the "Mafia" as "a shadowy, international crime organization" that was behind local and national organized crime. According to historian Lee Bernstein:

> The conspiracy theory of organized crime was fueled by the fear that there were few distinguishable differences between gangsters and "respectable" people. *Time* [magazine] tapped into this fear. The gangster "lives comfortably but not fabulously in a respectable neighborhood, contributes to charity, hobnobs with cafe society, is a friend to politicians, sends his children to summer camp and the big kids to college. . . ." In describing criminals and organized crime in corporate terms, the [Kefauver] committee and the press used a readily available frame of reference for their conspiracy theory. They looked like businessmen, lived in the same neighborhoods as businessmen, contributed to charity and political campaigns—all with the goal of getting their tentacles into "legitimate enterprises."[4]

The syndicate films were able to feed easily into this discourse by combining attributes and conventions of the gangster film with the topicality of the Kefauver hearings. This chapter will examine the historical and sociocultural contexts of the Kefauver-inspired syndicate films of the 1950s, and the emergence of this cycle of crime films will be located in the interplay of their generic traits with the cultural discourse of the era. According to Steve Neale, "Genres do not consist solely of films. They consist also of specific systems of expectations and hypotheses which spectators bring with them to the cinema and which interact with films themselves during the course of the viewing process."[5]

The syndicate films drew on topical sources to provide their audience with a depiction of the "greater menace" of organized crime as a primarily alien conspiratorial threat in postwar America. Engendered by the newsworthiness of the hearings themselves, the cycle fed on public fears of the pervasiveness of organized crime not only in urban centers but also in small-town America. Invoking a sense of authenticity through both narrative and semidocumentary techniques, the cycle aimed to make connections with audiences' understanding of the contemporary political culture. Cinematic attempts to narrate the story of organized crime produced several cyclical variants of the syndicate-film format: the city exposé, rogue cop films, and witness prosecution films, as well as intergeneric hybrids, testify to a proliferation of cinematic ways of capturing the topicality of the organized crime drama.

On January 5, 1950, Senate Resolution 202, calling for an investigation of organized crime in the United States, was introduced by Estes Kefauver, the Democratic senator from Tennessee. Kefauver had studied recent reports from crime commissions in California, Michigan, and Illinois and believed that the federal government needed to play an active role in assisting local governments with what he saw as a growing national problem. The Special Committee to Investigate Organized Crime in Interstate Commerce was formed in May 1950, and it included Kefauver, Senator Alexander Wiley (R-Wis.), Senator Charles Tobey (R-N.H.), Senator Herbert O'Conor (D-Md.), and Senator Lester C. Hunt (D-Wyo.). Acting as chief counsel for the committee was Rudolph Halley. The purpose of the committee was threefold: to make a complete investigation to determine whether organized crime utilized the facilities of interstate commerce; to investigate the manner and extent of criminal operations that were taking place and identify the persons, firms, or corporations involved; and to determine whether such criminal operations were developing corrupting influences in violation of state or federal laws. The most important criminal activity that interested the committee was gambling and the use of the wire service by organized crime. At one point Kefauver claimed, "The Public Enemy No. One in America today is the Continental Press Agency": wire services broadcasted racing news and other gambling information across many states, and the receipt of this information provided the base for many large syndicate gambling operations.[6]

Within its fourteen-month duration (May 1950 to July 1951) the committee traveled to fourteen cities and interviewed more than seven hundred witnesses, resulting in twelve thousand pages of public testimony. Kefauver's motive for traveling around the country was primarily to illustrate the extent of organized crime's influence across the nation. All of the cities the committee visited were large urban centers: Miami, Kansas City, St. Louis, Philadelphia, Chicago, Tampa, Cleveland, Detroit, New Orleans, Las Vegas, San Francisco, Los Angeles, Saratoga, and New York City. The committee hearings in New York generated the most publicity and were viewed as the climax to the proceedings. Several of the hearings had been televised on a local level. The New York hearings, however, were broadcast nationally, sponsored by *Time* magazine. Some of the most colorful witnesses testified during these hearings: Frank Costello, the reputed "Prime Minister of the Underworld"; Virginia Hill Hausen, "Mistress to the Mob" (who after her testimony told reporters, "I hope an atom bomb drops on you!"); Ambassador William O'Dwyer, the former mayor of New York; Albert Anastasia, alleged boss of Murder, Inc.; and Jacob "Greasy Thumb" Guzik.

Bernstein has suggested that the Kefauver hearings purposely created an atmosphere of entertainment. "The easily digestible narrative that contributed to the popularity of the hearings allowed many viewers to describe the proceedings as a 'performance.' One goal of the hearings was to gain popular support for the legislative goals of the Committee. To do so they enlisted the narrative conventions

1. Members of the Senate Crime Investigating Committee, June 1, 1950.
Left to right: Sen. Charles Tobey, Sen. Herbert O'Conor, Rudolph Halley,
Sen. Estes Kefauver, and Sen. Alexander Wiley. Courtesy of the Library of
Congress Prints and Photographs Division.

of popular entertainment and avoided academic research."[7] According to
Bernstein, "The *New York Times*'s Jack Gould explicitly described the hearings in
terms of their entertainment value: 'It has been an almost incredible cast of characters that have made their appearance on the screen. The poker faced Erickson,
the saucily arrogant Adonis, the shy Costello and the jocose Virginia Hill might
have been hired from Hollywood's Central Casting Bureau.'"[8] This type of narrative construction was also reinforced, according to Kefauver biographer Joseph
Gorman, through "the simplistic concepts of American politics conveyed through
thousands of high school government classes and textbooks. Good and evil, heroes
and villains — such black and white categorization made each specific encounter
between committee and witness easy to follow."[9] This is further illustrated in a full-
page advertisement in *Film Daily*, dated March 27, 1951 (during the New York
hearings), for a full-length news feature from *Movietone News* on the "Kefauver
Crime Investigation" held in New York City. The advertisement shows two col-
umns labeled "The Investigators" (Sen. Estes Kefauver, Sen. Charles W. Tobey,
Sen. Herbert R. O'Conor, Sen. Lester C. Hunt, Sen. Alexander Wiley, Chief Counsel Rudolph Halley) and "The Witnesses" (Frank Costello, Ambassador O'Dwyer,
Anastasia, Virginia Hill Hausen, Frank Erickson, Jacob "Greasy Thumb" Guzik).[10]
The advertisement resembles a listing of dramatis personae in a play, and one could
easily substitute as column headings, "The Good Guys" and "The Bad Guys."[11]

2. Mobster Frank Costello testifying before the Kefauver Committee. Courtesy of the Library of Congress Prints and Photographs Division.

The Kefauver Committee Report on Organized Crime was the official document that presented the results of the transcontinental investigation. Published in the fall of 1951, following the final hearings, the document begins with an examination of the "City Stories," summarizing the results of testimony in each of the fourteen cities the committee visited. The report concluded that organized crime existed on a national level: "Organized criminal gangs operating in interstate commerce are firmly entrenched in our large cities in the operation of many different gambling enterprises such as bookmaking, policy, slot machines, as well as in other rackets such as the sale and distribution of narcotics and commercialized prostitution." Further, the report suggested that a "sinister criminal organization known as the Mafia" was the "binder which ties together the two major criminal syndicates as well as numerous other criminal groups throughout the country." The national organization of crime, the committee stated, wielded considerable power and constituted a shadow government that regulated its own trade, enforced its own laws, and used the laws of the legitimate government to further its interests.[12] Yet the true significance of the committee was elsewhere. According to Joseph Gorman, "The significance of the hearings lay, however, not so much in the quantity of evidence gathered by the committee as in the incredibly effective manner in which it managed to arouse an interest among great masses of people in the nature and scope of the problem of organized crime and its relationship to political corruption."[13] Hollywood producers were quick to capitalize on the topicality of organized crime in the nation's newspaper headlines by reinvigorating the relatively dormant gangster genre with "Kefauverism."

Tied in with the discourse on organized crime that Kefauverism sponsored were the developing postwar discourses of nationalism and of liberal consensus. The concept of a "national imagined community" is particularly useful for placing the syndicate films and the crime hearings within the larger context of national discourses. In regard to these films, as well as early television programming, the "imagined community" also helped reinforce the basic precepts of the emerging liberal consensus. Benedict Anderson defines the term *nation* as "an imagined political community": imagined as "both inherently limited and sovereign." Anderson argues that a nation is an "imagined community" primarily because the members of that community will never know most of their fellow members, yet they have a deeply conceived image of their communion. This communion is visualized as a deep, horizontal comradeship, without class distinctions. It is sovereign because of its historical dimensions, which include both the decline of the dynastic realm and the new motivating force of capitalism. According to Anderson's definition the community is limited because of the geographical boundaries of the nation itself.[14]

In his essay "The Ideology of the Liberal Consensus" Godfrey Hodgson argues that the common values and beliefs that many Americans held in the 1950s represented a "liberal consensus" that described America as a perfect society free from any major conflicts. Hodgson identifies six core assumptions of the "liberal consensus" ethic: American free enterprise as democracy, increased production (economic growth), equality, freedom from social problems, the chief threat of communism, and the destiny of America to bring the free-enterprise system to the rest of the world.[15] These values and beliefs conceived of America in the 1950s as a perfect society *because* of capitalism, not in spite of it. The rise of production in postwar America and the increase in consumer spending had also contributed to a growing sense of affluence and economic growth. Such assumptions, in tandem with the ideological ascendance of a "national imagined community," were produced and reproduced in the mass media. Newspapers, Benedict Anderson points out, are addressed to the collective of an imagined community in that the "newspaper reader, observing exact replicas of his own paper being consumed by his subway, barbershop, or residential neighbors, is continually reassured that the imagined world is visibly rooted in everyday life."[16] Similarly, early television was a commodity that fed on a "congregational audience" that was primarily family centered and communal in the consumption of wholesome, nonthreatening entertainment.

Postwar cinema's relation to the production of imagined community is, however, a paradoxical one. Taking the films produced by Hollywood in the late 1940s, such as *Crossfire* (1947), *Gentleman's Agreement* (1947), *Pinky* (1949), and *All the King's Men* (1949), the period marks a tendency to engage with more difficult, more socially and politically contentious, issues. Yet the emergence of the Kefauver-inspired crime cycles would counterindicate an ideological dominance of a "liberal consensus" in which such progressivism was curtailed. Social critiques of America's imagined community were, rather, deflected toward its alien "others" as narrated by the crime film.

The early cycle of syndicate films, 1950–1952, addressed the topical issue of organized crime within the boundaries of postwar crime film techniques. During the late 1940s "semidocumentary" techniques within fictional film contributed to a move from the studio-bound look of many crime films toward greater social realism. According to Frank Krutnik these crime dramas "signaled a shift away from the 'tough' thriller's obsession with psychological breakdown and sexual malaise, or at least they recast these elements within a perspective which stressed the *normative processes of law and order.*"[17] Other factors, including the Paramount decrees, might explain such a shift given that these films were produced in an era of upheaval in Hollywood. The Paramount decrees of 1948 forced the major studios to divest their large theater chains.[18] One of the effects of this divorcement was a significant rise in independent production. The freedom of exhibitors to choose from outside the Hollywood system led to the production of more independent films. Producers, actors, and directors formed their own production companies. And since the majors were still in control of distribution, many typically distributed independent products. A number of independents jumped on the "topicality" bandwagon in regard to the provocative nature of the revelations of the crime committee. By constructing narratives couched in a semidocumentary visual/aural style, these films provided their audiences with crime dramas that reinforced many of the revelations and conclusions of the Kefauver Committee. Increasingly with the crime film and especially with the syndicate film, the "normative processes of law and order" are continually emphasized. Police, detectives, investigative reporters are typical protagonists in these films, whose closure stresses the adage that "crime does not pay," not even organized crime. These films celebrated the efficacy of crime-fighting institutions and upheld the "imagined community" view that America was a perfect society because it could eradicate any threat, internal or external.

Early syndicate films released during the existence of the Kefauver Committee share several characteristics that set them apart from other crime films. Because of the widespread publicity and popularity of the hearings, the public became familiar with names and terms that eventually spilled over into popular culture. Key concepts of the committee hearings were utilized by Hollywood to invigorate crime films with topical references, either within the film's narrative or in a film's advertising. Syndicate films are concerned primarily with organized crime and its activities (gambling, bookmaking, and so forth). Organized crime, therefore, becomes a key narrative element within these films, displacing the traditional gangster narrative form illustrating the rise and fall of a lone protagonist. The early syndicate films also show a tendency to be explicatory in defining new terms and concepts of criminal activities (for example, "the $2 bet" and other betting terms, a *hit*, a *contract*, and so forth). Also these films tend to show crime as a business enterprise. A collective term is generally utilized, often in film titles themselves, to describe the nebulous, far-reaching criminal organization: *The Mob* (1951), *Hoodlum Empire* (1952), *Chicago Syndicate* (1955), and *The System* (1955). Organized crime is often referred to in these films as "the mob," "the syndicate," or "the combination," reflecting the move from entrepreneurial criminal efforts to incorporation. As film historian Jonathan Munby has noted, "These films focused on the decline of individual agency before the power of organizations, collectively reflecting the inquisition climate of the Red Scare that had only exacerbated the general paranoia about institutional power." [19]

Joseph M. Newman's *711 Ocean Drive* was the first syndicate film to be released after the formation of the Kefauver Committee in May 1950.[20] The film is significant because of its subject matter — the racing wire service and its manipulation by organized crime. It is also one of the first films to portray the "mob" as being business-like in their criminal operations. The film was released on July 19, 1950, and its advertising touted it as an "Expose of the $8,000,000,000 Gambling Syndicate and its Hoodlum Empire!" A full-page advertisement in *Film Daily* emphasized the film's purported veracity:

> Because of the disclosures made in this film, powerful gambling interests tried to halt production with threats of violence and reprisal. In a real sense, this picture was made with a gun in its back and it was only through the armed assistance of the police in Los Angeles, Boulder Dam and other communities, that this story was able to reach the screen. It is the story of the $8,000,000,000 syndicate that has milked 150,000,000 people of millions of dollars . . . a truly explosive story . . . a real motion picture achievement.[21]

The ad copy was accompanied by the silhouette of a policeman's profile, on which was printed, "Filmed Under Police Protection." The film also contained a prologue by Senator Alexander Wiley, of the newly formed Kefauver Committee. Wiley extolled the film as an "honest picture" that "can be a tremendous constructive factor in informing the public of the meaning of that innocent $2 racing bet at the candy store." [22] Within its narrative structure the film combined semidocumentary technique with the traditional rise-and-fall pattern of earlier gangster films. Thus, *711 Ocean Drive* represents a transitional film, bridging the gap from the 1940s noir semidocumentary thrillers to the syndicate-dominated crime films of the 1950s.

The film opens in semirealistic fashion, with Lt. Pete Wright (Howard St. John) of the "Gangster Squad" on his way to arrest Mal Granger (Edmond O'Brien) for murder. The ensuing flashback relates the meteoric rise and fall of Mal Granger from anonymous telephone repairman to big-shot operator in the syndicate. It is Mal's technical savvy with electronics that boosts his career when his local bookie, Chippy (Sammy White), advises him that there is money and power to be made with his technical know-how. Chippy brings him to the attention of his boss, Vince

Walters (Barry Kelley), who runs a booking operation under the front name Libert Finance Company. Mal soon devises a relay amplifier modification that organizes all of Walters's books into a unified system. When Walters is killed by a bookie whom he has threatened, Mal takes charge of the operation. Mal's subsequent success gains the attention of the national syndicate boss, Carl Stephans (Otto Kruger). Mal joins the syndicate, and, on discovering that he is not receiving the amount of profits he expected, he turns the tables on them by past-posting race results after he has placed a large bet. Mal has also had Stephans's underboss, Larry Mason (Don Porter), killed in order to get Mason's wife. When the killer attempts to blackmail Mal, he kills him by running him off a cliff. The film's climax occurs at the Hoover Dam, where the syndicate has informed police that Mal Granger is located. A chase ensues, and Granger is shot by the police within the art deco environs of the monument. The film ends with a voice-over narrator warning the audience, "Only an innocent $2 bet you say! Well it's just as innocent as the germs in an epidemic. Spreading the worst kind of disease. The civic disease of criminals with a[n] $8,000,000,000 racket. Corrupting politicians, buying protection, fostering crime . . . all with your $2."

The semidocumentary style of the film placed an emphasis on technology as a criminal tool, especially in regard to gambling and the wire service. Mal Granger is an expert on telephones and electronics that he uses to help enhance the wire service for bookie operations. *711 Ocean Drive* is unique in that the technical wizardry of its criminal protagonist is utilized to further the aims of organized crime. Most semidocumentary "police procedurals," such as *House on 92nd Street* (1945), *13 Rue Madeleine* (1946), *Call Northside 777* (1948), and *T-Men* (1949), show technology being used to the advantage of law enforcement personnel. This educative component of the film was not missed by reviewers. *Commonweal* noted:

> *711 Ocean Drive* tackles a theme as timely as today's headlines: gambling and bookies. Our hero in this case has quite a knowledge of electronics which he is putting to good use for the telephone company in Los Angeles. But his small salary won't stretch, and when a bookie friend shows him how his brains could be used to more monied advantage by an organization running a wire service, he starts to work for people of extremely dubious repute. At this stage of the movie you get a thorough education in how bookies, helped by a wire service right from the race track to their place of business, cash in on split-second timing.[23]

A feature of the film that would become more prevalent as the decade progressed is the depiction of gangsters as businessmen. Dapper, well-dressed Otto Kruger portrays crime boss Carl Stephans as if he were the CEO of the syndicate: overlooking board meetings, traveling by plane, issuing assignments to "special departments." The "gangsters" in *711 Ocean Drive* dress and act like businessmen and upper-class executives. In fact, the syndicate's method of enticing Granger to join and then isolating him can be read as a parallel to the rise and dominance of corporate America in the postwar years. As Kefauver stated in *Crime in America*, following Prohibition crime had become "big business." "Hoodlums . . . started cleaning their fingernails, polishing up their language, and aping the manners and sartorial trappings of captains of industry."[24] This new corporate structure of organized crime becomes even more apparent in the Warner Bros. film *The Enforcer*, which was titled for its British release (more apropos of its subject matter), *Murder, Inc.*

Released on February 24, 1951, *The Enforcer* ran in New York City during the Kefauver hearings of March 12–21 of that year. What is especially noteworthy is that the subject matter of the film had relevance to the hearings themselves, particularly during the questioning of Ambassador O'Dwyer, the former prosecuting attorney of the "Murder, Inc.," trials of the early 1940s. In addition, the film was initially released with a prologue by Senator Kefauver himself.[25] The subject matter of the film was not concerned with the syndicate's interest in gambling or bookies but with another covert criminal enterprise: murder for hire.

The film's protagonist, District Attorney Martin Ferguson (Humphrey Bogart), is set on sending gangster Albert Mendoza (Everett Sloan) to the electric chair. When his key witness, Joseph Rico (Ted de Corsia), dies after falling from his cell window while trying to escape, Ferguson sifts through case records and tapes in an attempt to find more conclusive evidence of Mendoza's guilt. Through a series of flashbacks the film's narrative chronicles the police investigation into Mendoza's contract murder enterprise. The case against Mendoza is concluded when Ferguson realizes that an eyewitness to Mendoza's first contract slaying, supposedly murdered in a gangland hit, is still alive.

Although the name "Murder, Inc.," is never mentioned in the film, the parallels to actual characters and events would not have been lost to the film's audience. Albert Mendoza's real-life counterpart was Louis Lepke, the only top-echelon crime syndicate leader to be executed in the electric chair. Joseph Rico is clearly patterned after Abe "Kid Twist" Reles, known as the "canary of the mob." Reles was a killer for Murder, Inc., who after his arrest in 1940, began talking to prosecutors on the proviso that he would avoid prosecution for any murders that he committed. Reles provided plenty of names, as well as murder contract information, during his "canary act" until he mysteriously fell from his sixth-floor Coney Island hotel window while under police protection. The Murder, Inc., trials revealed a syndicate subsidiary that consisted of a special troop of killers based in Brooklyn, who were contracted for mob hits. Among the names "sung" by Reles were Pittsburg Phil, Happy Malone, Mendy Weis, and Chicken Head Gurino. The film's cast of characters also included such colorful monikers as "Big Babe Lazich," "Philadelphia Tom," and "Duke Malloy." The meeting place for the elite execution squad was in the backroom of a twenty-four-hour candy store called "Midnight Rose's." This was likewise depicted in the film as the store operated by Olga Kirshen, which serves as a front for Mendoza's murder-for-hire enterprise.[26] The most significant feature of *The Enforcer* was not its veiled references to the real-life characters and events of Murder, Inc., but its depiction of a conspiratorial organization and the paranoia it produced.

As Carlos Clarens has noted, the image of an "invisible, omniscient empire of crime" pervades the entire film.[27] Beginning with the film's opening, where an armored truck containing the witness, Joseph Rico, arrives in the bowels of the police station to deliver its protected human cargo, a sense of paranoia is present throughout. The film carries that paranoid fear through each of its characters, who fear the retribution of the unnamed organization should they run afoul of it. The concept of a shadowlike criminal organization was maintained throughout the Kefauver hearings. According to Bernstein, "Within the context of the 1950s, Kefauver was able to use crime as an issue to promote paranoia similar to that of McCarthy. He tied American gamblers into a worldwide ethnic conspiracy yet maintained that they were the 'scavengers of crime in America.' Kefauver wed metaphors of evil capitalists to animalistic foreigners to fuel his conspiracy theory of organized crime."[28] This conspiratorial element becomes a significant feature of 1950s syndicate films, in which the "combination" becomes a very real presence in the narratives.

Other early syndicate films incorporated topical references to the Kefauver hearings either into the film's advertising or preexisting material. For instance, Paramount's *Appointment with Danger*, starring Alan Ladd, was released on May 9, 1951, but it had been completed in 1949. The advertising for the film referred to Ladd's character as "the crime investigator who smashes the underworld's million dollar train robbery!" In addition the advertising emphasized the film's veracity by stating that it was "based on actual cases from the files of the Post Office Department."[29] Alan Ladd's character, Al Goddard, is actually a postal inspector, and the term *crime investigator* is never used in the film itself. Similarly, the film has no references to the "syndicate," and the intended robbery is an independent, local affair.

Howard Hughes's production of *The Racket*, released on December 13, 1951, was a remake of Hughes's earlier film version of Bartlett Cormack's 1927 play. The screenplay, written by W. R. Burnett (*Little Caesar*, *Asphalt Jungle*) added several scenes depicting a Crime Commission headed by Les Tremayne. These scenes were filmed by Nicholas Ray in June 1951, after the principal photography had finished (April–May 1951).[30] Also, the syndicate itself was identified through the personage of Connolly (Don Porter, who played a similar role in *711 Ocean Drive*). In typical syndicate-film fashion the mob boss is never identified in the film; he is a mysterious presence who is only contacted via his go-between, Connolly.

Hoodlum Empire (1952), released by Republic Pictures a year after the Kefauver hearings, contained numerous referents to the crime committee.[31] Although real names were not used, even reviewers pointed out the similarities between characters in the film and their real-life counterparts. The *New York Times* review began by saying, "It is fairly safe to state that the paying customers are bound to recognize similarities between 'Hoodlum Empire,' now at the Globe, and a certain Senatorial investigation into crime, which also had some entertainment values."[32] *Variety*,

3. Luther Adler portrays a mob boss based on real-life Frank Costello in *Hoodlum Empire* (1952). *Left to right*: Roy Barcroft, Adler, Forrest Tucker. Photo courtesy of Eddie Brandt's Saturday Matinee, North Hollywood, California.

referring to *Hoodlum Empire* as a "film version of the Kefauver investigation," stated that the "film industry's pat foreword, 'events and characters depicted herein are purely imaginary . . .' which generally accompanies title credits of every picture, must be taken with a grain of salt insofar as 'Hoodlum Empire' is concerned. For [Luther] Adler clearly portrays Frank Costello, [Brian] Donleavy [*sic*] recreates Sen. Kefauver and Miss [Claire] Trevor does a Virginia Hill down to the original camera-smashing incident. . . . Others who stand out are Gene Lockhart, whose use of senatorial rhetoric closely resembles the style of Sen. Tobey."[33]

In addition to the in-text parallels to committee members and witnesses the film provided information and revelations from the investigation. At one point Senator Stephens (Brian Donlevy) gives a speech concerning the "innocent $2 bet" and its consequences. Nicolas Mancani (Luther Adler) gives a lengthy explanation to his nephew of his new "business enterprise." Pointing to a map of the United States on the wall, Mancani explains, "What we don't own outright, we control outright!" In regard to the legitimacy of his newly formed syndicate, Mancani claims, "Everybody wears a nice clean front. . . . I'm in real estate, Charlie's in oil, and Sporty there is an art dealer. . . . [E]verybody's got something that's strictly legal." The infiltration of organized crime into small-town America is depicted with Mancani's organization establishing itself in Central City, where they attempt to place slot machines into a gas station owned and operated by Mancani's nephew, Joe Gray. Mancani again explains to his nephew, during a nighttime visit to his home, that the organization is spreading out even into small towns. The octopus-like tentacles of organized crime, as it established a stranglehold across America, was a primary concern of the Kefauver Committee. In fact, Bernstein notes, the octopus metaphor was a favorite of the crime committee and inspired a *Time* magazine cover featuring a smiling Kefauver "superimposed on a cartoon drawing of an octopus holding guns, drug paraphernalia, cards, and other tools of the crime trade in its numerous tentacles."[34] As the tagline for *New York Confidential* (1955) emphasized, "The syndicate *still* exists. The rules *still* hold. *This* is how the cartel works. *This* is New York Confidential!" This conspiracy theory of organized crime was also a staple feature of the urban exposé films of the mid-1950s.

Another cycle of syndicate films emerged after the Kefauver hearings were completed. These films found a rich source of material in the documented findings of the committee hearings as they were published in two books, *The Kefauver Committee Report on Organized Crime* (1951) and *Crime in America* (1951), written by Estes Kefauver. The latter was on the *New York Times* bestseller list in the fall of 1951. In addition Kefauver published a series of articles, under the title "What I Found Out in the Underworld," for the *Saturday Evening Post* in April 1951. The medium of television also profited from the committee hearings, not only through broadcasts of the hearings themselves but with programs that were engendered by them. During the 1951–1952 season alone five programs were concerned with crime: *Crime Syndicated* (CBS), *Crime Photographer* (CBS), *Treasury Men in Action* (NBC), *Man against Crime* (CBS), and *Crime with Father* (ABC). *Crime Syndicated* is especially of interest because it utilized crime committee members Senator O'Conor and Chief Counsel Rudolph Halley, as well as Kefauver, to introduce weekly crime dramas, supposedly based on facts gathered by the committee.[35] These publications and broadcasts continued to play to the public's curiosity, as well as the committee's brief, concerning organized crime and its influence in postwar America.

A subcycle of syndicate films, the city or urban exposés, followed in the wake of the Kefauver Committee hearings. These crime films associated themselves with the transcontinental investigation of the Kefauver Committee by treating their narratives as true exposés of crime and corruption in their designated cities. Many of them were located in metropolitan areas where the committee itself held hearings: *The Miami Story* (1954), *Miami Expose* (1956), *New York Confidential* (1955), *Chicago Confidential* (1957), *Chicago Syndicate* (1955), *New Orleans Uncensored* (1955), and *Inside Detroit* (1956). Others exposed criminal activity in such locales as Texas (*The Houston Story* [1955]), Alabama (*The Phenix City Story* [1955]), and Oregon (*Portland Exposé* [1957]). Will Straw writes, "Most of these films claimed, in their opening sequences or in the posters which advertised them, some link to a real-life investigation of municipal vice and corruption."[36] In addition they al-most always either alluded to or emphasized the involvement, and frequently the "otherness," of the "syndicate" itself in their respective locales, in keeping with the findings and conclusions of the Kefauver Committee. The template for the urban exposé cycle, however, did not contain a real location within its title; instead, its title emphasized the key image that binds this group of films, *The Captive City*.

The Captive City was the first production of Aspen Pictures, an independent pro-duction company formed by Robert Wise and Mark Robson. *The Captive City* was filmed entirely on location in Reno, Nevada. Robert Wise recalled, "We made the entire thing in Reno. We used the newspaper there, the city hall, the street. There was no process—we hung cameras on cars—we didn't shoot a foot in the studio. We shot it in 22–23 days. That was the first one I ever did entirely on location. Filming was completed in February, 1952 and the film was released on March 26, 1952."[37] Both Wise (who directed the film) and Robson had worked at RKO, as editors (both were editors on *Citizen Kane*) and as directors in the Val Lewton unit. Their expe-rience at RKO is apparent throughout the film, particularly in its technical aspect (it was photographed with a Hoge lens, which helped with many deep-focus shots) and the atmosphere of terror and paranoia maintained in the film. Wise's taut di-rection was rewarded with generally favorable reviews. The *Los Angeles Daily News*, for instance, stated, "Director-producer Wise builds each facet lucidly and perti-nently as the cancerous undergrowth, festering in out-of-state Mafia killings, is un-folded."[38] *The Captive City* took a different narrative approach to the syndicate film, exposing the "cancerous undergrowth" beneath the veneer of normalcy in a small American town. It was perhaps this approach and the way it was told onscreen that persuaded Estes Kefauver to provide an epilogue to the film.

Captive City begins with Jim Austin (John Forsythe) and his wife, Marge (Joan Camden), driving through the countryside in the early morning hours. They are be-ing pursued, but it is not clear by whom. They seek haven at the police station in the small town of Warren. While they await notification of a police escort to the capitol, Jim Austin uses a nearby tape recorder to relate the events that have transpired. In an extended flashback Austin reveals that he is a newspaper editor in the small town of Kennington. When he is contacted by a local private detective, Clyde Nelson, who is seemingly working on a harmless divorce case, things begin to change. Nelson wishes to expose the small town as a front for organized crime and, specifically, to expose one of Kennington's leading businessmen, Murray Sirak (Vic-tor Sutherland), whose divorce case Nelson was investigating. After talking to Chief Gillette (Ray Teal) of the Kennington Police Department, Austin dismisses the de-tective's conspiratorial ideas. However, when Nelson is murdered, Austin takes up the investigation. Accompanied by his photographer, Phil Harding (Martin Milner), Austin learns that the syndicate is using Kennington for its wire service fa-cilities. Nicolas Fabretti is the mob boss who visits the small town from time to time from his headquarters in Florida. Austin begins to receive pressure from various

4. John Forsythe and Joan Camden prepare to testify before a Senate Crime Committee in Robert Wise's 1952 film *The Captive City*. Photo courtesy of Eddie Brandt's Saturday Matinee, North Hollywood, California.

members of the community, including the police chief, to drop the investigation. Austin succeeds in uncovering the whole sordid business — the crime, filth, and corruption — with the blessing and help of local authorities. When his photographer is brutally beaten and Murray Sirak's wife (Marjorie Crossland) is killed, Austin decides to take his findings to the Kefauver Senate Crime Committee hearings at the Capitol. After driving all night and evading the mysterious car with Florida plates that is pursuing them, the Austins finally receive an escort and at the film's end enter the hearing room to testify before the crime committee.

In keeping with the mood of paranoia, the syndicate forces are never actually seen in the film. Their presence is alluded to by the "car with Florida plates" or newspaper and teletype reports, or even the mere mention of the name Dominic Fabretti. Only the front activities and those who are being used by the syndicate are actually seen. Chief Gillette, Murray Sirak, and others are the common people who are acting as agents or fronts for Fabretti and the mob, whether they know it or not. Many of the advertisements for the film also alluded to the "syndicate" as an unseen but very real presence. Most ads featured a gigantic silhouetted figure of a gangster carrying a machine gun in one hand, looming over a city skyline — and in his other hand, puppetlike, were strings leading to various parts within the city. As part of the advertising campaign the veracity of the film was noted. *Film Daily* touted the endorsement of Senator Kefauver: "The first and only motion picture to carry the personal endorsement of crime-buster Sen. Estes Kefauver."[39] Kefauver's epilogue to the film helped to mediate the fictional narrative with a nonfictional world. This was to become a staple feature for the many urban exposés that were to follow.

To reveal the vice and corruption hidden within the communities' "normalcy," there is a mediator within the narrative space. In *The Captive City* it is Jim Austin, a newspaper editor, who, through his voice-over narration (via the technology of the tape recorder) explicates the events of the film. In other urban exposés the voice-over is often a "voice of God"–style narration, which was frequently used in semi-documentary films of the late 1940s, such as *House on 92nd Street*, *T-Men*, and *The Naked City* (1948). This type of narration is utilized in *New York Confidential*, *The Miami Story*, *Miami Expose*, *Chicago Confidential*, *The Houston Story*, and *New Orleans Uncensored*. Some urban exposés add a prologue provided by a public figure. In *The Captive City* it is an epilogue by Sen. Kefauver; in *The Miami Story* a prologue is given by Florida senator George A. Smathers. *Miami Expose* is introduced by Mayor Randy Christmas, who warns the audience, "It could happen in your state"; and in *The Phenix City Story* the prologue is provided by the citizens of Phenix City, Alabama, themselves. The authenticity of the urban exposé narrative also extends to the use of on-location photography. Many of these films were shot on their respective locations, providing a travelogue not only to the well-known features of their locales but also to the "guilty" ones. These help to "reveal" the crime and corruption that provide the films with their primary audience interest. As Will Straw suggests, "[Urban exposé] narratives, nevertheless, are secondary to their cataloguing of vice, and to the formal organization of these films as sequences of scenes in night-clubs, gambling dens and along neon-lit streets."[40] *Variety* reported in its review of *The Miami Story*, "Apparently inspired by the U.S. Senate's frequent probes into crime, the Robert E. Kent script is a swiftly paced chronicle of how a gambling and white slave syndicate was supposedly smashed in Miami. A brief introduction by Florida's Senator George A. Smathers plus a liberal use of background footage of the Miami area give added authenticity to the yarn."[41] The *New York Times* commented, "Despite the documentary aura that surrounds the proceedings by virtue of a foreword spoken by Senator George A. Smathers and a 'voice-of-doom' off-screen narration, 'The Miami Story' is quick to get down to melodramatic cases."[42]

Because of their relative obscurity in geographical locations and distribution, Will Straw suggests, the films of this particular cycle blocked any participation in a "generalized, moral panic over organized crime."[43] The group of films can be seen in a larger context as another cycle of films that emerged after the Kefauver hearings ended. Kefauver himself wanted to show the extent of organized crime in small-town America but was unable (or unwilling) to do so. The fact that many of the first films to emerge from this cycle were set in locales visited by the committee attests to their relevance to the hearings themselves. As the cycle tapers off, more obscure locations are selected, such as *Portland Expose* (1957), *New Orleans after Dark* (1957), *The Houston Story* (1956), and *Damn Citizen* (1958).

Other generic variations of the syndicate film emerged following the Kefauver hearings. These films, generally, utilized the syndicate not as their primary concern but as a backdrop for their crime narratives. One such variant was the rogue cop films like *The Big Heat* (1953) and *The Big Combo* (1955). Both of these films revolve around an individualistic detective protagonist who sets out on a personal vendetta against the mob. In Fritz Lang's *The Big Heat* it is Detective Dave Bannion (Glenn Ford), who after several murders, including that of his wife, eventually breaks the grip of the syndicate chief, Mike Lagana (Alexander Scourby). Joseph Lewis's *The Big Combo* has Detective Leonard Diamond (Cornel Wilde) obsessively pursuing mob boss Mr. Brown (Richard Conte), who has secretly taken over syndicate operations. Both films conclude with the status quo being restored, by sparing the lives of their respective syndicate representatives and thereby not letting their heroes become a part of the crime and corruption that surrounds them. Tom Gunning states in his book on Fritz Lang, "By operating outside the law, the rogue cop affirms an ideal justice untrammeled by official corruption or incompetence, but he also risks becoming indistinguishable from the gangsters he fights. . . . Thus the plot must resolve the cop's quest not only by defeating the gangster, but with a renunciation of violence by the cop."[44] The male protagonist, however, was not the only one to fight the corruption of organized crime.

Two genre variations concerned female witnesses who are being escorted and protected in order to testify against the syndicate. Richard Fleischer's *The Narrow Margin* (1952) and Phil Karlson's *Tight Spot* (1955), both inspired by Virginia Hill's appearance before the Kefauver Committee hearings in New York, concern female mob witnesses who are cooperating with the law, but only after a narrative that highlights their trials and tribulations of escaping the reach of the syndicate empire itself. In *The Narrow Margin* crime film icon Marie Windsor plays Mrs. Neil, a mobster's widow, being escorted by Charles McGraw to act as a witness against organized crime. And in *Tight Spot* Ginger Rogers portrays Sherry Conley, who is offered freedom and immunity from prison if she testifies against mobster Benjamin Costain (Lorne Greene). At film's end, as she prepares to testify before the committee, she is asked to identify herself. She states, clearly and emphatically, "My name is Sherry Conley — Gangbuster!"

One of the most interesting and unusual syndicate genre hybrids combined elements of the syndicate film with the 1950s science fiction film. In Edward L. Cahn's *Creature with the Atom Brain* (1955), a Clover Production released through Columbia Pictures, deported gangster Frank Buchanan (Michael Granger), in association with former Nazi scientist Dr. Wilhelm Steigg (Gregory Gaye), places atomically controlled devices into the brains of recently dead former gangland associates.[45] With this army of robotlike zombies Buchanan murders the people responsible for his deportation, including the district attorney and gang members who testified against him. Police scientist Chet Walker (Richard Denning) and his homicide detective friend Dave Harris (John Launer) put the pieces of the puzzling crime spree together and eventually destroy the zombie "syndicate" along with their creators. This unusual combination of two 1950s-inspired genres — the syndicate film and atomic-age science fiction film — seems only logical given that both drew heavily on the public fear and paranoia of cold war politics and culture: both 1950s genres utilized semidocumentary techniques to reinforce the liberal consensus view of American scientific dominance and know-how. In many 1950s science-fiction films the scientist, working with the cooperation of the government (most often the military), destroys the alien invaders through some technological innovation. Similarly, in the syndicate film the "normative processes of law and order" are generally upheld at the end of the film with the breakup of the syndicate forces.

An arresting feature of the majority of syndicate films is the absence of ethnicity in regard to the criminal syndicate. Whereas the Kefauver Committee made a strong effort to emphasize the "otherness" of the Mafia by relying in its testimony and conclusions on "simplistic and nativist explanations for the causes of crime,"[46] the syndicate film did not make an attempt to weld critiques of the syndicate to issues of ethnic identity. Indeed, in some cases these films made a deliberate effort to avoid the issue. For example, Howard Hughes's remake of *The Racket* went so far as to change the name of the major mobster from "Nick Scarsi" to "Nick Scanlon." One possible reason for this was to reinforce the idea of the "imaging" of the "enemy within." Closely paralleling such cold war sci-fi films as *Invaders from Mars* (1953), *It Came from Outer Space* (1953), *Invasion of the Body Snatchers* (1956), *The Brain from Planet Arous* (1958), and *I Married a Monster from Outer Space* (1958), many syndicate films emphasized the dehumanization of the familiar through the threat of organized crime. As Vivian Sobchack notes regarding the 1950s sci-fi films noted above:

> While we may react with varying degrees of detached wonder to invading Martians or Metalunan Mutants who are distinctly seen as "other" than ourselves, our responses to those aliens clothed in our own familiar skins are another matter entirely. We expect unnatural behavior from something seen as unnatural, alien behavior from something alien. What is so visually devastating and disturbing about SF films' "taken over" humans is the *small*, and therefore terrible, incongruence between the ordinariness of their form and the final extraordinariness of their behavior, however hard they try to remain undetected and "normal."[47]

Thus the threat from within becomes even more salient in regard to syndicate films, especially when the protagonist finally recognizes the threat of organized crime for what it actually represents — a threat to the foundations of nation, family, and community.

Two films emerged at the end of the syndicate cycle that effectively reflect the parallel between racketeering and totalitarianism. Interestingly enough, in both, the dominant threat is toward the family unit. Whereas early syndicate films stressed the threat to the community (*711 Ocean Drive*, *The Captive City*) and to the nation (*Hoodlum Empire*, *The Enforcer*, *The Turning Point*), both *The Brothers Rico* and *Underworld U.S.A.* focus on the danger to familial relationships. By locating the threat within the domestic terrain of the home, these films reinforced the liberal consensus view of the danger of dissent (in the form of involvement with organized crime) and the "imaging" of a perfect democratic community (which is threatened by organized crime). Yet the threat in both films has the semblance of normality. As Carlos Clarens states, "In *Invasion of the Body Snatchers*, the peculiar behavior of seemingly normal people was accounted for by the fact that they were extraterrestrials: in *The Brothers Rico*, the explanation was that they were mobsters."[48]

Phil Karlson's *The Brothers Rico* (Columbia Pictures, 1957) concerns the efforts of ex-mobster-turned-businessman Eddie Rico (Richard Conte) to locate his younger brothers, Johnny (James Darren) and Gino (Paul Picerni), for the mob. Johnny was the hit man on a contract killing, and Gino was the driver. The syndicate feels that both may be coerced into testifying before the D.A. Eddie believes that kindly Uncle Sid Kubik (Larry Gates), the mob boss, merely wants to get Johnny and his pregnant wife out of the country safely. But, as he discovers, they want to kill Johnny and have been using Eddie as a "bloodhound" to trace his brother's whereabouts. Ultimately, unable to save his brothers, Eddie eludes an underworld dragnet to finally confront "Uncle Sid" and testifies before the D.A.

Karlson continually undermines the notion of "normalcy" throughout the film. Its Sirkian opening sequence, with a lyric underscoring by George Duning, shows Eddie and his wife, Alice, asleep in bed. The phone rings, Eddie answers it, and the sense of normalcy is suddenly interrupted—the phone call is from Eddie's former mob associates. The intrusions into the normal become more frequent as the film progresses. We learn that Eddie and his wife want to adopt a child. On the day of the meeting with the adoption agency Eddie is sent to a meeting in Miami with "Uncle Sid." Sid inquires about his family and particularly his younger brother's whereabouts. While this friendly, paternal meeting with Eddie takes place, his brother Gino is being beaten down the hallway. Karlson effectively layers his film with the revelation of criminal activity looking and behaving as if it were respectable and "normal." As Jack Shadoian notes, "Karlson records the American landscape with a diabolical equanimity. We see the environments as actual and authentic, but in the context of the film we see them with a fresh perspective. They are the rot—disguising fronts and facades we live among, and that makes them more sinister than any diagonalized dark alley."[49] The final shot of the film shows Eddie and Alice arriving at the adoption agency—order and family are ultimately restored with the demise of organized crime.

Samuel Fuller's *Underworld U.S.A.* (Columbia, 1961) depicts organized crime as a vast, dehumanized institution. Disguised by its legitimate front, called "National Projects," it is run as if it were a legitimate business operation. Executive board meetings are held with other "company" men. Heading the enterprise is its "CEO," Earl Connors, who accounts for production shortfalls and sends personnel into the field. The real enterprise here, however, is narcotics, prostitution, and labor racketeering. But as Connors stipulates at one of his "board meetings," "As long as we run National Projects, a 'legitimate' business operation, and pay our taxes on 'legitimate' income, and donate to charities and church bazaars . . . we'll win the war. We always have." This war metaphor is also reiterated by Driscoll, the chief counsel of the Federal Crime Committee, who is intent on breaking up Connors's organization. Driscoll gives a brief lecture to his committee members on the nature of the syndicate's organization: "The syndicate bosses in the field command the rackets, like generals in the field command divisions. And lording it over the syndicate wheels is the top brass, the underworld's combined chiefs of staff. Each chief commands a specific department — Gila, narcotics; Gunther, labor; Smith, prostitution . . . and so on. They all have substantial business fronts, pay taxes, wear respectable suits. And lording it over all of them is Earl Connors, their Chief of Staff."

Into the syndicate comes ex-con Tolly Devlin (Cliff Robertson), who uses his trust within the organization to avenge his father's death. Once his revenge is complete, Tolly is ready to quit his life of crime and lead a respectable life, marry, and have children. But Driscoll informs him that it cannot stop there — the syndicate must be eliminated. Tolly soon learns the truth when he is told by the syndicate bosses not only to wipe out an informant's family but also to kill the woman he intends to marry. At this point Tolly decides to eliminate Earl Connors himself. It is only when the threat to the family becomes evident that Tolly is spurred to take further action, an action not motivated by revenge but by duty and survival.

Inspired by the events and findings of the Kefauver Committee, as well as the postwar fear of communist domination, these films reinforced the liberal consensus view that America was being targeted from within, as well as without, its geographic boundaries. According to Jack Shadoian these films identified a parallel discourse with the anticommunist crusaders: "Crime, like communism, is against the American way of life. The evils of these poisonous systems are analogous. Americans must stick together and support whatever measures, however extreme or unsavory, that a courageous individual adopts to penetrate syndicate operations and hierarchies. . . . Crime is corruption that exacts from the public good a daily price. It must be annihilated at its source."[50] Concurrently with this cycle of films as it developed in the 1950–1952 period, then, a variant crime cycle emerged — anticommunist films. These films, which included *I Married a Communist* (1950), *I Was a Communist for the FBI* (1951), *The Whip Hand* (1951), and *Big Jim McClain* (1952), examined the supposed threat of communism in America. The substitution of communists for gangsters was not an entirely Hollywood concept. In a speech delivered at Columbia University on July 10, 1951, titled "Crime in America and Its Effects on Foreign Relations," Estes Kefauver compared racketeering and organized crime to totalitarian governments. Kefauver stated in terms that could equally be applied to communists: "The racketeer and the gambler are parasites on the community and the nation. They perform no useful service; they produce nothing. We found, during the course of our investigation, that these parasites drain from our people billions of dollars a year, which otherwise might be diverted into useful enterprises—which, instead of producing cases for the relief rolls, would produce substantial citizens working each day as part of a great team, to keep this a substantial country."[51] Kefauver's insistence on a "substantial" citizenry and country emphasized the dichotomy of the constructed "American" with that of foreign-born gangsters and communists. The syndicate films that were spawned during this period helped to reinforce those beliefs.

Film critic Peter Biskind has suggested that every film made during the 1950s was in some way affected by anticommunist rhetoric.[52] It may be equally true that every crime film made in the 1950s was made in the shadow of the Kefauver hearings into organized crime.

Notes

1. Frank MacShane, *Selected Letters of Raymond Chandler* (New York: Columbia University Press, 1981), 266.

2. *Life*, April 2, 1951, 25.

3. The phrase "greatest menace" is from a speech delivered by Illinois governor Adlai Stevenson in 1950 in which he stated that in regard to organized crime, "the greatest menace is that the public will come to accept organized crime as something inevitable, as a necessary part of our social system" (Lee Bernstein, *The Greatest Menace: Organized Crime in Cold War America* [Amherst: University of Massachusetts Press, 2002], 9).

4. Lee Bernstein, "The Greatest Menace: Organized Crime in United States Culture and Politics, 1946–1961" (Ph.D. diss., University of Minnesota, 1997), 133. The article from which Bernstein quotes is "Crime: It Pays to Organize," *Time*, March 12, 1951, 22–26.

5. Steve Neale, *Genre and Hollywood* (New York: Routledge, 2000), 31.

6. The best sources of information concerning Estes Kefauver and the Crime Committee are William Howard Moore's *The Kefauver Committee and the Politics of Crime, 1950–1952* (Columbia: University of Missouri Press, 1974), which remains the standard work; and Joseph Bruce Gorman's *Kefauver: A Political Biography* (New York: Oxford University Press, 1971). Also see Estes Kefauver, *Crime in America* (Garden City, N.Y.: Doubleday, 1951); and *The Kefauver Committee Report on Organized Crime* (New York: Didier, 1951).

7. Bernstein, "Greatest Menace," 137.

8. Bernstein, *Greatest Menace*, 75.

9. Gorman, *Kefauver*, 88.

10. *Film Daily*, March 27, 1951, 8.

11. The entertainment aspects of the Crime Committee hearings were noted frequently in the show business journal *Variety*. For instance, on March 21, 1951 (while the committee was holding its hearings in New York City), *Variety* reported that "TV's Kefauver Kayos B.O.": "Broadway will be glad when this new 'What's My Crime?' quiz show hits the road. The out-of-town preliminary probes were just so many road companies. This is the original cast—Frank Costello, Joe Adonis & Co.—and they're living, breathing characters on everybody's home." In the same column *Variety* quoted an editorial from the

New York Herald Tribune referring to the committee's televised hearings as the "perfect combination of information and entertainment."

12. *Kefauver Committee Report*, 174–178.

13. Gorman, *Kefauver*, 78.

14. Benedict Anderson, *Imagined Communities: Reflections on the Origin and Spread of Nationalism* (London: Verso, 1983), 15.

15. Godfrey Hodgson, "The Ideology of the Liberal Consensus," in *A History of Our Time: Readings in Postwar America*, ed. William H. Chafe (New York: Oxford University Press, 1995), 104–105.

16. Anderson, *Imagined Communities*, 22.

17. Frank Krutnik, *In a Lonely Street: Film Noir, Genre, Masculinity* (New York: Routledge, 1991), xiv.

18. For further information concerning the Paramount decrees see Michael Conant's classic study, *Antitrust in the Motion Picture Industry* (Berkeley: University of California Press, 1960). Also of interest, primarily because it concerns industry practices that were affected by the Paramount case, is Mae D. Huettig's *Economic Control of the Motion Picture Industry: A Study in Industrial Organization* (Philadelphia: University of Pennsylvania Press, 1944).

19. Jonathan Munby, *Public Enemies, Public Heroes: Screening the Gangster from "Little Caesar" to "Touch of Evil"* (Chicago: University of Chicago Press, 1999), 133.

20. There were several films released in the late 1940s that could be seen as precursors of the syndicate cycle. Significantly, these were made by independents. Most notable among them are Abraham Polonsky's *Force of Evil* (1948), which is concerned with the numbers racket and the syndicate and is told from the criminal perspective. Joseph H. Lewis's *Undercover Man* (1949) is a police procedural that combines semidocumentary techniques with a gangster narrative. This film also is one of the first to actually address the "Mafia" by name. Both films use narrative techniques that will be carried over into the 1950s syndicate cycle in the wake of the Kefauver hearings.

21. *Film Daily*, July 21, 1950, 12.

22. *New York Times*, July 20, 1950, 21.

23. *Commonweal*, July 21, 1950, 392.

24. Kefauver, *Crime in America*, 20.

25. According to William Howard Moore, Kefauver was so dissatisfied with the film that he asked that his portion be removed. The prologue does not appear in any video copies of the film. See Moore, *Kefauver Committee*, 224n27.

26. Carl Sifakis, *The Mafia Encyclopedia* (New York: Facts on File, 1999). Burton B. Turkus, *Murder, Inc.: The Story of "The Syndicate"* (New York: Farrar, Straus, and Young, 1951).

27. Carlos Clarens, *Crime Movies: An Illustrated History* (New York: Norton, 1980), 236.

28. Bernstein, "Greatest Menace," 151–152.

29. *Film Daily*, April 10, 1951, 5.

30. Lee Server, *Robert Mitchum: "Baby I Don't Care"* (New York: St. Martin's, 2001), 220–221.

31. William Dieterle's *The Turning Point*, released November 14, 1952, also concerned a crime committee headed by John Conroy (Edmond O'Brien). Perhaps its most recognizably Kefauveresque moment was having Ed Begley, playing mob boss Eichelberger, perform a nervous "hand ballet" (à la Frank Costello) during his testimony before the committee.

32. *New York Times*, March 6, 1952, 23.

33. *Variety*, Feb. 20, 1952, 6.

34. Bernstein, *Greatest Menace*, 67.

35. Alex McNeil, *Total Television: The Comprehensive Guide to Programming from 1948 to the Present* (New York: Penguin, 1996).

36. Will Straw, "Urban Confidential: The Lurid City of the 1950s," in *The Cinematic City*, ed. David B. Clarke (New York: Routledge, 1997), 111.

37. Frank Thompson, *Robert Wise: A Bio-Bibliography* (Westport, Conn.: Greenwood Press, 1995), 57–58.

38. Ibid.

39. *Film Daily*, March 28, 1953, 3.

40. Straw, "Urban Confidential," 111.

41. *Variety*, March 31, 1954, 6.

42. *New York Times*, March 31, 1954.

43. Straw, "Urban Confidential," 115.

44. Tom Gunning, *The Films of Fritz Lang: Allegories of Vision and Modernity* (London: British Film Institute, 2000), 423.

45. Other Clover Productions, released through Columbia Pictures, include the urban exposés *Inside Detroit*, *Miami Expose*, and *The Houston Story*. Actor Michael Granger appears as a gangster in both *Miami Expose* and *Creature with the Atom Brain*.

46. Bernstein, *Greatest Menace*, 70.

47. Vivian Sobchack, *Screening Space: The American Science Fiction Film* (New Brunswick, N.J.: Rutgers University Press, 1997), 120–121.

48. Clarens, *Crime Movies*, 246.

49. Jack Shadoian, *Dreams and Dead Ends: The American Gangster/Crime Film* (Cambridge, Mass.: MIT Press, 1977), 261.

50. Ibid., 259.

51. Estes Kefauver, "Crime in America and Its Effects on Foreign Relations," *Vital Speeches* 17, no. 21 (Aug. 15, 1951): 656.

52. Peter Biskind, *Seeing Is Believing: How Hollywood Taught Us to Stop Worrying and Love the Fifties* (New York: Pantheon, 1983), 4.

Two
Gangster Transgressions

Gender and Sexuality

Ladies Love Brutes

Reclaiming Female Pleasures in the Lost History of Hollywood Gangster Cycles, 1929–1931

Esther Sonnet

IVING DISTINCTIVE NARRATIVE FORM to emerging discourses of social change and fictional shape to the mass experience of immigration, industrial modernization, and urbanization, the putative "rise and fall" narratives of *Little Caesar* (1930) and *The Public Enemy* (1931)—and to a lesser but significant degree *Scarface: The Shame of A Nation* (1932)—have come to define the ideological terrain of early 1930s gangster film: salutary warnings to the lower orders to remain in their place within capitalist hierarchies or dangerous/pleasurable fantasies of mobility that offer the sight of wealth acquisition and luxury consumption without the real cost of exploited labor. These titles and, more pertinent, the critical tradition that has interpreted and reinterpreted them have largely determined the prevailing view that the proper provenance of a "gangster film" at this time was to embody cultural uncertainties produced by challenges to the racial, social, and economic borderlines that had previously maintained strict divisions between licit/illicit, legitimate/illegitimate, "upper" and "under" worlds. As film historians have contended, the gangster provided the late 1920s and early 1930s with a fictionalized figure on which uncertainties about civic authority, wealth, and social power could be projected.[1] Yet even a small sample of films produced during the 1929–1931 seasons indicates that *Little Caesar* and *The Public Enemy* were *atypical* in their concentration on the individualized life history of the ambitious lone gangster. Primary research into Hollywood film production during this time suggests, in fact, a radically different picture from that perpetuated by film critics in that a welter of titles show that the gangster figure was by no means confined to depictions of urban crime, law and order, or civic corruption.

Titles produced during 1930–1931 on the whole illustrate that the gangster figure was an ideologically potent character dramatizing unresolved social, economic, and class conflicts. However, a major dimension of its utility for exploring cultural insta-bilities around *gender* and *sexuality* has been "forgotten" or suppressed. For example, *Kid Gloves* (1929), *The Racketeer* (1929), *Ladies Love Brutes* (1930), *Dance, Fools, Dance* (1931), *A Free Soul* (1931), and *Corsair* (1931) form a distinct cycle of films within a wider range of productions in which the gangster figure operates as threat not only to the social and public realm of law and order but to the sexual and "pri-vate" sphere of gender roles, heterosexuality, and female desire. Previous critical ac-counts of the gangster genre in the early 1930s make little reference to films that over-whelmingly attest to the wider dissemination of the gangster figure in narrative forms underpinned by the plot structures now associated with "women's films"—romance and female-centered melodrama.

In a variety of formats films of this period weave stories around the dangerous and seductive gangster figure as a means to dramatize transgressions of heterosex-ual desire and, crucially, offer those cinematic pleasures to a female audience that has until now been entirely effaced from traditional accounts of the gangster genre. *Framed* (1930), *Roadhouse Nights* (1930), and *Playing Around* (1930) each exploit the seedy demimonde of the nightclub and the indeterminate sexual morality of the nightclub singer/hostess to play with distinctions between voluntary sexual activity and forms of coerced prostitution demanded by the morality of the gangster underworld. *Chinatown Nights* (1929), *Come Across* (1929), *Skin Deep* (1929), *Woman Trap* (1929), *The Cheaters* (1930), *Man Trouble* (1930), *The Big Fight* (1930), *The Good Bad Girl* (1930), *The Lawless Woman* (1931), *Hush Money* (1931), *City Streets* (1931), *The Guilty Generation* (1931), and *Bad Company* (1931) compose a body of films that are, variously, love stories and melodramas in which female protagonists are brought into close proximity to the gangster's crimi-nal underworld milieu in order to dramatize erotic relationships. Centrally con-cerned with sexual, personal, and familial relationships, the films are not typified by the kind of tropes defining the "classic" Prohibition gangster films *Little Caesar* and *The Public Enemy* in that they do not dwell on the public's perception of the gangster menace, violence, gang organization, gun battles with the law, personal violence, or an ethnic individual's drive for power and success. Instead, the gangster milieu is invoked in order to stage narratives that exploited the gangster figure for its capacity to destabilize normative assumptions governing heterosexual behavior. The dangerous, exciting, and coercive gangster provided an imaginative space into which transgressive fantasies of female desire could be projected: powerful enough to "force" women into sexual compliance, the gangster was constructed as a per-ilous seduction and catalyst in narratives that explored the boundaries of "decent" or "legitimate" female sexuality. Thus, against the restriction of critical interest in the cinematic gangster figure to the few canonical texts, this chapter asserts the im-portance of retrieving a "lost" history of films that command attention because they insist on the presence of *female* spectators in audiences for gangster films at this time. Further, the rich and diverse range of titles produced during 1929 to 1931 suggests the *primacy* of female audiences in shaping Hollywood's gangster narratives. This is not to make an argument for including newly discovered titles into the existing canon but for the concept of "gangster film" to be fundamentally reconceived in respect of a more historically grounded assessment of its constitution. But to do that it is crucial to ask, What might account for the submersion of such a significant body of film production?

For a feminist film historian it is tempting to assert that the evacuation of women as important consumers and shapers of Hollywood products from critical histories of the gangster genre is no more complicated than gender "blindness" by which male historians simply do not "see" forms of popular culture that are not explicitly given over to male concerns. However, to insert the historical dimension that is missing from so many of such accounts, it is essential to observe the institutional context formed at the beginning of the decade from the interface of Hollywood producers with the regulatory body, the Studio Relations Committee (SRC), that advised on controversial material, anticipated what might necessitate the censors' cuts, and negotiated with film producers on creative solutions to censorship difficulties.[2] In September 1931 a range of films was assessed by the SRC according to their conformity to the classification "Gangster Picture" (though also noted as "Gangster Theme"). To be labeled as either would ensure difficulties for the distribution in both home and international markets and draw critical examination from local censor and police boards, who could order cuts and even withhold exhibition on the basis of the SRC's classification. In this respect a persuasive argument as to why the titles discussed here have been "invisible" to film historians could be made from the point of view of their exhibition/distribution classification, since few of the films produced in the period with gangster interest actually attracted the full "Gangster Picture" label. A telegram from SRC representative Jason S. Joy to Maurice McKenzie in September 1931 delineates more amply the process by which the classification of titles shifted:

> Have rechecked situation today concerning gangster pictures not already released. There appear to be no gangster pictures in preparation. One and possibly three are in production. "Scarface" by Caldo is certainly a gangster theme. "The Guilty Generation" by Columbia is classified by Wilson as a gangster theme and by Trotti as a gangster theme with such modifications as to perhaps make it useable. . . . "Corsair" by United Artists will not fall in the classification of gangster themes if the studio has followed our advice. We will see finished picture in ten days. "Bad Company" previously called "A Gangster's Wife" "Gangster's Moll" and "Mad Marriage" is a gangster picture. . . . "Homicide Squad" by Universal was classified by us on July 23rd when we saw it as a gangster picture. We had on reading the script and in subsequent discussions advised changes which we thought would help to remove it from this classification.[3]

The very general strictures against the representation of crime codified in the Motion Picture Production Code of 1930 do not offer guidance specific enough to make clear the basis of classification, and the SRC's definition of a "gangster picture" proper is seemingly contingent on studios meeting the recommended suggestions from the SRC:

> On July 31st Junior informed me by letter that he would make these changes. On August 6th he advised Mr. Wilson that he had made all the changes which I had suggested and because the picture was overdue had shipped it East without giving Wilson an opportunity to see it. It may or may not remain a gangster picture.[4]

But it is apparent that the distinction between a "gangster film" and a "film dealing with crime" is a crucial one that would affect a number of important agents involved in the production, circulation, and exhibition of Hollywood films:

> Commitments had been made for all of the above stories before the discussions occurred here last April. That is not an excuse but a statement of fact. Do not believe that any company will undertake further gangster stories. For the triple purpose of protecting the Chief who is now charged in many quarters with broken promises whenever a legitimate crime picture is produced, in order to continue to make available crime as a proper source of drama and in order to clarify our own minds especially those charged with the responsibility of obtaining and developing stories we believe it to be very important to differentiate in minds of public and censors immediately the difference between gangster film and film dealing with crime. In former action centers around gangster warfare and ruthless struggle between rival gangs with little or no implication of law or order. In the crime story the conflict is between law on the one hand and a criminal or criminals on the other hand of which the gangster is only a part. "The Star Witness" illustrates what we believe to be a perfectly legitimate use of the crime and gang element.[5]

The practical effectiveness of this distinction might be questionable, but the intent behind it is clear: to thwart the passage of films about intergang warfare "with little or no implication of law and order." Yet this attempt to define precisely a "gangster film"—all the better to isolate the foundation of its pernicious effect—also worked to severely restrict the number of films that could be included in the classification. None of the film titles that will be discussed in detail here would have qualified. Thus, despite their testimony to the ideological potency of the gangster figure, these titles "disappear" beneath the purview of the kind of historical and critical attention drawn by *The Public Enemy* or *Little Caesar* that, since they clearly did conform to the classification, have largely precluded further investigation.

With a newly enlarged conception of the function of the cinematic gangster figure in the early 1930s, though, it becomes evident that it was deployed extensively enough to warrant reconsideration of the commonplace assumption that the intended audiences for the gangster picture were exclusively male. In this context the notion that audiences for films were bifurcated along gender lines suggests another explanation for the "invisibility" of films addressed to women but that revolve around gangsters. Published in 1933, a little after the period under review but consolidating widely held views, the volumes on cinema and social influence sponsored by the Payne Fund Foundation encapsulated prevailing assumptions that the deleterious "effects" of cinema on adolescents were differentiated by gender. As Lea Jacobs notes in her study of "fallen woman" films, Blumer and Hauser's influential *Movies, Delinquency, and Crime* "explicitly linked the gangster film with the problem of violent crime among boys in the urban tenements, and the sex picture — stories about gold diggers, flappers, and vamps — with delinquency and various forms of prostitution among young women."[6] That these notions formed the foundational principles for more conspicuous film regulation and censorship under the Production Code Administration, which superseded the SRC in 1933, testifies to the entrenchment of the conception of separate audiences for separate genres: the gangster film encouraged crime in males through imitation and the depiction of technical knowledge, and the sex picture encouraged sexual permissiveness and prostitution in females through identification with the glamour and luxury of the "kept woman." Jacobs's work on the post-1933 "fallen woman" genre fully illustrates that the institutional context forming from Hollywood producers, censors, and various reform groups was crucially "engaged in prolonged debates about how to foster normative definitions of gender roles, marriage, and family life."[7] She clearly illustrates how the production histories of the "fallen woman" films she selects exemplify the "pressure on the industry to regulate representations of sexuality" and that the negotiations are "best understood as a function of a set of assumptions about spectatorship, specifically female spectatorship, current in the thirties."[8] Those "assumptions" were predicated on the notion that it was the more impressionable and psychologically weaker female spectators who were especially susceptible to the morally degenerative effects of cinema, hence the concentration of regulatory concern on pictures exhibiting the "sex" picture's advocating of sexual transgression. Yet the overall effect of the identification of specific narrative types — gangster or sex picture — with either male or female film audiences obscures the historical reality of the many hybrid films that do not fit easily within either classification and that, crucially, invoke sexual transgression, female sexuality, and gangsters in quite different admixtures than the bipolar model suggests.[9]

The Racketeer, Ladies Love Brutes, A Free Soul, Dance, Fools, Dance, and *Corsair* exemplify films in which the gangster conjoined with romance-melodrama structures to provide the thematic concerns of the "society melodrama." As the phrase should itself make clear, a "*society* melodrama" dramatizes not only personal and emotional entanglements but also ones that register most forcefully as often irreparable infractions of social norms and codes. It is a narrative form that centers on the usually doomed consequences of illicit liaisons between lovers and intended partners ill-matched by birth, class, or wealth. In this variant of the society melodrama the narrative of sexual desire that is irreconcilable with social stricture is mapped explicitly against the pairing of upper-class socialite women with underclass men. These films are thus structured by a power dynamic generated by unequal class status, but here it is the *male* who is socially subordinate to the authoritative upper-class female. The gangster is thus constructed not primarily as a criminal outlaw but as an irresistible pole of sexual attraction whose social "illegitimacy" engenders a highly specific erotic relationship. This initiates complex interplays among sexuality, class, and gender and marks the gangster-inflected social melodrama as especially significant for potential disruptions to the normative gender roles of cinematic heterosexuality that proscribe representation of *active* female sexual desire.

Based on the stage play *Pardon My Glove*, by Zoe Akins, *Ladies Love Brutes* neatly encapsulates in its title the mildly sadomasochistic underpinning of the society melodrama's location of the underclass male on the terrain of social transgression and sexual attraction. The film opens with a panoramic view of a city shot from the top of a half-built skyscraper: among the construction workers getting their hands dirty on the girders is a "great guy" who is shown to be the millionaire owner of the Forziati Company. A rich man risen from the tenement slums of the East Side, where he still lives with his motherless son and the boy's grandmother, Joe Forziati (George Bancroft) climbs down, cheerfully whistling a vulgar blues version of "Frankie and Johnny," a narrative maneuver that confirms his lower-class origins.[10] Physically commanding and at ease with the laborers he employs, Forziati is not himself a criminal, yet the childhood milieu in which he was raised and now works is inextricable from the criminal underworld. The film dramatizes this when a former gang racketeer and labor agitator, Mike Mendino (Stanley Fields), operates an extortion racket to exact graft from all building subcontractors; this runs against Forziati's honest work ethic by embroiling his workers in a "protective organization," thus threatening the award from the city administration of a large building contract to Forziati. Successfully thwarting Mendino in a hand-to-hand fight, but thereby setting in motion a revenge plot, Forziati is awarded the contract.

The award brings him into association with the socially prominent men who control the city's building program, and through this association Forziati is made aware of his own social inferiority. Having established Forziati as physically commanding, streetwise, wealthy, and entrepreneurial, *Ladies Love Brutes* proceeds to make humorous play at the expense of the "Skyscraper King" and his déclassé attempts at social entrée. Longing for social acceptance, he persuades a tailor to dress him as befits the upper classes (a motif subsequently much repeated to chart the gangster's "rise" into social prominence). Prefiguring *Little Caesar's* Rico Bandello, Forziati is clearly marked by uncultured manners and behavior as both working class and as Italian immigrant, suggested not least when he puts a half-eaten biscuit in his pocket. From a faux coat of arms formed by a pick and shovel, to new shoes that pinch — "It's tough on the dogs to look like a gentleman" — or the tailored jacket stuffed with newspaper, Forziati's clumsy efforts offer comic commentary on the working-class tough guy's adoption of upper-class culture. Yet the social snubbing is serious: "What's the matter with me? They'll do business with me but I'm poison. I built a hundred swell apartments in the town and I don't expect to get invited to dinner at any one of them." While exploiting him to make money from the city building works, the upper-class business echelons exclude Forziati from their dining club, at which he'd generously offered to pay their bill — to "blow the crowd for lunch."

This scenario confirms David E. Ruth's contention that the gangster was a mythological construction "invented" by the American mass media to dramatize public anxieties over the role of corporate culture, the legitimacy of business practice, the meaning of ethnicity, and the breakdown of traditional class and cultural borders.[11] Within the enclosed social world of business the class and ethnic borders that separate men are thus clearly circumscribed, and full social mobility is denied to the presumptuous arriviste. Yet what distinguishes *Ladies Love Brutes* and other society melodramas of this type from the normative narratives of class infraction in *Little Caesar* or *The Public Enemy* is that the agent of disruption is not the gangster figure but *the sexually inquiring upper-class woman*. Forziati is introduced at the home of society leader Mimi Howell (Mary Astor) and her son and learns that she is separated from her husband, Dwight. Mimi is rich, cultured, educated, chic, elegant — and profoundly bored. Forziati's uncompromising masculinity, slum origins, and underworld connections provide Mimi with a risqué diversion to her stultifying marriage: "What do you see in him?" a horrified friend asks, to which she responds languidly: "I do like having someone in love with me. Every woman does." She encourages his evident infatuation, despite (or because of) social disapproval: "I don't understand how Mimi could invite a man like that." "It's perfectly simple. Ladies love brutes."

The evident power imbalance that characterizes the relationship between Mimi and Forziati works to eroticize a "forbidden" sexual liaison. Mimi, however, conjoins her erotic fascination to wider social dissolution of male control of female sexuality and offers a (class-determined) view of the emancipation of women that, in a world of economic abundance, social status, and privilege, relates solely to the personal assertion of sexual freedom and dissolution of traditional marital expectations. On upper-class strategies for coping with a stifling asexual marriage, Mimi contends, "Don't you know it doesn't matter who goes near whose wife anymore? Men and women don't just sit and look at each other over restaurant tables for years." Incorporating a vocabulary derived from popular feminism and liberalizing mores on adultery and divorce, Mimi refuses to agree that her position as a wife and mother is incompatible with the satisfaction of independent sexual desire and claims "equal rights" with adulterous husbands: "I've been stepping out myself, enjoying *my* freedom after nine years as a passive wife." Mimi's critique of monogamous bourgeois marriage seems to offer the possibility that she will forgo social privilege in favor of personal freedom and accept Forziati's offer of marriage. However, her active assertion of autonomous sexuality and independence is, ultimately, recouped by her class-determined maternal position as she tells him she can never marry him because she could not accept the social opprobrium that would accrue to her son. As with several films of this type, the temporary pleasures of contravening conventional heterosexual decorum through proximity to the virile, underclass male that are offered to female audiences are curtailed by narratives that demand the restitution of traditional moral order.

In the hope that his safe return will oblige Mimi to marry him anyway, Forziati arranges for his chauffeur to "kidnap" her son but is unaware that the chauffeur is, in fact, in the employ of Mendino, who has also arranged to kidnap Forziati's son as revenge for losing the building contract. The two boys are thus held together in a blackened cellar, and Mimi appeals to Forziati, who "knows everyone in the underworld," to secure her son's release with the reluctant promise of marriage if he does.[12] Mendino offers Forziati the choice of only *one* boy for release—Mimi's or his own—and the other for death. Recognizing his own folly in staging a kidnap plot, Forziati chooses to have Mimi's son released then risks all in a gunfight with the gangster racketeers to free his own boy. With both boys safe Forziati demonstrates superior moral character by relinquishing his claim on Mimi and thereby eases the passage for the absent father to return to the reunited family. Both fathers, in a gesture previously refused, shake hands in recognition that the "real hero is this family—that's where everybody belongs"—each child with his own father. Where class had divided the men, mutual recognition of their parental responsibilities as fathers offers masculine reconciliation in a transclass and transethnic paternal function. Consequently, the film's ending recasts the liberal sexual freedom initiated by Mimi as a disruptive, aberrant episode and the gangster figure as a threat to the family who must be expelled. In this sense Mimi's infatuation with a low-class male is a catalyst for resolving the tensions of the broken family.

Reaffirming the role of fathers in a weakened marital context, *Ladies Love Brutes* returns the sexually adventurous woman to the family unit. The status quo is maintained, for there is no social mobility for Forziati at all; rather, the film underlines his failure to transcend class/ethnic limitations and the incompatibility of class cultures: the film concludes with his chastened but welcome return to the house he was born in on the East Side.

The film's presentation of desire untrammeled by social convention is mediated to some extent by the fact that Forziati is not a gangster; rather, it is his proximity to the underworld that adds a frisson of danger to what is a basic class-defined social melodrama narrative. Nonetheless, although contained by a conservative narrative that returns class, ethnicity, and gendered sexuality to their socially approved places, *Ladies Love Brutes* opens spaces of identification that posit the production of pleasures for a female audience.[13]

The Racketeer, however, offers a more complex negotiation of the consequences of socialite fascination by incorporating a violent bootlegging gangster chief into a high-society melodrama but with a "fallen woman" plotline. *The Racketeer* opens on the streets with an intergang murder and a territory war between two rival bootlegging gangs. In the midst of this a drunk is picked up from the sidewalk and put into a taxi by Rhoda Philbrooke (Carole Lombard), an upper-class woman who draws the attention of one of the gang leaders, Mahlon Keane (Robert Armstrong). The following evening Rhoda attends a charity card game, and the gossiping socialites make it clear that she has for some time been a social outcast and is "terribly brave" for staking a claim to rejoin her peers. Rhoda's "crime" was to leave her millionaire sportsman husband to care and tend to a broken alcoholic violinist Tony Vaughan (Roland Drew). The gossip moves between character assassination of the "fallen woman" and support for her recuperation: she is "her own worst enemy," fully aware of the social cost of divorce yet unwilling to pay the price of social ostracism; but, for the young daughter of a disapproving dowager, Rhoda is the "bravest woman I ever heard of" for following her desire for a "mad musician," to which her mother responds, "I do believe I have given birth to a modern." Thus Rhoda is utterly "romantic" for choosing destitution over privilege and personal freedom over social constriction. Mahlon Keane also attends the charity function as part of his attempt to join legitimate society and spots Rhoda cheating at cards, which he covers to save her embarrassment. *The Racketeer* thus sets up a peculiar erotic triangle: a self-pitying, alcoholic musician who lives only for art, a "fallen" socialite, and a murderous but masterful and self-possessed gangster. Each is marked in some way as an "outsider," but Rhoda refuses Keane's easy assumption that her behavior is underpinned by sexual promiscuity. His own sexual experience mistakenly includes her as a "fallen woman": "Forget what I am. You know who I am. You know how I live. I've met many women at card tables." Rhoda's defense of her moral character is robust: "A woman who would cheat for money might not care to do other things. You can mark me as slightly damaged and put me on the bargain counter."

Complex circulations of desire are patterned through the three figures. Rhoda is held to have left her husband through strength of character and a protofeminist assertion of her right to sexual fulfillment. Yet her erotic enthrallment to the alcoholic musician demands a masochistic renunciation of self-fulfillment and ultimate abnegation of self. During one of his alcoholic binges Vaughan says, "If I had the courage, I'd kill myself," to which she replies, "I love you. When you're well and strong again, I'll go my way, but you must let me help you now." Her maternal "duty" to sacrifice her personal fulfillment for the good of art, to make Tony strong and well enough to play at his own concert, leads Rhoda to accept the financial assistance of Keane. Keane's own erotic attraction to Rhoda is filtered through a drive to connect with the high culture that the classical violin represents, and he takes control of Vaughan's physical rehabilitation, bankrolling the concert tour in the hope that Rhoda will accept him when Vaughan leaves her. The narrative flows around these characters: Vaughan's relationship to Rhoda oscillates between child-like dependency when he is drunk and brusque rejection when he has recuperated. When he is fully recovered, Vaughan rejects Rhoda, and she responds: "He doesn't need me. I've lost my job," and in a final abasement she accepts the gangster but, curiously, out of an infantilized desire for Keane to assume the dominant role, to "take care" of her. Despite struggling against Keane's offer of an easy life, Rhoda succumbs when the musician leaves to embark on a tour to great critical acclaim. The gangster books a passage for the pair on a cruise liner with the intention of taking his wealth and starting afresh without his increasingly murderous underworld connections. Even knowing that he can never command the erotic intensity of Rhoda's adoration of the sensitive, otherworldly violinist, Keane takes their impending marriage as an opportunity for reinvention—"all out in the clear, just you and I." Yet the impossibility of the union is figured in a mirror shot of the couple in the concert dressing room that explicitly triangulates the erotic scenario: a violin soundtrack and cutaway to Tony performing accompanies contemplation of their image as the future Mr. and Mrs. Keane. The ephemeral quality of the mirror offers instead misrecognition of union and self-completion. Keane's mistake of sending a gang member to kill his rival sets in train the denouement, in which he is killed just at the moment she will tell him she cannot marry him.

The gangster, then, is expelled from the erotic triangle to allow for the creation of the couple; the musician's "rejection" of Rhoda is explained as a passionate sense of *his* unworthiness: "Don't leave me. [Kiss] I couldn't help myself. I'll never bother you again. What have I to give to you? [Passionate kiss]." Rhoda achieves a reversal of her erotic subjectivity in commanding love based on Vaughan's masochistic abasement to her. In granting Rhoda her object of desire without punishment, it could be concluded that the potentially powerful destabilization of normative heterosexual relations that the film promotes works in favor of female gratification. *The Racketeer* utilizes the gangster figure to dramatize shifting scenarios of competing sexual subjectivities within both "fallen woman" and society melodrama narrative structures yet is not fully contained by either. There is some "excess" of meaning that is not accounted for by these narrative models that counteracts the neatness of narrative reconciliation and closure.

A *Free Soul* opens with a beautiful, perfectly coiffed Jan Ashe (Norma Shearer), dressed in flimsy underwear, offering herself for appraisal to a hidden man to whom she addresses the question, "Tired of me after one night?"[14] From her flirtatious banter and easy manner, the scene, set in a hotel room, suggests a lovers' breakfast. It is surprising, then, when the hidden man is revealed to be her father (Lionel Barrymore). The scene establishes the pair as unconventional members of the Ashe dynasty, an upper-class WASP family who regularly feature in society pages and enjoy the highest levels of traditional aristocratic privilege. Their relationship is

1. Female desire: gangster Ace Wilfong (Clark Gable) and Jan Ashe (Norma Shearer) in *A Free Soul* (1931). Photo courtesy of the British Film Institute.

unorthodox: they travel together; Jan calls him by his first name, Stephen; and they share a commitment to lives lived without self-deception and to self-assertion as antidote to the strictures of convention. From Jan's childhood, her father has fostered in her an independence of spirit and trust in personal choice not typically encouraged in young women, exhorting her to "think for yourself — make your own mistakes and live by them." Jan is engaged to a reticent and gentlemanly polo player, Dwight Winthrop (Leslie Howard), who, although decent and patient, offers no challenge to Jan. Disdaining their family relations for their narrow-minded views on personal behavior and the importance of "tradition," father and daughter are mirror images of each other and form a bond that excludes others by its intensity. Binding the two together is a mutual recognition that at the center of each personality is a flaw: Stephen Ashe is a chronic alcoholic, and Jan lacks emotional stability. Into this scenario enters the gambler-cum-gangster "Ace" Wilfong (Clark Gable), who hires Stephen as his attorney to defend him against a charge of murder. The scene in which Jan meets Ace for the first time at her father's chambers is exceptionally explicit in that it is cut to the measure of *her* desire: shots of her gaze are held long enough to make him the object of sexual attraction, thus opening a cinematic space for female identification with Jan as bearer of the objectifying look.

As in *The Racketeer*, the overall narrative of *A Free Soul* triangulates the socialite and the gangster, but in this instance it is the woman's father who serves as the third party.[15] This is readily suggestive of a classical Freudian reading, but, extraordinarily, the film is underpinned not by the story of male castration and renunciation of the mother but by the *female* passage through the Oedipus complex through which women acquire identities appropriate for hegemonic heterosexuality. The film traces Jan's psychical trajectory from a father-identified child who will achieve adult sexuality (and accession to "proper" female identity) only by renouncing the father as love object and assuaging "penis envy" by exchanging him for a replacement male. It will not, of course, be the gangster who finally assumes this patriarchal place but the socially equal, gentle, and considerate fiancé. In this sense Jan's entry into gender-appropriate adult heterosexuality is marked by a fantasy of erotic enslavement: the child's reluctance to relinquish the father as original love object demands coercion, and the dangerous appeal of the virile gangster provides a perfect scenario that is sexually seductive and compels compliance. That Jan and Ace exchange ties when they first meet confirms the view that she is unaware at this stage, as Freud would insist of all female pregenital sexuality, that she does not own the phallus but *acts as if she does*. In other words, Jan believes she is her father's equal in possessing the symbol of male authority, the phallus/tie, which keeps the father/daughter relation in a state that is undifferentiated by gender inequality. Offering her tie to Ace is a gesture grounded in an understanding that she is his equal, too, and in the belief that it is hers to offer. This provides psychoanalytical underpinning for Jan's contravention of dominant social norms of feminine gender identity and resistance to bourgeois marriage: her infatuation with Ace Wilfong is based on the fact that he is "the first really exciting man I've ever met," a man who would understand why she doesn't want to marry and let life "settle around me like a pan of sourdough." From Wilfong's tastefully and fashionably furnished penthouse Jan experiences what it is to be a "free soul": looking out at the city panorama, she declares, "I love it." "Love what?" "I don't know. A new kind of man for a new kind of world." The gangster figure, then, is the embodiment of antitraditional and urban modernity, a figure whose place "on top of the world" is testament to the socioeconomic transformations that had shaken the foundation on which traditional wealthy elites had rested before the 1929 crash. Jan's public affair with the sexually magnetic gangster, who is involved in opium, murder, extortion, and white slavery, initially satisfies her desire to shock her social scene and family by her choice of partner, believing this to be a true test of independent judgment. Yet her drunken father interprets the infatuation as an "illness," "disease," or "compulsion" on a par with his alcoholism and tries to separate them. He makes a withering attack on Wilfong's low-class origins and, in the process, betrays his seemingly liberal credo: "The only time I hate democracy is when one of you mongrels forgets where you belong. A few legal dollars, a clean suit, and you move across the railroad tracks." Accusing Jan of carrying on a "miserable backstairs affair with a miserable rat," Stephen confirms his sense of patriarchal "ownership" of his daughter's sexuality when he derides her for being "nothing but a cheap, common, contemptible . . ." Jan counters with the riposte, "I am not cheap," which asserts a claim to self-determine the meaning of her unorthodox sexual choice.

It is at this point that the dual perspective on active female sexuality that characterizes this and other films of this type is made transparent: Jan's "feminist" perception is that sexuality is a legitimate area for the expression of independent, free choice, but this view runs up against dominant mores, which account for her behavior quite differently. She cannot escape the patriarchal logic that equates active female sexuality with a despoiled self, with the destruction of "reputation" and social standing and, as here, a sexuality that is pathologized as a masochistic "sickness." The plot proceeds with father and daughter making a pact to swear off their chosen addictions and attempting to "withdraw" from alcohol and sex by walking the mountains for three months. On return, both fail: Stephen degenerates into complete drunkenness and falls into the gutter. Jan meets up with Wilfong, who, in her absence, has dropped the veneer of sophisticated, urbane lover and, in blackmailing her to marry him, reveals the brute beneath. Now physically rough and verbally vicious, Ace sneers at her compulsion to seek love among the bestial underworld: "It ain't polite but it's what you want." Wilfong calculates that no one will marry Jan when they discover that she frequently stayed nights at the Ritz with him, that her social reputation would be destroyed. Recognizing this to be true, Jan resigns herself to her fate and dolefully comments that it is "just the marriage I always dreamed about . . . but the moonbeams turned to worms and crawled away." She is a "marked" woman, but her "reputation" comes to matter only when she is expelled from her family and left without the patriarchal protection of tradition, wealth, and social privilege.

Yet, as in *The Racketeer*, the "fallen" woman does *not* pay. Former fiancé Dwight Winthrop steps in to protect Jan's reputation by shooting Wilfong (supposedly over a gambling debt) and goes to trial for murder. Jan drags her degenerate father, the only man she believes can defend Dwight successfully, from the drunk house, and, after his rehabilitation, Stephen Ashe's tremendous court performance ensures Dwight's freedom. Stephen dies a noble and redemptive death as a result of his effort, which, in the Freudian narrative, serves to ensure Jan's Oedipal trajectory toward adult female heterosexuality; with the patriarch removed, the way is left open for the reunion of the class-appropriate couple, thus carrying both social and psychical resolutions to their orthodox conclusions. *A Free Soul* is a highly distinctive narrative because it so explicitly represents the psychical foundations of hegemonic heterosexual female identity. Although the conventionality of its conclusion cannot be contested, the film does challenge the prevalent view within film studies that Hollywood cinema offers only Oedipal dramas from the point of view of the male spectator. The metonymic use of the gangster figure to represent "precivilized" female libidinal drive is a potent indication of unconscious pleasures addressed to the *female* spectator.

Ladies Love Brutes, The Racketeer, and *A Free Soul* assert that female desire is a destabilizing force that works to dissolve class boundaries and initiates a passage through sexual desire to its satisfaction, regardless of social consequences. It is a powerful agent that does not respect social order. Further, the gangster-inflected society melodrama demonstrates that class is an essential dimension to the organization of patriarchal gender relations although here it is manifest that white, upper-class females hold far greater socioeconomic and legal power than lower-class males. This overturns the foundation of normative heterosexual gender relations in that women are actually in a "dominant" position. Class differentials may be understood, then, as a socially sanctioned pretext for the staging of narratives of female sexual transgression. In other words, analysis of the appeal of "the lady and the gangster" format reveals how a power relation constructed on the basis of *class* difference works to license active and dynamic female desire. Simultaneously, the transgressive quality that typifies the format attests not only to the psychical pleasures afforded by the reversal of normative gender power relations but also to the *social* changes in representations of women at this time. It is therefore important to balance a reading of unconscious structures of pleasure with a consideration of how Hollywood film in this cycle responded to the widening socioeconomic parameters of modernity that were transforming perceptions of women's role in society in response to changing mores on marriage, divorce, and sex.

As evidence of the film industry's participation in promulgating cinematic fare on the basis of its "contemporary" and "modern" appeal, the press book accompanying the distribution of *A Free Soul* explicitly addresses the figuration of change and challenge to older stereotypes of female sexuality.[16] Clearly acting as a form of ventriloquism, "Innocent Screen Heroine of Old Out of Place in Modern Life States Norma Shearer" is a document fascinating for the way it conflates expectations of Shearer's star persona with direct address to her female fans on the subject of the changes in cinematic representation of women. The "Star Interview" opens with the pertinent question: "Where is the gelatin heroine whose virtue was her own and only reward, who wept copious tears when the facts of life were revealed by gentlemen with black moustaches, whose adolescent faith in mankind was akin to a belief in Santa Claus?" And the reply: "'I don't know,' opines Norma Shearer, 'I only hope they never find her again — for me at any rate.' Miss Shearer was at work on the final scenes of 'A Free Soul,' her new Metro-Goldwyn-Mayer starring picture that will come to the ——— Theatre. She played an 'emancipated' girl, one who learns the facts of life, who lives life, but is none the less a heroine." This acknowledges a contemporary lack of appeal — to women — of the fallen woman/victim character. "'Nobody,' said Miss Shearer, 'wants to see the heroine of a picture suffer anymore. Audiences prefer to see me, for instance, as a girl who doesn't wither under a blow. They like to see me go to the devil — but they want to see me come back again.'"

The studio publicity "interview" adeptly conflates onscreen character, star persona, and "real" actress: "Norma is frank, but with no intention of shocking any one.

She personifies the modern trend — in life and on the screen. She lacks all equivo-cation." Offering a thoroughly modernist expression of the importance of lived ex-perience in determining character, she continues: "Adela Rogers St. John wrote *A Free Soul* on facts in life — on actual experience, and that's why the novel struck popular fancy, she explained. And, as in 'The Divorcee,' I found that one could do the same thing on the screen." Thus cinema is identified as a positive agent in the challenge to represent women differently, and *A Free Soul* was promoted on the ba-sis of the vicarious pleasures offered to its female spectators: "I don't mean that every heroine should carry rebellion against conventions as far as this particular heroine, but it gives them a sort of satisfaction to see someone else do it, just the same." Ac-knowledging the potential for cinema to articulate social change (with box office success the measure of appeal), the interview nonetheless recognizes the distance between image and "reality" and is careful not to cede direct representational status to cinematic portrayals of women, either new or traditional:

> "Some fans have censured some of my roles of girls who defied conventions, of course. The box office, however, provided the real answer. Our new type of screen heroine really reflects, in a way, the new freedom every woman, secretly perhaps, dreams of. But in real life, when the truth is told, it doesn't quite exist. But then neither did the old time starry-eyed heroine with golden curls and the immacu-late innocence. This is what we call an era of sophistication, and men and women are on a more common ground. And I'll admit seeing a little of real life really helps some of us."

In this cycle, films pivot on the capacity for *female* sexual desire to disrupt and destabilize class and ethnic boundaries. It is essential, however, that this assessment does not ignore the historical specificity of films produced in the period from 1929 to 1933, from the Wall Street crash to the nadir of national economic collapse in the Depression. In this respect the critical shibboleth that the gangster is "invented" as an antihero symbolizing the post-crash dissolution of boundaries dividing legiti-mate from illegitimate capitalist entrepreneurship should be recast to include con-sideration of how such disorder might be figured in ways of immediate interest to female spectators. *Dance, Fools, Dance* and *Corsair* are both explicitly contextual-ized by a contemporary experience of the Depression, although each utilizes the gangster not only for his capacity to overturn the "natural" economic order of cap-italism but to transpose that capacity for signifying disruption to the private sphere of heterosexual relations.

As a *Variety* reviewer notes with amusement: "Probably 'Dance Fools Dance' is as good a title as motion picture titles go, but a metaphysician might have ex-hausted learning trying to reconcile it with the melodrama of newspapers and gang-dom in which Joan Crawford is featured."[17] Crawford's star persona by this time was built on roles that explored the moral, economic, and social consequences for women of modern sexual conduct. From *Sally, Irene, and Mary* (1925), *The Taxi Dancer* (1927), *Four Walls* (1928), *Untamed* (1929), and *Paid* (1930), Crawford was associated with women who, although often economically impoverished, were nonetheless determined and often physically magnetic. Often focused on stories of lower-class women to dramatize relational conflict, her films used narratives of courtship, marriage, or divorce to address themes of sexual jealousy, female autonomy, male ownership, and sexual initiation. In marked class contrast her "flapper" films, such as *Our Dancing Daughters* (1928), *Our Modern Maidens* (1929), *Our Blushing Brides* (1930), and *Montana Moon* (1930), centered on the romantic entanglements of the generation of postwar hedonistic and sexually permissive Bright Young Things and were characterized by numerous changes of risqué costumes, luxurious interiors, exuberant jazz and dancing sequences, and extended love scenes. The press book for *Dance, Fools, Dance* draws directly on both strands of Crawford's recent cinematic history to combine "social realism" with the visual appeal of the film for female spectators familiar with Crawford's representation of wealthy and sexually liberated socialites: "The thrills of 'Paid' and the youthful gayety of 'Our Dancing Daughters' and 'Our Modern Maidens' are blended perfectly in this picture. A meeting of underworld and society in an exciting, gorgeously mounted show that gives beautiful Joan the chance of her career. Swinging costumes, kissing, swimming costumes."[18] Indeed, the film invokes the period with a presentation of Crawford as visual spectacle when her character Bonnie Jordan hosts a party for a crowd of rich sophisticates aboard her own yacht. Their fathers play cards and discuss the value of their stock market dealings while wryly commenting on their indolent offspring's lack of discipline and understanding of the meaning of work. Between smooches with her boyfriend, Bob (Lester Vail), Bonnie performs a wild dance and, to stave off ever-threatening boredom, suggests a swimming party. The ensuing bathing scene, with its suggestion of nude bathing, drew close attention from the Studio Relations Committee.[19] It was the following scene, however, that caused more difficulty. Set in a cabin, the scene shows Bonnie (in negligee) and Bob (in pajamas) behaving intimately, and it is here that Bonnie sets out her personal sexual credo. Declaring that she is "not old-fashioned," Bonnie signals that she wants to enjoy Bob without the confines of marriage: "I believe in trying love out. . . ." "On approval?" "Yes, on approval." Her anticonventional "flapper" modernity of the right to love "on approval" rejects traditional feminine behavior and decorum as she demands, "Kiss me, Bob": the passionate kiss and fade to black that follow leave little doubt that the relationship is then sexually consummated.[20]

While maintained within her privileged social strata, Bonnie's sexual philosophy of independence presents no real ideological conflict, yet *Dance, Fools, Dance* poses the problem of how that philosophy survives without wealth and social influence to support it. Bonnie and her feckless brother, Rodney, are thrown into absolute penury when the Wall Street crash leaves their father penniless — he dies of a heart attack on the stock market trading floor. A montage of a carefree dancing crowd is superimposed onto the frantic melee of brokers on the trading floor scrambling to recoup massive financial losses. America's historical shift from economic prosperity and growth to national collapse and depression registers as Bonnie's ignominious "fall" from luxury to poverty. With this abrupt personal transition Bonnie is confronted with the logical consequence of her independent sexual philosophy. Out of a sense of "doing the right thing," Bob offers to legitimate their liaison through marriage as the "least I could do"; to live by her credo of sexual equality, Bonnie gallantly refuses him: "You don't have to be a martyr to the cause. Everything's fifty-fifty, you know that. There's absolutely no obligation on anybody's part so cheer up — there'll be no wedding bells for us." Although painfully aware of passing up possibly her last chance for the financial security and social standing that marriage to Bob would secure, Bonnie refuses to trade on the "obligation" that premarital sex conventionally places on him. With a brave but equivocal face, she states, "I like my freedom just as much as you do, Bob, and I intend to keep it." They part, and the picture shifts focus to Bonnie's adaptation to reduced circumstances and to the world of work.

After she has rejected what she defines as the "silly, stupid, conventional things" expected of "beautiful but dumb" women (teashop waitress, model, or beautician), Bonnie takes the "man-sized" job of cub reporter in the all-male environment of a Chicago newspaper office. Through this work she strikes up a friendship with an old-time reporter, Burt Scranton (Cliff Edwards), who is working on the lurid stories generated by the city's gangster warfare. Meanwhile, her brother, Rodney, earns his living in commission from persuading his former society contacts to buy bootleg liquor from charismatic gang leader Jake Luva (Clark Gable). The plot turns on Rodney's unwitting involvement as a driver in an early representation of the St. Valentine's Day Massacre, in which seven members of a rival gang are murdered. Rodney's alcoholic binges and weak nerves make him likely to reveal the perpetrators of the massacre, so Luva plots to ensure his silence by entrapping him further into the gang's illegal businesses. When Luva learns that Burt Scranton has succeeded in getting the story from him, Rodney is offered the choice of murdering Scranton or being killed himself, and he chooses the former.[21] Unaware of her brother's involvement, the loss of her friend spurs Bonnie to avenge Burt's killer, and she agrees with the newspaper heads to go "undercover" as a dancing girl in Luva's high-class nightclub to investigate. She is to take on the role of "Mary Smith," a "tough girl from Missouri, a cheap moll who hangs around nightclubs," and is told to use "any weapon you've got" to infiltrate the gang.

At the nightclub Bonnie's performance as a bare-legged, high-kicking dancer dressed in silver lamé draws the disdainful attention of her former socialite acquaintances (among whom is Bob), who sneer to see Bonnie reduced to the lowest social level. Ignoring them, Bonnie makes a seductive and conspicuous play for Luva and, supplanting his sophisticated, platinum crop-haired paramour, is soon invited up to his beautifully furnished private penthouse above the club. Before she joins him, Bob calls at her dressing room; assuming her to have "fallen" beneath redemption, he nonetheless admits to strong feelings for her but this time offers not marriage but a role as his mistress and "kept" women. Refusing again to capitulate to the patriarchal terms of this offer, Bonnie does not disabuse him of her real purpose in dancing at the club and, physically rebuffing his advances, rejects him: "Don't touch me. That's all over." Joining Luva in his apartment, Bonnie barely fends off his physical attention but, in the course of her visit, discovers her brother's involvement with the murderous gang and the death of Scranton. The plot then resolves with a three-way shoot-out at Rodney's apartment in which Luva, his chief henchman, and Rodney are killed. A brokenhearted Bonnie files the whole story, including her brother's role, and scoops the gangland murder cases for the newspaper. With the gangs broken, Bonnie decides to quit: as she walks through the office for the last time, she is met by Bob, who declares that what he has and now feels for her is true love and insists that she marry him. The request "Kiss me, Bob" indicates that she gets her man, not on his terms but on terms that satisfy *her* personal code of honor.[22]

Classified by the SRC as a "modern youth drama," *Dance, Fools, Dance* is a pertinent example of the way in which films in this cycle throw into relief the "double standard" controlling and ultimately limiting the extent of women's sexual independence. Bonnie's descent from upper-class heiress to working woman and then to "moll" also dramatizes the ways in which the meaning of active female sexuality is entirely class-bound, with the déclassé sexuality demanded of a female protagonist by a male gangster figure marking the point at which voluntary sexual activity melds with economic exchange. Understood in this way, representations of gangsters within the cycle's varying scenarios of active female sexuality become symptomatic of the way in which "disordered" socioeconomic relations become imbricated with "disordered" dominant positions within desire. The case of United Artists' *Corsair* is similarly instructive, although for the manner in which female-controlled cross-class desire is staged to carry a narrative that critically examines corporate business ethics in the context of Prohibition enforcement and racketeering rum-running.[23]

The film opens with a montage reprising the recent graduation of successful football player Johnny Hawks (Chester Morris) from a prestigious college and provides the story with the hitherto unidentified "social issue" of what to do with the "thousands of ambitious youths turned out of college as All-American football heroes."[24] Johnny is ambitious and rejects the tame idea of football coaching in favor of a job on Wall Street. He soon inveigles an invitation to a high society ball in the hope of meeting prospective employers. When Johnny enters the ballroom, the camera traces his eyeline to a svelte and glamorous young woman, shot from behind, who wears a backless evening gown and socializes effortlessly with her high society guests. The camera lingers on the conspicuously exposed back, but the suggestion that this gaze is "owned" by Johnny is broken when Alison Corning (Alison Loyd) returns the look, and her control over the scenario is further confirmed by the ensuing dialogue. Positioned as sexually experienced and fully capable of selecting her partners, Alison is casually informed that Johnny is "not her type" because "he comes from the West, washed dishes, worked his way through college and doesn't know how to wear clothes." Despite, or, by my argument, because of, the class imbalance, Alison toys with the idea of making Johnny part of a Pygmalion-type project of bringing him into "polite society" and immediately objectifies him. She asks if he is "afraid" of her and subjects him to lingering looks of desire: "I always know what I want and usually get it." When he fails to respond in kind, Alison derides his geographical and class origins, which at the same time derides his muscular, self-reliant masculinity, his "He-man 'son of the west' novelty stuff." The power imbalance of class and wealth is thus inscribed once again across gender lines and mapped against conflicting forms of sexuality. The dialogue demonstrates an acute consciousness of challenges to "proper" gender roles and awareness that sexual permissiveness defines the metropolitan "sophistication" of the socialite. In trying to fathom Johnny's resistance, Alison suggests that intimate contact with women of this social sphere would ruin him for more prosaic relations suitable for his class: "I suppose you don't want to go back West with any 'cold and lovely heiress' complex to come between you and your corn-fed girls?" His riposte that he has no girls back home reveals a popular familiarity with psychoanalytical terms: "If I had, they wouldn't have your complex!" For a solid, hardworking, ambitious, and physically adept working-class male the flagrantly active sexuality of upper-class girls is explained as a "complex," with erotic indulgence reduced to a form of neurosis. On parting, Alison wryly subverts social niceties: "Thank you for not making love to me" to which Johnny replies, "Why? I never thought of such a thing," which Alison sarcastically caps with, "You wouldn't, would you?" Set up in this way, it is clear why the review of *Corsair* in the November 20, 1931, *New York Times* could identify the film's contemporary reworking of older stereotypes in the fact that it is "not a case of the villain pursuing the heroine, but of the girl pursuing the bright young man." How, then, does this description warrant the view from the Studio Relations Committee that *Corsair* represents "gang philosophy in its very worst light"?[25]

With Alison's intervention Johnny is offered a job with her father, a hugely wealthy broker on Wall Street. One year later, though, Johnny has become thoroughly disenchanted with the practices he encounters. With stock market dealings in crisis, he learns from Steven Corning that the "cardinal rule for business success is to get out from under while the going is good and let the other fellow hold the bag." Criticism of financial institutions and their role in causing the misery of unemployment, starvation wages, and mass migration in the Depression is not softened: when Johnny offers his word of honor on a business deal, he is reminded: "What's honor got to do with it? This is Wall Street." The clash of values between the young man imbued with the Protestant work ethic and the older generation of corrupt brokers is marked; as a fellow stock trader suggests, "Steve is a crook and we're all crooks. Wall Street isn't a football field and Corning & Co. isn't the YMCA. It's a first-class gambling joint; only they use margin clerks instead of croupiers." Johnny discovers that Corning has made enormous profits by exchanging worthless stock for good securities, offered in good faith for investment by widows and on behalf of orphans, and that he makes money on illegally imported liquor, which he purchases from his gangster associate Big John (Fred Kohler). Johnny's sense of moral outrage combines with a mission to demonstrate that he has the right qualities of capitalist entrepreneurship to compete successfully in the Prohibition economy: he declares to Alison that "I'm going to put one over. . . . I'm going to take what I want out of the world just as your father does but I am going to use my own hands and take my chance." He equips a sailing ship, the *Corsair*, and embarks on a career of piracy, hijacking illegal liquor from the ships entering America by way of Canada and selling it back to Corning, who is unaware that he is, in fact, buying back the same liquor for which he has already paid Big John. Much of the picture is given over to external location scenes of Johnny's marine adventures and high seas skirmishes with guns and gangsters, thus fulfilling the hybrid combination of gangsterism and dangerous romance indicated in the description of *Corsair* as a "virile drama with a red-blooded raider zooming up to new heights of romance and realism."[26] From the studio's point of view, the story ingredients "romance" and "realism" are matched to the putative gendered interests of its audience. The strategy of constructing a film's appeal to capture the widest audience requires this type of "doubling" of address to both male and female spectators and is discernible in the suggested catch lines that attempt to appeal to dual interests: "Luxury, Wealth, Beautiful Clothes, Position. She had it all"; "A Savage in Combat, A Slave in Love"; and "The heart of a woman ruled him where the strength of the lawless failed."

For most of the film it is unclear whether Johnny has capitulated to the immoral ethics he seemed to reject in the bucket-shop brokers, and this marks his entrepreneurial business success with a high degree of equivocality. Accumulating vast profits by "stealing" from the rich, through his own labors, organizational acumen, and enterprising spirit, Johnny provides an image of a post-Depression era in which capitalism is reinvigorated: his young, self-reliant, rugged, go-getting masculinity stands in contrast to the old, corrupt, and moribund financial elite represented by Corning. Yet such a positive representation of masculinity sets up an interesting dilemma for the initiating narrative of female desire that frames the piracy action and gangster excursus. It would be extraordinary for the romance to be resolved with Alison rewarded with the object of her desire when Johnny, in addition to his lower-class origins, has been shown to be a violent, ruthless racketeer. To observe the parameters of this ideological constraint, the narrative concludes with the revelation that Johnny had actually been operating as a Robin Hood figure, sending his profits to support the widows and orphans that Corning had swindled. In other words, *Corsair* operates a form of masquerade in which the hero is able simultaneously to embody desirable masculine attributes and incite the same cross-class eroticism that

2. Gangster masquerade: John Hawks (Chester Morris) and Alison Corning (Alison Loyd, a.k.a. Thelma Todd) in *Corsair* (1931). Photo courtesy of the British Film Institute.

characterizes the cycle's deployment of the dangerous gangster. It is telling in this respect to note the absence of ethnic characterization: as with Forziati's Italian and Keane's imputed Irish ethnicity, *A Free Soul* underscored the "mongrel" status of its gangster protagonist by naming him Ace Wilfong—a curious German and Asiatic compound—while Johnny Hawks epitomizes the white American of solid native stock. Redeemed in this way, Johnny qualifies as ideologically suitable for the task of "remasculinizing" and reinvigorating financial capitalism. His entrepreneurial success and physical courage are rewarded with the presidency of an off-shore branch of Corning's empire (who is now reformed and imbued with social conscience) and with marriage to a compliant Alison, who declares that, rather than merely flirting and toying with Johnny, she had been genuinely in love "from the moment I set eyes on you." By such an ideological sleight of hand, the upper-class girl *is* rewarded with her "gangster." As a result, *Corsair* remains equivocal on several counts—in its representation of Wall Street as the metonym for corporate capitalism; in concluding with the "message" that "crime," if justified, does pay; and in the view that sexually desirous and experienced women can be rewarded with the hero. However, it is the fact that *Corsair* demonstrates the manly virtues of the masculine "hero" through the depiction of the activities of a bootlegging gangster that drew most attention from the SRC, which was exerting its influence on the preparation of pictures containing gangster elements. The surviving documentation catalogs the problems presented for the SRC by the proximity of the romantic male hero to the gangster.

From a concern for the deleterious effect of depictions of gangster crime on the morals of cinema spectators, the correspondence that details preproduction script meetings with Roland West centers on the negotiation between the director and the SRC of the need for different endings in order to avoid glamorizing Johnny as grid-iron hero turned "gangster." Already, the original treatment betrays a self-conscious attempt to anticipate the committee's concerns that the film would need to be "cleaned up" by a moral ending to compensate for the depiction of crime and its rewards:

> A boy (Chester Morris) is introduced as a dashing college football hero, meets the attractive daughter of a banker and stock broker on Wall Street who employs him as a stock salesman. At the end of the first year he resigns from the company because of his unwillingness to sell worthless stock to women. However, he has acquired the methods of Wall Street and the taste for big money. Together with some of his college chums, he equips a yacht in such a manner as that it can be made to appear to be merely a pleasure yacht, or, on short notice, can be transformed into a boat that resembles, in all outward respects, a United States Revenue cutter. The balance of the story is given over to the details of the hi-jacking. Briefly, he steals liquor from boats outside the twelve-mile limit and sells it to the stockbroker for whom he worked on Wall Street. During the process men are murdered and a woman is murdered; but through it all our hero becomes more successful and more wealthy until in the end of the picture he finally marries the daughter of his original boss, the stock broker. In an attempt to moralize, a tag has been written for it in which the hero is killed on the street in New York by the gang whom he has been hijacking.[27]

Director Roland West's letter to Jason S. Joy is evidently concerned to ensure the survival of the hero in that he offers the romance angle as possible solution: "It is a shame to kill the hero in the finish and if, in your opinion, it isn't necessary, let me know, as a love finish would be better." [28]

To avoid the patently conventional sop of having Johnny killed by rival gangsters, a telegram to Jason S. Joy from Will Hays suggests making Johnny an undercover police agent, "which would allow for even greater use of pirating scenes with beneficial rather than harmful consequences." Making Johnny an agent of authority "would inject the law wholesomely into the situation and disabuse [the] charge that police forces are depicted as helpless before bootlegging elements." [29] West was opposed to this idea, and it is at this point in the negotiations that the solution of donating the illegally gained money to the swindled widows and orphans is reached. The next agreed-on synopsis thus reads this way:

> The boy will come up from college as he does in the original story and accepts employment from Corning, the broker. However, he soon discovers that he is in a bucket-shop selling worthless stocks to women and orphans on margins. He also discovers that Corning (who is now to become the "heavy") is in the liquor business as a partner to Big John, the man from whom the hero in the original

version steals the liquor. Chester Morris leaves Corning's employ, denouncing his tactics in Wall Street and drawing healthy comparison between them and the legitimate activities of the Wall Street bankers and brokers. Motivated by revenge, Morris becomes a hi-jacker stealing only from Corning's ships and allowing other ships in the legitimate trade between ports to proceed without molestation. Ironically he sells to Corning the liquor that he has already stolen from him. When he has succeeded in breaking Corning financially, he exposes his plot, marries the girl and goes into legitimate business.[30]

The SRC was evidently concerned to ameliorate the film's highly explicit criticism of Wall Street's financial institutions and, as further correspondence attests, to encourage modifications to picture content to ensure that it did not classify the film as a "gangster" picture. It will be recalled that *Corsair* was one of a range of films in production in September 1931 that were assessed by the SRC according to their conformity to the classification "Gangster Picture" and that, accordingly, few of the titles considered here, either in brief or at length, would have qualified. Yet *The Racketeer, Ladies Love Brutes, Dance, Fools, Dance, A Free Soul*, and *Corsair* demonstrate that the gangster figure was an ideologically potent one that dramatized — and temporarily circumvented — the cultural boundaries describing the "legitimate" dynamics of gender, heterosexuality, and female desire. It is, therefore, now arguable that the single-minded focus of the SRC on the "gangster film" in terms of the representation of formal law and order obscured the potency of the gangster as agent of *libidinal* rather than criminal disruption.

The "lady and the gangster" cycle is only one of several in which early 1930s Hollywood figured female sexuality in relation to the male gangster. The complexity of cinematic significations of female sexuality in the period becomes yet more apparent when the figure of the "moll" in, for instance, *The Secret Six* (1931) and *Beast of the City* (1932) is addressed. The physical embodiment of the notion that women's only access to male power is through sexuality, the moll nonetheless combines elements of the "fallen" woman, "kept woman," prostitute, gold digger, and city girl, each indicative of the variety of cinematic figurations the period produced to articulate social changes to female sexual identity. Writing in 1937, Gilbert Seldes looked back to 1931 and to the watershed that he believed *The Public Enemy* represented for cinema audiences split by gender:

The cycle of gangster pictures — there were of course, dozens of them — was important in screen history for several reasons. In the midst of the world depression, the movies suffered with all other industries and the gangster pictures reanimated the screen and brought men trooping back to the movie houses which they had begun to abandon to women and children. It is a remarkable thing that while the handsome heroes of the screen are supposed to be attractive to women, the handsome women of the screen also attract women to the movies because they are supposed to represent the ideals to which they aspire: they are beautiful, well dressed and ultimately successful in love. But apart from Mae West, few of them became the "dream girl" of many men. . . . Men found the movies feminized and the great change came when Mr. Cagney in *Public Enemy* was being annoyed by Mae Clark and rudely ground half a grapefruit into her face. From that time on it became common form for the tough guys of the pictures to kick and slap their women around on the slightest provocation and roars of delight rose from the throats of men who had up to that time found nothing satisfactory in pictures except the newsreel and Mickey Mouse.[31]

Behind the history of male audiences who could find "nothing satisfactory in pictures" before *The Public Enemy* inaugurated the long tradition of the misogynist gangster film, Seldes indicates the contours of a "feminized" Hollywood that this chapter has also worked to reveal. In sum, the concealment of a cinema "abandoned" to women and children has been replicated in subsequent critical work on the gangster that forcefully underlines the importance of historical reclamation to reinstate the "lost" history of female cinema spectators and the films that included them in their address.

Notes

1. See introduction to this volume for general bibliography.

2. For a condensed history of the SRC in relation to later developments in regulation and censorship of the Motion Picture Producers and Distributors Association and the Production Code Administration see Richard Maltby, "The Production Code and the Hays Office," in *Grand Design: Hollywood as a Modern Business Enterprise, 1930–1939,* ed. Tino Balio (Berkeley: University of California Press, 1995); on the role of regulation and censorship in domestic and international markets see Ruth Vasey, *The World according to Hollywood, 1918–1939* (Exeter: University of Exeter Press, 1997); for a collection of essays on Hollywood regulation see Matthew Bernstein, ed., *Controlling Hollywood: Censorship and Regulation in the Studio Era* (London: Athlone Press, 2000); and for a specific study of regulatory "negotiations" see Lea Jacobs, *The Wages of Sin: Censorship and the Fallen Woman Film, 1928–1942* (Berkeley: University of California Press, 1995). The complex picture of institutional continuity and change in regulatory administration, together with the unevenness of patterns of "enforcement" that these histories suggest, makes the recent tendency to categorize Hollywood productions as either "pre-" or "post-" Code (with the 1934 Breen administration marked as the censorship watershed) very difficult to sustain. See, e.g., Mark A. Viera, *Sin in Soft Focus: Pre-Code Hollywood* (New York: Harry N. Abrams, 1999); and Thomas Doherty, *Pre-Code Hollywood: Sex, Immorality, and Insurrection in American Cinema, 1930–1934* (New York: Columbia University Press, 1999). Viera and Doherty both attempt to construct "pre-Code" Hollywood films as entirely free from regulatory practices and hence as characterized by gross violations of the Code's later strictures.

3. Jason S. Joy to Maurice McKenzie, telegram, Sep. 1, 1931, *Corsair* PCA file, Margaret Herrick Library, Academy of Motion Picture Arts and Sciences (hereafter cited as MHL-AMPAS).

4. Ibid.

5. Ibid. Nonetheless, the "gangster" and "crime" film debate had by 1931 led the SRC's role of advising studios on preproduction scripts toward a more active intervention in promoting its preference for films that glorified not the work of criminals but of law enforcers. Joy continues:

[*The Star Witness*] . . . illustrates the direction in which the minds out here are moving, that is there seems to be developing a cycle of thought in which the criminal and the underworld is the heavy and the representative of right living and those on the side of the law assuming the heroic roles. If all of the above is true is it not important that a statement which will reach the newspapers, police chiefs and censors be issued which will help them draw the necessary distinction between beer running gangsters and the kind of criminal stories which have had their proper place in literature and in pictures? Trotti goes further and suggests that this statement ought to take the form of a personal letter from the chief to each of the above named classifications and also the member companies and that the letter should be made public.

The fruition of the SRC's desire for pictures that glamorized the figures of law and order would come later—and after repeated iteration from the more robust post-1933 administration of the Production Code—with the glorification of the FBI or other government agency in G-Men in 1935 followed in 1936 by Let 'Em Have It, Men without Names, Public Hero Number One, Man Hunt, The Crime Patrol, Counterfeit, Special Investigator, Sworn Enemy, and the burlesque F-Men.

6. Jacobs, Wages of Sin, 5. See also Garth S. Jowett, Ian C. Jarvie, and Kathryn H. Fuller, Children and the Movies: Media Influence and the Payne Fund Controversy (Cambridge, U.K.: Cambridge University Press, 1996).

7. Jacobs, Wages of Sin, xi.

8. Ibid., 3.

9. Jacobs notes that both the gangster film and the fallen woman film were structurally similar in their "rise and fall" narratives and that both presented the censors with the problem of "glamour." An industry censor's comments on the 1932 film Red Headed Woman makes the connection in the following terms:

There is a striking similarity between the treatment of this character and the earlier treatment of the gangster character. . . . Because he was the central figure, because he achieved power and money and a certain notoriety, our critics claimed that an inevitable attractiveness resulted. And that was what they objected to in gangster pictures. They said we killed him off but that we made him glamorous before we shot him. This is what you are apt to be charged with in this case. While the Red Headed Woman is a common little creature from over the tracks who steals other women's husbands and uses her sex attractiveness to do it, she is the central figure and it will be contended that a certain glamour surrounds her. (Jason S. Joy to William A. Orr, June 14, 1932, Red Headed Woman PCA file, MHL-AMPAS [also cited in Jacobs, Wages of Sin, 18]).

10. For an extensive history of the blues song "Frankie and Johnny" and its use in Hollywood film see Peter Stanfield, "'Extremely Dangerous Material': Hollywood and the Ballad of Frankie and Johnny," in Classic Hollywood, Classic Whiteness, ed. Daniel Bernardi (Minneapolis: University of Minnesota Press, 2001), 442–465.

11. See David E. Ruth, Inventing the Public Enemy: The Gangster in American Culture, 1918–1934 (Chicago: University of Chicago Press, 1996).

12. Other than some minor amendments to dialogue, close-ups of guns, and a scene of Mimi and Joe drinking cocktails in a private dining room, the main concern for the Studio Relations Committee was the depiction of child kidnapping. Although the film was made before the kidnapping of the Lindbergh baby in 1932, representation of kidnapping was later incorporated into the Code's strictures governing rereleases. Ladies Love Brutes PCA file, MHL-AMPAS. A Production Code certificate to permit the reissue of Ladies Love Brutes was not granted in 1939 because of this "special regulation." The deleterious effect of the proximity of children to gangsters was also raised.

13. The film was sold largely on the strength of the star persona of now barely remembered George Bancroft—the biggest box office star in 1930—although this catalog of skills suggests areas of interest to both male and female audiences: "You will see him in denim jumpers on a lofty girder, driving home the last rivet in a towering skyscraper. You will see him immaculate in full-dress. You will see him winning a beautiful refined society woman. See him in a fierce hand-to-hand fight with a racketeering labor agitator. See him tender and sympathetic as he makes a decision that may send his own little son to death. See him in broad comedy as for the first time he squirms under the expert hands of a society tailor" (preproduction preview by Earl W. Wingart, Paramount, Ladies Love Brutes PCA file, MHL-AMPAS).

14. Original story by Adela St. John (novel); also staged as a play by Willard Mack. PCA files hold nothing on this original film production but include some material on a possible 1945 remake and

discussions of another MGM version later still, with Elizabeth Taylor and William Powell, *The Girl Who Had Everything* (1953).

15. Further evidence of uncertainty as to the centrality of active female sexuality, unconventional gender roles, and the role of the father in this melodrama is supplied by the press book for *A Free Soul* (British Film Institute, London). Following are the sensational and sometimes lurid catch lines created by MGM to be selected by cinema exhibitors to "sell" the film to their patrons: the differing semantic inflections are clearly considerable and attest to the mixture of the new (New Woman) and the formulaic (Fallen Woman):

She thought a woman could love two men — until she tried.

She thought a woman's soul could be free — but found that love held it a prisoner.

She loved a good man — and was infatuated by a gambler. The result almost wrecked her life.

The glamorous Norma Shearer of "Strangers May Kiss" — in a role just as gorgeous — but how much more dramatic.

She tried to toy with men's affections — and faced a terrible choice.

Morals were just words, she thought. Until morals rose up and almost smashed her life.

She was a gilded moth playing about the fires of pleasure. And how narrowly she escaped those flames!

A man died — a father sacrificed his life — to return her to the path of right.

She tasted the deepest depths of life — to find it bitter.

She tried to flit from love to love — but Fate barred her way.

She thought love something to play with — to extract new sensations from — but found it stronger than Life itself.

The drama of a woman who wanted to taste all of life.

In gilded palaces of society — in sordid depths of the underworld — she sought thrills. And she reaped the whirlwind.

She thought he was all man — too late she learned he was all beast.

Nothing could fetter her freedom, she thought. But that was before she really new love.

Should a child always follow her father's teachings?

Should a father teach a girl all the facts of life?

16. All direct quotes in this and the following paragraph are from the press book for *A Free Soul* archived at the British Film Institute, London.

17. *Variety,* no date given, PCA file 070 RM6b, MHL-AMPAS.

18. *Dance, Fools, Dance* press book, MHL-AMPAS. The *Motion Picture Herald*, March 7, 1931, applauded Joan Crawford's acting versatility in her "portrayal of two types of characters: the first as the wealthy dancing daughter with nothing to do but spend time and money and the other as hardworking and fast thinking newspaper woman. Both are done to perfection."

19. "[W]e believe [the swimming scene] to be a violation of the general principles and the claude [sic] prohibiting obscenity of the Code. We felt that, whether or not there is any suggestion in the action itself that the men and women are nude, the suggestion in the dialog that they are is offensive" (Jason S. Joy to Irving Thalberg, Nov. 17, 1930, *Dance, Fools, Dance* PCA file, MHL-AMPAS). "Since seeing *Dance, Fools, Dance* at its first preview we have had several conferences with Mr Stromberg and have looked at some retakes suggested for questionable scenes. We believe it is necessary to eliminate all that part of the bathing scenes on the yacht which shows the men and women starting and in the process of taking off their clothes and the line something to the effect that "it isn't decent" spoken by one of the guests during this action. Mr Stromberg has assured us that he is working this out" (Jason S. Joy to Thalberg, no date given [1930], *Dance, Fools, Dance* PCA file, MHL-AMPAS). "Both from the standpoint of the Code and that of the censor boards, there are a few questionable incidents in the picture . . . [the scenes where the boys and girls] . . . strip to their underthings and dive overboard. While there is no evidence of exposure, the scene is not essential to the plot and is a violation of the Code (Plummer, memo, Feb. 4, 1931, *Dance, Fools, Dance* PCA file, MHL-AMPAS).

20. "While we are very much afraid of the love scene in the cabin, we do not believe that the retake of this is sufficient to carry to story. However, it would help a great deal if the fade-out on this scene were to occur after Bonnie's line 'I believe in trying out love,' thus eliminating the words 'on approval,' said by Boy [sic] and repeated by Bonnie in the embrace" (Jason S. Joy to Thalberg, no date given [1930], *Dance, Fools, Dance* PCA file, MHL-AMPAS). As anticipated by Joy and Plummer (Feb. 4, 1931 [see note 19 above]), the "on approval" dialogue was cut by the censors of Massachusetts, Ohio, British Columbia, Virginia, New York, Britain, and Australia on release.

21. The parallel here is with the real-life gang murder in 1929 of *Chicago Tribune* crime reporter Jake Lingle: with the massacre the story line suggests the introduction of a degree of topicality to an already hybrid production.

22. *Variety*'s review (no date given) encapsulates the film's appeal to the female audience:

This picture will rock the b.o. Few films have emerged from studios with a more mixed up history. But if the story lacks coherency, the situations more than atone for it. It's of a society girl gone bourgeois through necessity. As a sobbie, she solves a gangster shooting that involved her brother unknown to her. Romance lingers throughout. It has sex, romance, punch, suspense and everything a deluxer can sell. Metro has tried here to have Joan Crawford show everything she had. She does. That's QED meaning b.o. with s.a. Maybe there's a trick to making talkers entertaining. This one is mostly tricks. It begins with the daring moment when men and women strip aboard a yacht for a swim in their undies. Hot all over even after that and mainly due to Miss Crawford. She's s.a. from toes to headlights. Behind her is a capable cast. Miss Crawford croons her baritone to tell the sweetie she would rather test love before taking it on. *There the women fans will thrill.* The dialogue keeps track of this thought. There are faults with that dialogue but it can't hurt the film. Had it been shaved a bit the film would have been finer. Some ritz lingo practically throughout . . . racketeer society and paper boys. *Another woman spot is at the finish when, with that Crawford shoulder shrug, the girl rolls a kiss request straight to her man after 79 minutes of most indifference.* Happening after three killings on the screen, with one the girl's brother who dies in her arms as he shoots it out to protect her from his gun mad pals. Her brother goes the way of booze collecting because he isn't used to hard work. She skips to a paper office where presumably a family friend placed her when her society snobbies give her air, now she's poor. Her lover did that too. That lover angle is a subtle point of the picture and keeps customers guessing if it's that way or just platonic. When he finds her dancing in a dive, he turns to proposition her. She gives him the chill with a tear. It's jake drama as the flops will have it. Then some moments of hoke meller stuff that you grin inwardly at but like, as the racketeers talk about "rides" and swat the girl's brother for being "yellow." (*Dance, Fools, Dance* PCA file, MHL-AMPAS; emphasis added)

23. For added authenticity the press book repeatedly notes that Walton Green, the chief investigator of Prohibition in Washington, acted as consultant on the film's depiction of illegal liquor run through the sea routes (United Artists' press book, British Film Institute, London) and that the film was based on the novel/memoirs published about his experiences. It also notes that *Corsair* features the first use of the radio telephone on film.

24. *Corsair* files, British Film Institute, London.

25. Jason Joy to Mr. Hays, memorandum, April 17, 1931, *Corsair* PCA file, MHL-AMPAS.

26. United Artists' *Corsair* press book, British Film Institute, London.

27. Roland West to Jason S. Joy, May 26, 1931, *Corsair* PCA file, MHL-AMPAS.

28. Ibid.

29. Hays to Joy, undated telegram, *Corsair* PCA file, MHL-AMPAS.

30. Jason S. Joy to Will H. Hays, June 18, 1931, *Corsair* PCA file, MHL-AMPAS.

31. Gilbert Seldes, *Movies for the Millions* (London: Batsford, 1937), 50–51.

A Gunsel Is Being Beaten

Gangster Masculinity and the Homoerotics of the Crime Film, 1941–1942

Gaylyn Studlar

S SCHOLARS HAVE OBSERVED, the gangster was virtually expelled from the center of class-A Hollywood productions during World War II.[1] This was an overdetermined occurrence. In part it reflected the intensification of a well-established prewar trend based on Hollywood's discomfort with regulating the appearance of gangsters as protagonists; starting in the early 1930s, these characters were the object of vocal criticism from various moral reform groups, state censorship boards, and social commentators.[2] In 1932 the Association of Motion Picture Producers (the West Coast sister-organization of the MPPDA) forbade its members from producing more gangster films.[3] In 1934 the Motion Picture Producers and Distributors Association (MPPDA) created a Production Code Administration in the process of Hollywood's attempt to self-regulate rather than be subject to government regulation.[4] Under the auspices of Joseph Breen, the Production Code Administration's new, stricter enforcement standards of moral self-regulation made the gangster unwelcome as a film protagonist: private detectives, federal agents ("G-Men"), and other assorted figures aligned with the law largely replaced gangster protagonists in A productions. In 1936 the PCA even refused its certificate, and thus permission for commercial rerelease, to Warner Brothers Studio's classic gangster films *Little Caesar* (1930) and *The Public Enemy* (1931).[5] At the end of the decade a limited cycle of nostalgic gangster films, including *Angels with Dirty Faces* (1938) and *The Roaring Twenties* (1939), was released, but these films were careful to emphasize the anachronistic futility of gangsterism as a masculine response to growing up as a member of the urban poor.

After war came to America in December 1941, the movement away from protagonists who overtly functioned as gangsters intensified as a reflection of government and industry concerns about the appropriateness of screen depictions of social problems during a time of national crisis. Carlos Clarens says that the gangster film "went off the agenda" in reaction to the United States government's call for Hollywood films to perform a role in boosting wartime morale.[6] Frank Krutnik cites the specific role of the Office of War Information in making it difficult to portray gangsters in U.S. films; the OWI was involved in a focused attempt to prevent U.S. film productions from depicting "lawlessness or disorder" as the "main theme of a picture."[7] Clayton Koppes and Gregory Black date a major change to December of 1942, when the Office of Censorship released a new code of regulations that took a tougher tack when it came to the depiction of gangsters and other lawless elements of American life unless the depicted offenders were punished.[8] However much it wanted to be perceived as upholding its patriotic duty, Hollywood rankled at government control over its product. Influenced by film industry executives, the U.S. Congress drastically cut OWI funding, but OWI's Ulric Bell remained in control of export licenses for films seeking foreign markets, and Bell was reputed to have a particular dislike for gangster films.[9] Bell's attitude toward the latter, combined with Hollywood's desire to gain access to newly opened foreign markets, may have played a significant role in gangsters' virtual disappearance from the screen between 1943 and the end of the war.

Although complicated by industry self-restraint and, ultimately, wartime regulation, crime films of the years 1941–1942 suggest a masculinity that could not be fully unhooked from the exaggerated violence or established visual iconography of gangster criminality. Those elements of criminality were made familiar to cinematic audiences by numerous gangster films of the late 1920s and early 1930s, as well as by extensive media coverage of real-world gangsters of the era, such as Al Capone and John Dillinger, who fascinated Depression-era Americans. Nevertheless, crime films of the 1941–1942 period are often difficult to situate critically, in part because of their relative scarcity. Films such as *The Maltese Falcon* (1941), *This Gun for Hire* (1942), *I Wake Up Screaming* (1942), and *The Glass Key* (1942) are sometimes regarded as being of a piece with films noirs of the postwar period.[10] Rather than debate whether this is a viable way of approaching such films, in this chapter I wish to address a small set of A-class Hollywood productions of 1941 and 1942 through a different framework of consideration. I argue that three highly successful films, *The Maltese Falcon*, *The Glass Key*, and *Johnny Eager* (1942), are unified in one important respect: they demonstrate Hollywood's fragile negotiation of homoeroticism within gangster-derived depictions of masculinity. With the exception of *Johnny Eager* these were not "gangster films" in the sense of having a gangster protagonist, but they often emphasized the gangster-derived characteristics of the hero and of the conventionally coded types who populate the world of men in which he lives — the supporting characters and antagonists/villains who sustain the idea of the all-male gang as a key icon of the American underworld.[11]

It should not be forgotten that these films had a relationship not only to earlier films but also to hard-boiled literature of the 1930s, including the novels of Dashiell

Hammett and Raymond Chandler, whose books often either inspired or, as in the case of *The Glass Key* and *The Maltese Falcon*, served as the direct, primary source material for films in the 1930s as well as in the early 1940s. Their work exemplified the literary fiction of the so-called *Black Mask* school, which often focused on detective heroes with ambiguous moral codes who rubbed elbows with the criminal underworld. These much-adapted literary sources often brought contradictory attitudes toward homosexuality into the arena of popular film and to the depiction of the masculinity of the gangster-derived detective hero and the denizens of the criminal underworld who inevitably surround him. Homosexuality is frequently referenced and even saturates the world in which the hero moves with some uncertainty — overtly expressed on the professional level but sometimes, more subtly, on the sexual one as well. For example, in Raymond Chandler's 1931 novel *The Big Sleep*, the hero, Phillip Marlowe, must unravel his rich clients' connection to a pornography racket run by gay men. An ambivalent, homophobic fascination is registered in Marlowe's first-person narrative as he encounters a young gay man who has just avenged the death of his older lover:

> The boy spun towards me and his right hand darted up. . . . His eyes were a wet shine in the glow of the round electroliers. Moist dark eyes shaped like almonds, and a pallid handsome face with wavy black hair growing low on the forehead in two points. A very handsome boy indeed, the boy from Geiger's store. . . .
> 'You must have thought a lot of that queen,' I said.[12]

This excerpt from *The Big Sleep* suggests how hard-boiled literature played a role in influencing the dialectic between homophobia and homoeroticism in the films under consideration, but I will be arguing that these films brought their own important resonance to the hard-boiled tradition of representing masculine sexuality. Among the most important was the casting of the hero, with its implications for the transgendered erotic appeal of the male protagonist, the ambiguity of the erotic landscape of narrative and dialogue; in addition, there are other specific textual patterns to consider, including framing, camera angle, shot perspective, editing, and focus. Drawing on this repertoire of techniques, these films construct masculinity in ways that threaten the fragile boundaries between the normative and the perverse.

I will argue that *The Maltese Falcon, The Glass Key,* and *Johnny Eager* trade on the ongoing appeal of "hard-boiled" screen masculinity even as they also unveil, in unexpected and sometimes inchoate ways, the erotic problematic of homosociality in screen depictions of gangster-derived masculinity. These films, I will argue, expose the continuum of "male homosocial desire" and the contradictions in filmic representation of that continuum that arise within the historical context of a triangulated negotiation involving (1) the demands of industry self-regulation and the U.S. government wartime imperatives placed on Hollywood product presumed to address a general audience, (2) Hollywood's generic conventions associated with a tough-guy masculinity, and (3) representational codes of depicting violence in the criminal underworld that constitutes an overwhelmingly same-sex environment. I will argue that the terms of this convergence, as well as the implications of textual specifics (such as casting), serve to call into question cultural representations of male-to-male bonding in these films that otherwise tend to be naturalized in classical Hollywood texts of the period.

In her seminal work, *Between Men*, Eve Kosofsky Sedgwick argues that "male homosocial desire" is defined as "the spectrum of male bonds that includes but is not limited to the 'homosexual'"; she argues that this desire must be controlled and contained in patriarchal society because these "heavily freighted bonds between men exist, as the backbone of social form or forms." As a result, the term *homosexual* functions as a regulatory definition that works to control not just a minority of men, who are homosexual in sexual behavior, desire, style or identity, but "the whole range of male bonds that shape the social constitution."[13] As a consequence, says Sedgwick, the expression of homophobia in society becomes "a tool of control over the entire spectrum of male homosocial organization."[14] By understanding this structuring role of homophobia and exploring the "dialectic between homosexuality and homophobia" in film texts, we may take Sedgwick's analysis of literary texts as a model for reading crime films of the 1940s also "as explorations of social and gender construction as a whole, rather than of the internal psychology of a few, individual men with a 'minority' sexual orientation."[15]

From such a perspective one may see how these crime-centered films of the early 1940s explored the sexual complexity of the bond forged between men within a homosocial underworld associated with gangsterism. Male homosocial desire finds one representation in the depiction of "platonic" male friendships and the traditional emphasis in gangster films of bonds on loyalty — and love between men. Of particular interest are representations that implicate gang structure and masculine friendship in homoeroticism, a largely unexamined undercurrent of the criminal underworld depicted in many 1940s crime films.[16] I explore how such friendship is ambiguously implicated in perverse (that is, homosexual and sadomasochistic) aspects of the structure of the gang, with its depiction of a homosocial world in which women can figure only marginally. This world is dominated by various kinds of antisocial behavior — including the possibility of homosexuality and perversity.[17] Although both homosexuality and other perversions (such as sadism, masochism, and fetishism) were officially forbidden representation under the Code, Hollywood had long depended on representational conventions "from which," as early Code enforcer Jason Joy noted, "conclusions might be drawn by the sophisticated mind, but which would mean nothing to the unsophisticated and inexperienced."[18]

Upon viewing, it is at once obvious that the films under consideration reflected a much more self-conscious approach to masculinity and the intersection of violence, pain, sexuality, and male bonding than most Hollywood gangster films offered in the 1930s. Yet those earlier films set the stage in at least one way for constructing masculinity in 1940s Hollywood crime film.[19] Masculinity attached to crime as a Hollywood generic mode became manifest through, and inseparable from, particular narrative and stylistic figurations of violence. Violence becomes an important element in representing homosocial desire, including homosexuality. This was especially so within a system of filmic representation that cultivated ambiguities of expression in order to suggest forbidden behaviors and conduct regarded as immoral by many censorship authorities (state and local boards) and the industry's own system of moral self-regulation (the Code). The MPPDA's Production Code demanded that Hollywood film depict the "correct standards of life."[20] However, as Lea Jacobs has noted, the code allowed the survival of transgressions to those standards but did so "at the price of an instability of meaning. . . . [T]here was constant negotiation about how explicit films could be and by what means (through the image, sound, language) offensive ideas could find representation."[21] With the PCA under Joseph Breen, suggests Jacobs, the MPPDA was "more careful . . . to monitor nonverbal aspects" of films than the old Studio Relations Committee; thus, after 1934 "the treatment of potentially offensive action shifted in the direction of greater ambiguity," but "ambiguity in the treatment of detail did not always work in the interests of censorship."[22] Perversions, including homosexuality, were forbidden depiction in film according to the industry's governing Production Code, but what were perversity's signs on the screen, and how might it be represented in the 1940s within an era marked by this "greater ambiguity"?

Although adapted for the screen twice in the 1930s, Dashiell Hammett's *The Maltese Falcon* was most famously brought to the screen in John Huston's 1941 film version, released a few weeks before U.S. entry into the war. In this film Humphrey Bogart brought to his performance as Sam Spade, the film's detective protagonist, a notable amount of the tough-guy volatility that had accompanied his typecasting as a gangster throughout the 1930s at Warner Brothers, including his appearance as Duke Mantee in *The Petrified Forest* (1936).[23] As in the original novel, a character named "Wilmar" appears in the film as the strong-arm of Kaspar Gutman (Sidney Greenstreet). In Huston's production Gutman is an overweight older man with refined tastes and a lilting British accent, and the performance of Sidney Greenstreet as Gutman suggests stereotyped upper-class British homosexuality. With Wilmar in tow, Gutman has been pursuing the black statuette of a falcon across several continents. Portrayed by Elisha Cook Jr., Wilmar is a diminutive young man garbed in a manner reminiscent of 1930s gangsters in their work mode: overcoat, hat, and a facial expression of intractable inexpressivity. Thus, Wilmar represents the familiar figure of the gangster assistant — otherwise labeled as a bodyguard, enforcer, gunman, hired killer, henchman, or stooge. In *The Maltese Falcon* he is a young man, not beautiful, not even particularly attractive, but remarkably youthful.[24]

Wilmar trails Sam Spade, who finds Wilmar's affectations of gangster toughness laughable and, as a result, spends a great deal of time showing up Wilmar's lack of real gangster skills. Spade humiliates Wilmar by having him removed from a hotel lobby by the hotel detective. At another point he takes away Wilmar's guns and tells Gutman that his gunman lost his arsenal to "a crippled newsy." In spite of his problems in doing his duties as a henchman, Wilmar's job never seems in doubt, and Gutman seems only to excuse him, as when, in a remarkable moment of affectionate indulgence, he surmises that Wilmar played with matches and set the ocean freighter *La Paloma* afire. At another point Gutman pulls at Wilmar's coat sleeve to keep him from responding violently to Spade's taunting. This gesture of tugging at Wilmar's sleeve may seem a curiously intimate gesture for a boss to employ with his gun-toting enforcer.[25] Its coded significance is suggested by Sam Spade, who implies through his choice of words that Wilmar performs in another way—a sexual way—for his boss: "Get out, and take your gunsel with you," he growls.

When Dashiell Hammett submitted *The Maltese Falcon* to his publisher, his novel's protagonist used the word *catamite* in this scene to describe Wilmar. In the version originally submitted for publication Sam Spade says to Gutman in the aforementioned scene: "Get out, and take your catamite with you." Hammett's editor refused to accept this dialogue since the longstanding definition of *catamite* was the passive partner in sodomy.[26] To satisfy his editor's objections, Hammett substituted *gunsel*, a slang word reputed to have Yiddish origins. Hammett's editor may have thought that this obscure word meant gunslinger: he accepted Hammett's substitution, yet this word had the same basic meaning as *catamite*—a young male homosexual kept by another man.[27] *American Speech* defines gunsel as "the boy who travels with a man and has many names—punk, gazooney, gantzel, supposedly used as slang in the 1930s among hobos."[28]

The editor's misunderstanding—or lack of understanding—of the connotations for the word *gunsel* were perpetuated by the Production Code Administration, or "Breen Office," when it issued a Production Code Administration certificate of approval to *The Maltese Falcon*. The PCA left the character of Wilmar, along with the word *gunsel*, transferred virtually intact from the novel.[29] Movies and movie critics alike have subsequently used *gunsel* to refer to any gunman or henchman—without connotations of his sexual function in the gang. In 1965, in the wake of the widespread use of the word in crime fiction and film, mystery writer Erle Stanley Gardner attempted to correct the record; he told readers of *The Atlantic* that *gunsel* is "a very naughty word with no relation whatever to a bodyguard, a gunman, or a torpedo."[30] Even so, in its 1999 edition, *The Oxford American Dictionary* definition is simply stated: "Gunsel: n.sl. a criminal, esp. a gunman."[31]

Extant files of the PCA give no indication that the Breen office had any objections to the character of Wilmar, nor was the word *gunsel* a subject of discussion with the studio. Was this indicative of a lack of vigilance to homosexuality? The PCA administrators regularly asked (in anticipation of British censors) for words such as *pansy* and *punk* to be excised from movie dialogue, and the Breen office was particularly concerned that overtly effeminate male characters would signal homosexuality to audiences.[32] Referencing a draft of *The Maltese Falcon* script, PCA

125

representatives told the studio that the character of Joel Cairo required action: "We cannot approve the characterization of Cairo as a pansy as indicated by the lavender perfume, high pitched voice, and other accouterments. In line with this, we refer you to Page 148, where Cairo tries to put his arm around the boy's shoulder and is struck by the boy for so doing. This action, in the light of Cairo's characterization, is definitely unacceptable."[33]

Joel Cairo and other effeminate film characters worried the PCA, who thought audiences would understand the common signifiers of effeminate homosexual style. Warner Brothers deleted the scene suggesting that Cairo is an aggressive homosexual on the make with his "arm around the boy's shoulder" at the request of the PCA. Nevertheless, in spite of the PCA's vigilance, Cairo appears in the film accompanied by gardenia rather than lavender perfume, and his voice is low and soft rather than high pitched, but he remains obviously coded as a gay man in the orientalized mode (Hammett refers to him as "the Levantine"). In his first appearance onscreen he is announced by Spade's secretary but without Effie Perine's declaration of his identity as provided in the book: "This guy is queer." The camera is set up to replicate the visual perspectives of the scene in which Brigid O'Shaughnessy entered Spade's office. However, when Cairo enters, the camera emphasizes Spade's reaction as it tracks in on the detective as he brings a cigarette to his mouth to lick the paper closed. His eyes open wide and his tongue literally hangs out as he watches Joel Cairo (Peter Lorre), who is then revealed in a reverse shot.

Cairo's entrance is thus coded visually to mark him as an aberration of masculinity that surprises even the jaded Sam Spade. After a bit of conversation, Cairo uses a gun to hold Spade up so he can search his office. Smiling, he starts to pat Spade down from behind, "to make certain you're not armed." By way of contrast, in both the novel and the 1931 film version, the frisking is face-to-face. Before he is touched, Spade quickly turns around. A low-angle shot holds on the two as Spade slowly walks Cairo across the room in a forced, wordless "dance" before Spade punches Cairo with the latter's own gloved hand. Yet Cairo, unflinchingly polite as ever, ultimately does get the best of him. He asks for his gun back, Spade gives it to him, and Cairo points the gun at Spade and announces his plan to search the office. At this reversal Spade laughs, "Go ahead, I won't stop you." In a later scene Spade will assault Cairo again and tell him, "When you're slapped you'll take it and like it." Thus, Spade seems to take great pleasure throughout the film in the homophobic humiliation of homosexuals, that is, "beating up on fags."

Nevertheless, there is an interesting dichotomy articulated in the film, mainly through performance nuance given to moments in the narrative that suggest more than sustained and unrelenting homophobia. The homophobic pleasure that Spade takes in the beating of Cairo and the physical and verbal taunting of Wilmar is counterpointed by Spade's casual, accepting attitude toward the gay men from whom he takes money (Cairo gives him a retainer) and who become his potential partners in retrieving the falcon. When Cairo returns to his hotel after a night of being grilled

1. Joel Cairo (Peter Lorre) is an aberration of masculinity that surprises even the jaded Sam Spade (Humphrey Bogart) in *The Maltese Falcon* (1941).

by the police, Spade is surprisingly empathetic, even solicitous: "Then you'll be wanting sleep." Cairo joins forces with Gutman and Wilmar, and the three become an ad hoc gang, one that is as overtly homosexual as Hollywood might offer at the time. Near the end of the film, Gutman asks Spade whether he would like to join him on his continued quest to find the falcon. Spade demurs; he does not join the gay gang (which we learn will be picked up by the police), but the film points to the possibility that Spade has, as Gutman recognizes, a great deal in common with these "eccentric travelers" and might have his apparently heterosexual masculinity comfortably adjusted into a homosexual criminal regime.[34] Indeed, the sympathetic attention and even admiration that accrues in the film around these "eccentrics" is extended in John Huston's informal sequel to and send up of *The Maltese Falcon*, the black comedy *Beat the Devil* (1953), a film that suggests just this kind of accommodation of its hero, Bogart's "Billy," to a similar gang of three gay crooks.

Because of their sexual predilection, the ad hoc gang of Gutman, Cairo, and Wilmar plays on the possibilities along the preexisting continuum of the homosocial structure of the criminal gang already familiar to audiences from gangster films of the 1930s. The prevalence of homosexuals among criminals in this film echoes homophobic psychoanalytic discourse of the era. One frequent commentator on homosexuality, Edmund Bergler, noted: "[I am continually amazed at] . . . the great percentage of homosexuals among swindlers, pseudologues, forgers, lawbreakers of all sorts, drug purveyors, gamblers, pimps, spies, brothel-owners, etc." [35] Yet Huston's film also suggests that these gay men are, at various moments, interesting, fun, and even sympathetic characters. Whereas Gutman and Cairo evoke the long-standing stereotypes of specific modes of foreign homosexuality (upper-class British and Oriental), Wilmar is more intriguing (yet less exotic) because of his link to American mob iconography. In that respect Wilmar's presence becomes a reminder of the sometimes ambiguous sexuality of the tough lads of the streets who rose to criminal success in early 1930s gangster films like *Little Caesar* and *The Public Enemy*, as well as those "boys" who inhabit the margins of the hard-boiled novel, as in Chandler's *The Big Sleep*. Yet the queerness of the "boy" Wilmar seems to have passed unnoticed by Hollywood's self-regulatory system.

The use of the term *boy* might suggest pederasty, but, if we draw on the work of George E. Haggerty, the definition of the *boy* as a sexual object determined by age and his function as a sign of "cross-generational desire" may be less important here than the notion of a sexual relation, as Haggerty suggests, "so rigidly hierarchical as to insist on power relations before any kind of desire can be articulated." [36] Haggerty argues that this kind of sexuality was associated in the eighteenth century with libertinism, which he defines as a sexual relation in which there is no crossover or reversibility between the male subject (who desires) and the male object of desire. [37] Haggerty's remarks on libertinism in the context of male-to-male sexuality allow us to consider the power dynamic created around the figure of the "boy" gunsel in *The Maltese Falcon* and in crime films in general. This articulation of sexuality in one in which the privileged subject (usually male) uses another person (in this case a man) as a sexual object in relations that can never be equalized or reversed, but which remain strictly hierarchized, no matter what occurs in the "acting" play of sexual positions. Perhaps this mode of homoeroticism is ultimately more radical as a threat to the status quo of culture than the overt criminal activity of these "sexual suspects." As we will see, the idea of the man who functions as the object of desire of another man is articulated in a different but related way in the other two films under consideration, *The Glass Key* and *Johnny Eager*. In these two films platonic friendship takes place between two men, one of whom is the "hired man" who may resemble the gunsel but is a participant in another kind of structured power relation that tests, in different ways, the patriarchal norms of homosociality and its delimitation of desire.

Problematizing cinematic norms of homosociality through different emphases from those we have seen in *The Maltese Falcon* is the 1942 screen adaptation of Dashiell Hammett's novel *The Glass Key*. This film demonstrates a complex articulation of male friendship to suggest contradictions in Hollywood's representation of male bonding, as well as instabilities in the broader cultural function of homosociality. In *The Glass Key* the relationship between political boss Paul Madvig (Brian Donlevy) and his hired adviser, Ed Beaumont (Alan Ladd), is represented as a platonic male friendship. On the surface this is in keeping with Hollywood's usual presentation of male friendship as exemplary of male-to-male love that supports rather than undermines the workings of the homosocially structured patriarchal system. In the story Ed Beaumont functions as an ad hoc detective who searches for the truth of Madvig's suspected involvement in the murder of Taylor Henry (Richard Denning), the upper-class playboy brother of Janet Henry (Veronica Lake). Even though Janet Henry thinks Madvig killed her brother, she allows herself to become engaged to Madvig for the sake of her father's political aspirations (Madvig's support is crucial to her father's candidacy for governor). Beaumont proves Madvig's innocence, and when Madvig realizes Beaumont and Janet are in love, he gives them his blessing to start a life together.

Blustering and violent, the middle-aged Madvig, like the classical gangster, has risen from the "wrong side of the tracks." Gangster conventions are inscribed in his overstated attire, as well as in his inability to catch on to the middle-class norms of demeanor and social decorum. In fact, Madvig is portrayed as the political equivalent of a gangster. He is extremely successful in controlling candidates and voting blocs, winning elections and doling out protection — providing the latter even to gangland types like Nick Varna (Joseph Calleia), a gambling boss who secretly owns the local newspaper. In the film's opening scene one woman bluntly says "he's the biggest crook in the state." This displacement of racketeering to the political scene may have satisfied protectors of wartime morality and morale, but it was not likely to fool many in the audience. The generic territory that was being retrod was clear.[38] Screen gangster conventions are also invoked in Madvig's very personal brand of violence, associated with his continually expressed impulse to use his fists — even at a funeral. Early in the film he sends a political cohort through a plate-glass window for merely casting doubt on his judgment.[39]

Although both Madvig and his best friend, Ed Beaumont, take Janet Henry as their ostensible object of desire, I will argue that the woman is not the erotic center of the film, but that Ed Beaumont is, and that the film produces several levels of homoerotic sexual signification that problematize and make ambiguous both the "platonic" male bonding of friendship and the heterosexual hegemony asserted through the presence of the female love interest. As I will argue, this "making strange" the norms of male-to-male friendship endangers normative male subjectivity and continually threatens, as George Haggerty has suggested in another context, to "expose the cultural function of male-to-male affection."[40]

A crucial element in this process of unsettling homosocial structures of male-to-male bonding and cultural norms of masculine sexuality occurs in *The Glass Key* through a continually asserted conflation between eroticism and violence, between kissing and hitting, between what the vernacular of the film might call "smacking" (as in a loud kiss) and "smacking" (landing a resounding blow).[41] In the opening scene Paul Madvig insults the Henry family in public. In response Janet Henry walks up to Madvig, slaps him, and, in a play on the name of her father's political party (the "reform" party), declares that Madvig should be "reformed out of existence." This encounter motivates Madvig to cheerfully proclaim to Beaumont in the next scene, "Hey Ed, I just met the swellest dame. She smacked me in the kisser." This dialogue (and encounter with the "dame") is absent from the 1935 film version of the novel, as is much of the sexual tension, since Janet Henry is reduced to a minor character who is not the subject of rivalry between Madvig and Beaumont. In the 1942 version this love-at-first-slap scene is the only explanation ever offered for Paul Madvig's desire for Janet Henry, a desire that will lead him to abandon his current candidate of choice for governor and back her father instead. However, the audience may take note of the fact that the diminutive, blonde, glacially beautiful, and facially inexpressive Janet Henry looks enough like Madvig's best friend and smoothly confident assistant, Ed Beaumont, to be Beaumont's sister, and the brother-sister bond is echoed in the pairing of Madvig with a younger sister, Opal (Bonita Granville), as well as in Janet Henry and her blonde sibling.[42]

This triangulation of Madvig/Beaumont/Janet Henry makes the latter more obviously a function of homosociality as a "form of a desire to consolidate partnership with authoritative males in and through the bodies of females."[43] Madvig's romance

2. Diminutive, blonde, glacially beautiful, and looking enough alike to be brother and sister; Janet Henry (Veronica Lake) and Ed Beaumont (Alan Ladd) complicate the "heterosexual" trajectory of Paul Madvig's desire in *The Glass Key* (1942).

with Janet Henry is thinly motivated, and Beaumont's erotic energies throughout the film seem much more bound to Paul than to any woman, including Janet. Beaumont and Henry are at cross-purposes: he seeks to clear Madvig of suspicions of murder; she's trying to prove Madvig is guilty even though she becomes his fiancée. At one point she tries to seduce Beaumont but declares in frustration as he moves away from kissing her: "Can't you forget about Paul for one minute?" Beaumont does flirt warily with Janet, as well as with a publisher's young wife and with a female nurse. The latter attempts to stop him from leaving the hospital by invoking the higher authority of the male doctor, a Dr. Redman. Beaumont kisses the protesting nurse and forcefully declares, "Send that to Dr. Redman." An articulation of male sexuality that is meant to be amusing in its domination of femininity becomes infused with homoerotic suggestiveness.

Not only does *The Glass Key* cultivate a sexual ambiguity around the Madvig/Beaumont/Henry triangle by virtue of the extreme quality of the bond between the two men, but a great deal of sexual ambiguity accrues around the casting of Alan Ladd. In attempting to pinpoint the star's appeal, film critic Richard Schickel identifies Ladd as "probably the first male star to achieve fame by combining beauty and somnambulism like the female of the species."[44] Ladd enjoyed a rapid rise to stardom at Paramount in two crime films that reflected that studio's defiance of the Office of War Information regulation (enforced by the Bureau of Motion Pictures) and the Breen office.[45] In rapid succession Ladd appeared as "Raven," a cold-blooded professional assassin in *This Gun for Hire* (released May 1942) and then in *The Glass Key* (October 1942).[46] In both films Ladd's almost feminine good looks provided an interesting combination with his deadpan, baritone delivery and highly controlled, inexpressive manner. Ladd's screen stardom traded on tough-guy roles that foreground the violence long associated with screen gangsters, but by virtue of his matinee idol attractiveness, his hard-boiled films were marketed during this period to women as well as to men. Of *This Gun for Hire*, advertisements proclaimed: "It's dramatic dynamite . . . with a new star who's romantic dynamite. Girls, mark down his name, because you're going to hear it plenty: Alan Ladd! When he looks at you, a girl just can't call her heart her own." Slightly more revelatory of the fact that Ladd played a psychologically disturbed murderer in the film, a publicity tag declared: "He's the 'KISS and KILL' Ladd they're all talking about!"[47]

Here, within the crime film, ostensibly a genre aimed at men, Alan Ladd provided a spectacle of eroticized male stardom. As I have argued elsewhere, certain male stars, such as Tom Cruise, may be presented in the narrative and treated by the camera in ways that challenge presumptions regarding the gendered divisions of sexual desire and identification, even within genres supposedly aimed at male viewers.[48] It is generally agreed that Hollywood film presumes to create the male star as a heteroerotic sign, but I argue that it cannot always control the slippage between that "normal" heterosexual appeal of the star and homoerotic viewer pleasure that takes the male actor as an object of same-sex desire rather than purely of narcissistic

3. Alan Ladd: screen stardom trading on tough-guy roles and almost feminine good looks.

identification.[49] This slippage creates troublesome implications for classical Hollywood's appeal to the sexual fantasies of a gendered audience. Hollywood's system of masculine representation required constructing a coherent male subjectivity, but the exhibitionist nature of male-centered cinema centralizes the threat of turning this subject into an object of erotic contemplation — for men, as well as for women viewers.

Alan Ladd's embodiment of masculinity, almost feminine in its perfect blonde beauty, suggests an erotic appeal that puts pressure on the regulation of identification and desire according to the dominate order of gender and sexuality. Ladd's stunning blonde good looks are often on display in flattering close-ups. The film offers up his beauty to the audience in fetishistic shots unmediated by the looks of other characters. This occurs in the scene in which Ed Beaumont tells Paul he has found the body of Taylor Henry in the street. Ladd is placed on the right of the frame, in medium close-up, facing the camera (and looking slightly to his right) as he observes Madvig's reactions to the news. Madvig's face is revealed to the audience in mirror reflection (as he shaves). Yet, in contrast to this type of image, which seems to follow Laura Mulvey's definition of fetishistic looking as being "in direct erotic rapport with the spectator," *The Glass Key* also seems to make a concerted effort to obscure and cover Ladd's body (often with a long coat) to a degree unmatched in its depiction of Paul Madvig (or in the treatment of George Raft as Beaumont in the 1935 version directed by Frank Tuttle).[50]

These techniques of obscuring Ladd's body through costume or shot selection would seem to follow the conventions of representing gangster henchmen (such as Wilmar), but they also resonate with the theories of Steve Neale, who argues that Hollywood films attempt "to disavow any explicitly erotic look at the male body." Neale claims that, in order to disavow the homoerotics of looking, male spectacle in classical cinema has been subject to a highly conventionalized method of representing the male body and male-to-male looking that does not acknowledge the male body as being constructed for the spectator. The male body cannot be offered to the spectator unless these looks are mediated by the gaze of other characters whose "looks are marked not by desire, but by fear, or hatred or aggression."[51] As a result, even though "male heroes can at times be marked as the object of an erotic gaze," says Neale, "the expression of any explicit avowal of eroticism in the act of looking at the male seems structurally linked to a narrative content marked by sado-masochistic phantasies and scenes." Why does this occur? Because, says Neale, male homosexuality is "constantly present as an undercurrent, as a potentially troubling aspect of many films and genres."[52]

Although the fetishizing close-ups of Beaumont call into question some elements of Neale's arguments, a scene in which Beaumont is tortured appears to confirm his theoretical formulation. However, there is an important difference. Unlike many of the scenes of ritualized violence that Neale discusses in male genre films, *The Glass Key* quite self-consciously suggests a spectacle of violence that is not a pure displacement for male-to-male eroticism but actually reveals to the viewer how the depicted violence is imbricated in homoeroticism. The scene occurs as the narrative result of Beaumont's pretense that he is interested in throwing in with the gambler-gangster Nick Varna. When Varna realizes that Beaumont has no intention of betraying Madvig, he allows his men to torture Beaumont. The camera reveals two henchmen, Jeff (William Bendix) and Rusty (Eddie Marr), playing cards in a dark and dingy apartment. We hear moaning coming from offscreen space. A tracking shot pulls back to reveal Beaumont, face down, on a small bed. His shirt is in tatters. The scene is played out with the camera staying remarkably distanced from Beaumont as he crawls across a room fragmented by darkness and disarray. Before he can reach the door, Beaumont is stopped. In response to his captive's feeble escape attempt, Jeff eroticizes the relationship of brutality between him and Ed with his patronizing patter: "Now, sweetheart, you know what I told you," says Jeff, before he grabs Beaumont away from the door and starts to beat him into unconsciousness. It becomes apparent that Jeff enjoys torturing Beaumont, so much so that fellow strong-arm Rusty worries that Jeff will "croak him." Jeff's dialogue is not exclusive to the 1942 film version, but here Jeff's hulking physicality and the perverse enjoyment of violence inscribed on his face make him a distorted doubling of Madvig, whose violence suggests that he also is an unrecuperated thug. This raises the question of whether Madvig's thuggishness also extends to experiencing the homoerotic pleasure in sadism.

Of course, the film refuses to answer this question, but a trenchant comparison is implicit in the parallel structure created between Jeff's gangster threat to Beaumont and Madvig's. The beautiful tough boy, Alan Ladd as Beaumont, makes the iconography of sexual seduction at one with the iconography of gang brutality. Without a point of view convergent with that of the camera's or the revelation of his face to emphasize his feelings, Beaumont is reduced in the scene of torture to the status of an object. Jeff's "romantic" comments feminize Beaumont, but they also suggest the perverse intimacy of torture and the possibility that Jeff's homoeroti-cized male relations reflect on all male violence as containing sexual pleasure. After Varna arrives, they dump the unconscious Beaumont in a cold-water bath to revive him before they start torturing him again. In response to Varna's asking him to work on Beaumont some more, Jeff says, "It's a pleasure," and we believe him. A medium shot shows Rusty staring in dismay at Jeff's brutality (which is offscreen). Later, Beaumont is left alone in the room. We see his face as he looks in the mirror and as he searches the medicine cabinet for something to assist him in his escape. With a razor blade he finds, he cuts up a mattress, sets it afire with a lighter, and, in the ensuing confusion, jumps out a window of the apartment while Jeff and Rusty beat out flames. He awakens in the hospital and immediately demands they get Madvig. Madvig arrives and, in turn, tells the hospital staff: "If that guy dies, I'm turning this hospital into a warehouse."

In his analysis of Hammett's novel *The Glass Key* Sean McCann talks about the ubiquity in hard-boiled novels of a trope where a woman is held captive and tor-tured in a "scene of terrible sexual cruelty" that is watched by the hero, who is un-able to intervene.[53] "It would be difficult to overstate how central scenes of this type were to the developing hard-boiled crime story," says McCann, who reads this "tab-leau of cruelty and submission" as "a tacit allegory of . . . the conflict between civic responsibility and unrestrained, irrational desire."[54] McCann's brilliant analysis of the novel is primarily interested in how scenes such as this offer a metaphoric in-terpretation of American civic life and politics, but he does acknowledge the sexual element in such scenes, as they appear in Hammett's novel.[55] I would prefer to em-phasize how this degrading violence extends "normal" male-to-male violence and links it to a sadistic violence imbued with an erotic intensity of a perverse acting out of male-male intimacy. This is more than a metaphor of civic responsibility and power. Using grotesque violence instead of the sexual act as the ultimate perfor-mative utterance between men, *The Glass Key* articulates a potentially terrifying revelation of sadistic homosexuality as the underside of American homosociality. Contrary to the novel, the film makes the violence in the Madvig/Beaumont rela-tionship overt rather than latent, thus exposing the parallel between the Beaumont/ Madvig relationship even more than does the novel.[56] Before Beaumont's fake defection to Varna's camp, Madvig and Beaumont come to blows in a bar scene where they have taken a private niche; Beaumont breaks a beer glass to hold off Madvig. Later, in a parallel scene with Jeff, he will do the same. Violence not only characterizes the erotic friendship between Madvig and Beaumont but is part of sexual desire in general; it will continue to be asserted in the film and implicated in modes of sexuality, as when Beaumont bends down to kiss the wife of the crooked newspaper publisher and suddenly a shot rings out to signal the publisher's suicide.

However, the film, even more acutely than the novel, suggests the homoerotic tenor in Jeff's relationship to Beaumont and the destructive force of male-male desire. Torturing Ed gives Jeff a sexual thrill that he now wants to reproduce. Although Jeff almost killed him, strangely enough, Ed gives him that opportunity. The ensuring scene erases the boundaries between opposing definitions of *friend* and *sodomite*. "What do you suppose gives me such a boot out of slugging you?" asks Jeff, when Ed goes looking for him and finds him in a bar, coded as extremely "low," not only by its basement location but also by its seedy furniture and down-and-out patrons. A close-up shows Jeff as he introduces Ed in terms that perversely echo Paul Madvig's first remarks on Janet to Ed Beaumont : "Meet the swellest guy I ever skinned a knuckle on." No wonder, in the novel, Jeff raises the possibility that not only does Ed like suffering but that there is a name, a category, a definition for someone like that: "'You see, he likes it. He's a —' he hesitated, frowning, wet his lips '— a God-damned massacrist, that's what he is.'" [57] Jeff has some cause to think this. After all, Ed has sought out Jeff. Jeff presses Beaumont to his side. Jeff's hands are constantly moving across Ed's upper body as he makes declaration to the bartender that Ed is the "best friend I got in the world." Because the casting of Alan Ladd as Beaumont raises the specter of the gunsel, the suggestion that Jeff is sexually attracted to Ed in a perverse way is unmistakable. Jeff suggests that he and Ed go up to a small private room where he says he will beat Ed. "We got to go up and play handball, me and cuddles," Jeff announces. Jeff is drunk, but he is astute enough to know that Ed has come to extract information from him. He leads Ed to a private room upstairs, sits down beside him, and puts his hands on him again. His voice gets more threatening as he alternately rings for drinks and calls Ed a "heel." Jeff pushes his body up against Ed and starts to make a threatening move toward him when the bartender enters. Just as Jeff is drunkenly confessing murder, Varna enters. He and Jeff get into an argument. Ironically, Jeff berates Varna for "pawing him." Jeff's sweating face looms over the camera in a grotesque close-up as he strangles Varna. Although he expects his "friend" to give him Varna's gun, Ed holds Jeff at gunpoint until the cops arrive to arrest him for murder.

The presumed reason for this dangerous encounter is Beaumont's friendship with Madvig. With Jeff's arrest, sadistic homosexuality is held at bay, but its possibility has been raised as only one menacing flange of the repertoire of sexual nonconformity within the gang as an all-male institution. Other modes of "normal" homosocial bonds between men have been contaminated with the possibility of homoerotic feeling. After having made visible the complex erotics in male homosocial relations, the film attempts to recuperate happy heterosexuality by tacking on a conventional Hollywood ending by securing Beaumont and Janet Henry as a couple. Yet the contradictions and disturbances raised in the homosocial world of the gang persist in memory.

The Glass Key is not the only crime film of the early 1940s to suggest the possibility of homoerotic feeling in its hero's male-to-male relations. The beautiful gangster of ambiguous sexuality is central to *Johnny Eager*, which was in production when Pearl Harbor was bombed and was released in 1942 to tremendous box office and excellent reviews. The film's first scene establishes its protagonist, a former gangster, as an apparently humble taxi driver. In the opening sequence of the film the physical beauty of Johnny Eager (Robert Taylor) is subject to discussion by half a dozen women, including two sociology students (one of them played by Lana Turner) who, for a class assignment, tour the city's parole office to explore how the other half lives. On the way home Lisbeth Bard (Lana Turner) wistfully remarks to her friend, "He looks like he would beat a woman." Johnny Eager is beautiful but heartless and sexually threatening.

The interest of women in Johnny Eager is counterpointed in the film's first sequence by Johnny's single-minded pursuit of a man. The film takes Johnny through a number of urban locations, where he repeatedly and determinedly asks the whereabouts of only one person: Jeff Hartwell. He finally locates Jeff (Van Heflin) in the apartment they share. Jeff and Johnny live together in domestic relations that look like homosexuality. Instead of the shabby apartment shared with female "relatives" that he occupies when he is tipped off to the visits of his parole officer, Johnny actually lives with a man in an expansive, expensive apartment hidden behind a secret door at the racing track office. Johnny's elegant apartment and fastidious appearance identify him "with [the] luxury, with obsessions with beauty and appearance" that Richard Dyer suggests typify noir's representations of effeminate — and villainous — homosexuality.[58]

In spite of his embracing of luxury, Johnny still trades on his past as a "tough boy" of the streets. In his operations he likes to remind other gangsters of the various criminal exploits they shared in the old neighborhood. However, these are not expressions of homosocial nostalgia but are depicted as Johnny's cynical attempts to manipulate his colleagues in crime, to encourage them to trust him. The film makes it clear that no matter how long he has known these men, he trusts no one — except Jeff Hartwell.

As in *The Glass Key*, the casting of the protagonist is noteworthy in forcing the recognition that the male body is actually constructed for the gaze of the spectator. The casting of romantic heartthrob Robert Taylor as Johnny Eager makes the character's appeal to women characters (and audience members) absolutely believable. But rather than secure the sense of Johnny as irrevocably heterosexual, the casting of Taylor, like that of Ladd in *The Glass Key*, opens the possibility that Johnny would be attractive to men, as well as women, as an object of desire. Eager's identity as an honest taxi driver is a mere masquerade to satisfy his parole requirements and cover his real ambitions, reflected, of course, in a name that harkens back to the Prohibition-era movie gangsters. He remains a successful racketeer, the mastermind of an elaborate gambling operation. He is in the midst of establishing a dog-racing track, but its opening is held up by an injunction issued by Judge John Benson Farrell (Edward Arnold), who once put Johnny away and regards him as "vermin." Johnny's identity as a cabdriver is not the only aspect of his life that is highly suspect.

Although women are exceedingly interested in Johnny, he appears no more interested in women than he is in driving a cab. Johnny is shown to be indifferent to them, even to his ostensible moll, Garnet (Patricia Dane). In one scene she showers him with kisses and compliments but gets not a one in return, nor even an interested look. Johnny's coldness to Garnet was the result, in part, of PCA instructions to MGM that Johnny and Garnett's interactions could not give the audience the impression that the two have been or are presently involved in physical sexual intimacy. Physical contact between them in any scene had to be limited, a policy that the PCA had developed as a broad strategy to cope with the presence of "illicit" (that is, nonmarital or adulterous) heterosexual activity in films.[59] This action by the Breen office had the unintended result of intensifying the homoerotic overtones in *Johnny Eager* of the protagonist's primary male-to-male relationship with his henchman and self-proclaimed "stooge," Jeff Hartwell. What is more, the narrative structure and visual compositions also have a similar effect, as Jeff and Johnny are often photographed alone together, with Jeff gazing in fascination at Johnny. The film ambiguously suggests through dialogue and action that this is more than platonic friendship, even though that is all it can be within the overt signification of the film. When Jeff Hartwell is introduced, the audience may be surprised to see that he is not visually rendered as a "gunsel" type but is a very young, curly-headed literati in rumpled tweeds. His ability to make classical allusions at every turn indicates he is obviously well educated, a member of the social elite, but he is an alcoholic.[60] Because he was drunk, he has failed to do the duties Johnny assigned him, but, like Gutman in *The Maltese Falcon*, Johnny does not seem to care if his assistant is incompetent. Instead, Johnny fixes Jeff a bromide and regales him about the dangers of his drinking. This is a relationship between men of very different backgrounds who share nothing from a common childhood history to suggest the motivation so often called on as explanation for intimate male bonding in the gangster film. It is a relationship, like that of the gunsel and the "boss," that is hierarchal, apparently based on money, yet also unusually intimate and emotionally codependent. Jeff says he regards Johnny as "unique," as "astute," but he continually assails Johnny for his lack of more tender emotions. Although he says he is a modern Boswell to Johnny's Samuel Johnson, Jeff's behavior suggests less of the biographer's objective observation than the well-bred idealist's awe-filled, homoeroticized admiration for an exciting "rough lad." If that rough lad is the beautiful Robert Taylor, then no complicated explanation for his fascination with a gangster is necessary.

It follows that, except for his attachment to Johnny, Jeff doesn't seem to have any reason to belong in this criminal underworld. His love for Johnny ventures beyond the familiar model of *The Public Enemy* or other films of the 1930s, like *Manhattan Melodrama* (1934), that focus on two pals growing up together into hooliganism. Instead, it ventures into the territory of cross-class romance that usually defines the gangster film's heterosexuality rather than its homosociality. Jeff's wild admiration for Johnny is registered in close-ups and sustained gazes, as in the final sequence, where Jeff holds on to Johnny's hand and tries to prevent his departure into the street fight that will kill him. Such close-ups suggest a sexual transgression of Hollywood visual conventions and smack of the same class transgression present in the classical cinematic trope of the sexual liaison between an upper-class socialite and a gangster. Found, most memorably, in MGM's *A Free Soul* (1931), this pattern is later reconfigured in films noirs in the relationship between a rich woman and the detective, as in *Murder, My Sweet* (1944) and *The Big Sleep* (1946). This trope is exploited in *Johnny Eager* in Jeff's relationship with Johnny, but it is also doubled in Johnny's romantic relationship to Lisbeth Bard, a wealthy sociology student who becomes enamored with Johnny even though her stepfather, Judge Farrell, is Johnny's sworn enemy.

The naked emotional extremism of Jeff's love for his beautiful gangster boss/ friend gives the impression that he would prevent any rival from invading his romantic territory (Johnny).[61] Initially, Jeff is shown reacting to Lisbeth as a rival, in repetition of an earlier moment when Jeff and Garnet vie for Johnny's attentions. In that scene the rivalry is painfully overt: Jeff tells Johnny to choose between them, and Johnny tells Garnet to go away. A close-up emphasizes Jeff smiling with satisfaction at his triumph. Later, when Johnny picks up Lisbeth in a nightclub, Johnny notifies Jeff that he will go home in a different car. As Lisbeth walks past his table, the camera lingers on Jeff, who is staring at her with an expression that can only be read as a mixture of curiosity and jealousy. "Mr. Freud, take a letter," he drunkenly slurs. As the relationship between Johnny and Lisbeth develops, Jeff becomes morally repelled by Johnny's scheme to exploit Lisbeth's feelings for him. This raises the interesting possibility that Jeff identifies with Lisbeth.

Johnny Eager has many nascent qualities of the gangster boss that will emerge in movies after the war. Like many noir gangster bosses/villains, including Whit Sterling in *Out of the Past* (1947) and Eddie Mars in *The Big Sleep,* he is smoothly mannered, stylishly presentable, and apparently Anglo-Saxon. He suggests the emergence of the new corporate-style hood who is exceedingly adept at sustaining a masquerade of law-abiding normality. Although he is marked by the film as morally repugnant, Eager retains his status as antihero, not only because he is beautiful to look at but, in part, because he is more like the Prohibition-era gangster in at least one respect: he is not yet the killer by remote control that so irritates the proletarian sensibilities of noir heroes such as Philip Marlowe in *The Big Sleep.*

In fact, reforming his heartlessness rather than his criminality per se underscores the film's narrative trajectory. Although he acts as though he's in love with Lisbeth, Johnny blackmails her stepfather by making him (and Lisbeth) think she has shot to death a hood that attacked Johnny in his apartment. The shooting was a setup, a confrontation staged wholly for the purpose of having Lisbeth incriminated in a shooting. Johnny forces her stepfather to lift the injunction on his racing track, but he does not anticipate that Lisbeth's bourgeois guilt will drive her to the brink of madness.

Giving Johnny Eager a heart occurs through the combined effects of Jeff's moralizing and Lisbeth's suffering. This goal of providing for the gangster's emotional reform, so necessary for the PCA's approval, dominates the narrative in the second half of the film, but it also contributes to the sexual incoherency surrounding the film's inscription of Johnny as both object and subject of desire. After Johnny hits Jeff for saying he is so selfish that he can't understand love, Jeff attempts to leave Johnny. This moment fulfills, in a perverse, homosexual articulation, the early assessment by Lisbeth that Johnny would be likely to hit a woman.[62] But Johnny has hit a man, a common occurrence in a gangster film. Yet this is not just any man but the man who clearly loves him, who is in masochistic submission to him, who has come to occupy the "feminine position." Jeff's femininity is inscribed again when, a few moments later, he returns. "Like poor Garnet, I came back for my purse," he says, referring to an earlier scene in which Johnny's girlfriend attempted to regain his attention. Jeff seems no different from all the women in Johnny's life who have loved him. Yet there is a difference, not only in his gender but in his intimate knowledge of Johnny's professional life, as well as his personal one. Jeff tells Johnny that when he left, he was intent on "turning the key" on Johnny, on singing to the district attorney and then committing suicide. An extended close-up shows Jeff with tears rolling roll down his cheeks as he recounts those plans that he attributes to his desire to help "that little girl" (Lisbeth). He has abandoned his plans because, "It's just like you said, you're the boss. You've got everybody over a barrel." This apparent reference to Johnny's status as the leader of a criminal gang is actually the basis for another, more intimate meaning. Who is "everybody," and what is this "barrel" to which Jeff refers? The answer is that Jeff and Lisbeth share the uncomfortable position of being in love with a remorseless gangster boss.

Reverse shots show glamorized close-ups of Johnny attempting to comfort Jeff. Johnny decides to tell Lisbeth the truth, which, he says to Jeff, he is doing "as much for you as for anybody." So that her life will not be ruined, he will show her the man she supposedly killed. A full shot lingers on Jeff, smiling broadly, as he follows Johnny out of the apartment. Johnny lures into the street the man Lisbeth "killed," but there are complications with the rival gang the man has joined. His hand is clasped over Johnny's, and he makes a final plea to Johnny to abandon his scheme and go away with him — to the mountains in the West.[63]

MGM's glossy house style attempts to outrun gangster movie realism in *Johnny Eager*, just as the film's heterosexual narrative agenda attempts to outrun the

4. Jeff Hartnett (Van Heflin) and Garnet (Patricia Dane) vie for the attention of the exciting "rough lad" Johnny Eager in *Johnny Eager* (1942).

"emotionalism" of homosexuality inscribed in Jeff's love for Johnny. The film ends up in the traditional territory of the gangster film: the streets, an orgiastic display of violence and homoerotic love. After Johnny sends Lisbeth and Jeff away from the scene, Jeff, armed with the telepathy of the ever-faithful lover, senses that something is wrong and returns. A shoot-out in the street with gang rivals has left Johnny dying in the dark, rain-slicked streets. Jeff runs to Johnny, calling his name. Jeff cradles the dying Johnny in his arms. "What's that highest mountain, where we're going?" Johnny asks before he draws his last breath. In an intense close-up Jeff tearfully delivers an epitaph for his friend, a speech that the PCA demanded to bring home the point to audiences that "crime doesn't pay" but one that inadvertently reinforces the homoerotic force of the "platonic" friendship between the two men: "This guy could have climbed the highest mountain in the world . . . if only he'd just started up the right one."[64] Surrounded by darkness, Jeff holds Johnny in a final embrace.

Johnny Eager is unusual among gangster films in the 1940s in representing homosexuality perhaps no less ambiguously than in other films but quite distinctly as being aligned with romantic idealism. Nevertheless, that idealism is affiliated with masochistic desire. Although that also might be said of Ed Beaumont's dangerous pursuit of the truth for Paul Madvig in *The Glass Key*, here Jeff's masochism is attached to a symbolic appropriation of a moralizing feminine consciousness and a self-abnegating double mimesis of the woman's traditional role in heterosexuality.[65] Even if we recognize the film's textual inscription of Jeff's desire as sexual, Johnny could still be read as the straight object of Jeff's erotic attachment. However, an against-the-grain reading might align him as the modern notion of the "butch clone," the gay man with a penchant for artifice of identity who encourages the perception that he is straight through his performance of normative homosocial masculinity. Jeff's romantic idealism is used by the narrative to the purpose of reforming his beloved object into embracing committed heterosexuality, as well as a heightened moral sensibility. Although this homoerotic idealism may seem far removed from the tone usually associated with the gangster film of the period, *Johnny Eager* suggests a mode of homosexual attachment that Hollywood would place at the center of the narrative in postwar films such as *Gilda* (1946) and *White Heat* (1949). However, in typical noir fashion, these later films twist male-to-male erotic idealism into something that seems sick and destructive rather than redemptive and reforming, as in *Johnny Eager*, a film that speaks to the power of Hollywood classical film of the early 1940s to problematize male identity — and homosociality — beyond the parameters usually ascribed to it under the Code yet, at the same time, manage to successfully adhere to that Code.

Certainly the protagonists of these three crime films all problematize the conventional cultural routing of homosocial desire; that is, they disrupt the sexual function the woman plays as the socially and sexually acceptable object who substitutes for a sexually taboo male object.[66] This disruption occurs in a number of ways in the cinematic criminal underworld to suggest an uninterrupted continuum between "normal" homosociality and "perverse" homoeroticism in the gang that society otherwise attempts to obscure or deny. Because of the Code and contemporary standards of sexual behavior, however, we never can expect to see the gangster involved in overt sexual acts of homosexuality in classical Hollywood films; instead, homosexuality must be implied through the absence of sexually charged heterosexuality, as well as through emotionally charged shows of intimacy between men, and through the visual language of cinematic composition, shot perspective, and cutting. These films can be seen as occupying a transitional period between the classic gangster films of the early 1930s and films noirs of the postwar period. On the one hand, they evoke certain aspects of gangster homosociality of the 1930s but with homoerotic complications that suggest a "disturbance in the sphere of sexuality" very different from the obsession with the femme fatale associated with film noir.[67] The sexual specter of the gunsel haunts male relationships in crime films of the 1940s, whether gangsters are explicitly part of a distinctly homosexual subculture (like the gang in *The Maltese Falcon*) or of a "normal" gang (as in *The Glass Key* and *Johnny Eager*). Thus, these critically neglected films of the war years provide the foundation for examining the complicity between expressions of violence and transgressive male sexuality in later films such as *Gilda* and *White Heat*. They also demonstrate how, as much as its moral regulators might wish otherwise, Hollywood film could not free itself from the homoerotic implications of patriarchal homosociality and its structured repression of homosexual desire. As a consequence, whether always intentional or not, these films take the familiar trope of male bonding attached to the depiction of a violent gangster underworld and provide the "slight shift of optic" that shows us how the Hollywood crime film, even under the restrictive domain of the Production Code, might reveal in unexpected and instructive ways how, as Sedgwick writes, "[f]or a man to be a man's man is separated only by an invisible, carefully blurred, always-already-crossed line from being 'interested in men.'"[68]

Notes

1. Frank Krutnik, *In a Lonely Street: Film Noir, Genre, Masculinity* (London: Routledge, 1991), 25; on the 1943 directive see 234n13. See also Clayton Koppes and Gregory Black, *Hollywood Goes to War* (London: I. B. Taurus, 1988), 126–131; on the control of moral content so that Hollywood's financial interests would be served see 138–140.

2. Tino Balio says that although the MPPDA publicly defended the cycle of gangster films in the early 1930s as deterrents to lawlessness, privately the organization admitted that these films had created a "prairie-fire of protest." See Tino Balio, *Grand Design: Hollywood as a Modern Business Enterprise, 1930–1939* (1993; repr. Berkeley: University of California Press, 1995), 51.

3. Balio, *Grand Design*, 52.

4. Lea Jacobs, *The Wages of Sin: Censorship and the Fallen Woman Film, 1928–1942* (1991; repr. Berkeley: University of California Press, 1999), 110.

5. In 1936 Warner Brothers sought a Code certificate for reissuing *Little Caesar*. The studio was told by the PCA to withdraw its application in a September 8, 1936, letter from Joseph Breen to Jack Warner. The film was finally issued a certificate in 1953 on the theory that the film had become a "period piece." Clipping and letter in *Little Caesar* PCA file, Special Collections, Margaret Herrick Library, Academy of Motion Picture Arts and Sciences, hereafter cited as MHL-AMPAS.

6. Carlos Clarens, *Crime Movies: An Illustrated History* (New York: Norton, 1980), 180.

7. Marilyn Yaquinoto, *Pump 'Em Full of Lead: A Look at Gangsters on Film* (New York: Twayne, 1998), 74–75, 180. See also Krutnik, *In a Lonely Street:* "the gangster-hero fantasy met with substantial resistance during the war. . . . [O]ne can see the gangster film as having been displaced by the 'tough' thriller" (198).

8. Koppes and Black, *Hollywood Goes to War*, 125–126.

9. Ibid., 126–132.

10. Krutnik, *In a Lonely Street*, 35.

11. Krutnik, ibid., concludes: "In general, the gangster as protagonist is found only on rare occasions in 1940s Hollywood cinema. . . . However, the gangster figure does figure in a somewhat transmuted manner in many of the 'tough' thrillers" (201).

12. Raymond Chandler, *The Big Sleep* (1939; repr. New York: Vintage 1992), 97.

13. Eve Kosofsky Sedgwick, *Between Men: English Literature and Male Homosocial Desire* (New York: Columbia University Press, 1985), 85–86.

14. Ibid., 115.

15. Ibid., 92, 115.

16. Krutnik, *In a Lonely Street*, 201. On the appearance of homosexuality in films of the 1940s see Vito Russo, *The Celluloid Closet* (New York: Harper and Row, 1981); Richard Dyer, "Homosexuality and Film Noir," in *The Matter of Images* (London: British Film Institute, 1993), 61–66; and Robert J. Corber, *Homosexuality in Cold War America: Resistance and the Crisis of Masculinity* (Durham, N.C.: Duke University Press, 1997), 11–15. In his pioneering 1977 article, "Homosexuality and Film Noir," Richard Dyer argues that the representation of homosexuality in film noir of the 1940s is negative, oppressive, and stereotypical, with the effeminate male homosexual typically marked as the villain, as in Otto Preminger's *Laura* (1944). He acknowledges that the discernible, iconographic presence of gay characters occurs "in a minority of films noirs," but he regards "their absence from all other types of film" as meaning that homosexuals "constitute a defining feature of film noir taken as a whole" (61). Although valuable for calling attention to the presence of gay characters in 1940s films, Dyer's argument is based on a questionable premise. Gay characters are certainly not absent "from all other types of film in the

1940s." One need only look, for example, at comedy and, more specifically, at the films of Preston Sturges, to find evidence that contradicts this view.

17. James Naremore says that censorship reports of the 1940s "reveal that classic noir was almost obsessed with sexual perversity. The villains in these pictures tend to be homosexual aesthetes" (James Naremore, *More Than Night: Film Noir in Its Contexts* [Berkeley: University of California Press, 1998], 98). From my perusal of PCA files, the Breen office files rarely recorded reactions to perversity, but filmmakers were obviously knowledgeable in how censors would react to depictions of it. PCA members tended to comment much more often on the drinking of alcohol in films than on perversity unless the latter was expressed in the form of effeminate homosexuality or extended, graphic scenes of physically violent sadism; such scenes drew their attention in the film noir *The Big Heat*. Breen wrote to the studio regarding the film's script: "an increased amount of violence and rather spectacular brutality has been injected into it, an[d] the accumulative effect of this, we think, is definitely not good. We must, therefore, respectfully request that some of these acts of brutality be eliminated, and the overall violence considerably reduced" (Joseph Breen to Harry Cohn, March 20, 1953, *The Big Heat* PCA file, MHL-AMPAS).

18. Jason Joy to James Wingate, Feb. 5, 1931, *Little Caesar* PCA file, MHL-AMPAS (cited in Balio, *Grand Design*, 416n5).

19. Scholars who talk about dispersal of gangster qualities include Krutnik, *In a Lonely Street*, 197–201.

20. Balio, *Grand Design*, 48.

21. Lea Jacobs, "Industry Self-Regulation and the Problem of Textual Determination," *Velvet Light Trap* 23 (spring 1989): 9.

22. Lea Jacobs, *Wages of Sin*, 112–113.

23. This gangsterlike volatility and physical intensity is completely missing from Ricardo Cortez's interpretation of Sam Spade in the 1931 film version of the novel. Missing also in this version is the light, humorous touch given to the presentation of Gutman, Cairo, and Wilmar.

24. The henchman is sometimes depicted in film as a grim middle-aged professional, as in the opening of *The Killers* (1946) or even as dim-witted, unattractive middle-age men, as in *The Big Sleep* (1946).

25. This gesture of tugging at the sleeve is repeated by Jeff Hartwell (Van Heflin) with the sleeve belonging to his adored boss, Johnny Eager (Robert Taylor), in *Johnny Eager* (1942).

26. This is the definition provided by the *Oxford American Dictionary* (New York: Oxford University Press, 1999), 117.

27. See an online discussion of *gunsel* in *Take Our Word for It*, no. 73 (Feb. 14, 2000), www.takeourword.com/Issue073.html. Erle Stanley Gardner's "Getting Away with Murder" (*The Atlantic*, January 1965) relates a tale of Hammett, in a story for *Black Mask* magazine, using the word *gunsel*: "The Editor of *Black Mask*, Joseph T. Shaw, deleted 'gooseberry lay' from Hammett's story, but passed over 'gunsel' and, as a result, says Gardner, 'writers of the hard-boiled school of realism started talking about a gunsel as the equivalent of a gunman'" (74). In an issue of *Entertainment Weekly* a character in the hit television series *The Sopranos* is referred to as a "ponytailed gunsel" in a usage of the word that sustains the modern, nonsexual definition. See Ken Tucker, "Television," *Entertainment Weekly*, December 20/27, 2002, 118.

28. *American Speech*, cited at *Take Our Word for It*, no. 73 (Feb. 14, 2000), www.takeourword.com/Issue073.html.

29. The 1931 film version of the novel significantly trims Wilmar's role. He speaks only in the scene where Spade suggests he should be the "fall guy." In this scene the detective refers to Wilmar as Gutman's "boyfriend," and Gutman is shown patting Wilmar's cheek on two separate occasions.

30. Gardner, "Getting Away with Murder," 74.

31. *Gunsel* is not present in the 1947 edition of *The American College Dictionary* (New York: Random House); see *The Oxford American Dictionary* (New York: Oxford University Press, 1999), s.v. "gunsel."

32. Members of the more lenient Studio Relations Committee of the MPPDA also objected to the depiction of a clothes tailor in *The Public Enemy* as excessively effeminate ("a 'fairy,' with hands on hips, Nice-Nellie talk, etc."). See Lamar Trotti to McKenzie, Milliken, Joy, et al., April 24, 1931, *The Public Enemy* PCA file, MHL-AMPAS.

33. Joseph Breen to Jack Warner, May 23, 1941, *The Maltese Falcon* PCA file, MHL-AMPAS.

34. The term *eccentric travellers* is cited by George E. Haggerty as a euphemism used in public reference to William Beckford and his male lover in their attempt to escape scandal by living in Italy, a country associated in the eighteenth century with sodomy. See George E. Haggerty, *Men in Love: Masculinity and Sexuality in the Eighteenth Century* (New York: Columbia University Press, 1999), 149–150.

35. Edmund Bergler, "Differential Diagnosis between Spurious Homosexuality and Perversion Homosexuality," *Psychiatric Quarterly* 18 (1944): 100–112.

36. Haggerty, *Men in Love*, 140–141.

37. Haggerty says that libertines may be "'homosocially' united, of course, but theirs is a homosociability of satiric individualism" (*Men in Love*, 25–26).

38. An earlier (pre-Code) film that clearly links politics and gangsterism is *Lawyer Man* (1932).

39. The violence of Madvig in the 1942 version of the novel is quite different from the 1935 version, in which Madvig (Edward Arnold) is so nonviolent a character that the public is portrayed as disbelieving that he could kill anyone (at first, before the newspapers start to work on him). Also, the sexual rivalry between Madvig and Beaumont for Janet Henry is eliminated, as is the extent of her duplicity.

40. Haggerty, *Men in Love*, 37.

41. See the *American College Dictionary* (New York: Random House, 1951), s.v. "smack."

42. In the novel and the 1935 film version Opal is Madvig's daughter. Madvig is also given an elderly mother in Hammett's original story and in the first film version.

43. Sedgwick, *Between Men*, 38.

44. Richard Schickel, *The Stars* (New York: Bonanza Books, 1962), 246.

45. Koppes and Black, *Hollywood Goes to War*, 125–126, 100, 102. Paramount refused to submit scripts to the OWI.

46. The first screen version of Hammett's novel was released in 1935 and starred George Raft.

47. Paramount Studio press book for *This Gun for Hire*, USC Press Book Collection, USC Cinema Archive of the Performing Arts, cited in Sheri Lynn Chinen Biesen, "Film Noir and World War II: Wartime Production, Censorship, and the 'Red Meat' Crime Cycle" (Ph.D. diss., University of Texas at Austin, 1998), 24. Biesen argues that Joseph Breen's temporary departure from the PCA in April 1941 to join RKO (lasting until March 1942) "resulted in an easing of PCA enforcement in 1941 and 1942" (17).

48. Gaylyn Studlar, "Cruise-ing into the Millennium: Performative Masculinity, Stardom, and the All-American Boy's Body," in *Ladies and Gentlemen, Boys and Girls: Gender in Film at the End of the Twentieth Century*, ed. Murray Pomerance (Albany: State University of New York Press, 2001), 173.

49. Ibid., 174.

50. Laura Mulvey argues that "a male movie star's glamorous characteristics are thus not those of the erotic object of his gaze [the male viewer] but those of the more perfect, more complete, more powerful ideal ego" ("Visual Pleasure and Narrative Cinema," *Screen* 16, no. 3 [Aug. 1975]: 28, 30).

51. Steve Neale, "Masculinity as Spectacle," in *The Sexual Subject: A Screen Reader in Sexuality* (London: Routledge, 1992), 285.

52. Ibid., 281, 284, 286.

53. Sean McCann, *Gumshoe America: Hard-Boiled Crime Fiction and the Rise and Fall of New Deal Liberalism* (Durham, N.C.: Duke University Press, 2000), 130.

54. Ibid., 130.

55. Ibid., 134–136.

56. Ibid., 136–137. McCann recognizes the "implicit analogy" made throughout the novel in pairs of men, O'Rory ("Varna" in the film) and Jeff, who strangles him; Senator Henry and Taylor, the son he kills."

57. Dashiell Hammett, *The Glass Key* (1931; repr. New York: Vantage Books 1989), 185.

58. Dyer, "Homosexuality and Film Noir," 65.

59. Louis B. Mayer to PCA, July 16, 1941, *Johnny Eager* PCA file, MHL-AMPAS. Mayer agrees to limit physical contact between the two characters. On the PCA's reliance on physically separating illicit lovers as a technique recommended for other films see Jacobs, *Wages of Sin*, 116–131.

60. Alcoholism was often linked to homosexuality in psychoanalytic discourse of the time, as well as in popular culture. The alcoholic protagonist of the novel *The Lost Weekend* is depicted as being homosexual.

61. This kind of defense of the gangster love object occurs with Otero's attempt to shoot his rival, Joe (Douglas Fairbanks), in *Little Caesar*.

62. The most startling moment in the 1935 version of *The Glass Key* is when Ed Beaumont (George Raft) decks Paul Madvig's daughter in order to keep her from accusing her father of murder. In the last scene they will go out on their first date, to the smiling approval of Madvig and his mother.

63. This trope of escape to the West also occurs in *The Killing* (1956), in the impassioned attempt of an old hood (Jay C. Flippen) to stay with the young "hooligan" (Sterling Hayden) and in *The Big Combo* (1955), in dialogue between the homosexual henchmen, Fanty and Mingo.

64. See July 16, 1941, report on conference between Considine, McGinness, Block, Mahin, Messinger, et al. to Mayer from the Breen Office, *Johnny Eager* PCA file, MHL-AMPAS.

65. *In a Lonely Street* discusses the male in noir who is "in thrall" to the woman as "the loved object" in terms that Krutnik regards as compatible with Freudian discourse. See Krutnik, *In a Lonely Street*, 83–85.

66. Sedgwick, *Between Men*, 3–5.

67. Annette Kuhn, *The Power of the Image: Essays on Representation and Sexuality* (London: Routledge, 1985), 94. Freud coins this phrase in his analysis of the case of Dora. See Sigmund Freud, *Dora: An Analysis of a Case of Hysteria* (New York: Collier Books, 1963).

68. Sedgwick, *Between Men*, 89.

Mother Barker

Film Star and Public Enemy No. 1

Mary Elizabeth Strunk

O N APRIL 3, 1936, BRUNO RICHARD HAUPTMANN was executed for the kidnap-murder of Charles and Anne Morrow Lindbergh's two-year-old baby boy. Yet Hauptmann, who had been denounced in court as "Public Enemy Number One *of the World*," was not commanding the attention of law enforcement the world over. In that same month FBI director J. Edgar Hoover revealed the identity of the "*Real* Public Enemy No. 1." The predominantly female readers of *American Magazine* were the first citizens privy to the story, which previously had been "locked in the archives of the Federal Bureau of Investigation." According to Hoover, America's worst villain wasn't Hauptmann or Al Capone or the still-at-large Alvin "Creepy" Karpis. Instead, Hoover's article declared, "[t]he most vicious, dangerous, and resourceful criminal brain this country [had] produced in many years" was none other than "Mother Barker."[1]

What made the timing of Hoover's pronouncement most peculiar was that by April 1936 "Mother Barker" had been dead for over a year. On January 16, 1935, Kate "Ma" Barker (as she was better known) and her youngest son, Fred, had been shot and killed in a gun battle with FBI agents at Lake Weir, Florida. Fred Barker's criminal activities were well documented. But, whether it had intended to kill her or not, the FBI would have more difficulty in accounting for the death of Fred's diminutive, sixty-three-year-old mother, who had never in her life been fingerprinted, arrested, or officially charged with any crime. Eyewitness reports of the shoot-out vary wildly, reflecting the tumult of the encounter. Depending on who tells the story, Ma Barker was too obstinate, too ignorant, or maybe too frightened to obey the lawmen's orders that she and Fred emerge from their cottage hideout. The only certainty is that Ma died out of sight, thus concealing both her reaction to the standoff and the true manner of her death. (The FBI was reluctant to claim credit for the bullet that allegedly pierced Ma's heart, attributing it instead to a self-inflicted gunshot wound or a mercy killing at the hands of her son.)[2]

With the appearance of Hoover's *American Magazine* article fifteen months later, Ma Barker was reborn. The sparse outlines of her meagerly documented life were altered and amplified to cast Ma as a criminal queen bee that the FBI was *forced* to destroy. Hoover's article denouncing Ma and justifying her demise ultimately launched her as a potent icon: that of an outrageous, apparently unnatural, mother whom the magazine proposed as "a lesson to every foolish woman who overindulges her children."[3] To this day Ma's name remains a part of the national vocabulary, an idiom most often used to denigrate an older woman as coarse, violent, or domineering. In popular culture representations Ma Barker has emerged as a cinematic trope, a campy monster useful for revealing the social anxieties of the particular historical moment in which a film or television program about her was created.

That the figure of Ma Barker has reappeared so regularly is not an accident but a reflection of her allegorical utility. Four feature-length films about Ma Barker emerged at roughly the rate of one a decade in the period 1940–1970: *Queen of the Mob* (1940; writing credit to J. Edgar Hoover), *Guns Don't Argue* (1957), *Ma Barker's Killer Brood* (1960), and *Bloody Mama* (1970). Each film stretched her character to more violent proportions. These celluloid interpretations, which reached new generations that could only know "Ma Barker" and the early FBI through their onscreen portrayals, are doubly informative. On one level the dramatic permutations of the films' common central character demonstrate the changing status of white American mothers in their imagined roles as nation-builders and citizens. By virtue of her familiar but flexible narrative, Ma served as a negative social barometer by which women's deviant behavior was defined and normative behavior reinscribed. On another level successive onscreen depictions of Ma's capture also speak to the declining authority of the state-sponsored family norms, particularly those advocated by Hoover's FBI.

This chapter asserts Ma as a palimpsest on whom has been written more than seven decades' worth of fluctuating perceptions of national civic ideals, federal policing, and the ways images of home, mothers, and nation relate to them both. Taking as its starting point the "official" Ma, the Hoover-created Ma Barker, who became the foundation for Ma Barker the recurring screen icon, I demonstrate how the figure of Ma Barker signified more than just a negative example of womanhood. In Hoover's writing, and elsewhere, she became the corrupted female foil to the virile and virtuous G-man, and a parable on the hazards of abandoning the domestic ideology Hoover repeatedly invoked as an antidote for crime.[4] As the following analysis of the films about Ma will show, she became in the 1940s and 1950s an emblem of national sickness, male weakness, and consumer-based degradation. In subsequent retellings of her story, in the 1960s and 1970s, she would be further reviled as the enemy and antithesis of all-American youth and manhood. Until the late twentieth century Ma's FBI-enhanced image would serve exactly the purposes for which it was originally designed: to justify state authority and to require that women — and notably mothers — be excluded as direct enforcers of that authority.

Little is known about the real Ma Barker, but there is little doubt that her life and ambitions were not quite what the 1936 "*Real* Public Enemy" article made them out to be.[5] All four of Ma's sons were criminals, and two of them participated in a pair of high-profile kidnappings of the 1930s.[6] Ma Barker's connection to these crimes is not known, but she did live for a time with her grown sons and some of their gang members. The official FBI report from 1935 describes Ma as "an average mother of a family which has no aspirations [and] evidenced no desire to maintain any high plane socially." Written after Ma's death, the report is rife with speculations designed to underscore the possibility of her guilt. For instance, "it is possible Ma became loose in her moral life" at the time she separated from her husband; and "inasmuch as she was more intelligent than her sons . . . she ruled them with an iron will." The FBI further concluded that "Ma Barker liked to live well. She purchased expensive clothing, furniture, and other necessities from the spoils of her sons' depredations."[7] In a curious departure from Hoover's published description, the official FBI record leaves out any reference to Ma as a mastermind of the midwestern underworld.[8]

The more excessive renderings of Ma's story had greater staying power, and potentially fabricated details from Hoover's article were readily accepted as fact. Many newspapers ran "first-person" descriptions of Ma Barker and her career by reprinting portions of the *American Magazine* article word for word, thus helping cement Hoover's version of Ma Barker into history.[9] Former Barker associate Alvin Karpis later complained that "Ma Barker never ran a crime school. . . . As a matter of fact, the legend of Ma Barker . . . only grew up in the years after her death and only then in order to justify the manner in which she met her death at the hands of the FBI."[10] In fairness, some of the embellishments to the Ma Barker legend appear not to have been the work of Hoover but may have been inserted by magazine editors. For example, the Ma Barker described in *American Magazine* exploited her "nice little old lady" appearance to case banks; "Ma Barker was an actress," and "[s]he could weep with the ease of a movie star and much more convincingly."[11] No such observation appeared in the original article draft. The magazine editors may have wanted to reassure readers that the lack of evidence connecting Ma to any of her sons' robberies or kidnappings was, in fact, evidence of her supreme duplicity.

Depicting Ma as an actress proved prophetic, for she would soon appear in Hollywood. With his ghostwriter from *American Magazine* Hoover also produced a full-length book, *Persons in Hiding*, in 1938. *Persons in Hiding*, like the articles that preceded it, was based on the real-life FBI cases on which Hoover and his public relations experts had rebuilt the bureau's beleaguered reputation. Each chapter was designed as a morality tale for a public that Hoover considered dangerously enamored with gangsters.[12] Of the four book excerpts translated into films by Paramount

Studios in 1939 and 1940, the two most successful were based on real-life women outlaws,[13] including Ma Barker.[14]

Although he did not appear in any of the *Persons in Hiding* films, Hoover's face and name appeared on many publicity posters alongside those of the principal characters. The *Motion Picture Herald* raved about the "solid gold proposition" of cashing in on Hoover's name and endorsement. Correspondence between FBI headquarters in D.C. and the writers at Paramount indicates that the FBI director kept close tabs on the adaptation of his book into screenplays. These letters reiterate again and again that Hoover would withdraw his support—and use of his image—unless he personally approved the final script. Hoover's team also insisted that FBI agents and technology at all times be shown in favorable light.[15]

Hoover did not always get his way, however, especially with the Ma Barker script. For instance, the censors would not accept Hoover's title, "The Woman from Hell," so Paramount released the film as *Queen of the Mob* in 1940.[16] *Queen of the Mob*'s Ma (renamed "Ma Webster" for the film) is also a far tamer character than the Ma Barker whom Hoover and his ghostwriter described in *American Magazine*. This first cinematic Ma helps plan her sons' crimes for a while but seems more interested in arranging clandestine visits with her only grandchild. The film also met with a serious production roadblock when test audiences rejected the final scene depicting Ma's shoot-out with the FBI. In the original Hoover script the film ended with Ma bidding some federal agents a bitterly defiant "Merry Christmas, G-men," as she lies dying beneath her Christmas tree. This scene was later reshot so that Ma could survive and concede, "All right, Mr. G-man. You win," before bidding a sorrowful farewell to her son, who, dressed as Santa, lies dead under the Christmas tree.[17] The G-men who lead Ma away, uninjured, take chivalrous care first to put away their guns. Hoover may have been surprised by this rewrite, but the revised ending represented a victory for the FBI. Test audiences got the film's message that Ma had been as corrupt as the G-men were righteous. Not public outrage at the FBI's actions but a squeamish aversion toward seeing grandmothers get shot seems to have dictated the new ending—one that made the federal agents even greater heroes than before.

Apart from its tidied-up finale, *Queen of the Mob* was faithful to Hoover's *American Magazine* account, especially as it enacted traits that would forever be associated with the "real" Ma Barker. These traits articulate the contradictions of the older woman's role in the social discourse of the late 1930s; she is simultaneously an object of comedy, derision, and danger. In *Queen of the Mob* Ma is shown to distrust all other women, especially younger female rivals for her sons' affections. She forbids her sons to associate with women and tears her one son's wife out of a family photograph. Ma also craves expensive consumer goods but does so, the film intimates, because she is keen to the prejudices of a legal system that make the world of high society one of the safest places for a criminal to hide. A wily manipulator, she also uses her appearance of vulnerability and innocence to rent hideouts and

1. Blanche Yurka plays the Ma whom test audiences wouldn't allow to die in *Queen of the Mob* (1940). Courtesy of the Academy of Motion Picture Arts and Sciences.

case banks. Ma therefore employs what is coded in her body by way of her sex, age, and whiteness to garner power in precisely those arenas where older women are presumed to have none.[18]

In keeping with Hoover's published denunciations of women criminals, *Queen of the Mob* condemns underworld women for more than their propensity for breaking the law. Ma's most egregious crimes are that of being a disruptive, rather than domesticating, influence, of having rejected traditional marriage and motherhood, and of possessing an ambition — and skill for moneymaking — far beyond that of the men around her. Paradoxically, however, the structure of power in the film's narrative is such that traditionally feminine attributes, positions, and practices also function as the very condition for Ma's capture. Ma is ultimately unreliable as a criminal because of family attachments — in this case an overwhelming devotion to her grandson. *Queen of the Mob*'s revised ending suggests that separation from the child, and not death, was for Ma the ultimate punishment. Thus, cultural norms double as a strategy for the enforcement of the law.

Subsequent cinematic representations of Ma Barker drew their story lines directly from Hoover's published accounts of her life, amplifying rather than mitigating his depiction of Ma as "she-wolf." That Hoover's version of Ma's story would prevail makes sense, given how often Ma's demise, along with John Dillinger's, was cited as the moment that the FBI had succeeded in ending the gangster era in the

United States. Recounted as having ushered in the FBI's newly professional period, Ma's 1935 death receives mention in the FBI headquarters' public tour, initiated in Washington, D.C., that same year.[19]

Flush with its mid-1930s success in the war against gangland, the FBI continued to make use of the "public enemy" formula in the shifting political climate of the early 1940s and beyond. Around the time the *Persons in Hiding* series went into production in 1939, Germany had invaded Poland and U.S. involvement in World War II seemed imminent. Suddenly, the gang-busting G-men found it necessary to morph into the spy-busting G-men. *Queen of the Mob* had done a reasonable box office, but by the time agents led her gently offscreen in 1940, Ma Barker was becoming something of an outdated symbol. It would be only a few years, however, before Ma resurfaced in popular culture.[20] Hoover's "*Real* Public Enemy" would prove an apt icon for a post–World War II culture preoccupied with cold war anxieties, child rearing, and rigid gender roles enacted in relation to the nuclear family and domestic space.

Ironically, the man who once rejected Hoover as lacking an understanding of show business happened to consider Hoover's "Mother Barker" rather well suited for it.[21] Radio personality and producer Phillips H. Lord wrote the script for Ma Barker's second onscreen incarnation, *Guns Don't Argue*. First broadcast piecemeal on television in 1955, the story was reissued by Visual Drama, Inc., as a feature-length film in 1957, by which time rural gangland stories were nostalgia pieces, representative of a simpler time. But the Ma Barker story line perfectly reflected contemporary fears of "Momism," or the destructive power of mothers over their husbands and sons. According to Philip Wylie, who coined the term in 1942, "Momism" was the dangerous product of a wartime tendency for "mother-worship"; women thereafter came to dominate and infantilize their offspring, rendering their male children particularly vulnerable to a self-serving "Gynecocracy."[22] *Guns Don't Argue* enacts the "Momist" vision of a deviant woman with the power to produce deviant men — either by dominating them or by giving birth to them.

Unlike *Queen of the Mob*, which avoided direct mention of the real-life characters on whom it was based, *Guns Don't Argue* purported to be a documentary about Ma Barker and other prominent underworld figures of the 1930s. (This absurd claim to authenticity is unintentionally opened to question by the film's tagline: "and dead men tell no tales.") The story opens with an FBI agent's voice-over dedication "to the men who overcame a period of gangster violence unmatched in criminal history." While the camera pans a quaint 1950s-style neighborhood, the offscreen voice (symbol of the continued authority of the state) intones how, in 1934, "your town, my town, *any* town in the USA" was in peril as criminals freely roamed the countryside. The film culminates with a fictional heist involving a who's-who list of 1930s baddies: John Dillinger, Homer Van Meter, Baby Face Nelson, and the Barker-Karpis gang. This final heist is contrived and directed by a Ma Barker closely resembling the Ma whom Hoover described in *American Magazine.* Actress Jean Harvey plays Ma as the violent puppeteer behind her "spawn of hell."[23]

Ma and two of her grown sons first appear gathered around the kitchen table. Son Dock Barker lifts a machine gun from the table and brandishes it admiringly before his brother Fred. "What a saxophone!" he whistles. The camera pulls right to reveal Ma, who jerks the gun from Dock's hands: "Make way for a music lover!" Physically, the 1957 "Ma" who snatches the symbolic phallus from her sons presents a stark contrast to the small and frail Blanche Yurka who played Ma in 1940. *Guns Don't Argue*'s Jean Harvey is a massive, wide-shouldered, broad-hipped woman who appears even larger with the help of black, thick-soled orthopedic shoes. Her costume is consistent throughout the film; she wears plain housedresses and aprons with her hair pulled severely off her face into a gray-white bun. After seizing the gun, Ma appears in close-up against a vacant backdrop; she shoots wildly and scowls into the camera as the voice of the FBI agent-narrator intones: "Crime breeds crime. And one gang of outlaws was linked to another. In the Middle West there was a church-going woman with four sons. To make certain her fierce pride in them would be justified, she taught them all she knew." Emphasized here are Ma's religious background and convictions (of which Hoover's article made conspicuous mention) and the contaminated nature of what Ma had passed on to her progeny, by way of knowledge or genetics.

"As a planner and caser of jobs, Ma Barker had no equal," says the narrator. Several scenes depict Ma as a criminal genius for whom all other outlaws aspired to work. In one especially improbable moment, Dillinger and Baby Face Nelson watch intently as Ma gives them orders on how to rob a bank she has cased. She demonstrates the particulars of the plan with a three-dimensional map, complete with toy cars. The success of the bank job depends on Alvin Karpis successfully delivering a baby carriage filled with guns. The carriage, apt trademark for a matriarchal gang, could be read as symbolizing the concealed menace of maternal caretaking and influence.[24] It may also have been a deliberate nose thumbing at Karpis, who, as the only one of the film's real-life gangsters still alive and still imprisoned, had allegedly vowed to kill and discredit Hoover for defaming Ma.[25]

Fred, Dock, and Lloyd Barker come across as puerile and weak. Ma must coerce them, with shouting and blows, to enact the schemes she designs. When Ma declares that their next job will be a kidnapping, the "boys" — in spite of their advanced ages, the "Barker boys" never became men — worry about committing a federal crime and the possibility of being pursued by "those G-men who can carry guns!" Ma scoffs at their fear: "The FBI . . . college boys! Get one of 'em in front of a machine gun, his hide's no tougher than the local laws'." The film then cuts to the narrator and another FBI agent, who confesses he is apprehensive about capturing Ma. The second agent sadly strokes his hat, noting: "'Ma,' that's what I call my mother." "Yeah, well, don't get sentimental about this one — it could kill ya," retorts the agent-narrator.

In fact, the men in Ma's life prefer death to the possibility of tangling with her. Eldest son Herman kills himself to avoid arrest because his mother taught him that the "worst sin in the world is to get caught." Ma's perpetually drunk second husband, Arthur, actually consents to being murdered rather than having to return to the overbearing Ma.[26] Only gang member Alvin Karpis displays any hint of rebellion. At one point Ma smashes Karpis's bottle of beer against a wall with the stern order, "In my outfit, no liquor and no dames!" Karpis starts from his chair, fists clenched, but the conventions of sex will not permit him to strike the elderly woman who is also his boss. Teeth gritted in frustration, he resumes his seat. But the "conventions of sex" have actually been muddied and *that*, the film intimates, is Ma's real crime. When Ma declares her outfit free of alcohol and "dames," she may be renouncing (for reasons of religion and self-discipline) two things her male compatriots are supposed to enjoy. But the no-dames rule also marks Ma out as not fully female and thus as a gender-confounding member of what Wylie dubbed Momism's "thundering third sex."[27]

As really did happen, Ma and Fred are ultimately cornered in their Florida cottage hideout. But *Guns Don't Argue* presents one significant inaccuracy: two agents stage the ambush alone. Ma somehow senses the lawmen's presence and orders her son to start shooting. When Fred protests, saying he would rather surrender and live, Ma becomes enraged: "You gutless little punk! Start shootin' or I'll slaughter you!" Even after Fred is hit by a bullet, she admonishes him to get back on his feet and keep firing. Only when Fred dies does Ma temporarily give up the fight, dabbing her eyes with her apron. Solemn music sounds as the narrator's voice chronicles the change: "Ma Barker, for a moment, softened. She became like a normal mother. Tenderness — a real sorrow — showed through the callus of viciousness."

Lest viewers feel any inordinate pity for Ma, her mourning lasts no more than a few seconds. In a flash she is back on her feet, shooting determinedly from the front window of the house. The audience watches her from a vantage point within the house, as though they, too, are members of her gang. With the FBI men offscreen and silent, Ma has the last word in the fight: "Those dirty butchers! Butchers! Dirty butchers!" She keeps shooting even when, presumably hit many times, she begins sinking slowly to her knees. A small painting of an American Indian on the rear wall — a reference to the belief that Ma possessed a "touch of Indian blood"[28] — becomes the final shot's focus as Ma slips out of view.

Only three years elapsed between the theatrical release of *Guns Don't Argue* and its near-remake, *Ma Barker's Killer Brood* (tagline: "No. 1 Female Gangster of All Time!"). The two films shared the same director and coproducer, but the latter's script was by F. Paul Hall, a little-known writer whom a *Los Angeles Times* review chastised for not having done more with "all the history" behind the nonfictional Ma Barker.[29] In fact, Hall drew his material from what were supposed to be the best "historical sources" available to him — the *American Magazine* article and the Ma Barker chapter from Hoover's *Persons in Hiding*. Hall's script therefore imagines

153

what the Barker boys might have been like when they were truly little boys and spec- ulates about the dynamic between Ma and the boys' father. Actress Lurene Tuttle's Ma Barker, although more emotive and physically vulnerable than Jean Harvey's creation, exhibits all the same traits of Momism as her predecessor: she is domi- neering, selfish, and materially acquisitive. But the Ma of *Ma Barker's Killer Brood* plays to other of Philip Wylie's famous complaints about moms, thus ratcheting up the character's parasitism, hypocrisy, and ruthlessness. Tuttle's Ma owes some of her wile to the cloaks of religious piety and hysterical tears, which she slips on and off with slithering ease.

As *Guns Don't Argue* implied with its pseudodocumentary format, *Ma Barker's Killer Brood* boldly declares that its story is true: "This story is true, documented from police records, newspaper files, and eyewitness reports. It is the sadistic career of Katherine Clark Barker, master of crime who taught her sons that the only crime was to 'get caught.' So cunning was this evil genius that in almost two decades of robbery, kidnapping, and murder, she herself was never once arrested. Ma Barker, mother to the underworld and Public Enemy."

The *Los Angeles Times* entertainment reporter couldn't resist a joke about how thoroughly "Mother Barker . . . the FBI's all-time pin-up girl," would appall child- rearing expert Dr. Benjamin Spock. "To think she isn't a fiction. Ugh!" [30] The *Los Angeles Mirror-News* echoed this sense of revulsion: "Miss Tuttle [as Ma] pre- sents a strong case against maternity." [31] By 1960, the Ma Barker tale's authenticity was accepted without question. The "evil genius" had also, by 1960, become the stuff of parody and camp (Ma as "pin-up girl" or as superlative parenting "don't"). But Ma Barker still represented ongoing anxieties surrounding motherhood and re- production as dangerously destabilizing when not contained by a system of mascu- line preeminence and mothering in service to the state. Any "case against mater- nity" was a case not only against the vision of a criminally violent Ma Barker but against any mother who, like Ma, challenged a cold war–era domestic ideology that relied on economically and politically subordinate women to serve as guardians of public morality.

Ma Barker's Killer Brood opens with the Barker family assembled in a church pew, the perfect family. Her smiling husband on one side and three neatly dressed little sons on the other, Ma casually confiscates a slingshot from her youngest, with a know- ing "boys-will-be-boys" glance. Both parents watch with pride as the eldest Barker child, Herman, plays the violin before the congregation. But when the Barkers return to their shabby home, all personalities except Mr. Barker's are instantly trans- formed. The boys throw off their church clothes with bitter complaints. Ma begins screaming at Herman for shaming the family at the service. Violins, she says, are only for the sissies she despises. When an ineffectual Mr. Barker attempts to stand up for his son, Ma grows angrier, grabs Herman's instrument, and breaks it over her knee. She orders her husband, who encouraged Herman's musical training, to take a look at their other, more productive sons. The three younger boys triumphantly step forward with the fistfuls of money their mother directed them to steal from the church's collection plate.

The audience is meant to sympathize with Herman, the only "good" son and, not coincidentally, the only one influenced by his father. When Herman is caught engaging in a petty theft that his mother ordered him to commit, Ma sobs and smothers him with kisses while in the presence of the sheriff. She also proudly asserts her son's regular church attendance. As soon as Ma gets Herman back to the house, however, she drops the loving mother act and strikes the boy fiercely. "Don't . . . get . . . caught!" A blow accompanies each word. The audience sees a high-angle close-up of Herman's face from Ma's viewpoint; the little boy looks terrified and then resigned. Ma will continue to test and mercilessly torment her oldest son, until he is driven to suicide.

When Mr. Barker resignedly suggests that he will begin whipping his sons for their misdeeds, and reluctantly unfastens his belt, Ma swings at him with a flyswatter. A fearful Mr. Barker warns Ma that God will strike her down for corrupting their sons. Ma mocks her husband's faith and argues that their children's delinquency owes to their father's failure as a male provider. Citing her own childhood poverty, and the cruelty of those who mocked her for it, as justification for her boys' crimes, Ma ridicules her husband's reliance on scriptures as a signature of the assenting poor: "Too much Bible and too little beef. Too many psalms and too little sowbelly. We don't need your chicken feed and we don't need *you*. So why don't you beat it?" The guilt-ridden Barker patriarch agrees to move out and will not consent to Herman's frantic pleas that he go along. Much later in the film, the Barkers are reunited at Herman's funeral. Mr. Barker tentatively approaches Ma, saying, "Katie, this didn't have to happen." She wails in response: "I know. If only you'd been a better father!" Mr. Barker's face contorts, and he slips out of the frame for the final time.

Ma arranges for another funeral in dispatching her second husband, Arthur, whose drunken ways have blown the gang's cover. She does not have her sons kill him, as happened in *Guns Don't Argue*, but instead forces Arthur to play Russian roulette. Laughs Ma, "I'm just about to divorce you — the quick way!" Her sons are delighted: "Ma, you are the slickest!" Ma's slickness in this film again extends to her role as the master planner and caser of bank robberies. But, in a departure from any written record, *Ma Barker's Killer Brood* imagines Ma as also participating in her sons' various holdups and kidnappings. Ma's presence adds an extra note of sadism to the Barker-Karpis gang's crimes, as in the moment when an enraged Ma crushes a guard between her automobile and his armored truck and then twice runs over him to ensure that he is dead.

In one final horrific crime Ma orders the death of a doctor who botched Alvin Karpis's and Fred's plastic surgeries. Her method of death is as cruel as possible. The doctor is trussed with ropes in the backseat of an automobile, doused with gasoline, and set aflame. Delirious with fear, the doctor pleads with his anonymous killer, represented only by a pair of male hands. When the doctor begins to burn, he reveals the name of she who ordered the killing: "It was Ma Barker," he squeals. "Ma Barker!" The flaming car hurtles off a cliff. The producers also utilized this scene under the movie's opening credits but edited it differently to imply that the offscreen assassin is, in fact, Ma.

The final, Florida-cottage scene in *Ma Barker's Killer Brood* resembles that in *Guns Don't Argue* but has far more dialogue and an extra scene in which the hubris of a pair of local police officers ("I'm gonna get the Barkers!") leads to their swift extermination. Ma also attempts to snare two FBI agents by making it appear that Fred is holding her hostage. The agents are skeptical, however, especially when Ma, as purported victim, whips out a rifle from beneath her apron. A shoot-out ensues, and Fred repeatedly tries to surrender. Ma's reaction, by this time, is predictable: "You gutless punk, you're as yellow as your old man! Stop shakin' and start shootin'. Start shootin' or I'll drill ya myself. I'd rather see one of my sons dead than a coward!"

When Fred dies, Ma has no moment of tender sorrow as she did in *Guns Don't Argue.* She weeps over his bloodstained form, but her reaction is still one of rage at the barriers of class and at the lawmen she regards as having unjustly murdered her offspring. She rips madly through the cottage's screen door, blindly firing her weapon and screeching: "They was always against us. Don't you see we had to fight? I'll kill you, ya butchers!"

Symbolically, at least, the discarded Barker father has the last word. At film's end Ma's narrative voice-overs are replaced by those of a stern-voiced male reciting scripture in the style of Mr. Barker: "For a good tree bringeth not forth corrupt fruit. Neither do the corrupt tree bringeth forth good fruit." Referring to the Barkers and other underworld characters, the voice concludes: "None left his mark. Each left his stain." But, as with all other Ma Barker movies, in *Ma Barker's Killer Brood* Ma leaves no literal stain at all. Unlike Fred, Ma never bleeds, perhaps because that image might lend truth to her characterization of the G-men as "butchers." Filled with bullets, Ma merely sinks to her knees and then flops dramatically into a swamp. The FBI agents stand with expressions of distaste over the dead body:

> First Agent: "If you didn't know the old witch, you'd think she was somebody's sweet old grandmother."
> Second Agent: "Yeah — like the wolf in Red Riding Hood!"

Ma's memory might have ended there but for the 1968 parole of longtime prisoner Alvin Karpis, who immediately produced a memoir denying Ma's role within the Barker-Karpis gang. Coincidentally, American International Pictures (AIP), a studio famous for churning out youth-oriented horror flicks, that same year had commissioned a Ma Barker script that might exploit the success of Arthur Penn's 1967 *Bonnie and Clyde.* Postponed in the wake of the Robert Kennedy assassination, AIP's Ma movie was finally produced under the direction of Roger Corman in

2. "The Family That Slays Together Stays Together." Ma Barker (Shelley Winters) and her murderous brood in a promotional still from *Bloody Mama* (1970). Courtesy of the Academy of Motion Picture Arts and Sciences.

August 1969, just as the Manson family murders hit the headlines. Suddenly, *Bloody Mama*'s tagline, "The family that slays together stays together," seemed less a parody of a slogan about family prayer than a tasteless exploitation of current events.

Of course, AIP had long specialized in monster and exploitation pics, and *Bloody Mama* delivers both. Shelley Winters's Ma Barker, who speaks approvingly of lynching and sports an oversized cross around her neck, is a caricature of southern Ozark prejudice and warped religiosity. The 1970 release features the usual host of Ma Barker traits but magnified to the level of outrageous perversion. For example, Ma's love for her unsavory sons goes beyond possessiveness. The Barker sons are presented as infantilized and sexually confused by the hyperbolized Oedipal love behind Ma's habit of alternately bathing or bedding them. In an early scene establishing Ma's contradictory relationship with her offspring, she chastises the boys for cursing, lies to protect them from rape charges, and then chastises them again — for raping a woman below their social class. She does all this while washing the "boys" (all grown men) in a wooden tub.

Ma's strange devotion to her children is explained by the near-silent opening sequence, in which teen-aged Kate Barker is accosted in a forest by her father and two brothers. After the implied incestuous rape, a tearful Kate fumes: "Gonna have me some boys and it wasn't any one of 'em who wouldn't kill for me and didn't kill for me or me for them. That's what you call family. Mama's boys!" Thus the film emulates a classic Freudian read of a victimized and frustrated woman as having given birth to sons to make up for her own "lack." However, Ma Barker ends up more often killing for her sons than they for her. And she takes particular satisfaction in torturing other women. For instance, to effect her sons' escape from a bank holdup, Ma forces four "fat ladies" of her own age to cling to the outside of the speeding getaway car. Citing the need to get rid of dead weight, Ma then pushes the largest and most frightened of the old women off into the road, where she is subsequently struck by a police car.

When perpetually high Barker son Lloyd (Robert De Niro) reveals the gang's identity to a young female vacationer, Ma insists that this security risk be eliminated and drowns her in a bathtub. The murder is eerily shot from an impossible viewpoint beneath the tub; the camera looks up at the panicked young woman's face, held underwater by Ma, whose own face is bathed in unnatural light. Ma's sons are also visible, standing around the tub in passive attendance of what their mother seems to be experiencing as a moment of religious rapture. Unlike previous versions of Ma, who consciously used piety as a disguise, *Bloody Mama*'s Ma is a true believer and master of twisting biblical teachings to her own ends. Whereas other cinematic Ma Barkers had moments of misgivings about their criminal activities, Shelley Winters's Ma never falters in her conviction of her own righteousness and state of persecution.

The Barker sons' prostitute-companion, Mona, confronts Ma after the drowning, backing down only when Ma threatens to drown her also. "There's nothin' you won't do, is there Ma?" says Mona. Ma responds philosophically: "It's supposed to be a free country, Mona. But unless you're rich, it ain't free and you know that. So I aim to be freer than the rest of the people." To cheer her family after the killing, Ma plays the piano, singing the pro-peace anthem "I Didn't Raise My Boy to Be a Soldier" and insisting that the others join in.

Condemned as a "vile exercise" and "Mommie and Clyde,"[32] *Bloody Mama* yet earned the praise of a few critics who lauded it as "more honest than *Bonnie and Clyde*" for refusing to mythologize its subjects. One such defender, writing in 1980, quoted Hoover's *American Magazine* article as proof that *Bloody Mama* got it right.[33] But *Bloody Mama* dramatically departs from the Hoover-endorsed Ma in that the G-man had become irrelevant, a stale symbol of antiyouth authority on par with Ma's out-of-touch parent. In previous films the Barker gang relied on its innocuous image as a multigenerational family. *Bloody Mama* subverts this logic, implying that the family is, in fact, an insidious social structure. Although the Barker sons do exhibit an intense loyalty to their mother, they also chafe under her control, and this tension seems manifest in the sons' various foibles: alcoholism in Arthur ("Dock"), drug addiction for Lloyd, and psychopathic urges in Herman. Fred is pegged as the homosexual lover of Kevin Dirkman (read Alvin Karpis) and is most distressed when his mother insists on sampling Kevin's affections.

The FBI is a nondescript, almost incidental force in the film, appearing only minutes before its conclusion. By the time agents move against the Barkers, the family has already started to disintegrate from within, thanks to the interventions of the millionaire Samuel Pendleberry, Barker kidnap victim. Pendleberry disturbs the sons with blue eyes that resemble their father's; he also indirectly chides Herman for being cowed by his mother/boss: "It's a hell of a thing to be without power, sonny boy." Herman is less infuriated than he is deeply moved by this observation and by Pendleberry's promise that "If I were your father, I'd take each one of you over my knee and give you the whaling of your lives."

After collecting Pendleberry's ransom, Ma spitefully insists that they kill him anyway because he rebuffed her amorous advances and rebuked her for swearing. Ma's reign as gang leader officially ends when the boys take Pendleberry into the woods and fire off their guns but set the prisoner free. Herman then officially wrests control of the gang by knocking Ma to the ground when she tries to give him an order. "You're an old lady, Mama. You just can't go beatin' up on grown men like they was little babies. It just ain't ladylike." Sprawled in an unflattering pose on the floor, Ma reacts with a bewildered senility that will remain with her until the movie's end: "Herman? Is that you, Herman?" Herman takes Mona's hand and leads her from the room, thus reasserting a "natural" order of male-led, heterosexual relations.

In an inaccurate re-creation of the final Florida shoot-out with the FBI, Ma is trapped in the cottage with all her sons except Lloyd, who has, moments before, died of a drug overdose. A pregnant Mona has previously fled. Kevin remains, but tries to bargain with the G-men. "I'm not a Barker!" he screams. "You bet your sweet ass you ain't," Ma says coldly, and guns him down. One by one, the remaining Barker brothers fall until only Herman and Ma are left. In a twisted and delayed version of Herman Barker's real-life suicide, Herman very deliberately kills himself in front of his mother. A crowd of picnicking families gather outside the besieged cottage and clap as Ma breaks a second-story window, props her submachine gun on a needlepoint Bible-verse pillow, and begins firing with a vengeance on the agents. The film freezes at the moment she is shot; Ma is never shown dying and, despite the title, never bleeds. *Bloody Mama* ends with a shot of a three-cent postage stamp depicting Whistler's Mother. The stamp logo bears sardonic witness to the film's message: "In Memory of the Mothers of America."

In the first twenty-five years after her death Ma Barker went from corrupt grandmother (1940), to unnatural amazon (1957), to wily, class-conscious coquette (1960). In these earliest films Ma did not stand as protagonist, nor was she a clear-cut villain. She was, instead, a screen on which the "secret threats" of a particular age could be most readily projected. Ma therefore stood for mothers (and women in general) deemed responsible for an increasingly consumer-oriented world, for the "male weakness" accompanying shifts in the economy, and for children raised not to embrace (or to embrace too fervently) the morals of a democratic, capitalist system.

Regardless of the time or style in which Ma was imagined, almost all films about the Barkers underscored the necessity of a heroic FBI. Each dramatization may have offered, for its audience's pleasure, the spectacle of the Barkers' grotesque behavior. But each also rearticulated the need for a state power that could defuse threats to a father-centered, heteronormative family unit by destroying inherently violent aberrations in that unit. In this way the Ma Barker films perfectly mirrored a half-century of bureau philosophy under the direction of J. Edgar Hoover.[34] That formula broke down by 1970, however, by which time both Ma Barker and Hoover's G-man were repositioned in popular culture as menacing, out-of-touch zealots.

Notes

Thanks to Margot Canaday, Robin Hemenway, Kate Kane, Lary May, Adam Sitze, and Kevin Strunk for their helpful feedback on this essay.

1. J. Edgar Hoover with Courtney Ryley Cooper, "The *Real* Public Enemy No. 1," *American Magazine*, April 1936, 16.

2. Hoover reminded journalists that "Ma told her boys never to be taken alive" ("Barker Gang Man, Woman Under Arrest," *New York Times*, Jan. 17, 1935). In "The *Real* Public Enemy No. 1" Hoover claimed that "there was no surrender in the heart of Ma Barker or that of her dominated son" (122–123). For other accounts of the shoot-out see Herbert Corey, *Farewell Mr. Gangster! America's War on Crime* (New York: Appleton-Century, 1936), 68–69; and Melvin Purvis, *American Agent* (Garden City, N.Y.: Doubleday, Moran, 1936), 166.

3. Hoover with Cooper, "*Real* Public Enemy," 17.

4. See, e.g., Hoover's address to the General Federation of Women's Clubs in 1938: "J. E. Hoover Urges Women Aid Work," *New York Times*, May 18, 1938, 22.

5. Hoover's *American Magazine* article was ghostwritten for him by former circus-reporter-turned-journalist Courtney Ryley Cooper. FBI records show that Cooper's research for "The *Real* Public Enemy No. 1" relied heavily on an interview with Ma's estranged husband, George Barker. Cooper's correspondence with Hoover and other bureau members indicates that he did not conduct this interview himself and, in fact, had never met any of the Barkers. Yet the article contains descriptive flourishes written in the first person to deliberately imply that he (Cooper writing in the person of Hoover) had personally spoken with George Barker. It also implied that Hoover had stared into Ma's eyes, which had, in the language of the article, "always fascinated me [Hoover]. They were queerly direct, penetrating, hot with some strangely smoldering flame, yet withal as hypnotically cold as the muzzle of a gun. The same dark, mysterious brilliance was in the eyes of each of her four sons" (17, 118).

6. The Barkers kidnapped the wealthy St. Paul brewer William Hamm and ransomed him for $100,000. A year later the gang snatched Edward Bremer, a prominent Minneapolis banker, and demanded twice as much ransom. They again were successful in collecting the money and releasing their hostage. However, Arthur "Dock" Barker left a fingerprint on a gasoline container, making it possible for the FBI to connect the gang with the crime.

7. FBI file 7-576-241, "The Kidnaping of Edward George Bremer" (Nov. 19, 1936), 3–4. FBI Freedom of Information Act Reading Room, Washington, D.C.

8. See Hoover with Cooper, "*Real* Public Enemy," 121. The *American Magazine* article describes Ma as a shrewd crime consultant whom "[c]riminals from a dozen penitentiaries sought . . . out." In fact, Ma's deviance seems to have been limited to her willingness to harangue those who would punish her sons' wrongdoing, especially when they were very young. When they were grown, she wrote near-illiterate letters to their jailers, decrying both their poor treatment in prison and her own dire poverty without their support. See, e.g., FBI file 62-21526-252, "Courtney Ryley Cooper" (June 20, 1936). FBI Freedom of Information Act Reading Room, Washington, D.C.

9. Abridged versions of Ma's biography—most lifted word for word from "The *Real* Public Enemy No. 1"—instantly appeared in the *Nashville Banner, Hartford Courant, Tulsa Daily World, Milwaukee*

Journal, and the *Kansas City Star.* These accounts were later cited verbatim in crime biographies and FBI histories.

10. Alvin Karpis with Bill Trent, *The Alvin Karpis Story* (New York: Coward, McCann, and Geoghegan, 1971), 80.

11. Hoover with Cooper, *"Real* Public Enemy," 121, 118.

12. As in his *American Magazine* articles, in *Persons in Hiding* Hoover identified himself as a lone crusader for the truth: "I'm going to tell the truth about these rats. I'm going to tell the truth about their dirty, filthy, diseased women. I'm going to tell the truth about the miserable politicians who protect them and the slimy, silly or sob-sister convict lovers who let them out on sentimental or illy-advised paroles. If the people don't like it, they can get me fired" (J. Edgar Hoover, *Persons in Hiding* [Boston: Little, Brown, 1938], xviii).

13. The first film to emerge from the series took its title from the book *Persons in Hiding.* It has frequently been misidentified as a Bonnie and Clyde story but is really a blended tale based on Bonnie Parker and Kathryn "Mrs. Machine Gun" Kelly. The composite central character in this film is "Dot Bronson," the ruthless, materialistic daughter of poor farmers. Dot's desire for wealth is symbolized by her obsession for a certain, expensive perfume, a brand dreamed up by Hoover himself, which he named "Tantalizing." The tagline for the film *Persons in Hiding* was "The Girl behind the Man behind the Gun," an indication that the male crook would never have become so successful or so thoroughly deviant without the encouragement of his "girl" and acquisitive wife. Ultimately, Dot's telltale "tantalizing" scent leads to her capture and imprisonment when she can't resist purchasing just one more bottle before attempting to flee the country.

14. Paramount reportedly paid Hoover $100,000 for the right to transfer four of his stories into screenplays. See *Persons in Hiding* MPAA file, Margaret Herrick Library, Academy of Motion Picture Arts and Sciences (hereafter cited as MHL-AMPAS). The studio had reason to expect a good return on its investment. *Persons in Hiding*—which served up its solemn, "What's-wrong-with-America?" sermons in a format that was part how-to manual, part crime novel, part gossip column—had proved so popular that it had to go through several extra press runs in its first year out. The *Persons in Hiding* films also fit neatly with the (anti-)gangster films that proliferated in the wake of the 1934 Motion Picture Production Code.

15. The Motion Picture Production Code Administration dispatched an early version of the *Queen of the Mob* script to the Department of Justice. In response the assistant to the district attorney, Joseph Mulcahy, wrote to PCA chief Joseph Breen a frank letter in which he condemned the script for "exploiting the accomplishments of a Ma Barker type of lawbreaker and for no good purpose." Mulcahy also earnestly warned Breen that "no one seriously engaged in law enforcement would approve the picture." Mulcahy's letter was dated January 16, 1940. A spate of testy memos among Breen and Will Hays and the Paramount scriptwriters followed. On January 22 word arrived from D.C. that "Mr. Mulcahy was wrong in his comments since J. Edgar Hoover, who *is* seriously engaged in law enforcement, has read and approved the script" (italics added). This correspondence further noted that Mulcahy had been "eliminated from the Department of Justice a few days ago." See Joseph A. Mulcahy (Justice Dept.) to Joseph Breen, Jan. 16, 1940; Luigi Luraschi to Joseph Breen, Jan. 22, 1940; both letters from the *Queen of the Mob* MPAA file, MHL-AMPAS.

16. Press packets for *Queen of the Mob* shouted of a "Reign of Terror! Ruled by a Queen of Crime Ten Times Tougher than the Toughest Man!" Hoover's face appeared on this third of the *Persons in Hiding* posters, a little larger now that the series was becoming more established. Oddly, the film's official promotional packet also connected Ma to a larger tradition of well-received outlaws such as Robin Hood, thus underscoring the ambiguity behind the appeal of entertainment based on criminal legends.

17. *Film Daily, Motion Picture Herald,* and the *New Yorker* gave the film favorable reviews. They also frequently misidentified the story line as strictly based on the facts of the real Ma Barker's life. Only a reporter for *Variety* wondered if the whole thing weren't perhaps "handed a sugary coating in several episodes." *Queen of the Mob* MPAA file, MHL-AMPAS; "Queen of the Mob," *Variety,* July 3, 1940, 18.

18. In speeches and written reports of the 1930s Hoover worried often about women being underestimated in their capacity as criminals. As he wrote in *Persons in Hiding,* "When a woman does turn professional criminal, she is a hundred times more vicious and dangerous than a man . . . [and] acts with a cold brutality seldom found in a man" (quoted in Anthony Summers, *Official and Confidential: The Secret Life of J. Edgar Hoover* [New York: G. P. Putnam's Sons, 1993], 69).

19. A head shot of Ma Barker, enlarged and mounted on a cutout of a woman's silhouette, appears in the FBI tour of today. Similar cutouts appear of Bonnie and Clyde, George "Machine Gun" Kelly, and Pretty Boy Floyd.

20. Indeed, the Ma Barker–inspired "Ma Jarrett" would appear in 1949's *White Heat.*

21. At midcentury gangster stories had not disappeared entirely from the public radar, as the long-running radio series *Gangbusters* could attest. Phillips H. Lord had initiated the series as *G-Men* in 1935, with the cooperation of Hoover and his FBI. Exasperated by the bureau's insistence that *G-Men* scripts avoid sensational details common to the action-detective genre, Lord terminated the partnership after only thirteen episodes. He then relaunched the series as the unauthorized, but far more colorful, FBI drama *Gangbusters*, which stayed on the airwaves until 1957 and, in 1954, crossed over to television. Richard Gid Powers, *G-Men: Hoover's FBI in American Popular Culture* (Carbondale: Southern Illinois University Press, 1983), 207–216.

22. Philip Wylie, *Generation of Vipers* (1942; rcpr. New York: Holt, Rinehart, and Winston, 1955), 194–217.

23. Hoover with Cooper, "*Real* Public Enemy," 16.

24. Michael P. Rogin, "*Kiss Me Deadly*: Communism, Motherhood, and Cold War Movies," in *Ronald Reagan, the Movie: And Other Episodes in Political Demonology* (Los Angeles: University of California Press, 1987), 243–244.

25. Karpis with Trent, *Alvin Karpis Story*, 80–91.

26. Late in her life the real Ma Barker did keep company with Arthur Dunlop but never married him. Dunlop did turn up murdered, and popular accounts, including Hoover's, fingered Ma as the culprit. Karpis insisted Ma knew nothing of the killing, which he claimed was carried out by persons outside the Barker-Karpis gang.

27. Wylie, *Generation of Vipers*, 204.

28. FBI file 7-576-241, 3.

29. Charles Stinson, "Dr. Spock Would Rap Ma Barker's Method," *Los Angeles Times*, Feb. 5, 1960, 24.

30. Ibid.

31. *Mirror-News*, "Petty Thievery," Feb. 4, 1960.

32. Charles Champlin, "Crime Saga of Ma Barker," *Los Angeles Times*, 1970.

33. Louis Black, "Bloody Mama," *Cinema Texas Program Notes* 19, no. 1 (Oct. 13, 1980): 86. Black specifically cites Hoover's alleged description of Ma's eyes (see note 5 above).

34. The contrast between benevolent, paternal G-men and destructive, out-of-control Ma was enacted most blatantly in another film on which Hoover collaborated, *The FBI Story* (Warner Bros., 1958), starring Jimmy Stewart as a saintly agent who must balance his responsibilities as a family man with his responsibilities to the bureau. Ma makes a cameo in a montage representing the gangster era. Armed, angry, and dark-complexioned, she appears in an upstairs cottage window. Stewart's voice-over ironically refers to Ma as a "sweet country gal" as he carefully aims his rifle . . . and executes her. Ma dies an awkward death at the hands of one of the United States' most beloved movie stars, further ossifying the "official" myth of Ma Barker as secret and under-appreciated peril.

Sometimes the hat makes the man. Sometimes the man makes the hat. Sometimes the man is the hat; sometimes the hat is the man. And sometimes the hat is simply a good place to aim the gun.

—MAX ERNST, in Nick Tosches, *Where Dead Voices Gather*

"Why are you so interested in the hat? Is it so important?"

He shrugged. "I don't know. I'm only an amateur detective, but it looks like a thing that might have some meaning one way or another."

—DASHIELL HAMMETT, *The Glass Key*

FOLLOWING THE CREDIT SEQUENCE and some simulated 16-mm amateur footage of a Las Vegas pool party, *Mulholland Falls* (1996) opens outside a Sunset Boulevard restaurant. The screenplay for the film describes the scene: a "6,000-pound Buick convertible pulls up in front of the restaurant. The car is black with red upholstery, and filling the seats, front and back, are FOUR VERY BIG MEN in suits and hats." The big men in suits and hats are the "mob squad," led by Maxwell Hoover (Nick Nolte), an elite yet officially unrecognized unit in the LAPD. Their job is to keep Los Angeles free of organized crime. With emphatic physical presence the four enter the restaurant and are solicited by the maitre d'hôtel: "Good evening, gentlemen," he says; "can I check your hats please?" The greeting is an unremarkable commonplace, noteworthy only insofar as it functions to authenticate the picture's re-creation of the codes and social customs of the time in which it is retrospectively set—the early 1950s. The four big men of the mob squad ignore the maitre d'hôtel's offer to check their hats and instead force their way into the restaurant to intimidate a visiting Chicago mobster and Hollywood film starlet dining with a large entourage. In the ensuing fracas, through which the mob squad's physical and quasi-legal authority is asserted, the hats remain firmly fixed. By the end of the movie, however, the credits play out to a sound-track finale entitled "Hats Off," a musical coda to an investigative narrative that has concluded with the pointed image of the mob squad's fedoras resting on each of their coffins. This convention draws on countless film images of military or police funerals, although, in the context of this film, it also suggests a symbolic reading in which the hats and their wearers have historically "checked in," that is, that the period of American history in which *Mulholland Falls* is set — an era of men and hats — is over. Indeed, the seismic cultural transformation that the film's date of 1953 presages is similarly underlined in the novelization of the film: "Elvis Presley was a year away from recording his first record, and Maxwell Hoover was only dimly aware of something called rock 'n' roll."[1] Unlike Maxwell Hoover, Elvis Presley did not wear a hat.

As a period gangster narrative set in the early 1950s, *Mulholland Falls* is emblematic of a welter of films that appeared in the wake of the success of *The Untouchables* (1987), which inaugurated a distinct cycle of gangster films sharing a common concern for crime-led narratives located in *historical* rather than contemporary settings. The predominant thematic "return" made by these films is to the pre-*Godfather* gangster figures of Prohibition and the Depression of the 1920s and 1930s. With most appearing during 1990 to 1993, the decade following *The Untouchables* produced *Miller's Crossing* (1990), *Mobsters* (1991), *The Lost Capone* (1991), *Billy Bathgate* (1991), *A Rage in Harlem* (1991), *Oscar* (1991), *Bullets over Broadway* (1994), *Devil in a Blue Dress* (1995), *The Funeral* (1996), *Last Man Standing* (1996), *Trigger Happy* (1996), *Hoodlum* (1997), *The Newton Boys* (1998), and *Lansky* (1999). Historical periods subsequent to the Prohibition era were also exploited as imaginative period locations for gangster films: for the 1950s *Havana* (1990), *Bugsy* (1991), *The Marrying Man* (1991), *Hoffa* (1992), *Mulholland Falls* (1996), and *L.A. Confidential* (1997); invoking the 1970s, *GoodFellas* (1990), *Carlito's Way* (1993), *Casino* (1995), and *Donnie Brasco* (1997).

The historical period of the early 1950s was one of major change in America's self-identity: emerging out of the shattered world order of the Second World War, national consciousness was shaped by the newly global context of political and economic realignments induced by the cold war and by the concomitant self-appointment of the United States as the world's policeman. This new world role is represented in *Mulholland Falls* by criminal investigations into the operations of the·industrial-political-military complex in secret government experimentation with nuclear testing. Domestically, big crime at this time is "organized," a corporate activity barely distinguishable from legitimate enterprise and embodied in the unidentified mob control and development of Las Vegas as a popular gambling resort. In the depiction of the early 1950s the deserts of Nevada are simultaneously occupied by both organizations, and both government and gangster organizations are given to be democratically unaccountable, hierarchical, obsessed with secrecy, violent, and corrupt. The diseased and unhealthy figuration of political and cultural power is offset by the unyielding masculinity of the mob squad, and their hats are emblematic of a nostalgic construction of masculine integrity. In this, hats function as a highly condensed signifier of the overall ideological project of *Mulholland Falls*: to offer its spectators an American past in which the national condition is mirrored by an uncorrupted form of masculinity that will be superseded by the events and transformations of the late 1950s and 1960s. Given the specific outline of the historical epoch that the film invokes, then, the earlier request for, and refusal of, the men to relinquish their head wear assumes far greater significance than simple social decorum.

As Thomas Frank illustrates, the 1960s "were hard on the American hat industry."[2] The late 1960s and early 1970s saw massive shifts in the traditional male garment industry; the domination of adult male business outfitting in the 1950s by the largely unchanging staples of hats and tailored clothing of dark suits, jackets, and trousers was ended by an economic, industrial, and cultural "revolution" that brought male clothing into the same fashion cycle that organized the production and consumption of women's dress. In February 1968 Johnny Carson wore a Nehru jacket designed by Oleg Cassini on *The Tonight Show*, precipitating an "overnight mania for the garment."[3] The "changes that followed constitute one of those highly visible and instant mass shiftings that are so often pointed to as distinguishing one historical era from another: square middle America became hip almost overnight": "Sartorial propriety seemed to vanish in many social circles and years of stasis gave way instantly to a plethora of fantastic garments. Beads and chains with large pendants were worn with the Nehru, as were square silk scarves. Nehru was soon joined by the Edwardian look, with its tight-fitting, double-breasted jacket, and then coats with the enormous 'Napoleonic' collar. Printed patterns allowed diversity amidst diversity. Flared trousers appeared."[4]

Frank's inventory of rapid style change from 1969 includes the introduction of brightly colored shirts with exceedingly long collar points, which "began to eclipse white shirts," "jackets with extremely wide lapels, extremely wide ties, extremely wide trouser cuffs, and bright colors and vivid patterns on everything."[5] After decades of relative stasis in which male business dress barely shifted from the uniform conformity of the three-button suit, white shirt, tie, and overcoat, the 1960s witnessed a tremendous speed-up of style turnovers, with stylistic novelty followed rapidly by obsolescence, that suggested that men's fashions entered a phase of rapid change in trends that brought it very close to the cycles and textures of feminine dress. The revolution in male attire conjoined with "unisex" social philosophies that sought to obliterate the meaning of sex/gender differences: "*Men's Wear* ran a feature on 'Trans-Sexual Fashion,' in which writer Jack McCloskey noted the rising popularity among the young of 'flowing scarves and look-alike vests, psychedelic prints, and perhaps even he/she caftans, serapes, djellabahs and burnooses.'"[6] Although it may ultimately have been an opportunity cynically seized by a stagnant capitalist market to increase sales on the principles of obsolescence, the overt threat to gender traditionalism and conformity expressed in the "New Individualism" of male dress was nonetheless licensed by the newly emergent social and political countercultural agencies with vested interests in challenging the hegemonic authority of white, middle-class, heterosexual, and patriarchal men: feminists, gays/lesbians, blacks and civil rights advocates, students, youth and antiwar proponents, hippie and "alternative" anticonsumerists. In this context the loss of the hat and suit suggests the further erosion of clothing to distinguish and deliver "difference"; here it is not the erosion of class distinction but the fashion system's capacity to deliver absolute *gender* distinction that is in doubt. The retro gangster films set in the 1970s (*Carlito's Way, GoodFellas, Casino, Donnie Brasco*) thus offer spectacles of male gangsters dressed to kill in pink pastel shirts, open-necked sport tops, bright checked jackets with nonmatching colored trousers, stack-heeled boots, velour tracksuits, and ethnic jewelry. The influence of countercultural style is felt too in the profligacy of facial and head hair: "Mexican" moustaches, mutton-chop sideburns, and "Afro" permed hair.

With special costuming by world-famous apparel designer Georgio Armani, *The Untouchables* marks the onset of the 1990s retro gangster film cycle; in its rehearsal of the early 1930s Chicago of Al Capone the film exemplifies a regime of signification in which the hat and suit are not simply markers of historically "authentic" male dress but are used as visual shorthand for a broader ideological operation — to reclothe male protagonists, and thus their spectators, in the garb of a bygone mode of masculinity. Putatively offering a historical enactment of the story of Capone's imprisonment not for murder, extortion, theft, or corruption but for the "soft" white-collar crime of tax evasion, *The Untouchables* is most effectively read as a male-addressed costume drama, a fictional form that uses the past to license fantasies for its contemporary audiences. As has been proposed of the welter of female-addressed literary adaptations that also proliferated during the same period, costume dramas offer the "pleasures of a spectacle of history immune from contemporary uncertainties around gender identity, personal and political struggles for economic independence, and personal autonomy in marriage, relationships or parenting."[7] Entirely compatible with contemporary conservative "backlash," "antifeminist," and "profamily" imperatives, *The Untouchables* exemplifies narratives that invoke the past as a nostalgic "return" to unchallenged patriarchal masculine integrity. And, within a framing style that repeatedly composes its male figures as objects of sartorial display, hats are central to an imaging of prefeminist male civic authority and male power. However, the reduction of hats to an unambiguous symbol of male authority, gender conformity, and masculine self-possession should be understood as a response to the gender concerns of the 1990s because, in confining the hat to fantasies of stable, hegemonic masculinity, films in this cycle efface the role played by the hat in gangster fictions of the historical period they attempt to simulate. In other words, hats in the first and subsequent cycles of 1930s gangster films were given thematic, formal, and symbolic emphases quite distinct from those that

1. Elliot Ness (Kevin Costner) in *The Untouchables* (1987), suit by Armani.

2. Al Capone (Robert De Niro) in *The Untouchables,* the best-dressed gangster in town.

characterize the 1990s retro gangster cycle. Even a short cultural history of hats in titles of this period suggests an intimate connection between the gangster film and the shifting historical configurations of masculinity through its "dressing." To illustrate more fully that the 1990s retro cycle exploits the hat in a highly specific way to create falsified *certainty* around masculinity, previous uses of the hat in gangster film and popular fictions can be examined to demonstrate the 1990s cycle's shift away from the hat's primary historical function in an "underworld" circulation — as signifier of cultural *inversion.*

Discussing men's apparel in "tough guy" and proletarian literature of the 1930s, scholar Kingsley Widmer noted that the "narrow-brimmed felt hat — by the Thirties a cliché identifying the movie 'gun' — was favored by the hobo as a distinction over the usual workingman's cap."[8] Both the "movie gun" and the hobo saw the cap as a symbol of the proletarian class, identifying the wearer as an exploited wage earner. A fedora, conversely, announced membership of the nonproductive classes that clearly (self-)defined both the hobo and the gangster.[9] In his 1926 autobiography one-time bum and yegg Jack Black writes, "My prestige grew and I came to be accepted everywhere as 'Stetson,' which, in the language of the road, means first class."[10] The petty criminals in Edward Anderson's classic Depression-era novel *Thieves like Us* (1937) exemplify this claim to class distinction through dress: "'I know one thing,' Chicamaw said. 'I'm going to be wearing me a fifteen-dollar Stetson and a sixty-dollar suit here pretty soon or it might be a black suit with some silk plush around me, but I'm sure not going to be wearing no overalls.'"[11] White blues singer and "father of country music," Jimmie Rodgers, in his song "Blue Yodel #8," suggested his protagonist shared a similar propensity with Jack Black for smart headgear and nonproductive activity: "I'm going to town honey, what you want me to bring you back?" asks his paramour. "I want a pint of booze and a John B. Stetson hat," he replies. The John B. Stetson hat company made all kinds of hats for both men and women, and only since the 1960s has it become synonymous with cowboy hats: here, in their desire to own a Stetson hat, the protagonists in Jimmie Rodgers's song and Anderson's story signal their ideological separation from honest wage earning toil. The distinct meanings attached to various hats by figures on the borders and in the margins of mainstream society form a context in which masculinity can be negotiated around the poles of production (work) and consumption (leisure). In the sense that the woman in Rodgers's song is providing the booze and hat for her man, the male character types defined through nonproductivity and love of hats—petty criminals, hobos, and gangsters—are enlarged to include the figure of the pimp.

In his informal history of the ballad of Frankie and Johnny, John Huston writes of the milieu from which the song emerged and of the folk that peopled its bars, gambling houses, and brothels:

> [The mack] invented styles that took the eye of the sporting world at large. . . . The St. Louis flats, heel-less, and of extra length for the men off the steamboats who had gone barefoot so long they could not stand the cramp of regular shoes. Mirrors were set in the toes. Gaiters matched the velvet trouser cuff, the vest, and hat,—the Stetson high roller, with nudes and racers inlaid with eyelets in the crown. The linens were of fine quality, with starched, embroidered bosoms and cuffs,—the cuffs worn low so that the diamond solitaire on the little finger just showed. . . . And the wealth of jewelry, solvent diamonds,—diamond suspender clasps, sleeve garters, diamond initials on the watch ribbon, diamonds in the teeth.[12]

This emphasis on masculine sartorial display focused on the hat is echoed in memoirs and biographies of pre–World War II jazz musicians who, like the pimp, petty criminal, hobo, and gangster, are defined as being neither productive worker nor petty bourgeois by their excessive exhibition of "self" through costuming. Self-styled inventor of jazz, and sometime pimp, Jelly Roll Morton described how he liked to dress in his early twenties: "Those days, myself, I thought I would die unless I had a hat with the emblem Stetson in it and some Edwin Clapp shoes." Morton eventually got the hat and a pair of shoes called St. Louis Flats that "turned up, I'm telling you the truth, nearly to my ankles." Other flaneurs of his acquaintance had shoes with electric light bulbs in the toes, "so when they would get around some jane that was kind of simple and they thought they could make her, as they call making um, why they'd press a button in their pocket and light up the little bitty bulb in the toe of their shoes and that jane was claimed. It's really a fact."[13] The rather more respectable musician and composer W. C. Handy confirms Huston and Morton's images of male dress on the streets of America's emerging metropolitan centers. Recalling his nights spent on Memphis's Beale Street, Handy writes, "Scores of powerfully built roustabouts from the river boats sauntered along the pavement, elbowing fashionable browns in beautiful gowns. Pimps in box-back coats and undented Stetsons came out to get a breath of early evening air and to welcome the night."[14] Louis Armstrong recalled an image from his youth of an evening's entertainment at the notorious Funky Butt Hall:

> At the end of the night, they'd do the quadrille, beautiful to see, where everybody lined up, crossed over — if no fights hadn't started before that. Cats'd have to take their razors in with them, because they might have to scratch somebody before they left there. Fighting was only to be expected. If a cat wanted to show respect for his chick, which was rare but not unheard of, he would ask her to stick out her elbow, and he would balance his hat on it. The hats were Stetsons, brand new, and very expensive, as much as six months' salary. And if anyone so much as grazed that Stetson balancing precariously on a chick's shivering elbow, there would be hell to pay. "Did you touch my hat?" the offended party would demand. And if the other cat admitted he did, which was the manly thing to do, "he hit him right in the chops."[15]

Here the hat is a sign of a man's standing among his peers. Like many other anecdotes of Armstrong's life reported in Lawrence Bergreen's biography, this is little more than personal mythmaking that corresponds less to reality than to widespread images of black American urban life at the turn of the century (in this particular instance, to the myth and ballad of Stack O'Lee). This is a story cultural critic Greil Marcus claims "black America has never tired of hearing and never stopped living out, like whites with their Westerns."[16] A less racially essentialist reading may claim otherwise, but whether by whites or blacks the story has been tirelessly repeated.

Stack O'Lee, Staggerlee, or some other of the dozen or so variations of the name is the emperor of the many "bad man" songs that first began to appear around the turn of the century. The story centers on a dispute between Stack O'Lee and Billy Lyons that leads to Billy Lyons's murder — justified by Stack O'Lee on the grounds that Billy "dun ruint my Stetson hat, and I'm bound to take [his] life."[17]

The historical figure and the myth of Stack O'Lee was nourished in the underworld of East St. Louis's brothels and saloons, with the myth given voice and form by the area's ragtime piano professors. "You dun stole my Stetson hat and I'm bound to take your life," Stack O'Lee tells Billy Lyons in one version of the song. While not ubiquitous, the Stetson hat forms the centerpiece of most retellings of the tale — "Now what do think of that! Old Stackalee shot Billy Lyons about a damn old hat." Stetson hats appear not only in the story of Stack O'Lee but also in other "bad man" ballads such as King Brady. The denouement of one version finds him "struttin' in hell with his Stetson hat."[18] The same sartorial elegance and a similar predicament is also evident in Stavin' Chain: "Stavin's Chain is dead and gone, He's in hell with his Stetson on."[19] But it is Stack O'Lee who best defines the idea of a "bad hat," the Victorian slang name given to a bully and a rogue.

Jelly Roll Morton recalled how, in 1900, New Orleans resident Robert Charles was denied the opportunity to get his hat when the police arrested him following an altercation with his wife. Charles broke away from his captors and barricaded himself inside his house, where he set to shooting any policeman who came within his sights, thereby starting one of the worst race riots in the city's history.[20] Actually, Morton got his facts wrong, but he was close to a poetical truth. The facts behind the race riot, as reported in William Ivy Hair's study, were that Charles was wearing a brown derby hat, a white shirt, black coat, and dark striped trousers when he shot his first policeman.[21] He was still wearing the brown derby when he was shot down five days later after having shot and wounded twenty white persons and killed seven, including four policemen, with his Winchester rifle.[22] The *New Orleans Daily Picayune* considered Robert Charles the "boldest, most desperate and dangerous negro ever known in Louisiana."[23] Desperate he may have been, but according to clothing store salesman Hyman Levy, Charles liked to dress well; he was "what you call a stylish negro."[24]

In these examples the hat appears to give purpose and reason to acts of seemingly irrational brutality, yet the universality of mass-produced male head wear, such as that worn in America in the first fifty years of the twentieth century, counters the value of the hat as object and symbol and its stated significance for its wearer, suggesting not the high value in which individual lives are held but how cheaply life can be exchanged for death — over something apparently as meaningless as an argument about a hat. This is because it is not the hat itself that is of paramount importance; rather it is what it represents. Writing in 1653, James Naylor, the English evangelist and protestor against the enclosure acts, explained why he refused to remove his hat or bow his knee to those in positions of authority: "The Scripture saith he that respects persons commits sin." This message of insubordination was rebuked by punishing his body with 310 lashes at the cart's tail, the branding of his forehead and the piercing of his tongue with a red-hot iron. Naylor had answered all charges against his person without taking off his hat.[25] Respect for one's peers (or lack of it) is shown at one remove through the regard given to a hat, which in a democracy suggests, as Bob Dylan has written, "a man's hat [was] his crown"[26]—it is the mark of individual sovereignty. Yet the historical processes of industrialization, and specifically mass production under modernity, clearly challenge the authenticity of claims to the hat's capacity as index of individuality; in the emergence of mass fashion and consumption during the twentieth century the hat occupied the center of emerging tensions between self and society, mass and individual, unique and standardized. It is popular fiction that will attempt to mediate between these contradictory experiences, using the sartorial infractions of the gangster to perform anxieties around the dissolution of stable class boundaries.

Echoing the milieu of the Stack O'Lee myth, *The Bowery* (1933) represents pre-Prohibition gangland through the legendary figures of old New York's saloon culture that was so ably fixed as an image in Herbert Asbury's "informal history of the underworld," *The Gangs of New York* (1927).[27] Wallace Beery plays Chuck Connors, who runs the Bowery's most popular concert saloon. When first introduced, he is having his shoes polished as he buffs his "skimmer" (a beautifully blocked derby) with his forearm. In the next scene Connor's arrival at his saloon is announced by following the progress of his hat as it is passed from punter to punter with great care and ritual, as if it were a king's crown, before finding its resting place on a common hat rack near the bar. Connors is a braggart and exhibitionist, a comic character. Circumstances have lifted him above the mob composed of his fellow Irish Americans; he is above the horde but never apart from it, until the end of the film when he leaves the Bowery and joins the army as a private to fight in the Spanish-American war. His social standing outside the culture of the saloon cannot be sustained; as such, Connors's elevated position among his peers depends less on his economic, political, or cultural status than on his ability to stage a continuous performance of self-importance, maintained and symbolized by the overelaborate display of respect given to his hat. In this instance the hat's function is less a symbol of absolute respect (as in the ballad of Stack O'Lee) than a contribution to a sense of character defined through class and ethnicity. In *Underworld* (1927)—a film that shares a similar sensibility with *The Bowery* in its representation of gangsters as lower class—a minor character flamboyantly enters a racially mixed subterranean joint by spinning his derby on the end of his finger and rolling it down the length of his arm, giving it a final twist in the air as he bows to one and all, the routine completed as he returns the hat to his head. The hat announces character in both senses of the term: as personality and as a figure in a drama in which class and ethnicity, it is implied, are a matter of performance.

Fashion in hats changes. By the 1930s the derby's symbolic significance was increasingly used to suggest that the gangster belonged to an earlier era—an anachronism waiting to be expelled from the narrative and from the world at large. This is particularly marked in *Interns Can't Take Money* (1936), the first film based on Max Brand's character Dr. Kildare. With its glass and white walled architecture, the Moderne clean, open, and feminine space of the hospital and the production-line efficiency of the medical staff are contrasted to the obsolete Victorian and masculine world of the saloon. The oppressive effect of heavy wooden panels that create the numerous small and dark rooms is echoed in the figure of the gangster slouched against the bar in his dark suit and tilted derby, a figure lost to the modern world.

In the Prohibition drama *The Beast of the City* (1932), which focuses on antigang law enforcement, family man and chief of police James Fitzpatrick (Walter Huston) is a paragon of white, professional, middle-class virtue. He wears a beautiful cream homburg. The height of the hat's crown and its light coloring confirm a sense of the character's decorum and distinction and gives authority to his person in compositions where he is surrounded by his minions, who wear dark fedoras. His homburg is also utterly distinguished from the derby worn by the head of the gangsters. Significantly, there is none of the exhibitionist display around hats found in the subterranean spaces of *The Bowery* or *Underworld*; the hat's function in *The Beast of the City* is understated, mute, a perfect symbol of bourgeois reserve and cleanliness.

Bourgeois reserve and cleanliness are entirely absent from *City Streets* (1931). The film begins with a montage documenting bootlegging from production through to consumption. In the brewery "Big Fellow" Maskal (Paul Lukas) extorts money from a rival racketeer, and a wad of cash is produced from inside the rim of the racketeer's black derby, revealing the initials "R. Z." Following a dissolve from fermenting beer inside a barrel to swirling river water, the same hat is seen twisting and bobbing downstream. Much later in the film an automobile's car door is opened and a hat rolls out into the street; in both cases the unattended hat is a metonym for the death of its owner. The forsaking of one type of head wear for another similarly symbolizes a passing or crossing over. The Kid (Gary Cooper) is an ex-cowboy and one-time rodeo rider who is down on his luck and has taken a job working in a shooting gallery in a fun fair — he is introduced via a close-up of the back of a western-style hat he is wearing. The Kid is courting Nan Cooley (Sylvia Sidney), a gun moll who works with her father in the beer racket. She tells The Kid he should show more ambition and get into selling beer: pretty soon, she explains, he will have "cars, servants, and everything." The Kid, however, wants to play it straight, and only after he believes Nan to have been set up by the police on charges of accessory to murder does he become involved in the racket. Donning a derby and a double-breasted overcoat with a large fur collar quickly and economically represents The Kid's transition from sideshow cowboy to gangster. On Nan's release the rough underling's garb of derby and coat has gone, replaced by a beautifully cut three-piece suit, matching felt hat, and combination shoes. He has the smart automobile as well, but such superficial trappings of success no longer impress Nan; time in jail has taught her that there is no honor among the racketeers and that prison or death is always the final payment for a life of crime. Nan and The Kid eventually throw over the mobsters and leave the rackets behind. The Kid's basic goodness is underscored as he is, at best, innocent of any misdeeds and, at worst, naive in his involvement in gang activities. Furthermore, he is contrasted to the true villain of the piece, "Big Fellow" Maskal, whose affected sophistication is undercut (like Paul Muni's gangster in *Scarface*) by his ethnic accent and against whom the guileless straight shooter appears unimpeachably Anglo-American. He may only be a sideshow huckster, but the cowboy hat he is wearing when he is first introduced suggests honesty because at some level it still refers to its origin as the head wear of laboring workers. On the other hand, the derby and felt hat he wears while working for the racketeers are affectations, markers of the gangsters' misappropriation of socially legitimate clothing.

Similarly, the hats sported by the young arriviste gangsters in *Doorway to Hell* (1930), *The Public Enemy* (1931), *Scarface* (1932), *Quick Millions* (1931), and *Little Caesar* (1930) are part of a display of conspicuous consumption. As David Ruth has so cogently argued, the Prohibition gangster was "an oversized projection of the urban American seduced by the promises of consumption."[28] The image of the gangster in newly acquired suit and hat surveying himself in mirror or shopwindow is a motif common to all these films. Ruth writes:

> As they dressed the criminal in fine clothing, adorned him with jewelry, and placed him in a luxurious nightclub, writers, filmmakers, and their audiences explored the abundance of goods that had transformed their society. Through the gangster image Americans previewed new paths to individual fulfillment apparently opened by a mass-consumption economy. At the same time they pondered how the new standards of consumerism affected older categories of social order, especially class and ethnicity. These were crucial concerns, and the gangster offered not just illumination but guidance as well. The inventors of the public enemy used him to promote values about the urban consumer society he epitomized.[29]

The mass production of clothing and the concomitant promotion of style through advertising, large-circulation magazines, and department stores had the effect of negating previously identifiable signs of social difference. This development was most accentuated in the shared sartorial dress of the gangster and the banker, an image of a dissolute society Brecht had portrayed in *Threepenny Opera*. The bandit MacHeath, writes Walter Benjamin in his study of the play, was a "model of social behavior," belonging to the "new school" of criminals/bourgeois: "He misses no opportunity to take center of the stage. And he is a different man in front of bankers, a different one in front of the owners of the B. shops, a different one before the court and a different one again before the members of his gang." He proves that "one can say everything if only one has an unshakeable will."[30] This world of uncertain and unstable identities was also of concern to Brecht's French contemporaries, as Robin Walz writes in his study of surrealism and "insolent" popular culture of the 1920s and 1930s:

> The criminal element ceased to be an inferior cadre of humans, the product of biological degeneracy or environmental squalor, and instead assumed the status

of a *parallel society*, whose machinations operated at all social levels. The most dreaded criminals in the reconstituted "army of crime" were no longer working-class ruffian muggers, nor the small time swindlers dressed in overcoats and bowler hats — not even the notoriously violent Parisian *apaches*. Rather the most dangerous criminals of the 1930s were the "smiling man" of bank scams (*l'homme souriant*), the "elegantly dressed" heroin dealer (*l'homme en habit*), and the suave drug lord (*l'homme en robe de soie bleue*). "There are crooks among millionaires, just as there are crooks among beggars," warned true crime author Xavier de Hauteclocque.[31]

But whatever the truth in the dissembling of social hierarchies, there was a converse thrust to reestablish difference, as Ruth argues for the figure of the American gangster. The apparent erasure of class lines was mitigated by an overemphasis in popular cultural representations on the gangster's ethnicity that appeared to insure against assimilation. "Style," writes Ruth, "continued to provide crucial information because the gangster, in his frenetic pursuit of fashion, revealingly overstepped the boundaries of good taste. . . . [T]he over-adorned gangster buffoon carried a clear message to people from working-class and ethnic backgrounds: attempts to use possessions to rise above one's proper place in society are futile."[32] Furthermore, as the fate of the cinematic gangsters testified, access to the world of consumption was only permissible for a limited period. In death the gangster symbolically returns to the gutter from which he was born.

The gangster figure demonstrates a specific relation to dress and display, a correlation in which criminality relates as much to the gangster's exposure of the cultural instability of the categories of class, ethnicity, and consumption as to formal law breaking: the progress of the ascendant gangster is marked through visual codes in which the hat (derby vs. fedora) functions as the signifier of his temporal and figurative distance from the simply criminal. As such, the gangster's hat symbolizes a larger experience of modernity in which troubling dissolutions of traditional moral, economic, and class parameters are signified through the conflation of crime with social dissembling.

The role played by hats in American gangster culture evidently attests to a dense symbolic exchange around the liminal and provisional status of criminal identity. Further, hats are charged with political significance in their provocation of questions as to the legitimacy of class, wealth, and self-ownership. Yet the hats in the retro gangster films appearing in the 1990s make no reference to this history; indeed, the cycle itself has been defined by the very absence of any social, economic, or political resonance. As clear examples of Fredric Jameson's "le mode retro," the retro gangster cycle offers material evidence to support Jameson's observation that the postmodern cultural condition is one "beyond history."[33] Jameson's seminal analysis argues that the historical pastiche film, which demonstrates a deeply disturbing failure of real historical consciousness, is an "alarming and pathological symptom of a society which has become incapable of dealing with time and history."[34] For Jameson "historical perspective" is the marker of "critical distance," but the contemporary proliferation of aesthetic replays—pastiche, remake, adaptation, replay—of past historical forms and narratives denies this, offering "intertextuality" in its place as a "deliberate, built-in feature of the aesthetic effect," as the "operator of a new connotation of 'pastness' and pseudo-historical depth, in which the history of aesthetic styles displaces 'real' history."[35]

James Naremore also identifies the complexity of cinematic signification produced when intertextuality conjoins with "retro" settings: *Mulholland Falls* is not simply another vacuous postmodern pastiche of 1940s or 1950s crime movies but filters its "aesthetic replay" through primary visual reference to *Chinatown* (1974), itself a "retro" film already overlaid with pastiche 1940s/1950s imagery, clothing, dialogue, and narrative structure. *Mulholland Falls* is, however, distinguished from its most recent cinematic antecedent by its absolute semantic vacuity; *Chinatown*, for Naremore, offers at least *some* dimension of political critique in its exposure of corruption at the heart of families and of city politics, whereas the retro gangster films of the 1990s are "about" nothing of narrative or political substance, about little more than the "look" generated by "wide-angle lenses, low-level compositions, tracking shots, and the monochromatic look of masculine rooms with leather upholstery and parquet flooring."[36] In the same vein, the Coen brothers' *Miller's Crossing* "is 'about' smoking a cigarette in the dark while sitting next to a black telephone, with oriental rugs spread over hardwood floors and gauzy curtains wafting in the night breeze. Perhaps most of all, it is 'about' the glamour of men's hats." Accurately identifying the centrality of the hat to the signification of the retro gangster cycle, Naremore continues to elucidate the role it plays within *Miller's Crossing*:

> It begins with a surreal black hat blowing through the woods, and it repeatedly shows us gangsters peering beneath the down turned brims of their fedoras. The protagonist (Gabriel Byrne) wears a particularly dashing hat that he likes to hang on his foot when he sits in a chair with his legs crossed; at one point, making an emergency exit from his room late at night, he behaves like a latter-day cowboy, grabbing his hat and his gun rather than his shoes. Such attention to fetishistic detail is appropriate to the genre, but *Miller's Crossing* differs strikingly from any of its predecessors in its refusal to engage seriously with American political or social history. Unlike Hammett, unlike the Warner gangster films, and unlike 1970s movies such as *Chinatown* and *The Godfather*, it is incapable of (or uninterested in) creating a sense of tragedy. Moreover, in contrast to even the most conservative forms of comic parody, it does not even make us laugh at the things it imitates.[37]

Gangster pastiche films of the early 1990s are, then, critically purposeless and historically "depthless." Without the critical distance that would permit meaningful

3. Opening credit from *Miller's Crossing* (1990).

historical connection to the past, retro films overinvest in the presentation of surface styling and in generating surface connotations of "pastness" through "period" architecture, dress, interiors, fabrics, fashion, hair, and makeup. Yet, as several critics have countered, the kind of postmodernist conceptualizing that does not ask what *specific* ideological function retro films perform for their contemporary audiences is guilty of a wholesale dehistoricization of the very cultural artifacts it seeks to explicate.[38] The emphasis on surface qualities and an overly pronounced underlining of the costuming of men in tailored suits with beautifully shaped and fitted felt hats clearly does characterize the retro gangster cycle (and most emphatically in productions released around the middle of the decade). But beyond Jameson's mourning for the loss of some ill-formulated version of "real" history, or Naremore's lament for the absence of progressive social politics, ahistoricized notions of pastiche cannot address the real complexities of the recent "turn" to period film, confining their cultural significance to the "waning" of historical consciousness and domination of nostalgia in late twentieth-century Western postindustrial cultures.

It is a mistake, however, to dismiss retro films as simply the cinematic triumph of vacant style over cultural meaning. Rather, critical engagement with the proliferation of gangster films staged in "the past" must be grasped in their *connection* to—rather than evacuation of—contemporary concerns. This connection requires that titles such as *Miller's Crossing* or *The Untouchables* be located within a more effective framework to produce more critically and politically nuanced readings: what is specific to the 1990s gangster film's mutation into "period costume drama," given that this is not the first "retro" Hollywood trend to exploit Prohibition/Depression gangster stories?[39] What does the re-presentation of gangster narratives set in "the past" permit that contemporary scenarios might not? Anna Friedberg has trenchantly noted that nostalgia is an "*algia*, a painful return," but it also "offers up pleasures, albeit bittersweet ones."[40] What specific pleasures do retro gangster films offer to their contemporary audience, and how is that audience to be conceived? What is at stake here if a psychoanalytical explanation of the retro cycle suggests that the "compulsion to repeat is based on the desire to return"? Posed in these terms, the concept of empty pastiche lacks any explanatory value for analysis of a popular cinematic genre that is marked by a profound *politicization*. The mode that such politicization takes is, however, not to be found in the form that Naremore or Jameson find absent. Rather, the retro gangster cycle of the 1990s operates on the more covert terrain of sexual politics, where the nostalgic invocation of period setting is ideally placed to articulate fears and pleasures in the recuperation of "lost" gender certainties. In other words, the historical convergence of gangster narratives with the visual and aesthetic spectacle of history secured by the contemporary cinematic costume drama constitutes a powerful articulation of "nostalgia" as the vehicle for retrogressive, antifeminist, and "hypermasculinized" ideologies.

The work of "masculinization" is figured in the retro gangster genre through two operations: the resurrection of the dress codes of hegemonic masculinity and the literal and symbolic elimination of women. Taken together, the retro cycle underlines a notion that the gangster film has historically been inseparable from ideological explorations of masculinity and that each historical juncture has used the genre to give shape to prevailing concerns and uncertainties around the meaning of dominant male identity. If the logic of postmodern "nostalgia" is to sever aesthetic artifacts from the "historicity" of culture, the relocation of the hat outside of the flow of sociopolitical experience might suggest that contemporary concerns and uncertainties are better explicated through an interpretation of its *sexual* symbolism derived from Freudian psychoanalysis. Another of Louis Armstrong's anecdotes illustrates how readily the hat performs a symbolic function. Compounding a stereotypical image of the emasculating black woman, Armstrong's biographer (presenting the story as historical fact) writes that Armstrong was "wearing his best vines, out of hock for the day: a black suit, patent leather shoes, and, most impressively, a brand new Stetson hat." His wife, Daisy, appears, "flourishing her razor in his face." Louis takes off at a gallop but loses his hat: his friend, Little Head, stoops to retrieve it. "Daisy swiped his ass with her razor" and, then, "crazed with jealousy, Daisy fetched [Louis's] hat and ominously shredded it with her razor."[41] In this context the hat and phallus are coterminous, as Armstrong has lost control over both his hat and his marriage. That this is an "unnatural" state is assured in the comic tone in which the anecdote is told and, in this sexualized context, of having a friend called "Little Head"; as Stack O'Lee insisted, real men are mostly in command of their head wear. This instance classically situates the hat as detachable signifier of penis, phallus, and heterosexual masculinity; in the larger psychoanalytical story of male power, masculine identity is produced through fear of castration. It is a paradigm in which masculinity, never able to reach the illusory state of fixed identity, must continually confirm its presumption of phallic authority by rehearsing narratives that expunge castrating fears of "the feminine." The resurrection of the hat in the retro gangster films of the 1990s might, then, indicate deep-rooted anxieties about the current formation of masculine identity. This would explain why the films' overriding concern is to narrate the literal and figurative expulsion of whatever is "not masculine," in which the role played by women is pivotal.

In *The Untouchables* the *only* female role in a social order consisting entirely of men (running across the boundaries of legitimate/illegitimate) is the wife of Eliot Ness (Kevin Costner). Framed in close-up and physically static in the sentimentalized space of the domestic, the "wife at home with the children" provides the ideological anchor for the Federal Treasury rookie, set adrift in an amoral, corrupt, and brutal environment. Yet, as a classic trope in the coding of masculinity, the feminine/maternal is simultaneously the source of male vulnerability. With cursory narrative motivation the wife and children are shipped out from Chicago to a place of safety beyond the reach of Capone-authorized reprisals. Once dispensed, the male bonding that has assembled the unlikely group of "untouchables"—incorruptible law enforcement agents—intensifies. In an emotional environment in which women and children are emotional liabilities, and the personal ethics of other men—gangsters, businessmen, politicians, police, and the judiciary—are indistinguishable, *The Untouchables* invokes a paranoiac atmosphere in which only Ness's relationship with the veteran Irish beat cop Jimmy Malone (Sean Connery) is secure. As father figure to Ness's naive son, Malone functions as mentor to guide Ness not only to the capture of Capone but to the assumption of a properly "tested" manhood. Through "trial by action thriller ordeal" Ness and the audience are reassured by the film's definition of a truly masculine ideal: physical, rugged, independent, resourceful, "untouchable." There is no doubt as to what a Real Man's Man is—the Man Alone or, better, the Man without Women. With the bloody sacrifice of Malone's life comes the restitution of normalized heterosexual relations; Ness is reunited with his family, although the intensity of the men's emotional connection is recalled when the film closes with Ness sentimentally clutching Malone's officer's badge in his hand. It would seem that the wife and family element is included simply to prevent the film's adulation of homosocial attachments from slipping into the more dangerous realm of homoerotic desire.

If *The Untouchables* uses conventions from the gangster genre to protect the heterosexual domestic space by exclusion of the female from the homosocial sphere of law enforcement, in *Mobsters* (1990) women are incorporated into the spectacle of history from the point of view of the all-male world of the gangster but, again, only to be excluded. Focusing on the Prohibition-era gangsters Italian-Jewish Young Bloods Charlie "Lucky" Luciano (Christian Slater), Ben Siegel (Richard Grieco), Frank Costello (Costas Margalor), and Meyer Lansky (Patrick Dempsey), the film is an intricately plotted tale outlining the gang's organization and consolidation through the early underworld's greatest power struggle, the Castelammarese Wars. Literally, the only female role to feature in the film—beyond that of Siegel's next opportunistic lay—is Luciano's showgirl lover, Mara Motes (Lara Flynn Boyle). Partly to authenticate the film's "hot" approach to the period setting (which is announced by a supposedly contemporary 1920s flapper display of sexual liberation), her active sexual agency is here rather unimaginatively represented by an extended scene of "erotic" heterosexuality with Luciano on a billiard table. Filmed as a soft-porn interlude, this is something of a departure for a cycle that frequently attenuates sexual activity to the blowjob. The motif of the blowjob is an important signifier of the role sex plays in coding contemporary gangster masculinity; it is intended simultaneously to invoke the male position of privilege, in what a feminist critique would analyze as its power relation, *and* connote a prostitute/john transaction. *Mobsters*, however, utilizes the narratively redundant erotic scene to achieve two aims: to "soften" Luciano, which contributes to the overall romanticization of the Prohibition gangster figure in this cycle, and, as in *The Untouchables*, to heterosexualize a dangerously all-male domain. Once grafted into this domain, it remains for the film to play out the scenario that Luciano's emotional/sexual attachment to Mara is the source of male vulnerability and weakness. As site of punishment meted out between warring males, Mara is shot dead, significantly, in bed and thus expunged from the concerns of the narrative. However, the symbolic value of the punishment needs consideration. Is the meaning of the punishment to be found in taking from Luciano what he most desired? Or can this be pushed further so that it is heterosexual desire itself that can be said to be the target, that Mara's death is punishment for wanting intimate (rather than prostitute) connection with women? Whichever, male exposure to the claims of the feminine is clearly coded as psychical and physical risk.

Fear of feminization in this cycle reaches its apotheosis in *Bugsy* (1991). As a biopic of gangster Ben "Bugsy" Siegel (Warren Beatty) the film follows the conventional "rise and fall" structure: the brutal and hypersexual henchman of the Lower East Side gang, *Bugsy* opens on Siegel's life with his post-Prohibition relocation to California, his infatuation with the 1930/1940s Hollywood glamour Dream Factory, and evolution into a maverick entrepreneurial visionary. It is Siegel who sees the syndicate's future in legitimate gambling and, in the empty Nevada desert, initially hallucinates then builds one of the first casinos to found Las Vegas. The story will end with the elimination of Siegel at the syndicate's behest (for overinvesting Mafia money in his project without their permission and/or skimming off $2 million for himself). But interwoven with the gangster mythology is the dysfunctional "love story" of Siegel and Hollywood starlet Virginia Hill (Annette Bening). In the representation of this heterosexual coupling, the historical trajectory of the gangster genre reaches the stage at which masculinity in mainstream Hollywood film is increasingly represented as "hysterical."

The invocations of patterns of sexual exchange to frame exchanges of violence between men proliferate. When Siegel physically confronts an older but lower-order gang member with the knowledge that he knows he has ripped him off, the violent confrontation is initiated by the following: "Do you want to rape me? Do you want to fuck me?" Cut to the bewildered face of the elderly underling then continue for Bugsy's explanation: "You stole from me and stealing is a form of rape. . . . [I]f you steal from us, you rape and humiliate us." The act of men stealing money from other men (which has its own nonsexual motivation) is reconfigured within a dynamic of violence (of powerful/powerless) that utterly dissolves whatever may border heterosexual masculine power from homoerotic sexual fantasy: to be stolen from, to be raped, is thus to be symbolically "fucked" and thus "feminized." The proximity of both fear and desire in this fantasy of male penetration is underlined by what follows—a demonstration of sadomasochistic "degradation" role play: Siegel exhorts his "victim" to crawl on all fours and "be the dog you wish you were decent enough to be. . . . Come on, bark . . . bark." Outside the door, Virginia hears her lover crying out "Yes, that's good, that's good . . . ," and her reading hardly needs interpretation. Indeed, what is fascinating about such an interlude is just that—that they make critical interpretation redundant. Is the panoply of Freudian or Lacanian psychoanalysis really needed to "expose" the "underlying" conflation of hysterical male sexuality, fear of feminization, and performance of violence when it is so overtly marked? Or, as later in the film, when Siegel's obsessive jealousy precipitates a showdown with one of Virginia's abundant ex-lovers? Asking for an apology for calling her a whore and a slut, Siegel's ironic invocation of the codes of gentlemanly honor is met with "You can suck your apology out of my dick." Knowingly making the erotic movement toward a blowjob is, of course, Siegel's prelude to a sadistic beating for the insouciant victim.

In its thematic "return" to pre-*Godfather* (1972) gangster figures of Prohibition and the Depression, the retro gangster cycle demonstrates fear over the loss of masculine control, where representations of masculinity are overly marked as "hysterical" and meaningful distinctions between homosocial, heterosexual, and violent impulses are collapsed. This fear signifies the end point of a longer historical process by which male gangster protagonists have acceded to a profound psychologization, indeed, pathologization. In particular, these films suggest how sexual pathologization is the logical terminus of contemporary anxieties around male identity. But if the retro cycles of the 1990s revisit the "hats and suits" past in order to play out fantasies that are intended to be reassuring of the male self, do retro films that invoke the 1960s/1970s work to the same end, given the conspicuous *absence* of the hat and suit?

As enthusiastic participants in the Peacock Revolution, the protagonists of the retro gangster films set in the 1970s are, for audiences in the 1990s and early 2000s, ambivalently placed. At the center of historical processes that will leave a radically altered American culture, the detachment of male clothing from conformity and tradition into color, texture, and visual display is the sartorial corollary of a wider cultural dissolution of the gender and sexual certainties that guaranteed the ideological value of the hat and suit. It is, of course, a function of ideology to naturalize the assumption that masculinity was *ever* intact in the way *Mulholland Falls* or *Miller's*

Crossing proposes: the notion that masculinity is under threat or at risk of being "feminized" is one that has stood frequent reinvention. In the 1990s the semantic reinvigoration of the suit and hat in the pre-1960s retro films sat alongside post-1960s gangster films that offered instead the spectacle of its decline. *GoodFellas* and *Carlito's Way* thus offer complex spectatorial pleasures: narratives of exclusively male physical, economic, and social power are framed by a historical recognition of the reduced role that such hegemonic masculinity has come to have. Indeed, these are fictions that are themselves imbued with nostalgic regret for the loss, in the face of disloyalty, drug running/drug taking, and lack of personal discipline, of a system of organized crime that allowed every man to know his place within a firmly delineated hierarchy. It is in this vein that the 1970s retro gangsters rejoin their pre-1960s "brothers" in expelling forces that threaten male-defined masculine integrity.

Martin Scorsese's *Casino* (1995) records the history of the syndicate's development of organized gambling in Las Vegas from unsettled frontier through to its Disneyfication by "legitimate" big corporations. Told from the point of view of a casino manager employed by the syndicate to skim 25 percent from the gambling operations, Sam Rothstein (Robert De Niro) is characterized by an absolute need to control; through the video surveillance system, he is drawn to freewheeling Ginger (Sharon Stone), a prostitute successfully scamming the punters and the tables. In a peculiar inversion of the love-interest angle, Rothstein enjoins Ginger in a pragmatic marriage (the terms of which include producing a child before the wedding and a prenuptial financial settlement in the event of the marriage's failure). Despite the combined enticements of wealth, glamour, clothes and jewels, status, marriage, undemanding motherhood, and mob "respectability," Ginger explicitly refuses to collude in regarding the marriage as a personal or emotional one. That Rothstein has rather bizarrely chosen *the* most inappropriate woman to conform to the maternal and domestic ideal he seeks to "own" is confirmed in the course of the narrative. As Rothstein extends the surveillance techniques that regulate every aspect of the casino's operations to Ginger herself, the whore's logic is to repudiate the suffocating constrictions he has placed on her in his attempt to confine her in this way. Although located within the morally disturbed and psychotically violent province of gangsters, *Casino* depicts Rothstein as a man obsessed with conformity, with replicating heterosexual masculinity as it is constructed in dominant discourses of male possession. Against this, Ginger's defiance and assertion of independence are registered by her refusal to relinquish her previous relationship—begun when she was fourteen—with her small-time sleazebag pimp (James Woods). Within the ideological matrix of the film the moll figure is not the female criminal *equivalent* of the gangster, his immoral mirror, but is perversely positioned as an emblem of female rebellion against him.

It would be tempting to conclude that Ginger's prostitute "honesty" and inability to play the standard roles of kept woman or gold digger amount to a critique of Rothstein's assertion of patriarchal orthodoxy. However, the prostitute woman as transgressive agent is here a problematic construction in that her "free" choice of relationship with her pimp is also locked within the circuit of the male ownership of economic and sexual exchanges. Further, as she dies a penniless, ignominious, and pathetic drink/drugs death in the company of anonymous lowlifes, the covert message of *Casino* becomes clear. Signally failing to live up to patriarchy's/Rothstein's version of woman, Ginger is dehumanized and reduced to the parody of an unreconstructed hooker whose leitmotif is basely monetary ("I want my money . . . I want my jewelry"). It is for this that the audience is rewarded with the comforting spectacle of her mental and physical (self-)destruction. She is expelled "outside" of both gangster underworld and legitimate social order.

In terms of the overall narrative of *Casino*, Ginger's part as the doubly fallen woman is sidelined by the larger dynamic of Rothstein's relationship to his vicious thug protector (Joe Pesci). This mutually dependent male-male relationship supplies the emotional connection, the sense of shared purpose, trust, and loyalty, that is utterly absent from the marriage, and Ginger is damned at least as much again for her role as catalyst in its climactic breakdown.

The literal and symbolic marginalization of women within the 1990s gangster cycle is directly related to the pathologization of the gangster as portrayed in films such as *Casino*. The overly emphatic display of hysterical masculinity, however, may not be readily visible if all that can be recalled from the emergence of the Hollywood gangster cycle proper in the late 1920s/early 1930s is the "Big Three": a sexually inadequate Rico Bandello (Edward G. Robinson) eschews women altogether in favor of his relationship with his male dancer friend in *Little Caesar*, Tom Powers (James Cagney) is a brutal misogynist with a mother fixation in *The Public Enemy*, and Tony Camonte (Paul Muni) is condemned to an unrequited incestuous love for his sister in *Scarface*. In these iconographic tough-but-sexually insecure guys there may be evidence for suggesting generic continuity. However, as most of the chapters in this collection have noted, earlier cycles of gangster films have showed a marked concern with delineating and commenting on current discourses on criminality and society. Alongside concerns for the experience of modernity and the city space, previous gangster cycles have foregrounded class and ethnicity as important ideological matters. By comparison, the 1990s cycle appears etiolated and its superficial appeal to style a denial of substantive social engagement. Yet the parodic and solipsistic retreat into cinematic "nostalgia" conceals a retrenchment into outdated gender orthodoxies that underlines the continued relevance of political analysis as response to the reinvigoration of gangster film cycles.

Notes

1. Robert Tine, *Mulholland Falls* (New York: Signet, 1996), 35.
2. Thomas Frank, *The Conquest of Cool: Business Culture, Counterculture, and the Rise of Hip Consumerism* (Chicago: University of Chicago Press, 1997), 269.

3. Ibid., 191.

4. Ibid.

5. Ibid., 192.

6. Ibid., 191–192.

7. Esther Sonnet, "From *Emma* to *Clueless*: Taste, Pleasure, and the Scene of History," in *Adaptations: From Text to Screen, Screen to Text*, ed. D. Cartmell and I. Whelehan (London: Routledge, 1999), 59.

8. Kingsley Widmer, "The Way Out: Some Life-Style Sources of the Literary Tough Guy and the Proletarian Hero," in *Tough Guy Writers of the Thirties*, ed. David Madden (Carbondale: Southern Illinois University Press, 1968), 3.

9. Ibid., 257.

10. Jack Black, *You Can't Win* (1926; repr. London: AK Press/Nabat, 2000), 156.

11. Edward Anderson, *Thieves like Us* (1937), republished in *Crime Novels: American Noir of the 1930s and 40s*, ed. Robert Polito (New York: Library of America, 1997), 257.

12. John Huston, *Frankie and Johnny* (New York: Albert and Charles Boni, 1930), 107–108.

13. Alan Lomax, *Mister Jelly Roll* (London: Pan Books, 1959), 28, 33.

14. W. C. Handy, *Father of the Blues: An Autobiography* (New York: Da Capo Press, 1991), 118.

15. Laurence Bergreen, *Louis Armstrong: An Extravagant Life* (New York: Broadway Books, 1998), 39–40.

16. Greil Marcus, *Mystery Train: Images of America in Rock 'n' Roll* (London: Penguin, 1990), 66.

17. Sigmund Spaeth, *Weep Some More, My Lady* (Garden City, N.Y.: Doubleday, Page, 1927), 131–132.

18. Carl Sandburg, *The American Songbag* (New York: Harvest/HBJ, 1990), 198.

19. John A. Lomax and Alan Lomax, *Our Singing Country: A Second Volume of American Ballads and Folk Songs* (New York: Macmillan, 1941), 306.

20. Lomax, *Mister Jelly Roll*, 58.

21. William Ivy Hair, *Carnival of Fury: Robert Charles and the New Orleans Race Riot of 1900* (Baton Rouge: Louisiana State University Press, 1976), 116.

22. Ibid., 171.

23. Ibid., 179.

24. Ibid., 96.

25. Peter Linebaugh and Marcus Reiker, *The Many-Headed Hydra: The Hidden History of the Revolutionary Atlantic* (London: Verso, 2000), 95–96.

26. Bob Dylan writes, by way of an explanation of his 1993 cover of Frank Hutchison's version of the ballad of Stagger Lee, in the notes accompanying Bob Dylan, *World Gone Wrong*, Columbia 474857 2, CD, 1993.

27. Herbert Asbury, *The Gangs of New York: An Informal History of the Underworld* (New York: Garden City, 1927).

28. David E. Ruth, *Inventing the Public Enemy: The Gangster in American Culture, 1918–1934* (Chicago: University of Chicago Press, 1996), 69.

29. Ibid., 63–64.

30. Walter Benjamin, "Brecht's Threepenny Opera," in *Understanding Brecht* (London: Verso, 1998), 80.

31. Robin Walz, *Pulp Surrealism: Insolent Popular Culture in Early Twentieth-Century Paris* (Berkeley: University of California Press, 2001), 150.

32. Ruth, *Inventing the Public Enemy*, 73–76.

33. Fredric Jameson, "Postmodernism and Consumer Culture," in *Postmodern Culture*, ed. Hal Foster (London: Pluto, 1983), 117.

34. Fredric Jameson, "Postmodernism, or, The Cultural Logic of Late Capitalism," *New Left Review* 146 (July–August 1984): 53–92, 67.

35. Ibid., 67.

36. James Naremore, *More Than Night: Film Noir in Its Contexts* (Berkeley: University of California Press, 1998), 212.

37. Ibid., 214–215.

38. Barbara Creed, "From Here to Modernity," *Screen* 28, no. 2 (1987): 47–67; Anna Friedberg, *Window Shopping: Cinema and the Postmodern* (Berkeley: University of California Press, 1993); Roberta Garrett, "Costume Drama and Counter Memory: Sally Potter's *Orlando*," in *Postmodern*

Subjects/Postmodern Texts, ed. J. Dowson and S. Earnshaw (Amsterdam: Rodopi, 1995), 89–99; Sonnet, "From *Emma* to *Clueless*, 51–62.

39. See, e.g., the cycle of films inaugurated by *Baby Face Nelson* (1957), which included *Machine Gun Kelly* (1958), *The Bonnie Parker Story* (1958), *The Purple Gang* (1959), *Pretty Boy Floyd* (1960), *Ma Barker's Killer Brood* (1960), and *The Rise and Fall of Legs Diamond* (1960). This cycle is discussed in Carlos Clarens, *Crime Movies: An Illustrated History* (New York: Norton, 1980), 251–256.

40. Friedberg, *Window Shopping*, 189.

41. Bergreen, *Louis Armstrong*, 140. For a Freudian analysis see Cecil Brown, "Stagolee: From Shack Bully to Cultural Hero" (Ph.D. diss., University of California at Berkeley, 1993), 249–251.

The beast in me is caged by frail and fragile bands,
Restless by day and by night rants and rages at the stars
God help the beast in me.

–NICK LOWE, "*The Beast in Me*"

PERCEIVED AS HYPERMASCULINE FARE, the gangster picture is generally understood to be popular because of its explosive virility and its close connection to "reality." Yet despite these entrenched truisms about gangster films, the situation is more complex. Specifically, David Chase's cable television series, *The Sopranos* (1999–2004), touted as a departure from its gangster saga predecessors, is a pressing challenge to received wisdom about the definition of "crime entertainment." An extended narrative of the world of fin de siècle New Jersey mob boss Tony Soprano (James Gandolfini), *The Sopranos* reveals the gangster as the core of a highly emotional mode of storytelling in which the pleasures of action and violence exist to speak not only about macho aggressiveness "ripped from today's headlines" but also about vulnerabilities that the display disguises and about troubling cultural conditions. *The Sopranos* is clearly an elegiac, self-conscious, tragicomic meditation on America's lost innocence; but, less obviously, it is also about the otherness of body and family to American corporate culture, and, above all, it is about the undying connections human beings have to each other despite a social system that maintains its hold through a divide-and-conquer strategy. *The Sopranos* may seem to be an inversion of generic tradition, but, in fact, it develops thematic elements that have long been present in gangster narratives.

To explore *The Sopranos* as a revelation of a thickly disguised emotional subtext of gangster stories, I invoke the generally accepted definition of this category of entertainment set by the canonical films *The Public Enemy* (1931), *Little Caesar* (1930), *Scarface* (1932), *The Godfather* trilogy (1972, 1974, 1990), *Prizzi's Honor* (1985), and *GoodFellas* (1994).[1] Received critical wisdom on these films underlines three essential characteristics. First, the protagonists with whom we empathize reverse our usual patterns of identification by engaging us and our feelings with career criminals, often to the exclusion of empathy with law-abiding citizens (our ordinary social definition). This happens within a dense social context, which is the second essential trait. The gangster picture is highly social, epic in nature, generally painting a panoramic picture of society and its values, a departure from the usual emphasis in Hollywood on the purely personal and individualistic. Gangland protagonists are embedded in a well-articulated hierarchy of colleagues whose relationships may be turbulent but remain crucial to their well-being; they are not romantically isolated criminals—who also reverse our normal pattern of identification but, unlike the gangster protagonist, operate in a free-for-all manner against a dimly perceptible, adversarial social configuration. For this reason the final essential characteristic of the "classic" gangster film is its unusually even matching of the opposing claims of the personal and the social, unusual in that Hollywood almost always weights the scale for the personal. The "transgressive" nature of the "classic" gangster film permits a unique audience catharsis that speaks of the violence that erupts specifically because we *are* and need to be connected to other people. The catharsis is unique because its nuanced depiction of human connections, particularly with family, allows a forbidden look at "sacred" ties, which, despite the saccharine pronouncements of radical right-wing politics and much popular domestic drama, not only allure but also trouble us. In the gangster drama, as in our lives, strong desire for filiation complicates autonomy and the drive to succeed in a competitive economic system.

The gangster's dilemma strikes a chord in the law-abiding public, resonating against the secret knowledge of the ordinary moviegoer that in a competitive capitalist society the emotional claims of the family are in crucial ways "other" to materialist success. Thus it is no accident that crime families in the gangster films are often noticeably foreign, immigrant, and with an extended family. Their "foreignness" serves well as a vehicle for portrayal of the ancient, pre-American call of family ties, whereas modern success is conveyed by the "clean-cut Americans" on the police force and in the FBI who, not coincidentally, are almost always presented without reference to their families or to any connections that are not official. In a deft twist of point of view the law officers are too clean; the gangster's passions take center frame. The police establishment may be in the mainstream of the society depicted, but it operates as "otherness" to audience empathy. At varying levels of consciousness, the gangster film draws the audience into a radical alliance with an inversion of the usual definitions of "like" and "other," making American audiences adhere to the foreign.

The audience's surprising compact with the foreign element of blood and family connection in the gangster story makes possible a number of alternative

1. Generational rage: Livia (Nancy Marchand) with son Tony in *The Sopranos*. Courtesy of Anthony Neste/HBO.

perspectives, one of the most important being identification with a masculinity that is at once intensely virile *and* other to the standard self-contained masculine image. The gangster protagonist is, in the most profound way, a family man who gives the audience a means of obliquely exploring family life, free from the stigma attached to emotions and "women's entertainment," often erroneously identified as the whole of melodrama. What is ordinarily identified as family melodrama is feminized and openly emotional, whereas the domestic melodrama of the gangster picture is muscularized, displacing emotion onto the tumult associated with violence.

The Sopranos, as the inheritor of a long line of suppressed texts about familial tensions, brings this displacement to the surface. When Tony Soprano's mother, Livia (Nancy Marchand), conspires with his uncle Corrado "Junior" Soprano (Dominic Chianese) to have him killed, they are operating confusedly within the compulsions of a gangland struggle for rule of the Northern New Jersey mob. But each is also trenchantly expressing garden-variety familial anger: Livia a familiar generational rage because Tony has put her in a nursing home, and Junior a familiar fury about rank in families because he has been passed over and the leadership of the mob given to his nephew. What also distinguishes the gangster melodrama from the domestic melodrama is how directly and intensely emotions are expressed in the domestic melodrama, whereas in the crime melodrama the emotions of the situation are displaced onto the violent crime story. In *The Sopranos* Junior and

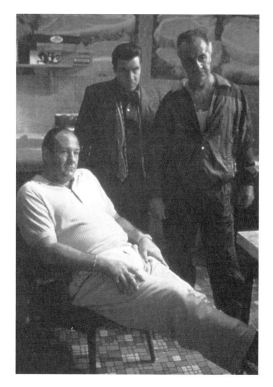

2. James Gandolfini as mob boss Tony Soprano, with his two "soldiers" (Steven van Zandt and Tony Sirico) in *The Sopranos.* Courtesy of Anthony Neste/HBO.

Livia give each other permission to rid themselves of Tony with such minimalism that the audience is not sure what has transpired between them until the plans to kill Tony are put into violent motion. The violence in the scenes in which an attempt is made on Tony's life obliquely expresses their rage with such displacement that they are not even present. Displacement of emotion, of course, protects the virility of the genre and gives access to emotional situations not seen in directly emotional terms.

The thinly disguised familial drama in *The Sopranos* is not a new wrinkle. In *The Public Enemy,* when Tommy Powers (James Cagney) collapses in the rain, murmuring, "I ain't so tough," the low emotion/high violence scene, as with the scene of Tony's near assassination, utilizes an action sequence to raise the issue of family conflicts. Tommy's collapse is the result of a gangland shoot-out, but its import is dramatized in relationship to his mother as it sets the scene for her impending discovery of his final appearance as a mummified corpse, in appearance horrifically evocative of a swaddled infant, a discovery so shattering that it is set in the unrepresentable emotionalism of her future discovery that never appears onscreen. On one level Tommy's crime agon is a shoot-em-and-die blood circus. But any gangster entertainment that is purely that is doomed to oblivion. The abiding relevance of *The Public Enemy* is its early use of the gangster milieu as a metaphor for the complex tensions between individuation and family. It is an early example of the self-image of a culture awash in pious pronouncements about the value of both individualism and family but that fosters no way to integrate the blood ties of family with the isolating drive necessary to individuals bound for success.[2] Comparison with *The Public Enemy* and other classic gangster films is encouraged by *The Sopranos*, which contains numerous allusions to *Scarface, The Godfather* trilogy, and *The Public Enemy.* In the second episode of the third season Tony watches *The Public Enemy* the day his mother dies, with specific emphasis on scenes between Tommy Powers and his mother. Indeed, after her funeral Tony watches the "I ain't so tough" scene and the scenes with his mother that the collapse sets up. The series is fully aware that Tony Soprano's thwarted attempts at meshing family and individuation are part of a long tradition. What is new in current gangster entertainment is that blunt, self-reflexive awareness of the genre's dark secret. *The Sopranos* deals openly in representations that were "suppressed" in the earlier classics. In the first image of the series, gang boss Tony Soprano is openly in dialogue with familial confusions, specifically the maternal influence. The series begins with Tony sitting in the office of a female psychiatrist, completely framed by the legs of a female nude sculpture, and thus recalling his origins in the birth canal and the power of the mother. His curious gaze upward at the nude sculpture is a radical reversal of the conventionally possessive male gaze.

Tony begins the series already having discovered that he "ain't so tough," collapsing as he periodically does from panic attacks, a debilitating condition whose cause, we later discover, is his extremely troubled connection with his mother and father. Tommy Powers never got a chance to process that thought, but like all other classic gangster figures, he was suffused with ambivalence about mothers, sisters, wives in the context of a similar confusion about brothers and father figures and the sexual and territorial implications of that ambiguity. *The Sopranos* offers Tony the opportunity for therapy and with a woman doctor, thereby making almost explicit its displaced investigation of the American family.

Linda Williams's seminal essay "Melodrama Revised," exploring the melodramatic infrastructure of Hollywood entertainment, suggested a way to pierce the layers of historical misperception of the classic gangster film. Williams examines a structuring tension between (realistic) action and (certain intensities of) melodrama as the inner dynamic of most Hollywood entertainment, giving us a vocabulary for speaking of the perennial importance of emotion, family, and women, although much veiled, in the gangster classics. Williams theorizes that the Hollywood action genres are versions of melodrama staged within a variety of discreet action conventions that each play out a narrative of misprized innocence: "If emotional and moral registers are sounded, if a work invites us to feel sympathy for the virtues of beset victims, if the narrative trajectory is ultimately more concerned with a retrieval and staging of innocence than with the psychological causes of motives and action, then the operative mode is melodrama."[3] She effectively argues that this is the foundation and center of most American films.

In its definitive formation, the gangster film reveals that the protagonist's drama *is* the staging of his innocence and his victimhood, although not in the tropes associated with domestic melodrama. The gangster's behavior is related to a social setting that has coerced a capable, forceful man into extortion and murder. Misprized innocence, relative to the gangster, is more complex than it is in domestic melodrama, since clearly, the gangster *is* guilty at the most literal level. The assumption is that the gangster is corrupt; in fact, shining through the Hollywood gangster's villainous deeds are the remnants of what his initial innocence might have been like. There is a longing in the gangster film for its protagonist's lost purity, staged on the level of the physical, for the Hollywood gangster typically has an "innocent," spontaneous relationship to his body and physicality in general.[4] Almost all the action is written onto the bodies of the gangsters, in a genre that places great emphasis on physical touch in general, often on drinking, and sometimes on food. The infamous grapefruit-in-the-face scene in *The Public Enemy* is as much a deeply embedded evocation of loss for Tommy as it is an abuse of Kitty (Mae Clarke). Tommy assaults Kitty because she is concerned about his welfare; apparently he needs to summon up considerable energy to deny that kind of filiation with anyone but his mother.[5] In *The Sopranos* an overt consciousness of the relevance of food and touch to this genre are everywhere, but this is not a simple awareness. Kisses and shared meals are both powerful and ambiguous signs: perhaps of connection, perhaps of betrayal and rejection.

Tony Soprano's rich physicality is a particularly important part of his characterization, a primary vehicle for our experience of his intricately marbled guilt and innocence; we know that he has a history behind him pushing him involuntarily into mob life, and we also share his pleasure in the body of the world, in both its perverse and sweet aspects, which makes a powerful suggestion to the audience that Tony could have been a very different person given other historical circumstances. Moreover this physicality contrasts favorably with the unsatisfying, sterile aphysicality of the law-abiding citizens, which makes us feel that Tony had (or perhaps has) the potential to be much better than they are. Tony touches and is touched, a source of his immense appeal. The inverse of the typical Hollywood hero, James Gandolfini has become an arresting sex symbol despite his potbelly and balding head because of his frank involvement with the sensual body. Gandolfini has made touch an integral part of Tony's management technique: embracing, kissing, shaking, and smacking the men he leads. Tony's relationship to food is unashamedly enthusiastic. Not only does he conduct much business over meals, but he appealingly expresses affection with food in a way that also expresses his power, as for example, in a good-night ritual with his son when he sprays whipped cream from a can into his own mouth as a bedtime treat and then sprays some into his son's mouth. The paternal and even maternal warmth he displays is the positive side of his gangster tendency to understand the world in purely physical terms. The emphasis on Tony's body is also a seminal mode of representing his problematic allure; although he lives a life shockingly contained by physical orientation, in which murder is just another form of saying "that's the way it is," the warmth of his engagement in the touchable world points up a lack in the characters who occupy a variety of moral and ethical positions: a physical coldness. With this troubling irony Chase permits sophisticated viewers a new insight into a fundamental aspect of what has always been the enigmatic attractiveness of gangsters. Tommy Powers was much more physically alive than his wooden, good, older brother Michael. We find the same contrast in many of Tony's predecessors.[6]

Thus, much of the gangster film, and certainly *The Sopranos*, unlike some of its detractors, is as complex as Herman Melville's *Billy Budd* in exploring the issues of innocence and crime. Just as Billy is judged guilty of murder despite the sweetness of his innocent body and the fact that he was irresistibly goaded into violence, Tony Soprano's guilt of murder — and more — is complicated by the fact that he was born (did not choose) to rule the Northern New Jersey mob and by his utterly spontaneous, childlike joy in physicality. The series follows in the footsteps not only of the "gangster classics" but of many important classics of American literature that represent the moral double bind. In contrast, the "moralist" critics of gangster film and television have shown themselves to be simplistic: reductive criticism of the gangster film has a venerable history, as the essays in this volume contend. Mainly, critics of *The Sopranos* raise their voices in horror at the violence and ethnic representation of Italian Americans yet fail to note critiques of so-called good citizens of all types.[7]

The Sopranos portrays a broad spectrum of characters, not only Italians, with extremely clear ethnic markings. Many of these characters are building lives as career criminals. The series depicts the sniveling hypocrisy of mainstream middle-class Caucasian professionals (clergy, teachers, lawyers, therapists, politicians, doctors) who are supposed to be guardians of the public sphere but who are cowardly and morally derelict in varying ways. However, *The Sopranos* is not using the mob simply to make good citizens more thoughtful about their own compromised actions in the climate of contemporary America. Rather, the series is trying for a much more profound interrogation of our blind spots relative to the pleasure we take in the infantile innocence of the gangster.

At the end of the first season, Tony Soprano tells his wife, Carmela, in the aftermath of the failed contract on his life put out by his hateful mother and his much-beloved uncle, "Cunnilingus and psychiatry brought us to this," a twenty-first-century translation of "I ain't so tough." The *this* of Tony's statement is the nub of the significance of this television series for the gangster tradition. For Tony "this" expresses his exasperation with the strains modern life has placed on the gangster's macho code. For the viewer, however, "this" is the possibilities inherent in modern life for a new understanding of the ambiguous charm of the gangster. Tony's mob issues are actually pretty standard, but they become new in *The Sopranos*, which insightfully reconfigures the delicate balance between right, might, and delight that has historically made the gangster film such a seething cauldron of unresolved drives. Its drama of competing kinds of innocence will be approached in this chapter through three seminal reference points: Tony's interlude with a family of wild ducks, Uncle Junior's image crisis when his interest in cunnilingus is made public (both episodes in the first season), and the unusual counterpoint between Carmela and Dr. Melfi that threads all three seasons. The series begins by posing the paradox of the ducks and then works episode by episode, season by season to establish a complex point of view that inevitably requires us to acknowledge, despite its power over us, the insufficiency of Tony's charm in the face of murder and other forms of social devastation.

Central to the series' take on the appeal of the immediacy of the gangster is its revelation of a dark secret about family through a juxtaposition between the role of Carmela and Dr. Melfi in Tony's life. Instead of comparing an innocent family with a guilty career, the series juxtaposes Tony's criminal activities with a family held together by his wife's unacknowledged, self-destructive attachment to the excitement and allure of Tony's violence, to which she is blinded by a reductive attitude toward religion that serves as a powerful form of denial rather than as a mode of fighting against evil. Only Melfi's psychiatry, with its ethical roots deeply anchored in a conscious connection with the beneficial aspects of the subconscious, can offer any hope of dealing with the attractions of the innocence (and power) of gangster spontaneity. In this *The Sopranos* represents a signal development over both the rigid code of ethics and morals in the 1930s gangster film and the post-Code relativity instigated by Francis Ford Coppola, neither of which dealt honestly with its material. In post-studio Hollywood, post-*Godfather* gangster narratives tended to follow Coppola's simplistic lead in relativizing values, which disappeared into the maelstrom of Michael Corleone's id and ego, seemingly lost forever in the glamour of gang potency. In contrast, the romanticizing of the gangster in the Godfather series is commented on in *The Sopranos*, particularly in the second-season episode "Commeditori," when Tony and the guys go to Italy expecting the operatic glamour from Coppola's films and are disappointed by the putrifaction and emptiness under the pretty surfaces of the Italian crime scene.

In *The Godfather* there is no moral center apart from Vito Corleone (Marlon Brando), the Godfather. Despite the film's graphic presentation of violence committed in Vito's name, the film promotes the clear sense that Vito Corleone and his son Michael (Al Pacino), with their warm sense of personal and family honor, are the most positive forces in a world in which the establishment is coldly corrupt, a radical destabilization of the traditional delicate balance between immediacy and ethics in the gangster project. *GoodFellas* takes this relativism a step further into total confusion, where it is completely impossible to explain the difference between criminal and legal activity, except that the hedonistic immediacy of the criminals is rich and exciting. *Prizzi's Honor* marks a subtle turn away from relativism. Everyone in the cast of characters is corrupt in a significant way, but the presentation of the story, using inversions of gangster film clichés to provide an ironic comment on the seeming normality of murder and crime in these lives leaves the audience with, at the very least, an uneasy feeling about the charm of spontaneity attached to mob politics. But gangster films continued to display ethics-free narrative, until the mid-1990s when more subtle shifts toward an increasingly explicit, complex ethical presence, for example in Martin Scorsese's *Casino* (1995) and Steven Soderbergh's *Out of Sight* (1998). *Casino* relies on subtle, implicit depiction of the rapid, irreversible degeneration of the undeniable glamour of "the life" into hopelessness. *Out of Sight* marks out a liminal area of the gangster film as it depicts a loosely organized gang terrain, more directly pits a highly ethical federal marshal, Karen Sisco (Jennifer Lopez), against the attractions of a career gangster, Jack Foley (George Clooney). Part of the innovation in this film is the highly sexual, attractive nature of Karen Sisco, a representative of the legal establishment who desires Foley but ultimately can make no sense of a life in which she betrays her commitment to law for him. *The Sopranos* is a part of this new trend.

The continuous thrust of *The Sopranos* is an examination of the way Americans (even gangsters themselves) are bedazzled by impulsive human desire that mesmerized Coppola, Scorsese, and Soderbergh.[8] Chase deliberates the need to use our human capacity to mediate desire so as to allow for important longer-range needs and interests. Tony's interlude with the ducks in the first episode, his pure delight in nature's gift to him, is the series introduction to the viewer of the problem of Tony's seductive "innocence." The ducks come to Tony literally out of the blue, bringing their natural bodies and their unsullied family behavior smack into the middle of Tony's contradiction-ridden home and business life. Tony's relationship with the duck family is not just a "nice touch" but a strikingly original element. The positioning of the ducks creates the maximum of complexity about Tony, coming as it does after a main title that contains a mass of aggressively virile resonances: Tony Soprano returning home to New Jersey from New York, a huge cigar in his mouth, driving through a maze of evocations of masculine power in America — bridges, highways, electric wires, and industrial sites. The sequence is shot from the driver's POV, further emphasizing Tony's dominance as he negotiates the twists and turns. Aurally, the montage is scored by a guttural rendition (by a group called Alabama Three) of "Woke Up This Morning," a song with the refrain "got yourself a gun."

These images immediately collide with Tony's position of subjective, childlike confusion in the psychiatrist's office (bracketed between female legs) and his discomfort as he meets Dr. Melfi for the first time. As he speaks with Melfi, almost simultaneously, we see Tony, suppressing the information about his violent operations and frolicking in his pool, like a delighted child, with a mother duck and her ducklings, clad — childlike — only in an open robe and his boxer shorts: "Listen, if you don't like that ramp, I'll build you another one. Maybe it's the wood." The entrance of the ducks into the analysis puts a strain on the already powerful imbalances of Tony's characterization.

In this episode these dissonances and contrasting fragments are bracketed by the linearity of Tony's conversation with Melfi. Unexpectedly, it is a curative rather than a repressive linearity that makes its first dent in Tony's macho defenses as he fulminates about the weakness involved in going to a psychiatrist. Melfi keeps him focused, finally thwarting his evasions as she insistently repeats the question, "Are you depressed?" He finally stops spinning his cover stories and answers reluctantly, "Yeah, since the ducks left." What to make of a protagonist who thrives on brutality and grieves at a profound level for departed ducks? Ultimately, a great deal. For Tony's infantile obsession with the ducks is a distillation of his confusion about immediacy — a confusion shared by everyone in the show but his therapist — which he is able to sentimentalize and compartmentalize so that his worship of his own visceral responses blocks him from experiencing a mature sting of conscience about his life of crime.

Tony's retreat into Melfi's inner sanctum suggests the possibility that he can gain the needed insight and marks an enormous change in the life of the gangster. Unlike the seminal media gangster, Tommy Powers, Tony Soprano does not have to have his body destroyed in order to cut through his defenses. Unlike Henry Hill (Ray Liotta) in *GoodFellas*, the gangster project Chase considers "the Bible" for his creation, Tony is not forever lost in the false glamour of the gangster life, in comparison with which ordinary life is a second-rate business that makes "schnooks" of all of us.[9] Tony has begun a quest that will slowly and with great pain, sorrow, and difficulty lead to other possibilities than the unthinking release of chaotic energy and false glamour that have locked previous gangsters into a doomed cycle of savagery.

Not for one second does *The Sopranos* deny the moment-to-moment pleasure of this infantilized life that the American media gangster leads, grabbing as appetite impels him, as did the classical gangster pictures that repeatedly asserted that Powers, Scarface, and Little Caesar were beasts at whom we should be horrified, a futile attempt to deny one of the film's most profound truths: the audience was secretly enjoying the explosive energy of these wild men. But neither does *The Sopranos* fall into the moral confusion of *The Godfather* trilogy and its descendants, which are so enchanted by spontaneous pleasure that they have barely a shred of defense against the infantile, violent sprees of their protagonists. In a flash of insight *The Sopranos* takes heed of that oddly seductive innocence in all its thrilling excitement and chilling myopia.

The characteristic myopia of Tony and his colleagues threads the series, continually provoking ambivalence about the gangster's spontaneity, one of the most revealing episodes being "Boca," the ninth of the first season. The episode is woven of two central stories, one about Uncle Junior's taste for cunnilingus and one about sexual abuse of one of Meadow Soprano's friends by Don Hauser (Kevin O'Rourke), the coach of the girls' soccer team at Verbum Dei, Meadow's high school. "Boca," which means "mouth" in Italian, is also the nickname for Boca Raton, the upscale resort town in Florida to which Junior takes his main squeeze, Roberta "Bobbi" Sanfillipo (Robyn Peterson), for some rest, recreation, and cunnilingus. (The pun will not be lost on anyone.) The juxtaposition of Junior's time out from the male world of the mob and the abuse story sets up a set of contrasts that suggest the problematic nature not of Junior's particular and perfectly innocent sexual desire but of its proscription by a male subculture that, ironically, enthusiastically endorses a wide variety of other instinctual drives that are dangerous and destructive. When Tony learns of Junior's sexual preferences, Junior must terminate his relationship with Bobbi, and the reflection cast by the Hauser story pairs these events to imply that all aspects of the lives of the gangsters are occasions for male self-indulgence, as long as they fit within the conventional macho image. This protocol "Boca" renders extremely problematic.

The soccer coach thread begins as Tony and the other suburban gangster fathers and their satellites are beside themselves with joy at the spectacle of their daughters' triumph on the soccer field. However, the thrill of victory relegates their daughters to the back burner and foregrounds their male sense of dominance. They do not take their daughters out to celebrate. They take the coach for a drink at Bada Bing, a topless bar. Their infectious euphoria turns slightly unpalatable when it generates an equally spontaneous anger at the news that Hauser has contracted to leave for the University of Rhode Island for financial gain. Impulsive forms of intimidation to get him to stay morph into an immediacy more alarming when the final shoe drops and it becomes clear that Hauser has sexually abused one of the girls on the team, and Tony and his soldiers decide to kill him. This complicates audience relationships with the characters. The "good fellas" are suddenly not amusing but frightening. Yet at the same time there is a nagging admiration for the gangsters: who is not outraged by child molestation? Except that, cleverly, Chase makes us confront the problem of dealing with such rage spontaneously.

Tony is the fulcrum of this episode because only he, by virtue of the combination of his gangster power and his analysis with Melfi, can begin to mediate the huge energies in play. He finds himself unable to blithely indulge his instincts, to enjoy without reservation either the damage to Junior's reputation because of his pleasure in giving Bobbi pleasure or the plan to avenge the young girl by killing Hauser. The newly emerging Tony is no longer completely proof against doubt. He aborts the contract on Hauser primarily because Melfi asks him a question he can neither answer nor ignore. In a yelling session with her Tony heaps contempt on the solutions posed by what he sees as the ineffective legal and psychiatric communities. "Who's gonna stop him? You?" But in the context established by the episode it becomes clear to the audience and to Tony himself that Tony is not motivated by anything but some dubious needs of his own for control and domination in seeking to kill Hauser, and the enthusiastic endorsement of those needs by Tony's soldiers contrasts suspiciously with their proscription of Junior's sexual indulgences. The physical spontaneity of cunnilingus is too openly emotional, too tender for the

3. Tony with his psychiatrist, Dr. Melfi (Lorraine Bracco) in *The Sopranos.* Courtesy of Anthony Neste/HBO.

soldiers, sounding yet a further note of warning about the limitations of the lure of gangster immediacy. The warnings become ever more insistent, and awareness for both characters and audience grows as the series continues.

Some awareness is born out of this situation. For Tony there is a modicum of new insight because Melfi demands repeatedly, despite Tony's energetic evasions, to know why Tony Soprano has to control everything. For the audience, although there is a certain attractiveness to Tony's "take charge" position, since we know the problematic relationship between legal justice and sex offenders, there is also a certain horror inherent in his propensity toward murder. When he finally calls the "hit man" and cancels the job, Tony feels not liberated or evolved but radically out of control, and to commemorate the loss that ethical behavior inspires in him, he floods his system with alcohol and Prozac, babbling that he hasn't hurt anyone. Like Tony, the audience is and continues to be in a conflicted position in which it is difficult to reject either Melfi's moral stance, with its long-range implications, or the short-term immediacy of Tony's practical approach toward survival. Yet at the end of "Boca" Tony is at a tantalizingly different place from any gangster in the history of the genre, because of psychiatry and cunnilingus.

This conflict is actively refracted in every transaction and relationship in the series but particularly in the juxtaposition of Tony's wife and his therapist. Having profited from Coppola's infusion of a new vocabulary and a more overt portrayal of family and gangster vocation into *The Godfather* films, Chase takes on the task of restoring values to mass culture fiction about gangsters, but with an unprecedented complexity and a new twist for the genre. The problematic nature of the joy associated with Tony's spontaneous virility is most uniquely confronted in the juxtaposition of Carmela's problematic, self-serving form of Catholicism and the painful integrity of Jennifer Melfi's commitment to our human relationship to the subconscious.

In films such as *Angels with Dirty Faces* (Warner Bros., 1938) a priest was used to pass harsh judgment on the infectious excitement of the gangster mayhem. Ironically, this worked nicely to liberate audiences from their ordinary limits by permitting them to enjoy the gangster while taking in the obligatory pieties at the same time. *The Godfather* series exploded this disguise not only by implicating the Church as a financial dependent of the Corleones but through the magnificent cross-cutting in *The Godfather* in which Michael is taking a principal role in the baptism of his nephew while his "family" is killing all the principal members of the rival mobs. As Michael is being asked, "Do you renounce Satan?" his will is being carried out by numerous assassins, a chilling evocation of the Church as the house of Satan in this world. The Church being unmasked as a fraud, and there being no other source of values in *The Godfather*, the vitality of the gangster assumes an uncontested sovereignty in the film, never to be questioned seriously by any ethical position, not even in the last Godfather film, in which Michael is broken by the loss of his beloved daughter. This murder only consolidates the position of violence as the dominant value. Michael has been overcome by violence greater than his own. In contrast, Chase also envisions a corrupt Church financially beholden to the mob, but *The Sopranos*, by placing Tony between Carmela and Dr. Melfi, raises to the surface from the depths of the gangster tradition the possibilities of human allegiance to ethics through taking heed of the energy of the subconscious.

Along with the Catholic Church, the subconscious has always played a role, albeit shadowy, in the gangster film but never before as a potential source of values. It has always lurked as the negative source from which gangsters draw nervous energy and the reason they are subject to fits. Often it is presented as part of their charm; Rico Bandello, Tony Camonte, and Tommy Powers are arresting because of the intimation of psychological disorders in their physical gestures and impulsive behavior. After World War II the psychology of criminal behavior became more explicit, as in *White Heat* (Warner Bros., 1949), which linked Cody Jarrett's (James Cagney) migraine headaches with his incestuous relationship with his mother, and ostensibly both with his propensity toward violence. After *The Godfather*, interestingly, abnormal psychology was relegated to the lesser gangsters, Vito and Michael Corleone becoming the templates for the gangster as hero in a totally degenerate society. But the series casts a cold eye on Tony's belief that he is of the latter type and suggests his lack of connection to subconscious energies.

The juxtaposition of Carmela and Dr. Melfi enables the melodrama of Tony's choices, not a sexual choice — the cliché of sexual competition between women is present only if it is imposed by a clichéd reading of the series — but a choice of values: Carmela's travesty of morality that actually enables him to continue in a life or crime and Melfi's honest confrontation of the subconscious that might aid him in coping with the infantile charms of criminal mayhem. That Carmela is married to the mob works on more than one level. She is, in many ways, an allegory for the confusion in the general American public about deviance. A devoted mother, with a sincere concern for other people and community as she understands it, she is, nevertheless, unaware that she is sexually excited by transgressive behavior, and especially by violence. She is a metaphor for the good citizen who thrives on films and news reports that feature bloody action. Endlessly tinkering with her Catholicism to imagine herself on the high road while Tony treads on lower ground, she is also an unmasking of the obligatory priest of the old gang sagas who thrived on chastising the "bad guys." (What other purpose did he ever serve?) But Carmela's piety is explicitly revealed, in part, as self-deception by her sexuality. She becomes aroused with Tony only in response to his criminal behavior. When he brings home a stolen fur coat, she expresses her appreciation by initiating sex: fascinatingly she is the partner on top. In an even more chilling and utterly unprecedented sequence in gangster lore, Carmela initiates unusually warm and tender sex when Tony, in an episode entitled "From Where to Eternity," returns from murdering a twenty-three-year-old boy. This is not a deed of which Tony has explicitly informed her, but the sequences before and after indicate that she knows the basics of his intent, a situation that patently horrifies and arouses her. It is noteworthy that her physical approach to Tony is linked to the infantilization that the worship of immediacy spawns; she caresses his face and body as a mother might caress a baby. In fact, Tony's relationship to his home stresses the infantile; he spends a disproportionate amount of time in his bed, like a baby in its crib, as Henry Bronchtein, the director of the episode, has noted.[10] Tony's home is not built in opposition to his gang life but on a disguised attraction to the "bad boy" energy of the criminal.

The audience, too, would like to stay in its crib, fiercely fighting what Chase reveals about Tony through the polarities inherent in Carmela and Melfi. Chat rooms buzz with audience desire to get lost in erotic fantasies about Tony with both women. But the series relentlessly chips at those fantasies, revealing some hard home truths about sexual attraction/repulsion concerning Tony. Chase links Carmela's morality to an infantilized relationship with the Church through her psychosexual liaison with the parish priest, Father Intintola (Paul Schulze). It says much about this character that if you say his name quickly, which they all do, it conjures up thoughts of "Rin-Tin-Tin." Father Philip Intintola spends cozy evenings with Carmela in front of the Home Entertainment Center, watching great old films and drinking good wine. He even spends the night once, ostensibly for practical reasons, while Tony is away, and they have a close brush with sex. But, as Carmela realizes and tells Father

Phil, he has made a lifework of arousing needy women and enjoying the whiff of sexuality without going anywhere with the passions he rouses. Would that Carmela could turn her formidable insights on herself. Even in the third season, when she can no longer endure her own complicity with the poisoned wellsprings of her affluence, she escapes into rhapsodies about the innocence of the baby Jesus in paintings in the Metropolitan Museum of Art, her version of Tony's fixation on the ducks. And when she consults a psychologist who bluntly refuses to let her pay him with what he calls Tony's blood money and tells her that her only productive recourse is to leave her husband, Carmela decides that this Jewish doctor "can't understand" the Catholic attitude toward marriage. Chase contextualizes this attitude in a less than flattering light when Carmela accepts the counsel of a priest (not Father Intintola) who insists that she honor the sacrament of marriage by taking from the marriage only that which isn't tainted by Tony's criminal activities, a stunning exercise in sophistry that continues to lock Carmela into her painful dynamic with Tony and results in no more than her renunciation of some flashy jewelry Tony has given her.

Chase also frustrates the fantasies that the audience wants to cultivate about Dr. Melfi. Although there is some subtextual sexual interest aroused in Jennifer Melfi by Tony Soprano, in contrast with Carmela she is prepared to deal with and fight it, fortified by her position as a conscious fisher of the subconscious. Paying what must be one of the highest compliments ever accorded psychiatry on television, Chase suggests that beyond the clichés that associate permissiveness with therapeutic treatment, clichés Tony hurls in Melfi's face periodically, exists a core in the psychiatric process that fosters an honesty about the attractions of the gangster way of life that may be our only hope, even if it cannot promise a complete solution to the problem.

From the moment Tony Soprano first enters Dr. Melfi's office, he attempts to ensnare her in the exercise of raw power that passes for sexuality and even love among the women with whom he deals. (It passes for love between Tony and the men too.) Often his displays toward her take an "adorable" childlike form of impetuousness, impulses unimpeded by any form of control, spontaneity, and socially immature gestures — putting his feet up on her coffee table and flapping them back and forth, for example. But his attempts to create a crib away from home for himself are not successful. Melfi will not give in to any of his gangster erotics — sudden attempts to kiss her, his attempts to extend the protection of his power to her — or to his belief that violence can change the truth. His declaration of love in the first season is met with her calm analytical approach to transference. His theft of her car to fix her starter as a "surprise" gift for her is met by her insistence that he will receive credit on his bill for the cost of the repair. She does let him get her and her date a table at a crowded, exclusive restaurant to prevent a scene, but when he threatens her with extreme physical violence at her analytical suggestion that his mother is behind the attempt on his life, she leaves him to deal with the doubts she has encouraged, doubts that cannot be pounded into submission. When Tony's violent way of life reaches into Melfi's life, forcing her to go into hiding, she terminates her association with him on what she assures him is a permanent basis. There seems to be no temporizing on her part, as there is with Carmela's, until in the middle of the second season, when she decides to resume therapy with Tony, plagued by dreams about abandoning him, despite the urgent pleas of her therapist ex-husband Richard La Penna (Richard Romanus) and her control psychiatrist Eliot Kupferberg (Peter Bogdanovich) to stay away from Tony, whom they deem a dangerous sociopath essentially beyond therapy. Their doubts stand unanswered in the second season. *Is* Melfi in the process of giving in to her own adolescent longings about Tony?

In the third-season episode "Employee of the Month" we must come to the conclusion that Melfi has important, mature, professional—not personal and infantile—reasons for continuing to treat Tony. The show, primarily about the rape of Dr. Melfi by Jesus Rossi (Mario Polit), who, as employee of the month at the local fast-food restaurant that Jennifer Melfi patronizes, is but one more example of social misprision of male qualities, quashes the innocence of spontaneity within the violent context. Whereas Carmela has permitted violence to be hidden and eroticized, the violence in Melfi's life is too available in all its ugliness to call forth anything but horror. Rossi's attack on Melfi is a motiveless hatred unleashed on her in a spur-of-the-moment urge, the worst aspect of spontaneity unmasked. Even for the audience, which, given the evidence of Internet chat rooms, was charmed by Tony and Carmela's postmurder bedroom scene, this is an act impossible to romanticize. Melfi's demeanor is utterly businesslike, as she descends a metal staircase in a cinderblock stairwell, a surrounding devoid of any sensual ambience, when Rossi assaults her. Her response is an unambiguous struggle to escape him. For the audience, trained by decades of gangster lore, sentimentalization is displaced onto its yearning for this terrible moment to foster in Melfi a desire to turn toward Tony as her protector and avenger.

A selective interpretation of the episode can suggest that this is a desire encouraged by the show. The police have casually released Rossi because of procedural snafus, and there is no one but Tony who can give Melfi the immediate gratification of vengeance. Melfi feels the same childish impulses to avail herself of that solace—she finds herself yelling at Dr. Kupferberg with the same rage that Tony directed at her when she suggested that Hauser be turned over to the police instead of dispatched by efficient mob execution: "That employee of the month cocksucker is back on the street, and who's gonna stop him, you?" But a more comprehensive understanding of events reveals that the show raises this desire in order to reject it. Despite her rage, Melfi's use of Tony to avenge her is restricted to the world of the imagination: the proper place for a gangster fantasy. It is important that Chase does not construct her as being above the desire to throw herself on Tony's mercy, for her ambivalence reflects the audience's divided position. Indeed, Melfi is overtaken by a spasm of fear during a therapy session with Tony, a typical symptom of rape victims, which upsets Tony, who intrudes on the distance between analyst and patient by walking over to comfort her. The moment is filled with unspoken feelings and ideas, as Tony searches Melfi's bruised face for some clue to this unprecedented outburst, and Melfi wrestles silently with a decision that has hovered over this episode. "What? Do you want to say something?" asks Tony, genuinely concerned, expressing the tenderness that is embedded in his rich access to physical immediacy. The camera lingers on Melfi's now impassive swollen and bruised face. "No," she says, and the episode cuts abruptly, with finality, to black. Tony's momentarily naive openness cannot be accepted because of its place in a much larger constellation of unacceptable behavior.[11]

In raising our fantasies that Tony will be Melfi's hero, and then dramatizing her ethical rejection of that childish romanticism about gangsters, *The Sopranos* as a postmillennial gangster entertainment, stakes its claim to generic complexity on the high ground of morality. It refuses to make things easy for us. On an emotional level, all people in this series are equal. Tony has many a genuine and profound emotional response. Even the most brutal and heedless of the gangsters might have one now and again. Yet if the human common denominator of intense feeling is a basis for empathy and identity with characters at times, that empathy does not become a substitute for ethics in this series. A melodrama, *The Sopranos* stages the innocence of its protagonist: Tony has a certain purity of heart. But that innocence is more troubling than elsewhere. *The Sopranos* proclaims, and loudly, that although the innocence of bodily immediacy is attractive, that is not enough. Tony's disregard for ethics and law cannot be condoned. Wife Carmela represents that untenable attitude of the mass audience excited by the lies unspoken, whereas Melfi will not lose herself in them, although at times, to quote Sam Spade, everything in her wants to. This is no valentine, as Mario Puzo's novel is to Vito Corleone.[12] Nor is it an arch wink at the joke the gangster world has played on straitlaced America, as in Richard Condon's *Prizzi* series.[13] David Chase and his creative community are inviting us to be very adult in our consideration of crime culture and very sophisticated about its role as a metaphor for the tangled desires of our daily lives.[14] We might even say that with *The Sopranos* mass culture comes of age as entertainment works as a truly popular examination of important popular realities. Would a public who could learn the lesson Tony provides continue voting for presidential candidates on the basis of a perceived warmth and spontaneity that annihilates known facts about the insufficiency of their administrative records and/or unacceptable ideological commitments?

Notes

1. The most current texts in print all adopt a position that the terms *crime* and *gangster* are reasonably interchangeable. Although there is an awareness that a certain imprecision is involved, there is no awareness that this is in any way significant. *The BFI Companion to Crime*, edited by Phil Hardy (Berkeley: University of California Press, 1997), an exhaustive encyclopedic work, makes no attempt whatsoever at establishing definitions. Douglas Brode's *Money, Women, and Guns* (New York: Citadel

Press, 1995) is also encyclopedic in nature but opts to cover in more detail than in the BFI book fifty postwar crime films it presents as generically significant. It establishes no criterion by which *GoodFellas* can be generically distinguished from the Dirty Harry series. *Hollywood Gangland*, by John McCarty (New York: St. Martin's, 1991), is specifically focused on "mob films" but makes little distinction between films in which the mobsters are protagonists and those in which they are antagonists, in terms of how the films make meaning. Carlos Clarens's *Crime Movies: An Illustrated History of the Gangster Genre from D. W. Griffith to Pulp Fiction* (New York: Da Capo Press, 1997) is remarkably free of interest in structural questions for a study devoted to the nature of the genre. *Dreams and Dead Ends: The American Gangster/Crime Film*, by Jack Shadoian (Cambridge, Mass.: MIT Press, 1977), announces in its title the interchangeability of generic characteristics.

2. The inevitable doom of the integration of individuation and family connection is a major feature of the "classic" gangster film, from Tommy Powers in *The Public Enemy* to Michael Corleone in *The Godfather* trilogy, to Charley Partanna in *Prizzi's Honor*, although the mother is not always the focus of this failure. In *Scarface*, a film contemporary to *The Public Enemy*, Tony Camonte (Paul Muni) individuates from his mother (his father is nowhere to be found) and the tiny, poverty-filled horizons of her life, in an attempt to become something more, but the violence of the process confounds and destroys him. However, in *Little Caesar* Rico (Edward G. Robinson) and his close friend Joe (Douglas Fairbanks Jr.) split the functions of the gangster protagonist so that the struggle between the two of them about whether Joe will form a family with his dancing partner, Olga (Glenda Farrell), or forsake her to be Rico's right-hand man is an individuation dilemma portrayed as a fight between brotherlike friends. For Michael Corleone (Al Pacino) the mother plays a marginal role. His love for his father draws him into the gangster scene, and his attempt to be his own man as well as a loyal son has tragic consequences. Charley Partanna (Jack Nicholson) has no visible mother; his attempt to individuate as a member of the Prizzi crime family ends when, to be his father's son and a successful gang member, he must kill his beloved wife, Irene (Kathleen Turner).

3. Linda Williams, "Melodrama Revised," in *Refiguring American Film Genres: Theory and History*, ed. Nick Browne (Berkeley: University of California Press, 1998), 42.

4. The spontaneous body of the gangster protagonist is always rendered appealing; in other genres of crime entertainment, where the gangster is an antagonist, that spontaneity is generally rendered repulsive; indeed, it is often inscribed as a nauseating violation of cleanliness, proportion, and order. It is no accident that James Cagney, a dancer, was so effective in gangster films. The attractions of his lithe, feline, grace set him apart from the wooden, if morally correct, bodies of the good men and the slothful, obdurate bodies of lesser gangsters. Paul Muni's representation of Tony Camonte's psychotic pleasure in violence was inflected by the charm of his exuberance and the sly humor of his physical satire of the ways of good citizens. Even Edward G. Robinson's portrayal of Rico Bandello, although never as sexually appealing as the performances by Cagney, Muni, and the later mobsters conveyed by Al Pacino, Ray Liotta, and Jack Nicholson, brought to the role a physical energy charged with electricity that was not available in other mobsters or "good guys." Compare this allure with the sensations of physical repulsion evoked by the criminals in the Dirty Harry series and the sleazy, greasy stereotypes of the unpalatable foreignness of mobsters in police entertainment when the Mafia is the target of their investigations. Certainly, however, the gangster film is not the only crime genre that celebrates the immediacy and beauty of the deviant. Films that followed in the "romantic bandit" tradition of *Bonnie and Clyde* also feature the physical appeal of the other side of the law.

5. Cagney's Tommy Powers is a fascinating mixture of corporeal immediacy and physical isolation. His quicksilver body sharply and even brutally shrugs off intimacy with other bodies, disavowing the kind of openness to touch that is so often a part of the gangster's nature, particularly Tony Soprano. Only with his mother is Powers warmly open to the ministrations of touch.

6. In nongangster crime entertainment the coolness of the policeman's body is often one of his central attractions, the heat of the gangster's body being associated with putrifaction and fetidity. Clint Eastwood's Dirty Harry is a prime example. Humphrey Bogart's physical coolness is also the center of his character when he fights crime, a hallmark that made him in many ways a more memorable lawman than he was a criminal. A withholding sexuality typifies the lawman in nongangster crime stories. (Bogart could play both sides of the street in this respect though. When Bogart played a criminal well, as when he played Duke Mantee in *The Petrified Forest* [Warner Bros., 1936], his chameleon body directed a dark form of anger into a warped energy that made him physically repellent and quite memorable.) In the gangster film the physical coolness of the lawmen is asexual, antiseptic rather than enticing. Despite Camonte's brutality in *Scarface* it would be a rare audience member who identifies with the mission of

the chief of detectives (Edwin Maxwell), who not only is so anonymous as to have no name but also projects no corporeal charm. In *Prizzi's Honor* the police are equally anonymous and so cold that we find no way to connect humanly with the legal system, as we do with Charley Partanna. In *The Sopranos* the police and the FBI are much in evidence and, for the most part, are of unquestionable integrity. Accordingly, they are clean-cut, if somewhat indistinguishable from each other. Their cool detachment from their work, in which there is no personal body, works similarly against audience empathy with their plans to get evidence on Tony, even if we know that it is the right thing to do.

7. Uncomprehending moralizing critics are as continuous a feature of the popular culture landscape as the gangster film itself. The historical fear that gangster entertainment would provide bad models of behavior and thought are echoed today by current social action challenges to *The Sopranos*. Marge Roukema, a conservative Republican congresswoman who admits to never having seen the show, has made public her desire to have Congress condemn the show because, "They do ethnic stereotyping and it's Mafia, homicide, cheating, corruption, financial corruption, denigrating women and families, all of it" (J. Scott Orr, "'Sopranos' Hits Low Note on the Hill," *Newark (N.J.) Star-Ledger*, May 9, 2001). The American Italian Defense Association has filed a lawsuit against the show, HBO, and AOL–Time Warner for violating a provision of the Illinois state constitution prohibiting stereotyping that might incite violence, hatred, abuse or hostility. (See Matt Zoller-Seitz, "Next on 'The Sopranos': Free Speech Goes to Court," *Star-Ledger*, April 6, 2001.) Essex County in New Jersey has banned the show from filming on county property on the grounds that it reinforces negative ethnic stereotypes. (Matt Zoller-Seitz, "'Sopranos' Welcome in Other Counties," *Star-Ledger*, Dec. 19, 2000). In each case the stereotype objected to is that of the Italian American, even though other ethnic and racial groups are much less flatteringly represented.

8. Much more objectionable to the Production Code Administration (PCA) than ethnic stereotyping was the presentation of the rot of legitimate professionals and cultural institutions, which it absolutely forbade. The PCA even tried to foreclose the possibility of any humor at the expense of sacred institutions like the family. It was willing to grant that perhaps one middle-class father might be corrupt but never the entire class. The making of the frothy musical *The Gay Divorcee* (dir. Mark Sandrich, 1934) was opposed by the PCA because it made light of divorce and thereby of the family itself. *The Sopranos* unflinchingly suggests wholesale corruption of the legal system and of the upper middle class and makes very light of the structure of marriage in some of its crueler jokes; however, no one is taking up those cudgels.

9. An unrepentant Henry Hill, in the witness protection plan at the end of *GoodFellas*, mourns, in the final frames of the film, his loss of "the good life": "We were treated like movie stars with muscle. We had it all just for the asking. . . . It didn't matter when I was broke. I would go out and rob some more. We ran everything. We paid off cops, we paid off judges. Everybody had their hands out. Everything was for the taking. And now it's all over. And that's the hardest part. Today everything is different. There's no action. I have to wait around like everyone else. . . . I'm an average nobody, get to live the rest of my life like a schnook." Scorsese took this speech verbatim from Henry Hill's statements in *Wiseguy*, by Nicholas Pileggi (New York: Pocket Books, 1985), 283–284. The film gives us no reason to second-guess Henry; it implies the existence of nothing that is as worthwhile in life as having "everything for the taking."

10. Henry J. Bronchtein, Commentary, "From Where to Eternity," Disc 3, *The Sopranos: The Complete Second Season*, DVD, HBO Home Video, 2001.

11. One of the most searing depictions of the pitfalls of mistaking Tony's lovable charm and intelligence for character occurs in season two, in an episode titled "The Happy Wanderer." David Scatino (Robert Patrick), one of Tony's childhood buddies, has grown into a compulsive gambler who wants to play with the big boys. Scatino bets far beyond his capacity to pay and is stunned when the once kindly friend, Tony, turns into a savage loan shark who bleeds his sports equipment business dry to facilitate his own cash flow.

12. Mario Puzo, *The Godfather* (Greenwich, Conn.: Fawcett, 1969). Vito Corleone emerges from the pages of Puzo's novel as a natural aristocrat, whose criminal modi operandi are mitigated by his great sagacity in knowing when and how to administer extreme punishment and when to refrain. Puzo's novel depends on a fantasy medieval, personal hierarchy, in which Vito rises to the top because his supremely warm, generous instincts and mental acuteness enable him to manage the affairs of human beings while an abstract legal system flounders. It is a profoundly relativistic book that idealizes men who "know how to use violence," the tone of which is perfectly translated to the screen by Francis Ford Coppola: "Don Vito Corleone was a man to whom everybody came for help, and never were they disappointed. . . . It

was not necessary that he be your friend, it was not even important that you had no means with which to repay him. Only one thing was required. That you, *you yourself*, proclaim your friendship" (14).

13. Richard Condon's *Prizzi* trilogy is an elaborate joke about the United States, proposing the gangster as the quintessential American: a person with absolutely portable ethics and identity, rooted in nothing but the exigencies required for success. In the trilogy Charley Partanna begins as a simple, obedient, but thoroughly effective, mob solider, who, by the last book, *Prizzi's Glory*, despite his history of murder, has been remade by his father and the don of the Prizzi family into a captain of legitimate industry and then, in the capacity of an adviser, the de facto president of the United States. The trenchant irony of the tale speaks of the blindness of American society from a perspective outside of American relativism that locates the trilogy as an ethical statement. *Prizzi's Honor* (New York: Coward, McCann, and Geoghegan, 1982); *Prizzi's Family* (New York: Putnam, 1986); *Prizzi's Glory* (New York: Dutton, 1988).

14. Although the *Sopranos*'s online chat rooms give no evidence of a broad spectrum of sophisticated viewers, they also give no indication that the fears of the would-be censors are justified. The enthusiastic participants do not express negative attitudes about ethnic groups. Nor do they seem to lose respect for cultural institutions, in fact quite the reverse. By and large the audience is intrigued by questions of loyalty to family and among "soldiers," although they are also swept up by sexual interest in the obvious objects of desire: Tony, Dr. Melfi, and Carmela.

The string dedicated to James Gandolfini, for example, on the HBO *Sopranos* chat room, on June 3, 2001, contained the following representative dialogue (I have preserved the idiosyncratic spelling and punctuation in all the interchanges that follow):

"Shellshell: I think what makes me like Tony so well, is the way he carries himself and protects his family. . . . It seems to that we are all missing the Point of the Show. Yes I know it has to do with the Mob and stuff. But it is also showing us that Family should always come first. We have all in some way or another forgot that Family is so important. . . . Family should always comes first . . . and with Tony it does.
Sweetpea: If you people could keep to the subject at hand it would be nice!! James Gandolfini is a great actor and he makes Tony come to life!!! You love it when he's a good boy and you love it even more than he's bad!!!!!
Novato Bon: shell~very well put. . . . I just hope the story arc doesn't come down to family vs Family!!!! T just has to side with Carm and da kidz <crossin'self> sweetpea~we have posted VOLUMEZ of praise of our guy James. . . . please don't presume we aren't in awe of his talentz!"

Striking here is the ability of fans to think of a murderer as a family man. Striking also is the awareness that they are watching a performance. Can we assess this kind of discounting of Tony's violent acts as a numbing of the public to violence? That purported desensitization may be mythological. Certainly, it was not noticeably in evidence during the attack on the World Trade Center on September 11, 2001. Perhaps the audience's ability to love Tony, even though the series explicitly depicts him committing brutal murder, can be attributed to the innate understanding that the show is fiction, not reality, and to an inherent, unanalyzed sense that *The Sopranos* partakes of a figurative mode that hyperbolically expresses the difficulty of connectedness. Interestingly, if this is so, fan chat coexists with the "Carmela Syndrome," common among "good people," the tendency expressed above to love Tony even better when he's bad unencumbered by an interest in emulating his acts of aggression. It is noteworthy that the audience became analytical about this erotic fascination with Tony only regarding the subject of the rape of Melfi, which forced them to debate at great length about the desire to see Melfi put herself under Tony's protection. As reported in the *New York Times*, even Lorraine Bracco's father emotionally implored the actress to "tell Tony" (*New York Times*, Dec. 29, 2001, A13). Audience debate, however, which continues even at this writing, is increasingly aware of the importance of Melfi's refusal to do so.

Three
"Other" Gangsters

Race, Politics, and the Gangster Film

Black Hands and White Hearts
Southern Italian Immigrants, Crime, and Race in Early American Cinema
Giorgio Bertellini

Half the people in "the Bend" are christened Pasquale. . . . When the police do not know the name of an escaped murderer, they guess at Pasquale and send the name out on alarm; in nine cases out of ten it fits.

> —JACOB RIIS, *How the Other Half Lives,* 1890

My Italian, at least I like to believe, is true to life in that he is emotionally akin to the members of the audience. . . . The likeness is an inner quality of the heart; the unlikeness or the dissimilarity is a matter of externals, which, none the less, add to his distinction and individuality.

> —GEORGE BEBAN, *Photoplay Characterization,* 1921

I am not Italian. I was born in Brooklyn.

> —AL CAPONE

THE EXTRAORDINARY POPULARITY of the HBO series *The Sopranos* (1999–2005) has generated a full-fledged publishing industry of its own centered on the figure of the Italian American mobster. Titles range from academic film and television studies to cookbooks and even how-to guides to tough business practices.[1] In many respects this is not news. The fascination for film gangsters has a long history in American journalism and criticism. Since the 1940s, film reviewers and commentators and, from the 1960s and 1970s, film historians have devoted attention to gangsters in film, pursuing questions of genre, iconography, authorship, and signifying conventions.[2]

Another approach to the gangster, also of long-standing tradition but rarely mentioned or incorporated in film criticism, pertains to the racial and sociocultural impact of mobster films, that is, to the larger, controversial issue of Italians' racial representation as dissonant subjects, inadequate for full American citizenry. Mafia stereotypes, first developed from the late nineteenth century and unquestionably enhanced by the countless representations of Italian mobsters in American cinema, have repeatedly prompted vehement protests of racism from Italian American constituencies. In the first part of the twentieth century these objections circulated mainly within Italian media outlets, the Italian-language press, radio programs, and various theatrical representations.[3] The 1960s civil rights movement gave a different tone and amplification to these complaints. That decade of radical political engagement fostered a major reexploration and reevaluation of Italians' cultural and ethnic identity and promoted its proud circulation in America's *national* public sphere. The ensuing founding of immigration archives, center for migration studies, and national associations devoted to the study of Italian American history and culture (such as the American Italian Historical Association [AIHA]), and the intensification of antidefamation lobbying by Washington-based Italian American advocacy organizations (for example, the Order of Sons of Italy in America [OSIA], the American Committee on Italian Migration [ACIM], and the National Italian American Foundation [NIAF]), resulted in an energized ethnic militancy against Mafia and racist stereotypes of Italians.[4] Furthermore, the post–civil rights emphasis on the history of American racial order informed Italian American racial studies, which over the decades have been particularly productive in the realms of political and cultural history, as well as literature and film studies.[5] This scholarship has shown a particular sensibility to the range and genealogy of Italians' racial discrimination in American media and public discourses and thus to the founding event of Italians' experience in America — the mass immigration from the south of Italy occurring from the early 1880s to the mid-1920s.

At the risk of polarizing the scholarship on the subject, I would argue that the critical literature on the media representation of the Italian criminal reveals a chasm between racial and film scholars, whose critical trajectories have all too rarely intersected. Quite often researchers working in Italian American studies operate from within departments of literature and history, more rarely in film, have a personally vested interest in issues of Italian American racial representations, and place an emphasis on issues of racial stereotyping in film and American culture as a whole.[6] Differently from film historians, race scholars rarely look at the cinematic figure of the gangster along the continuum of cinema as an aesthetic enterprise, a tradition of genre conventions, a highly ideologized cultural and entertainment industry, and a complex terrain of moral and social regulations (that is, censorship). By the same token, film critics and historians writing on film mobsters tend to overlook the continuum of American cinema's attraction for the racialized figure of the Italian immigrant, whether gangster or not. In so doing they tend to ignore the range of Italians' representations circulating over the decades in American media, particularly before the period of Prohibition (1920–1933).

As if looking through a stereoscope, in this essay I will attempt to merge the two pictures of the gangster film articulated by film and racial histories into a single one. Specifically, I am interested in placing the figure of the Italian gangster in American cinema within the context of turn-of-the-twentieth-century U.S. racial culture. An understanding of how American cinema addressed from the very beginning the issue of racial difference will enable us to grasp the range of various racial representations of the so-called Italian racial type, of which the gangster is but one of the most famous manifestations. A discussion of how the racial order of American cinema addressed Italian immigrants should help us to better comprehend the gangster films' changes in ideology and mode of address, namely, how American audiences first looked at racialized Italian criminals with cultural distance and moral distaste and how, gradually, audiences became intrigued by gangsters' still racialized individuality and cultural universe, defined by pleasure seeking and sexually free defiance and evolving into the most radical, yet American, challenge to the native capitalist and moral ethos. The transformation from "othered" racial types to American antiheroes par excellence is indeed tied to Prohibition, the Depression, and the introduction of sound, but it must also be viewed within a larger cultural dynamic germane to American racial culture.

In the heat of the post-1880s waves of immigration from southern and eastern Europe, scientific and political arguments converged in a common, nativist preoccupation with the biological effects of this influx for the American republic and, more specifically, for American urban life. Cosmopolitan in scope, but jingoistic in purpose, these research enterprises compared world races throughout history with a presumed Anglo-American distinctiveness. The resulting taxonomies, compiled in the name of a "biological science of racial hygiene and improvement," known also as eugenics, presented at their center a multitude of racial distinctions rather than a mere black/white juxtaposition.[7] Furthermore, this form of social Darwinism correlated racial stocks with inherent national and cultural qualities and connected racial classes with scales of human development and worth. European but also Asian, Mexican, American Indian, and African American populations were thus divided in terms of outer physical traits, from craniology and height to hair type and skin color but also in terms of alleged national characters, such as criminal attitudes, literacy, and civic stance toward Americanism. The range of these different racial groupings was impressive — forty-five according to the 1911 Dillingham Commission's Report on Immigration — and widely acknowledged, and it forces us to reflect on current linguistic habits. The correlation between distinct racial pedigrees and national characters contrasts with today's use of the term *ethnicity*. A mere discussion of cultural traditions, divorced from bioracial makeup — as the recent connotation of *ethnicity* suggests — was not current.[8]

Differently from earlier arrivals, European newcomers, particularly Italian Catholics and eastern European Jews, were visibly more diverse and "alien" in dress, customs, and religion. Without resorting to color-coded forms of racial discrimination (as in the case for Asian and Latino migrants and for Native and African Americans), the racial affiliation of southern and eastern European immigrants was initially viewed as a cluster of inherited and thus unchanging linguistic, cultural, devotional characteristics. Such features were often seen as un-American and explained according to the racial taxonomies and hierarchies developed by the increasingly popular thesis of social Darwinism. At the same time, immigrants' deplorable living conditions and visible squalor stemming from less noticeable labor exploitation and prohibitive rents became a common subject of interest for a range of urban, "ethnographic" discourses interspersing America's highbrow and popular racial culture. Apart from anthropology, sociology, and eugenics, urban crowds and racial characters were a favorite subject for mainstream (and sensationalist) journalism; reformers' writings; pioneering social photography (for example, Jacob Riis and Lewis Hine); the new "realist" literature of William Dean Howells, Theodore Dreiser, and Henry James; the so-called tenement melodramas of Abraham Cahan, Fanny Hurst, and Israel Zangwill; and countless vaudeville scenarios. It is worth remembering that by the turn of the twentieth century the relationship between American popular culture and racial diversity was not itself a novelty. For years popular forms of entertainments had grown accustomed to addressing foreigners and national *others* and to commercializing racial impersonations. The "cheap literature" of Ned Buntline, A.J.H. Duganne, and George Lippard; the world of the Bowery B'hoy and G'hal; slave narratives and stage melodramas; blackface minstrelsy, vaudeville shows, and comic strips — all paraded beer-guzzling Germans, tomahawk-waving Indians, dim-witted yet amusing African Americans, gesticulating Jews, pigtailed and wily John Chinaman, Italian blackhanders, and inebriated and carefree Irish Pat and Bridget.[9] Furthermore, the new global networks of commercial relations, American imperialistic endeavors in Asia and in the Caribbean, and the entire spectrum of "migrations" to and within the United States patterned American popular culture's penchant for complex and pervasive racial representations.[10]

Since the 1880s the process of Americanization of European immigrants constituted a challenging adaptational dynamic that, although granting them the status of "nonnative whites" (an advantage of civic equality denied to Latinos, Asian Americans, and African Americans), was nonetheless marked by the persistence of allegations of racial distinctiveness and inadequacy. If Italians in general were racialized in terms of lower moral standards, intellectual faculty, and assimilative aptitude (or lack thereof), while also being blamed for popery and political radicalism, southern Italians, who constituted the vast majority of Italy's immigrants, were even more heavily racialized. They were in fact described as showing *natural* tendencies toward deceitfulness, crime, and oversexualization. These allegations betrayed an Italian genealogy. Since the formation of Italy as a nation in 1861, the association of southern Italians and brigands or criminals had been a trope of new nationalistic Italian political and scientific discourse. Scholars and politicians, in fact, even when

1. An exemplary (and literal) newspaper characterization of Italian "Black Hand" delinquency: "Wake up, Sam!" *Life*, April 8, 1909.

of southern Italian origin themselves, viewed southerners' indifference or hostility toward the process of political "unification" (indeed an annexation) and "civic modernization" as stemming from a dissonant racial heritage. The influential and deterministic theories of criminologist Cesare Lombroso (1835–1909) and Sicilian anthropologists Giuseppe Sergi (1841–1936) and Alfredo Niceforo (1876–1960) identified southern Italians as Mediterraneans or Euro-Africans, as opposed to the Aryans of northern Italy, and equated them to other "lower" categories, including women, children, and crowds, all subsumed into the domain of the "natural criminal type." Often called *popolo-femmina* (female people) and *popolo bambino* (child people), southerners allegedly lacked northerners' civic responsibility and industrial efficiency and instead were described as intellectually challenged, inherently unable to exercise emotional and physical restraint from violence. For Niceforo, southerners' undisciplined individualism and amoral familism explained their barbaric, degenerate, and highly delinquent living habits as a direct effect of their degraded race.[11]

Beginning in the 1860s and 1870s, Italian politicians and social scientists linked the notion of race to that of a specific criminal activity, known as brigandage. Southern Italian brigands were violently opposing the presence of the new state, perceived as the expression of foreign occupation and responsible for repressive taxation and widespread misery. Understandably, the local populations viewed these brigands as heroes. Resurfaced in reaction to the new political order, brigandage had a connection with century-old local underworld societies generally known as *mala vita*, formed in each village as a parallel system of law and instituted to defend local populations from the abuses of foreign populations and feudalism. The *mala vita* had different names and modi operandi according to its regional origin.

In Sicily it was known as *Mafia*, in Calabria as *'ndrangheta* (or "honored society"), and in Naples as *Camorra*. These various underworld societies did not present high degrees of formalization or centralization: they did not have a Grand Council or an elected boss of bosses.[12]

At the beginning of southern Italians' immigration to the United States, reports about the arrival of members of the Mafia, Camorra, and southern brigandage in general abounded. As early as 1875 the *New York Times* emphasized the difference between northerners and southerners in stark, criminalizing and racializing terms:

> Until within the last three years . . . [t]he Italian colony was made up almost ex-
> clusively of industrious and honest people from Genoa and the towns of the Li-
> gurian coast, with a few emigrants from Piedmont and an occasional Livornese.
> Three years ago, however, there arrived here a large number of immigrants from
> the south of Italy. . . . It is to this latest addition to our Italian population that the
> Italians belong who are now so frequently guilty of crimes of violence. They are
> extremely ignorant, and they have been reared with the belief that brigandage is
> a manly occupation, and that assassination is the natural sequence of the most
> trivial quarrel. They are miserably poor, and it is not strange that they resort to
> theft and robbery. It is, perhaps, hopeless to think of civilizing them, or of keep-
> ing them in order, except by the arm of the law.[13]

At first limited to the urban press of New York and Chicago, the association of Italians, and Sicilians in particular, with Mafia criminal organizations gained wide national notoriety in the fall of 1890. On the late evening of October 15 the widely admired police chief of New Orleans, David G. Hennessy, who had been implicated in the arrest of numerous mafiosi, was shot dead. His alleged statement that "the dagos" had done it prompted the arrests of numerous Sicilians, part of a colony of Italian islanders who had settled in New Orleans for decades. Nine of them were tried but found not guilty for lack of evidence. Immediately after the verdict local politicians, businessmen, and angry civilians called for a public convention of outraged citizens, estimated between five thousand and twenty thousand. The vigilante mob attacked the prison where the defendants were still held and lynched them. The Italian government vehemently protested and threatened military action, and several American and foreign newspapers reacted with dismay at the news of the barbaric act. What the media coverage of the New Orleans events accomplished was not just the popularization of the term and concept of *Mafia* as a specifically Sicilian phenomenon. Most important, the national press gave the term a larger linguistic and cultural currency: every southern Italian "criminal" activity began to be described as linked to an underground society of ruthless thugs coming from the Old World and threatening the institutions of the new one.[14] Countless references to southern Italians' alleged general affiliation with the Mafia repeated and reinforced the familiar eugenicist allegation of their racial inadequacy for citizenship. Italian American papers, however, vehemently and repeatedly rejected the intertwined allegations of Italians' racial inferiority and proclivity for violence and criminality.

In the following years criminal gangs — self-described as "La Società Camorrista," "La Mala Vita," or "Mafia" — intensified their activity by kidnapping, blackmailing, and racketeering members of the Italian American professional and business class. Although these criminal acts took place throughout the country, they mainly held a local news interest, until the fall of 1903, when another expression associated with Italians' illegal activities gained widespread coverage. In April of 1903, in the Lower East Side, a gruesome crime, known as the "Barrel Murder Case," was committed (a beheaded body was found in a barrel in an empty lot between East Eleventh Street and Avenue D). In the following months the press closely followed the case by publishing related articles about Italians as victims and perpetrators of Mafia-style blackmail. That September, in a *New York Herald* article, an anonymous journalist named one such gang "The Black Hand" (*La Mano nera*), after a similar Spanish occurrence, and explained its workings. A letter was usually received by a wealthy Italian immigrant. In broken English or poor Italian the letter would threaten the kidnapping of a loved one, the bombing of property, or the murder of a family member, unless the recipient agreed to pay a large ransom.[15]

The sensationalist coverage gave the expression a contagious publicity. Several gangs, including non-Italian ones, used this cover to instill fear and thus reach their goal. Between 1903 and 1908 newspaper headlines used it freely to refer to crimes committed by Italians, often superseding previous mentioning of Mafia and Camorra activities.[16] Reports of the Black Hand were limited to the Italian American community, which perhaps made the news about it something between a detective narrative and an ethnographic revelation.[17] By 1908 the "Black Hand" had become more than a common expression: it had acquired the semblance of a popular myth, a media obsession, and an easy confirmation of broad racial typecasting narratives against southern Italians.[18]

Alongside sensationalist press and entertainments the tradition of racializing southern Italians as prone to antisocial and criminal acts included the ethnographic narratives of social workers and moral reformers. The figure of Jacob Riis (1849–1914), the famous Danish Protestant immigrant working as a police reporter turned social worker, writer, and photographer, is quite important in a discussion of how Italians were narrativized by American media. Describing southerners as "avowedly the worst of the Italian immigration," Riis, too, insisted on their alleged primitive and violent inclination: "they wash less, and also plot less against the peace of mankind, than they do in the north."[19] Riis's racialization of southerners included the familiar dimension of criminalization. Adopting and expanding a deterministic stereotype common to Italian academic and popular culture, Riis also referred to Neapolitans and Sicilians as ruthless brigands or members of Camorra or Mafia organizations engaged in daily violence and blackmail against other, more vulnerable Italians who, in turn, became objects of pity and sentimental pathos.[20]

Riis's sketches of racialized traits exemplify the way in which the American racial order of the time comprised, both conceptually and idiomatically, such different discourses as public welfare, social sciences, literature, theater, and journalism. Anthropology, sociology, criminology, and social work had learned from the literary habitus of characterization to draw coherent "racial types." Writing about Riis, a reviewer for the *Indianapolis News* remarked: "[he] knew how to put scientific and sociological truths in such a way as to make one think he was reading romance." [21] Similarly, "scientific" notions about characters' racial customs and heritage had become features of literary and theatrical characterizations.

Together these trends were part of a larger discourse about the city as theater of immigrants' perverse corruption of the American civic and moral culture. As America's center of cultural industry and a prominent ethnographic field in and of itself, New York City (more than Chicago and Boston) was positioned at the critical intersection of all of these social and discursive practices. Furthermore, as center of film production, prototype of spectatorial reception, and port of entry for European and Mediterranean migrants, New York City deeply affected how American films addressed and articulated racial diversity. Participating in the public cultural life of the city, early American cinema learned a great deal from the non-color-coded, racial characterizations sketched by moral reformers, political commentators, novelists, and vaudeville performers, both in their dominant emphasis on biological and cultural heredity and in their nascent environmental development. Caught between the need to address its immigrant constituents and the aspiration to gain wider cultural respectability and stronger commercial viability within the dominant, Anglo-Saxon U.S society, early American cinema was compelled to tell stories about old and new Americans. American films often resorted to racially inflected plots about city life, crime, white slavery, and battles between frontiersmen and Native Americans. With the predominance of story films over protodocumentaries (known as "actualities") occurring at the time of the national mushrooming of nickelodeons around 1905 and 1906, the production of urban dramas, western films, romantic narratives, and comedies consistently asserted the moral and cultural superiority of Anglo-Saxon culture and lifestyle through more or less overt displays of a racialized nationalism. This process instated the *racialness*, or intrinsic racial quality, of the American film image.[22] The conditions of possibility for the emergence of the Italian criminal in film need to be discussed in light of this racialness.

Over the decades D.W. Griffith's negrophobic film *The Birth of a Nation* (1915) has achieved a unique prominence in the historiography of early cinema and race. Griffith's ambitious and controversial twelve-reel feature film was the highest grossing American silent film, caused an unprecedented series of debates regarding national and local film censorship, and elicited a phenomenal barrage of protests by African Americans.[23] No other American film stirred more racial antagonism, and no other American film used more powerfully race-as-color as a definitive discriminatory tool. The film epitomized a filmmaking tradition that had and would regularly depict African Americans, as well as Asians, Latinos, and Native Americans, as subjects racially *extraneous* to the realm of American polity and thus constitutionally "unfit" to assimilate within "white" American mainstream society.[24]

This historiographical emphasis presents significant shortcomings. Although *The Birth of a Nation* is a crucial exemplum of belligerent racism in American popular culture, the film has motivated discussions of race in early American cinema premised on a juxtaposition of black vs. white — a polarization that we can term "critical biracialism."[25] The privilege of this dyadic tension results in the overlooking of parallel forms of racial discriminations not necessarily tied to the same color-coded visual evidence. An important distinction must be made here. It is unquestionably true that by sharing the political, economic, and social perks of whiteness, white European immigrants, like Italians, did not experience the same unbending exclusion endured by Latino Americans, Native Americans, Asian Americans, and African Americans. For Irish, Jewish, Italian, and Slavic populations adaptation and assimilation were not denied in principle but simply questioned and problematized with variable results.[26] Yet to reduce the notion of whiteness to a single, one-dimensional realm of advantage fails to account for the spectrum of its own internal, highly racialized taxonomies that were so often narrativized and displayed in early American cinema.[27] Color aside, a whole range of racial signifiers were used to mark the distinctiveness of European immigrants, and Italians in particular, within the complex and varying connotations of turn-of-the-twentieth-century urban views of race.[28] This, of course, was particularly true in New York.

Historically contemporaneous and geographically overlapping, moving picture productions and migrations to New York affected each other. The presence of immigrants in New York and the nationalistically and racially charged public debates around their culture, religion, and lifestyles inflected American cinema's ideological, aesthetic, and social fabric by prefiguring films' subject matter, settings, characterizations, genres, and, ultimately, civic educational mission.[29] As the most problematic, controversial, yet successful synthesis, the nonurban film *The Birth of a Nation* was the tip of the iceberg of a national cinema and an urban film culture both obsessed with and fascinated by race — and not just color.

Italians' position amid the other races could have relied on a uniquely revered cultural endowment: Italy's artistic, literary, and intellectual past glory. The American and European fascination for classic Italian humanism and its timeless civilization informed the antiquity taste of political culture, academic education, painting, literature, and stage. At work was the long-standing set of images and stereotypes of the Grand Tour that since the eighteenth century had granted Italian political and artistic history an ideal position of universal prominence within American cultural imagery. This idealism vigorously excluded southern Italian immigrants for whom, instead, a combination of hostility, resentment, and condescension was reserved. Despite its Eurocentrism, in fact, American culture promoted a separation between Italy's past artistic and cultural heritage, embodied in the nation's cities and museums, and the recent newcomers from Sicily, Naples, and neighboring regions. Richard H. Brodhead has referred to this split by describing the conflicting coexistence of a "touristic-aesthetic Italy," embodied in artworks and exotic sceneries, with an "alien-intruder Italy," constituted of immigrants at once picturesque and dangerous.[30] Aware of this pervasive American inclination, between 1906 and 1916 early Italian film companies produced dozens of historical dramas for the United States, the world's largest film market. Designed to satisfy the genteel and antiquarian taste of the American middle class, such lavish historical epics as *The Last Days of Pompeii* (Ambrosio, 1908 and 1913), *Nero; or, The Burning of Rome* (Ambrosio, 1909), *The Fall of Troy* (Itala Film, 1911), and *Quo Vadis?* (Cines, 1913) ended up becoming both strong commercial competitors of American cinema and influential aesthetic exemplars.

In many respects Italian immigrants' national origin, by signifying closeness to the artistic heritage of Western civilization, contributed to their potential ascription to America's white republic. Yet their widely illustrated racial typecasting, predicated on alleged terms of incongruous physicality, violent and hyperemotional regimes, and padronelike brutal abuse, also signified the tenuous state of a spurious citizenship. A frequently recurring measure of racial underscoring was *the law*, with its sets of rules and regulations defining a social contract that Italians were depicted as naturally breaching. At times benevolently rendered in folkloric and picturesque terms, this "racial dissonance" signified the unlikelihood of Italians' full equivalency with native white characters.

The equation of Italians with mafiosi, camorristi, and, later, blackhanders recurred fairly regularly in vaudeville sketches, newspaper articles, and cartoons. Beginning with the mass production of story films, the Mafia topic quickly became a popular subject for American moving pictures. Duplicating the yellow press sensationalist reports about saloon gambling, prostitution, and terrible brutalities taking place in Little Italy and satisfying a growing ethnographic interest in Italians' life in New York, early U.S. cinema made visible but also magnified (and fictionalized) what many Americans imagined about the inner circuits of the American metropolis where they were too afraid to venture. As early as the mid-1900s, cinema was singling out Italian blackhanders (more than Chinese and Jewish criminals) when addressing the widespread anxieties about the criminal outgrowth of the city's dark, seedy, yet never too distant, immigrant ghettos.[31]

Yet since the early 1900s, "protogangster" films did not cast all Italians as Mafia criminals. Often the story line divided immigrant characters into two clear-cut groups or created a space of moral indecision within a single character. The distinction between "good" and "bad" Italians was a profitable narrative compromise. Embodying the Italian community's racial difference in the figure of the Latin criminal, these films reaffirmed mainstream middle-class cultural prejudices and granted cinema the high moral ground of documenting and denouncing real delinquency. Simultaneously, by exhibiting Italians' honesty and frequent victimization and integrity, they pleased the self-image of Italian and, generally, immigrant spectators, who constituted a remarkable portion of New York's film audiences. Throughout all these possibilities the racialized topographies of New York City—early American cinema's master setting—could visualize scenarios of innocence, guilt, and successful adaptation and malign (self-)exclusion. Films could do so by exhibiting the abandonment of past traditions and customs and the acquisition of new habits or by focusing on the city's narrow and dark alleys, where enclaves of defiant Italians could exhibit their linguistic and cultural isolation. Italians' urban (self-)segregating settlements, in fact, from Manhattan's Little Italies to the tightly knit "suburban" communities of the Bronx or Brooklyn, well supported and enforced the perception of an abiding racial disjointing *within* mainstream "white" society.[32]

At the forefront of the "Mafia genre" was the Biograph 1906 one-reeler *The Black Hand*, with its significant expositions of the stark divide between Italian honest citizens and merciless criminals, by then often referred to as the "Black Hand Society."[33] In its combination of realistic rendering and moral/racial legibility the film's story line, which repeated countless newspaper reports and commentaries, became paradigmatic of the crime film genre featuring Italians produced throughout the following decade. In this "true story of a recent occurrence in the Italian quarter of New York" an honest Italian butcher, Mr. Angelo, receives a letter written in broken English by two Italian mafiosi who threaten to kidnap his daughter, Maria, unless he pays them one thousand dollars. In contrast with most newspaper reporting about Italians' distrust for law enforcement,[34] Mr. Angelo does not hesitate to call the police—a significant event signaling his deference for the order of the (American) law. Meanwhile, the gang kidnaps little Maria in what appears to be an authentic outside shot of Seventh Avenue in New York. Eventually, a clever scheme by the city's detectives enables the arrest of the gangsters, the rescue of Maria, and the long-awaited family reunion.

Despite its short length, *The Black Hand* offers numerous interesting insights. The Italianness of the gangsters is made visible through negative and stereotypical coding, from Old World costumes to drunkenness and fierce brutality. Mr. Angelo's and his family's racialness, however, is made rather invisible. They appear to be the assimilated and Americanized immigrants: hardworking, literate, honest, and, perhaps most important, confident in the American police force. Furthermore, the visual and narrative device of having a letter being written and read is a reminder of the crucial issue of literacy, which was the subject of a constant argument employed by the Immigration Commission to recommend immigration restrictions to Congress and which in the film functions to distinguish between "good" and "bad" Italians.[35] In the film's opening images, in fact, a close-up of the letter written and signed by the two ethnic kidnappers to demand the extortion reveals numerous spelling and syntactical errors: "Bewar! We are desperut! Mister Angelo we must

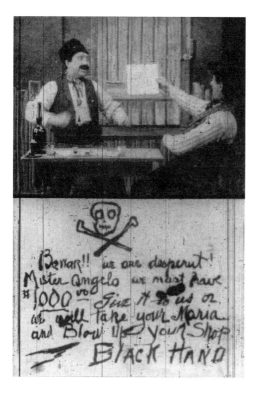

2. Inebriated Italian Blackhanders and their ungrammatical yet unambiguous blackmail note from *The Black Hand* (Biograph, 1906). Frame enlargements courtesy of the Library of Congress Motion Picture, Broadcasting, and Recorded Sound Division.

have $1,000.00, give it to us or we will take your Maria and Blow up your Shop. [signed] BLACK HAND."

Unlike these mafiosi, Mister Angelo, his wife, and their daughter appear wholly at ease with the English language. Images of his shop have several impeccably written labels. In addition, Maria's liberation occurs thanks to a note of written instructions secretly handed over to her by the American police and perfectly understood and put into practice by the little girl. Without much subtlety the film appears to suggest that unassimilated Italian criminals are often illiterate: they have not abandoned past customs and old ways. Instead, the honest ex-migrants display their honesty and drive to integration through a greater command of the language of the New World.

The Black Hand was not entirely a serious and dramatic portrayal of Italians' impassionate criminality. Fooled by a little girl's intelligence, the delinquents of the Biograph film resembled other blackhanders whose screen treatment was both sinister and comedic. In connection with an antiradical attitude toward Italians, a few films equated criminality with radical political activism and emphasized the shared foolhardy, hotheaded, and ultimately ludicrous traits of common gangsters and bomb-throwing agitators. Two examples of what Michael Slade Shull has called "genre intermingling" were *A Bum and a Bomb* (Champion, 1912) and *Giovanni's*

Gratitude (Mutual, 1913), which combined the gang film genre with the bomb parody cycle.[36]

Following *The Black Hand*, similar narratives of mob delinquency *within* the Italian community emerged in various American films, partly inspired by events selectively reported by the press.[37] At the end of 1906 the *New York Times* had followed the public outrage about the city's crime statistics by pressing for the establishment of a special police force to combat the Italian mob. At the time, the "Black Hand Society" of the New York Mafia was wrongly perceived as a well-organized, syndicate organization. Two years later Italian-born police detective Lieutenant Joseph Petrosino, who did not believe that the Italian criminality had achieved remarkable levels of centralization and organization, was nominated head of the special squad. Petrosino had immigrated with his family to the States at the age of thirteen. The story of "Italians chasing Italians" had an obvious attraction for American public opinion. The sensationalism of this confrontation intensified the racial profiling of Italians as a single cultural and moral entity, whose members, whether individually close to the Mafia or not, were inherently in tune with its habits and methods.

In January 1909 Kalem released the racial thriller *The Detectives of the Italian Bureau*. In the film nine-year-old Rosa is kidnapped by the Mafia. She escapes and is able to alert the detective of the Italian Bureau. The bureau's quick response enables the arrest of the blackhanders. The film's racial premise is made explicit in a review published in *Moving Picture World*, the leading film trade periodical of the time. Because American detectives "had little or no knowledge of the Italian language and were not sufficiently familiar with the methods employed by the blackmailers and kidnappers who come to our shores from the dregs of Italy," the reviewer argued, only "courageous and honest men of Italian birth" had the capacity and the practical skills to catch Italian criminals.[38] Quite explicitly, the theme of blood kinship among Italians ("Italian birth") was, according to *Moving Picture World*, what allowed even honest individuals to understand, by native and cultural sympathy, the acts and thoughts of criminal fellow-countrymen. Such a notion of "sympathy" speaks volumes about the resilience of ideas about Italians' racial and cultural dissonance from American society.

Less than two months after the Kalem film had been released, a tragic event occurred. On March 12, 1909, Petrosino was killed in Palermo by, as it emerged later, the local Mafia.[39] Petrosino's death increased the American public's hostility toward Italians, but it also inspired nationalistic and eschatological connotations.[40] It augmented the dualism contrasting the moral uprightness linked to American assimilation with the wickedness associated with its refusal. The outcry over the cold-blooded murder of a virtuous and assimilated Italian American at the hands of perverse Old World Italians elicited two contrasting effects. It emphasized a sense of defeat for the American nation's progressive and collective destiny. But it also tragically signified the moral superiority of the assimilated Italian over the indigenous one, regarded as *still* violent, ruthless, and subhuman. The ensuing intensification

3. Advertisement for The Adventures of Lieutenant Petrosino (Feature Photoplay Co., 1912), *MPW*, Nov. 23, 1912.

of the criminal prejudice against Italians ran parallel to an increasing demand for immigration restrictions.[41]

The assassination of the Italian American detective also had a remarkable impact on American film culture. In 1912 Feature Photoplay Co. released a four-reeler titled *The Adventures of Lieutenant Petrosino*, produced with the "special permission of Madame Petrosino." *Moving Picture World* emphasized how the film allowed a form of "ethnographic" access to the Mafia's inside customs: "the film makes the alleged machinations of the so-called Black Hand Society its most prominent feature and there are many blood-curdling scenes in showing the workings of that mysterious band of the underworld."[42]

In 1915 the newborn company Neutral Film released *The Last of the Mafia*. As a kind of avenging reenactment of Petrosino's murder, the film told the story of a famous Italian detective, Guila Ferrati, who is sent by the Italian government to investigate the illegal activities of two Italian mafiosi. Their American criminal connections are proven, but Ferrati is killed. Meanwhile, an Italian American merchant is blackmailed by the same Black Hand Society that has welcomed the two Italian criminals. The two villains threaten to kidnap his child, but he intends to resist and challenge their intimidation. With the collaboration of Lieutenant Cavanaugh, who despite the surname is of Italian parentage, the child is eventually rescued, the local band rounded up, and the two mafiosi are extradited to Italy.

Addressing the American reaction to Petrosino's tragic story, the film articulates an opposition between Old and New World and charges it with an assimilationist twist. In America criminal threats against family unity and personal justice do not go unchallenged. The figures of "good" Italian *Americans*, whether citizens or detectives, ultimately disrupt and defy the criminals' plans. The ideological overtones of the film's story line turned the film into "a popular offering" due to its assimilationist and redemptive payback.[43]

Another interesting example of intra-Italian conflict over Mafia abuse is *The Padrone's Ward* (Powers Co., 1914), which stages the conflict between a despotic

Italian padrone, or abusive employment agent, who is a gang leader, and an Italian American banker who, according to a classic puritanical archetype, is honest and wealthy. The former is abusing and exploiting a young girl whom the latter wants to save. The gang threatens the banker and sends a hit man to do the job. As a response the banker shows the degree of his assimilation to American society by seeking "the aid of protective association," the police. The Mafia's hired gun, however, is a crippled man who is in love with the young girl. Torn between his obedience to and fear of the gang's chief and his love for the girl, the hit man first attempts to carry out the orders then repents and warns the girl about the looming danger against her protector. The banker survives the menace, and the mobsters are eventually arrested.[44]

These protogangster film narratives and racial framework relied on the idea that for Italians assimilation was a challenging, but not impossible, process of moral domestication and adjustment. The racialized dimension of innate violence and delinquency prevented the entire community from redeeming itself from old attachments and habits. Yet a crucial sign of Italians' proper standing was their respect for the sacredness of work ethic and family life. Work endurance ("Sicilian indefatigability") and devotion to the family were some of the rare values the Anglo-American culture most admired in Italian customs. As a result characters that were shown sharing the principles of mainstream American morality were socially and also economically rewarded. If not, their racialization was further underscored.

Although allegations of natural criminal inclinations remained a constant narrative subplot, other films of the period found different ways to accentuate Italians' racial and cultural diversity. The theme of violence remained a constant presence. A number of titles, for instance, insisted on Italians' pathological jealousy and on their impetuous anger, as well as on their artistic and professional talents — in a combination of ethnographic realism and curiosity.[45] In other instances Italians' temper, passions, and inclinations for *vendetta* were ambiguously justified in the face of dreadful adversities and coupled with their allegedly intense attachment to family bonds. In *The Wop* (Independent Moving Picture Company, 1913) a widowed father named Luigi, after being unfairly jailed because of a strike he could not afford to support, "breaks down and wild with rage, curses the judge and . . . is possessed of but one idea — to kill the child of the man." Eventually, only the sight of his own daughter, who has in the meantime been adopted by the judge, stops his fury.[46]

The new poetic direction that still racialized Italian characters while stirring poignant participation and passionate involvement from the audience because of blatant discrimination and dreadful adversities was not a novelty in American media. It was part of a larger tradition spanning different venues that included, for instance, the popular literary genre of slave narratives of the late nineteenth century and the *humanizing* immigrant autobiographies of the early 1900s.[47] This "theater of white Americanness," to use Laura Browder's expression, was functional to a dialectic production of Americanness as white, civilized, and superior, and it turned immigrants and outsiders into an adaptable and entertaining commodity in the name of an attraction to sensationalism, otherness, and "local color." The plasticity of these racialized representations is an important factor in the progressive familiarization of the American audience with the Italian type, whether criminal or not. Still kept at a certain distance by a number of "othering" signifiers (type of narrative, neighborhood of origin, dress code, and acting style), Italian characters were gaining a steady and recognizable position within American cinematic imagery.[48] Over time, their increased visibility through racial markers contributed to solidify the perception that Italians' melodramatic characterizations, even in narratives of vicious and excessive violence, ultimately held a high degree of realism.

In the 1910s the growing combination of melodramatic pathos and ethnographic curiosity had an unquestionable broad marketability. Economic misery, life misfortunes, and moral redemption, in fact, especially within the narrative contours of social integration, were both gripping and educational subjects capable of attracting the highest emotional response of native and racialized audiences alike. Cinema's aspiration for the widest popular consent may explain why, since the early 1910s, American films developed more racially tolerant formulations of American civic identity. On the eve of World War I, when nativist slogans like "100 per cent Americanism" were aggressively calling for national cohesion and loyalty, several films addressing immigrants' experience in America entertained cosmopolitan ideals of universal tolerance and harmony. This emphasis on enduring racial traits, however, was a two-edged strategy. Without alienating either its immigrant or its middle-class audiences, in the mid-1910s American cinema engaged in the "realistic" and universalistic representation of racial and cultural diversities. By addressing immigrants as both picturesque and ill-fated, U.S. films struck a balance between the encouragement of emotional identification and the maintenance of nativist, bourgeois detachment.

Two such examples of realistic and "pathetic" racial film melodramas were released in 1915 with unprecedented nationwide success. Titled *The Italian* and *The Sign of the Rose* (or, alternatively, *The Alien*), the two films were feature-length productions presenting sentimental and sympathetic portrayals of Italian immigrants as victims of racial prejudice and terrible adversities. Starring the stage actor George Beban, who for years had specialized in impersonating French and Italian comedic characters, *The Italian* and *The Sign of the Rose* problematized the defensive, nativist, and often racist positions of the established crime film genre.

Beban's career is a shorthand of the relationship between American cinema and race. Born Malcolm Arnold in San Francisco in 1873, George Beban started his theater career as a comedian in the 1890s on the vaudeville circuit. Uninterested in moving pictures, his initial aspiration was to embark on serious dramatic performances onstage and decline comedic roles. By 1911 he had played the leading role for more than a year in the four-act racial melodrama, *The Sign of the Rose*, with which he toured England and the States and established himself as the Italian impersonator par excellence. In 1915 the play was adapted into a nine-reeler film, starring Beban himself, and even celebrated as a masterpiece of American cinema. Before examining *The Sign of the Rose*, however, we must turn to the film that, produced a year earlier, initiated Beban's success into the cinematic representation of wronged Italian characters.

In 1914, under the pressing invitations of Thomas Ince, Beban had taken part in the Los Angeles filming of what today is mistakenly considered his most famous film, *The Italian*. Originally titled *The Dago*, produced by Thomas H. Ince, directed by Reginald Barker, and released by Paramount, *The Italian* was an operatic tenement melodrama set in Italy and in New York's Lower East Side.[49] As a six-reel feature film, the film was also "confessedly aimed at a more cultivated public than has been reached by that useful trinity, bathos, sentimentality and melodrama."[50] *The Italian* operates through an ambiguous multidimensional address, already adopted in the stage editions of *The Sign of the Rose*: at the center of the narrative there is a character afflicted by abuses, misfortunes, and misery who nonetheless, differently from nonimmigrant characters, is denied the redemptive closure of final justice.[51]

As the film begins, curtains open onto the library room of a private residence. Sporting an elegant evening robe, George-Beban-as-himself appears as an upper-middle-class reader, quietly sitting in his book-filled studio and reading a novel titled *The Italian*. At the end of the film the same scene reappears. This time Beban closes the book as stage curtains signal the end of the show. Through this "literary" framework Beban intends to dissociate himself from the negative, highly stereotyped characterizations that one- or two-reelers had generally created about Italians (and immigrants in general) and that duplicated the racial typecasting of the vaudeville scene. Instead, he is explicitly signaling his plugging into the traditions of realist and sentimental literature and legitimate theater remindful of *Uncle Tom's Cabin*, which maintained a respectable, Anglo-Saxon ideological cast while treating still racialized individual characters with the romantic touch of universal humanism.

The first part of the film is set in Italy, where the title character, a decent and honorable gondolier, Beppo Donnetti, is in love with Annette but cannot yet afford to marry her. He then decides to immigrate to America. Landing in New York's Lower East Side, he finds work as a bootblack, saves his money, and a year later sends for Annette, whom he marries on her arrival. One intolerably hot summer, their only child becomes sick and is likely to die without pasteurized milk. Beppo begs everybody for help, including Mr. Corrigan, a heartless local boss who feels disrespected and has Beppo beaten and incarcerated. Without appropriate nutrition his child dies. Plotting revenge, Beppo decides to kill the boss's daughter. The cruelty of the American environment — the film seems to suggest — may easily turn the honest, yet still 100 percent Italian, Beppo into a criminal, spontaneously resorting to familiar Black Hand–style violence. Fortunately, he repents after noticing that Corrigan's daughter sleeps with the same babylike posture he had admired so much in his own child. The last image is that of Beppo at his son's grave and an intertitle

4. Beppo (right), played by George Beban, celebrates the birth of his baby at a bar on New York's Lower East Side. *The Italian* (1915). Courtesy of Kevin Brownlow.

that reads: "At the eternal bedside of his baby where hate, revenge and bitterness melt at the crucible of sorrow."

Despite his good heart, *The Italian* implies, Beppo did not hesitate to obey the pressing law of his race, which called for a violent, personal vendetta. Behind the facade of a suffering father still lurked the Italian nature of a violent man. Had he not been stopped by a last-minute distraction, his intrusion in the residence of the despicable Corrigan could have resulted in the cruel murder of an innocent child and in the destruction of a family unit. At the same time, Beppo's various misfortunes, particularly the loss of his child, are not narratively transformed into punishment for his abusers. The film denies him not only the right to express his rebellion and avenge himself but also his right to justice. After all, he remains an Italian immigrant and, as such, not unfamiliar with brutal violence. What the film exacts from its audience is not compassion for a peer but a purely sentimental pity undermined by the suspicion of a sudden and vicious transformation. In its melodramatic combination of realism, pathos, and racial prejudice, *The Italian* carefully preserved a racialized legal and ideological distinction between Italian and American individuals, while bringing the audience somewhat closer to a character of goodwill whose misfortunes could have easily (and "naturally") prompted familiar criminal actions.[52]

The same year, Beban reinforced his reputation as the most virtuoso Italian impersonator by bringing to the screen *The Sign of the Rose*, his signature stage play. Marketed also as *The Alien*, at nine reels *The Sign of the Rose* was a racial melodrama of shocking adversity and cruelty, displaying the perverse outcome of racial prejudices, sentimentalizing along the way the miserable Italian protagonist.[53] A financial dispute between two American brothers ends with one of them kidnapping the other's daughter and accidentally running over and killing Rosina, the only daughter of an Italian widower, Pietro. Distressed over his loss, Pietro is indicted as the kidnapper simply because he happens to be in the flower shop where the ransom was supposed to be paid to a man identified by "the sign of the rose." More than in *The Italian*, the film's ideological address openly sympathizes with the Italian character's emotional outbursts, which this time do not include a vendetta plot, following his family tragedy and his unjust accusation. Yet, once more, *The Sign of the Rose* narratively and visually racializes the protagonist through the realism of costumes and setting, the "authenticity" of Beban's unrestrained acting performance, and, quite prominently, the lack of a fair closure. Once racialized, in fact, Pietro's legal standing falls to substandard levels: nobody is indicted for the death of his daughter. The audience's emotional response is reduced to a partial compassion. Pietro appears as an imperfect, deficient, and "pathetic figure:"[54] only a partial identification is possible with him. This, however, is an important development when compared to previous representations. Although the story denies him justice, by requesting from him only a sense of childish and fatalistic submissiveness to the authority that failed to protect him, Pietro, just like Beppo in *The Italian*, has not failed to gain our sympathies and understanding. As the alternate title indicates, Pietro is and remains an "alien," although his emotions and even motivations have not remained alien to his audience.

Beban's characterizations, which continued to crowd American screens until the mid-1920s, are crucial for understanding the racially inflected sympathy that later representations of Italian types would enjoy.[55] To put it briefly, he quite consciously perfected a formula of "compassionate realism" whereby realism is a persuasive racialization of physical traits and outward actions, based on excess and picturesqueness, and whereby sympathy derives from the audience's emotional solidarity based on the character's tragic vulnerability and victimization (pathos).

In his *Photoplay Characterization*, a booklet-lecture published in 1921, Beban explained how his Italian characters' distinct outward traits were a matter of national and racial origins, as well as ingrained cultural manners, whereas their inner humanity had to be kept akin to the familiar sensibility of mainstream audiences and, as such, appear as universally true: "The likeness is an inner quality of the heart; the unlikeness or the dissimilarity is a matter of externals, which, none the less, add to his distinction and individuality. . . . We must understand the characters of a play, and understanding comes only when we feel, think, desire, and act in a similar way. A character whom we do not understand makes no appeal to us; we are likely to say that his character is impossible and unconvincing. We are cold in our attitude towards him and consequently unsympathetic."[56]

In the American cinema of the mid-1910s, and specifically at the time of the intense psychological characterizations enhanced by D.W. Griffith's cinema and when nativist slogans seemed to discourage attention for things un-American, Beban popularized a closeness with racialized, non-American characters. Although preceded by a number of shorter melodramas of crime and oppression, his feature films, without fully questioning contemporary Anglo-American racial prejudices, mediated both nativist antagonism and newcomers' grievances by pasting ideals of universal solidarity onto stories of white immigrants' indigence, discrimination, and injustice.[57] In the context of American cinema's ambition for a higher and more unanimous vocation—the notion and myth of moving pictures as "universal medium" before the startling diversity of its spectators—his sentimental tragedies furthered a sense of social inclusion and interracial kinship. This was not, however, an impulse to democratize representations from a racial standpoint. From westerns' racial pageantries to racial melodramas American cinema remained tied to an Anglo-American sense of cultural entitlement and racial supremacy.

The convergence of these poetic transformations around 1915 was not casual. Italy's siding with Western armies in World War I restrained U.S. films' inclination to depict Italians as "natural" criminals. Meanwhile, as the Great War increased American patriotism, the Great Migration of African Americans into urban cities and the arrival of other peoples of African descent from the Caribbean supported the emergence of the New Negro Movement in a period also shaped by race riots, labor strife, and visible protests that engendered, in Guterl's words, "a national mass culture obsessed with the 'Negro' as the foremost social threat." The former nativist emphasis on racial heterogeneity was complemented and then eclipsed by a dawning biracial polarization of black vs. white, best epitomized by the 1915 unprecedented success of *The Birth of a Nation*.[58] The equating of racial difference more directly with color made space for racial narratives that cast European immigrants in less antagonistic and more sympathetic and even sentimental tones. By then, American cinema was displaying a growing interest in characters' psychological rendering, and, in general, the new racialized consumer society was commercializing familiar racial differences for spectacular, emotional, and entertaining purposes.[59]

There were also other reasons why the Black Hand film genre faded away. The historical reality of Black Hand criminal organizations was in decline. After Petrosino's death the New York Italian Squad intensified its operations against racketeering and extortions, this time with major political backup. The same occurred in other American cities. Together with the emergence of anticrime groups among private citizens, the enforcement of federal laws prohibiting the use of mails to defraud led to the decline of the Black Hand during the late 1910s and its virtual disappearance in the 1920s.[60] Regarding the situation in New York City, the contributions of journalist Frank M. White chronicled the success of the Black Hand up to 1913 and its progressive demise resulting from the aggressive and relentless strategy of the city's new police commissioner, Arthur Woods.[61] The downfall of the Black Hand and its increasingly risky and less profitable extortionist racket in the Italian quarters did not mean the end of criminal activities involving Italians.

As many commentators have pointed out since the 1920s, the most fundamental reason for the end of the Black Hand was the enforcement of Prohibition laws in 1920.[62] The illegal sale of privately manufactured alcohol could reap immense profits. Both older and newer Italian groups abandoned older criminal practices and moved into the "booze game" with remarkable consequences. The amount of money made and the increased antagonism between gangs required an expansion of organizational size (for protection and control) and activity. More efficiently structured criminal associations became active in prostitution, gambling, counterfeiting, labor racketeering, and narcotics trafficking. This transformation extended the range of action of Italian criminals beyond the border of the Italian colony and implied the strategic co-optation of non-Italian gang members, mostly Jewish and Irish.[63]

What one witnesses in the 1920s are generational, structural, and geographical changes. The immigration laws drastically reduced the number of Italians arriving every year, and second-generation Italian Americans, who had grown up surrounded by the myth of quick material success and were accustomed to interacting with the world beyond Italian quarters, were beginning to take the lead. If the Black Hand was not a cohesive society, the emerging criminal syndicates were a radically different enterprise. As the operating director of the Chicago Crime Commission wrote in 1919, "Modern crime, like modern business, is tending toward centralization, organization, and commercialization. Ours is a business nation. Our criminals apply business methods."[64] Furthermore, the unforgiving strategy of New York authorities, backed by the political will to eradicate the Black Hand, had produced a move of criminals toward the Midwest. At the end of the 1910s Black Hand activities were reported in Kansas City and, most important, in Chicago. By 1924 the old Italian squad that Petrosino had headed and that had served as the model for protagonists of a number of films in the 1910s, all set in New York, was dismantled.

After 1915 and throughout the 1920s American cinema apparently discontinued its attention to Black Hand narratives. Alongside Beban's numerous films of the period, what one encounters among American films devoted to Italians are similar stories of social betterment, kidnapping, and mistaken identity, consistently woven with parallel story lines of romantic entanglements and personal sacrifice.[65] Although still displaying the ethnographic registers of the distant and picturesque, these films participated in furthering an emotional intimacy with racialized subjects. This time, however, the production of filmed racial melodramas featured both male and female characters. Highly emotional male subjects and a new, unprecedented spectrum of female protagonists — often played by established all-American icons such as Lillian Gish and Mary Pickford and dramatized by an increasing number of female screenwriters[66] — were cast in passionate, highly sensual, and quite controversial love stories set between the Old and the New Worlds. New York City's Italian ghettos were often adopted as a recurrent backdrop in these stories to explore, without pedantry, issues of social freedom, sexual expression, gender, and interracial relations, as well as cultural resistance and assimilation. The newly introduced circulation of Italian female figures in American cinema of the late 1910s and 1920s, protagonists of narratives of love and romance, adds the crucial dimension of gender to the racialized representation of the "Italian type" in American cinema. In these films Italian American women often demanded from their men and their family a modernization of gender customs and thus the abandonment of old ways in favor of an alignment with America's modern, consumer culture. Rather than simply dramas of the ghettos, these modern stories of class and gender advancement and participation in the urban promises of 1920s consumerism could be shared by millions of Americans. The figure that in this climate most decisively (and controversially) crossed the racial line of popular identification was Rudolph Valentino, the gallant Latin lover, in many respects a product of the New Womanhood of the 1920s.

Racially positioned between alterity and familiarity, Valentino was biographically coded as an Italian nobleman, the protagonist of a Horatio Alger success story in 1920s Hollywood, and clearly distanced from the familiar narratives featuring the average immigrant. That he could become an exotic object of sexual desire beyond undue fears of miscegenation tells of a resilient yet malleable racial difference, for decades articulated as socially dysfunctional and, at best, sentimental and picturesque, now turned sensually appealing and offered for public consumption.[67] Yet his characterization went a step further, particularly in the light of the many instances in which his character endured, and not just initiated or demanded, seduction, sacrifice, and violent punishment.[68] Champion of both barbarian virility and romantic passion, Valentino catalyzed and participated in a reformulation of mainstream masculinity in ways that were quite different from the Victorian codes of self-control, self-mastery, and self-restraint. Through the display of such traditionally feminine attributions as penchant for fashion, vulnerability, and even sadomasochism—both at the level of diegetic role playing and choreography of gazes with his female lovers—his films celebrated a morality of "passions" centered on the (racialized) "star being beaten," a cinematic and cultural configuration that was quite distant from the one enjoyed by such all-American male idols as Douglas Fairbanks, master of adventurous "actions." Through and beyond Beban's sympathetic realism, Valentino's decadent and masochistic characterizations opened the way for more complex forms of proximity, sympathy, and even identifications that were both transsexual and interracial. This ideological and spectatorial reconfiguration of the racial character (and star's popularity) could be profitably added to narratives that had crime, and not romance, at their center.

The new gangster, as we have seen, was radically different from the old blackhander. First and foremost, his emergence and "characterization" was an American affair and, as such, entertained a different relationship with the American people.

Differently from racketeering and extortions, in fact, bootlegging affected millions of formerly law-abiding Americans who were ignoring the new legislation and were patronizing illegal bars ("speakeasies") operated by Italian Americans. The so-called Italian criminal, in fact, was no more a foreigner migrating from the southern Italian countryside but an urban American of Italian origins, working within a business system and applying business models with which most Americans were familiar.[69] As David E. Ruth writes about the figure of the "public enemy" in American culture of the 1930s (an appellation often used to describe Chicago's Mafia leader "Al" Capone):

> The public enemy, energetic and confident, was successful in a competitive, highly organized business. A model of stylish consumption, he wore fine clothes, rode in a gleaming automobile, and reveled in expensive nightlife. He rebelled not only against the law, but against established behavioral codes, especially involving gender, and his lovers flouted the conventions of female propriety. In all these characteristics he was resolutely urban, a product of the city and an enthusiastic participant in its culture. . . . [T]he gangster was a central cultural figure because he helped Americans master this changing social world.[70]

As such, the gangster was the most fascinating emblem of the challenges faced by millions of Americans, caught in the dream and opportunities of individual fulfillment in a social context that sold consumption and display as never before. The introduction of synchronized sound (1927) gave him more than a voice: although the accent betrayed his marginal origins, his words spoke familiar ambitions and constraints. The post-1929 crash season of gangster films, particularly *Little Caesar* (1931) and *Scarface* (1932), could emphasize the biologically driven crimes of a figure that immigration restrictions should have kept out of the national borders but whose actions and ambitions could be recognized as 100 percent American.[71]

Although still a villainous figure, from the early 1930s the mobster literally gained the ability to speak out his desire for inclusion and participation in America's myth of individual success. His very American ambition clashed against the marginalizing reality of social origin and racial identity. The racialized gangster's violent rebellion against the restrictive and discriminatory laws and regulations, developed to exclude outsiders like him, was understandable if not admirable. The extensive showings of daring, yet ultimately vulnerable and tragic, individuals trying to buck the system far outweighed the moral reformism of gangster films' happy endings. The gangster's popularity signaled an alternative model of morality and lifestyle, increasingly undermining the WASP social order. If Beban's aesthetics of melodramatic pathos had replaced unsympathetic Black Hand criminality, a series of historical and cinematic factors, from the detested Prohibition legislation to Valentino's popular sadomasochistic romances, was transforming the still racialized portrayal of Italians into national emblems of widely felt moral and cultural changes. Many gangster films of the early 1930s, detailing the rise and fall of sensual, violent, and ambitious individuals, looked at Italian mobsters as the most assimilated challenge to the American way of life, or to paraphrase *Scarface*'s subtitle, as the "shame of the [American] nation."

Notes

Some of the material included in this essay has appeared in *Urban History* X, no. X (200X): XX. For their most helpful suggestions and precious comments on earlier drafts, I would like to thank Richard Abel, Catherine Benamou, E. Summerson Carr, Kristen Whissel, James Boyd White, my fellow Fellows at the Michigan Society of Fellows, and, in particular, Philip J. Ethington and Lee Grieveson. This is for Summerson.

Abbreviations are as follows: MPW (*Moving Picture World*); MPN (*Motion Picture News*); NYDM (*New York Dramatic Mirror*), PIA (*Il Progresso Italo-Americano*), and NYPL-TC (New York Public Library, Theatre Collection).

1. Apart from special issues and reportage appearing in daily newspapers and periodicals, a series of recent publications, academic and commercial, touch on issues of ethnic customs and representation, Italian cuisine, and general wisdom. See, e.g., David Lavery, ed., *This Thing of Ours: Investigating the Sopranos* (New York: Columbia University Press, 2002); Regina Barreca, ed., *A Sitdown with the Sopranos: Watching Italian American Culture on T.V.'s Most Talked-About Series* (New York: Palgrave, 2002); Simon David, *Tony Soprano's America: The Criminal Side of the American Dream* (Boulder, Colo.: Westview Press, 2002); Glen O. Gabbard, *The Psychology of the Sopranos: Love, Death, Desire, and Betrayal in America's Favorite Gangster Family* (New York: Basic Books, 2002). See also Allen Rucker and Michele Scicolone, *The Sopranos Family Cookbook: As Compiled by Artie Bucco* (New York: Warner Brothers, 2002); and Chris Seay, *The Gospel according to Tony Soprano: An Unauthorized Look into the Soul of TV's Top Mob Boss and His Family* (New York: J. P. Tarcher, 2002); Deborrah Himsel, *Leadership Sopranos Style: How to Become a More Effective Boss* (Chicago: Dearborn Trade Publishing, 2003); and Anthony Schneider, *Tony Soprano on Management: Leadership Lessons Inspired by America's Favorite Mobster* (New York: Berkley, 2004).

2. Consider, among others, Robert Warshow's fundamental essay "The Gangster as Tragic Hero," in *The Immediate Experience* (Garden City, N.Y.: Doubleday, 1962), 127–133 (originally appeared in 1948 in *The Partisan Review*); Jack Shadoian, *Dreams and Dead Ends: The American Gangster Film* (New York: Oxford University Press, 1977); Eugene Rosow, *Born to Lose: The Gangster Film in America* (New York: Oxford University Press, 1978); Thomas Schatz, "The Gangster Film," in *Hollywood Genres* (New York: Random House, 1981), 81–110; and, more recently, Jonathan Munby, *Public Enemies, Public Heroes: Screening the Gangster from "Little Caesar" to "Touch of Evil"* (Chicago: University of Chicago Press, 1999); Thomas Leitch, *Crime Films* (New York: Cambridge University Press, 2002); and Fran Mason, *American Gangster Cinema: From "Little Caesar" to "Pulp Fiction"* (New York: Palgrave, 2002).

3. A significant exception is represented by the work of Gino Speranza, a native Italian intellectual, lawyer, and civil rights advocate, author of "How It Feels to Be a Problem," *Charities* 12 (May 7, 1904): 457–463.

4. OSIA was established in 1905, the ACIM in 1952, and the NIAF in 1975.

5. The literature is now too copious to quote here. For an initial bibliography see Fred Gardaphé and James J. Periconi, eds., *Bibliography of the Italian American Book* (Mount Vernon, N.Y.: Italian American Writers Association, 2000), the dozens of proceedings of the AIHA, and the contributions of such periodicals as *Italian Americana*, *VIA*, *Forum Italicum*, and *Italian American Review*. Although dated, the best work on racial discrimination against Italians remains Salvatore J. LaGumina, *WOP! A Documentary History of Anti-Italian Discrimination in the United States* (New York: Arrow Books, 1973; repr. Toronto: Guernica, 1999).

6. One must point out that Italian American racial studies' attention to cinema is often restricted to the sound period and particularly to the post-*Godfather* productions. See, e.g., John Paul Russo, "The

Hidden Godfather: Plenitude and Absence in Francis Ford Coppola's *Godfather I* and *II*," in *Support and Struggle: Italians and Italian Americans in a Comparative Perspective*, ed. Joseph L. Tropea, James E. Miller, and Cheryl Beattie-Repetti (Staten Island, N.Y.: AIHA, 1986), 255–281; Robert Casillo, "Moments in Italian-American Cinema: From *Little Caesar* to Coppola and Scorsese," in *From the Margin: Writings in Italian Americana*, ed. Anthony Tamburri, Paolo Giordano, and Fred Gardaphé (West Lafayette, Ind.: Purdue University Press, 1991): 374–396; and Francesca Canadé Sautman, "Women of the Shadows: Italian American Women, Ethnicity, and Racism in American Cinema," *Differentia* 6/7 (spring/autumn 1994): 219–246. See also the recent volume edited by Anna Camaiti Hoster and Anthony Julian Tamburri, *Screening Ethnicity: Cinematographic Representations of Italian Americans in the United States* (Boca Raton, Fla.: Bordighera Press, 2002).

7. Emerging in England at the end of the nineteenth century, eugenics quickly developed in the United States, where its "scientific" tenets were popularized in the press and lay culture and ended up informing the biological engineering of the body politic of early twentieth-century immigration restrictions. See William H. Tucker, *The Science and Politics of Racial Research* (Urbana: University of Illinois Press, 1994); and Marouf Arif Hasian Jr., *The Rhetoric of Eugenics in Anglo-American Thought* (Athens: University of Georgia Press, 1996).

8. George W. Stocking has been the most acute reviewer of the "richly connotative nineteenth-century sense of race." "At the end of the 19th century," he writes, "'Blood'—and by extension 'race'—included numerous elements that we would today call cultural; there was not a clear line between cultural and physical elements or between social and biological heredity. The characteristic qualities of civilization were carried from one generation to another both *in* and *with* the blood of their citizens" (G. W. Stocking, "The Turn-of-the-Century Concept of Race," *Modernism/Modernity* 1, no.1 [1994]: 6; emphasis in the original).

9. For an initial bibliographic orientation see Laura Browder, *Slippery Characters: Ethnic Impersonators and American Identities* (Chapel Hill: University of North Carolina Press, 2000); on literature see Werner Sollors, *Neither Black nor White yet Both: Thematic Explorations of Interracial Literature* (New York: Oxford University Press, 1997); Werner Sollors, *Multilingual America: Transnationalism, Ethnicity, and the Languages of American Literature* (New York: Oxford University Press, 1998); on minstrelsy see Eric Lott, *Love and Theft: Blackface Minstrelsy and the American Working Class* (New York: Oxford University Press, 1993); and, more specifically on film, see Michael Rogin, *Blackface, White Noise: Jewish Immigrants in the Hollywood Melting Pot* (Berkeley: University of California Press, 1996).

10. Between 1880 and 1915 more than fourteen million southern and eastern Europeans arrived in the United States; from 1850 to World War I approximately a million Asians (Japanese, Chinese, Koreans, Filipinos, and Indians), despite numerous restrictions, landed on the West Coast, and, through the imposition of a border, more than a million Mexicans and Mexican Americans found themselves "migrants" in a new country. Furthermore, in this period thousands of African Americans, approximately half a million after 1916, had begun moving north to urban environments away from the South. Historian Carole Marks reported that 168,000 blacks moved from the South between 1890 and 1900, 170,000 between 1900 and 1910, and 453,000 between 1910 and 1920. See Carole Marks, *Farewell—We're Good and Gone: The Great Black Migration* (Bloomington: Indiana University Press, 1989).

11. See Cesare Lombroso, *L'uomo delinquente studiato in rapporto all'antropologia, alla medicina e alle discipline carcerarie* (Milan: Hoepli, 1876); Cesare Lombroso with Guglielmo Ferrero, *La donna delinquente. La prostituta e la donna normale* (Turin: Bocca, 1892; translated into English as *The Female Offender* [London: T. Fisher, 1895]); and Cesare Lombroso, *Criminal Anthropology: Its Origin and Application* (New York: Forum, 1895). For a general discussion of Lombroso's theoretical position see Randy Martin, Robert J. Mutchnick, and W. Timothy Austin, *Criminological Thought: Pioneers Past and Present* (New York: Macmillan, 1990), 21–44; also see Stephen Jay Gould, *The Mismeasure of Man* (New York: Norton, 1981), 122–142. Sergi's and Niceforo's most influential works were, respectively, *Origine e diffusione della stirpe mediterranea. Induzioni antropologiche* (Rome: Società Editrice Dante Alighieri, 1895), translated into English as *The Mediterranean Race: A Study of the Origin of European Peoples* (London: Walter Scott, 1901); and *L'Italia barbara contemporanea* (Milan-Palermo: Sandron, 1898). In the early 1910s renowned American sociologist Edward Alsworth Ross (1866–1951) popularized and expanded the theories of Lombroso and Niceforo in North America. He wrote that "the ignorant, superstitious Neapolitan or Sicilian, heir of centuries of Bourbon misgovernment, cannot be expected to prove us his race mettle" and "with the dusk of Saracenic or Berber ancestors showing in their cheeks . . . they lack the conveniences for thinking" (E. A. Ross, "Racial Consequences of

Immigration," *Century Magazine,* July 1914, 619; E. A. Ross, "Italians in America," *Century Magazine,* July 1914, 444–445).

12. Humbert S. Nelli, *The Business of Crime: Italians and Syndicated Crime in the United States* (Chicago: University of Chicago Press, 1976), 8–17. Early accounts of the Sicilian Mafia include Antonio Cutrera, *La Mafia e i Mafiosi* (Palermo: A. Reber, 1900).

13. "Our Italians," *NYT,* Nov. 12, 1875, quoted in LaGumina, *Wop!,* 41. Three years later the *New York Times* described how fitting the new environment was for Italy's older criminal groups: "New York City affords excellent opportunities for brigandage of the genuine Italian model. A band of brigands would find the rookeries of Mulberry Street more comfortable than the Calabrian forests, and much safer" ("Brigands at Home in the Italian Quarter," *NYT,* Sep. 26, 1878). For a general survey on how the *Times* viewed and discussed the presence of Italian immigrants in America see Ivan Hubert Light, *Italians in America: Annotated Guide to "New York Times" Articles, 1890–1940* (Monticello, Ill.: Council of Planning Libraries, 1975). Although news about the presence of mafiosi starts appearing in New Orleans in the early 1880s, in connection with the increase of the newly settled Sicilian populations, the correlation of southern Italians and criminality was early on a quick one. See "A Natural Inclination toward Criminality," *NYT,* April 16, 1876, quoted in LaGumina, *Wop!,* 28. On a national level the distinction between Italy's northerners and southerners was widely popularized by a series of articles that had appeared since 1890 in *Harper's Weekly* titled "The Foreign Element in New York City." See *Harper's Weekly,* Oct. 18, 1890, 817–819. Senator Henry Cabot Lodge had also expanded on the concept in an influential essay where he described southern Italians in terms of anarchism and antistate brigandage. See Henry Cabot Lodge, "The Restriction of Immigration," *North American Review* 152 (Jan. 1891): 27–35.

14. "The New Orleans Massacre," *Nation,* March 19, 1891, 232; "The Italian Trouble," *Nation,* April 9, 1891, 294; "New Orleans' War on the Mafia," *Illustrated American,* April 4, 1891, 318–323; "The Mafia and What Led to the Lynching," *Harper's Weekly,* March 28, 1891, 226–227; "The Mafia in Sicily," *Living Age,* June 1891, 633; "The Spirit of the Mafia," *Fortnightly Review,* Jan. 1901, 107–108, quoted in Nelli, *Business of Crime,* 275. For a general account on the New Orleans lynching see Nelli, *Business of Crime,* chaps. 2–3; and Richard Gambino, *Vendetta: A True Story of the Worst Lynching in America* (Garden City, N.Y.: Doubleday, 1977).

15. See *New York Herald,* Sep. 13, 14, 18, 19, Oct. 3, 1903. The most complete study on the phenomenon is Thomas Monroe Pitkin and Francesco Cordasco, *The Black Hand: A Chapter in Ethnic Crime* (Totowa, N.J.: Rowman and Littlefield, 1977), see esp. chap. 1 ("A New Name for an Old Crime").

16. Former president of the United Italian Societies of New York Gaetano D'Amato and well-known muckraker Lindsay Dennison later demystified both the organizational complexity and the newness of the Black Hand by emphasizing its links with the Mafia and Camorra. See Gaetano D'Amato, "'The Black Hand' Myth," *North American Review* 182 (April 1908): 544, 548; and Lindsay Dennison, "The Black Hand," *Everybody's Magazine,* Sep. 1908, 293. According to D'Amato the expression had first been used in Spain in the 1880s by a group of thieves and murderers who fashioned themselves as protectors of the common man against wealthy abusers. For him "some Italian desperado . . . had heard of the exploits of Spanish society and considered the combination of words to be high-sounding and terror-inspiring" (544). A Black Hand organization was said to be active in Puerto Rico in 1898.

17. As Humber S. Nelli writes: "Although Black Handers worked on all levels of immigrant society, they limited themselves geographically to Italians living or working in the colonies. . . . A computer-assisted study of 141 Black Hand cases that took place during 1908 in New York, Boston, Philadelphia, Baltimore, Chicago, Pittsburgh, Cleveland, New Orleans, Kansas City, and San Francisco uncovered the fact that not one Black Hand case reported in the press took place outside an immigrant district" (Nelli, *Business of Crime,* 79).

18. The fame of the Black Hand was troublesome to the Italian community, which vehemently opposed the unremitting representations of Italians as bringing into America the Old World criminal workings of Mafia and Camorra. It is interesting to note that in 1908 Alessandro Mastro-Valerio, publisher and editor of Chicago's *La Tribuna Italiana Transatlantica,* suggested that it was Carlo Barsotti, editor of the largest Italian American paper, the New York–based *Il Progresso Italo-Americano,* who had coined the term to better explain how Italian American crime was a *response* to the American environment and not a holdover of age-old southern Italian customs.

19. Jacob Riis, *The Battle with the Slum* (1902; repr. Montclair, N.J.: Patterson Smith, 1969), 176–177.

20. A useful discussion of Riis's attitude toward Italians is in Joseph P. Cosco, *Imagining Italians: The Clash of Romance and Race in American Perceptions, 1880–1910* (New York: State University of New York Press, 2003), 21–60.

21. The review was apropos Riis's *The Making of an American* (1901). See Keith Gandal, *The Virtues of the Vicious: Jacob Riis, Stephen Crane, and the Spectacle of the Slum* (New York: Oxford University Press, 1997), 12.

22. On the notion of racialness in early and silent American film see Jane Gaines, "The Scar of Shame: Skin Color and Caste in Black Silent Melodrama," *Cinema Journal* 26, no. 4 (summer 1987): 3–21; repr. in *Representing Blackness. Issues in Film and Video*, ed. Valerie Smith (New Brunswick, N.J.: Rutgers University Press, 1997), 61–81.

23. For an excellent survey of the film's critical literature see Robert Lang, ed., *"The Birth of a Nation": D.W. Griffith, Director* (New Brunswick, N.J.: Rutgers University Press, 1994). A fundamental work on the formation of African American film discourse is Anna Everett's *Returning the Gaze: A Genealogy of Black Film Criticism, 1909–1945* (Durham, N.C.: Duke University Press, 2001). On African American film representation and film practices see Donald Bogle, *Toms, Coons, Mulattoes, Mammies, and Bucks: An Interpretative History of Blacks in American Films* (New York: Continuum, 1999); Thomas Cripps, *Slow Fade to Black: The Negro in American Film, 1900–1942* (New York: Oxford University Press, 1993); and Pearl Bowser, Jane Gaines, and Charles Musser, eds., *African-American Filmmaking and Race Cinema of the Silent Era: Oscar Micheaux and His Circle* (Bloomington: Indiana University Press, 2001).

24. The distinction between whiteness and nonwhiteness mattered (as it still does) a great deal onscreen and off as it defined, in legal, social, and representational terms, civil entitlements that certain individuals enjoyed, while others did not. For the period, I am referring to rights to acquire citizenship, contract loans, purchase real estate, and freely choose marital partners.

25. I am referring here to the "biracialism" that emerged within the new "race consciousness" of the mid-1910s in the works of such authors as Madison Grant, Lothrop Stoddard (who coined the term), W.E.B. Du Bois, and Marcus Garvey. See Matthew Pratt Guterl, *The Color of Race in America, 1900–1940* (Cambridge, Mass.: Harvard University Press, 2001), esp. 6, 12. A biracial framework is at the basis of two remarkable film studies by Jane Gaines and Linda Williams. Examining respectively the so-called race movies produced for black audiences between 1913 and 1931 and examples of cinematic and televisual melodramas starring African American characters, Gaines and Williams have firmly remained within, without ever questioning, a black/white conceptual dyad, at the expense of other concurrent forms of racialization. See Jane Gaines, *Fire and Desire: Mixed-Race Movies in the Silent Era* (Chicago: University of Chicago Press, 2001); and Linda Williams, *Playing the Race Card: Melodramas of Black and White from Uncle Tom to O. J. Simpson* (Princeton, N.J.: Princeton University Press, 2001). Similarly Daniel Bernardi's anthology, *The Birth of Whiteness: Race and Emergence of US Cinema* (New Brunswick: N.J.: Rutgers University Press, 1991), focuses mainly on a color-based bi- and multiracial structure.

26. The very fact that assimilation was *open to question* was itself remarkable: most European groups hold what Matthew Frye Jacobson has termed a "probatory whiteness." As Jacobson has shown, the arrival of European immigrants problematized the inclusivity of the 1790 naturalization law ("free white person") by fracturing the monolithic notion of whiteness into a hierarchical ordering of distinct white races. See M. F. Jacobson, *Whiteness of a Different Color: European Immigrants and the Alchemy of Race* (Cambridge, Mass.: Harvard University Press, 1998), chaps. 2 and 3.

27. Similarly, the very few studies of southern and eastern European immigrants in American cinema have described these populations' experience of racial discrimination and their alleged failure to fully assimilate with the newly coined terms *nonwhiteness* or *off-whiteness*, thereby reducing the question of racial difference to shades of dichotomized color. See Diane Negra, *Off-White Hollywood: American Culture and Ethnic Female Stardom* (New York: Routledge, 2001).

28. As Peter Kolchin writes in his excellent critique of whiteness studies: "The unresolved issue here is the extent to which Americans conceived of *whiteness* (rather than other criteria such as religion, culture, ethnicity, and class) as the main ingredient separating the civilized from the uncivilized" (P. Kolchin, "Whiteness Studies: The New History of Race in America," *Journal of American History* 89, no. 1 [June 2002]: 1–41; 22 [emphasis in the original]).

29. I have discussed the methodological importance of migration in the study of early cinema in *Encyclopedia of Early Cinema*, ed. Richard Abel (New York: Routledge, 2005), s.v. "Migrations."

30. Richard H. Brodhead, "Strangers on a Train: The Double Dream of Italy in the American Gilded Age," *Modernism/Modernity* 1, no. 2 (1994): 1–19; see also John Paul Russo, "From Italophilia to

Italophobia: Representations of Italian Americans in the Early Gilded Age," *Differentia* 6/7 (spring/autumn 1994): 45–75. Riis had made this distinction also. He adopted for Italian migrants the less ideal conception of "low domestic barbarism" made particularly virulent by comparison to Italy's past and genteel "high cosmopolitan civilization." Back in Italy, he noted, "in the frame-work of Mediterranean exuberance, [Italians] are the delight of the artist, but in a matter-of-fact American community [they] become its danger and reproach" (Jacob Riis, *How the Other Half Lives: Studies among the Tenements of New York* [1890; repr. New York: Dover, 1971], 43).

31. The filmographic sources used for this overview are Zita Eastman, Vincent J. Aceto, and Fred Silva, eds., *Film Literature Index* (Albany, N.Y.: Film and Television Documentation Center, 1973–1979); Mirella Jona Affron, "The Italian-American in American Films, 1918–1971," *Italian Americana* 3 (spring/summer 1977): 232–255; Patricia King Hanson and Alan Gevinson, eds., *The American Film Institute Catalog of Motion Pictures Produced in the United States. American Films, 1911–1920: Film Entries* (Berkeley: University of California Press, 1988), esp. 337 (hereafter cited as AFI Catalog); Alan Gevinson, ed., *Within Our Gates: Ethnicity in American Feature Films* (Berkeley: University of California Press/AFI, 1997), esp. 1559; Paola Casella, *Hollywood Italian. Gli italiani nell'America di celluloide* (Milan: Baldini and Castoldi, 1998), 541–549. Particularly useful is Kevin Brownlow's discussion of early American films addressing Italian immigrants' experience in his *Behind the Mask of Innocence* (London: Jonathan Cape, 1990), 309–320.

32. Writing about a "nest of Italian thugs" living in the Mulberry Street area, Riis noted that they were all famous Neapolitan criminals who had been charged with every conceivable crime. Tied to what he perceived as a southern Italian custom of unruly violence that emerged in Italy as brigandism, for Riis the Black Hand phenomenon was a most un-American custom. See Riis, *How the Other Half Lives*, 52.

33. The topic of Black Hand activity was very much news of the day when the film was released. Although we do not have exact release dates, the copyright of the film (March 24, 1906) is remarkably close to the publication of a double-page special on the Black Hand in the *New York Tribune Sunday Magazine* on May 27, 1906.

34. Richard Gambino, *Blood of My Blood: The Dilemma of the Italian-Americans* (1974; repr. Toronto: Guernica, 2000), 278.

35. On the history of the literacy campaigns within the debates on immigration see John Higham, *Strangers in the Land: Patterns of American Nativism, 1890–1925* (1955; repr. New Brunswick, N.J.: Rutgers University Press, 1994), 103–108, 111–112, and 128–129.

36. Michael Slade Shull, *Radicalism in American Silent Films, 1909–1929. A Filmography and History* (Jefferson, N.C.: McFarland, 2000), 22.

37. Some titles include *The Black Hand, or Condemned to Death* (Vitascope, 1913), *The Black Hand* (Kalem, 1913), *A Blackhand Elopement* (Selig Poliscope, 1913), *Black Hand Conspiracy* (Apollo, 1914), *The Black Hand* (Royal, 1914), *The Black Hand* (Rolma Films/Metro Pictures, 1917). Among the foreign titles consider the French *The Black Hand* (Éclair, 1912). Éclair had already seized on the popularity of the American dime novels by releasing a Nick Carter detective film series beginning in 1908.

38. *MPW*, Jan. 30, 1909, 125. Other references are in *MPW*, Feb. 13, 1909, 173; and *MPN*, March 22, 1913.

39. Petrosino had gone to Sicily to further his investigations on the connections between Italian and Italian American Mafias—which he rightly suspected as rather flimsy since Italian criminality in New York had not yet become an organized syndicate. For an overview of Petrosino's figure and career see Arrigo Petacco, *Joe Petrosino*, trans. Charles Lam Markmann (New York: Macmillan, 1974); and George E. Pozzetta, "Another Look at the Petrosino Affair," *Italian Americana* 1 (fall 1974): 81–92.

40. "Petrosino's murder in 1909 . . . was decisive in the minds of many. In a leap beyond logic they concluded that his killing proved despite all evidence that the dreaded society did exist, that it was responsible for many if not all unsolved crimes in American cities, and further that all Italian-Americans were to blame" (Gambino, *Blood of My Blood*, 283).

41. The news prompted outrage from both the American and Italian American press. The former radicalized its prejudice and allegations of criminality against southern Italians. For instance, the *Brooklyn Daily Eagle* proclaimed "The Black Hand is everywhere!" The latter called for prompt action among all Italians to defy the Black Hand in the name of the honesty and integrity shared by Italian immigrants. Newspapers such as *L'Araldo*, *Il Telegrafo*, and *Il Progresso Italo-Americano* were quite aware, as George Pozzetta put it, that "the incident proved to be an important factor in establishing the specter of Italian criminality in the American mind and reinforcing the supposed undesirability of Italian immigrants. . . . The final success of the restrictionist movement owed no small debt to the death of Joseph Petrosino."

See Pozzetta, "Another Look," 89. For a discussion of the press reactions to Petrosino's assassination see Pitkin and Cordasco, *The Black Hand*, 106–136.

42. *MPW*, Nov. 16, 1912, 668. Over the years the story of Petrosino has remained well known. Several remakes have been made, from *Black Hand* (1950), with Gene Kelly, to *Pay or Die* (1960) with Ernest Borgnine.

43. *MPW*, March 20, 1915, 1784. In other cases films set in New York City and linked to Mafia-related urban crimes and vendettas pitted Italian gangsters against racially uncoded victims. This is the case in *The Cord of Life* (Biograph, 1909) and in later and longer productions like Griffith's much-praised *The Musketeers of Pig Alley* (Biograph, 1912).

44. *MPW*, Oct. 24, 1914, 540. Rather different is the case of *The Criminals* (Mecca, 1913). Here the police's misunderstanding of the situation is complete and surprisingly tragic, that is without a positive closure. A father has his child first kidnapped and then murdered by the Mafia. Still he ends up in prison, incriminated with the charge of being a mafioso himself. The ideological point of view of the film recognizes the injustice for the Italian character but apparently refuses to act on it. Without any opportunity of redemption for the racialized protagonist, the film did not appear particularly appealing to a popular audience. See *MPW*, April 5, 1913, 49.

45. Consider the racialized stories of passionate love and violent frenzy of *In Little Italy* (Biograph, 1909), *The Italian Blood* (Biograph, 1911), *The Violin Maker of Cremona* (Biograph, 1909), and *The Italian Barber* (Biograph, 1910)—all directed by Griffith—as well as *The Organ Grinder* (Kalem, 1909) and *The Immigrant's Violin* (Imp, 1912).

46. *MPW*, July 5, 1913, 83–84.

47. Written by both real and presumed slaves, slave narratives served the political purposes of emancipation or antiracism: these narratives of overcoming hardships and oppression ultimately stirred readers' emotional sympathy and sentimental concern. See Shirley Samuels, ed., *The Culture of Sentiment: Race, Gender, and Sentimentality in Nineteenth-Century America* (New York: Oxford University Press, 1992).

48. Italians' acting style was a mark of unmistakable difference, signaling their disproportionate reactions and emotional outbursts. Within the melodramatic metagenre underpinning American cinema as a whole, the difference between operatic stock figures and psychologized individuals (often all played by American performers) marked a crucial separation, charged with racialized connotations. It exhibited the divergence between clear-cut narratives whose characters' behavior was shown as reactive, instinctual, or perfunctory—as in later gangster films—and psychological story lines emphasizing characters' rational choices through inner turmoil and clear motivation. American actors and actresses did not have to invent such "excessive" performative styles: they could easily imitate them by visiting the numerous venues in New York hosting Italian opera and dialect theater. Since the second half of the nineteenth century, the trope of histrionic talent and melodramatic impersonations had informed the American (and worldwide) success and reputation of famous opera singers such as Enrico Caruso and Luisa Tetrazzini but also of stage actors such as Tommaso Salvini, Ernesto Rossi, Adele Ristori, and Ermete Novelli. Furthermore, since the 1890s, New York was home to a wealth of Italian vernacular plays, mostly in Neapolitan and Sicilian and comprising highly sentimental plots of love, jealousy, and revenge, as well as tear-jerking stories of sudden misfortunes or widespread deprivation, child death, kidnapping, and personal wretchedness. See Emelise Aleandri, "A History of Italian-American Theatre: 1900 to 1905" (Ph.D. diss., CUNY, 1983); and Emelise Aleandri, *Images of America: The Italian-American Immigrant Theatre of New York City* (Charleston, S.C.: Arcadia, 1999).

49. Beban changed the original title from *The Dago* to *The Italian*, apparently not out of sensibility but because he did not want to be a protagonist in a "common" program, as he desired instead to be associated with a special feature. Interestingly, the film was written by C. Gardner Sullivan, who had also scripted the aforementioned *The Wop* (Imp, 1913).

50. *NYDM*, Dec. 30, 1914, 26.

51. As Charlie Keil has rightly pointed out in his discussion of the film: "*The Italian* employs a heterogeneous audience address, which often operates in a contradictory fashion. . . . At the risk of being too schematic, one could argue that the film enfolds the material of its core narrative (which would seem to possess particular appeal for a working-class/immigrant audience) within a narrative frame which seems to work toward the cultivation of middle-class taste" (Charlie Keil, "Reframing *The Italian*: Questions of Audience Address in Early Cinema," *Journal of Film and Video* 42, no. 1 [spring 1990]: 37–38). Keil's essay on the film's textual strategies has provided an important starting point for my discussion, even though an analysis of the context of Italian immigrants' film reception remains out of its scope.

52. Several reviews praised the pathos of the narrative, the realism of the setting, and the poignancy of the acting performances. Particularly appreciated was Beban's histrionic acting ability and the sentimentality of the film's story line. See *NYDM*, Dec. 30, 1914, 26; and *MPN*, Jan. 2, 1915, 81.

53. The film had opened on April 12, 1915 as *The Sign of the Rose* at the Clune's Auditorium in Los Angeles, where *The Birth of a Nation* had just finished its nine-week run. In New York it opened on May 31 under the title *The Alien*. The film was mostly shot in Hollywood, and a few scenes were shot in New York. See *MPN*, Feb. 6, 1915, 35.

54. George Blaisdell, "The Sign of the Rose," *MPW*, May 1, 1915, 740.

55. His other racial melodramas include *Pasquale* (1916), *His Sweetheart* (1917), *Lost in Transit* (1917), *One More American* (1918), *Hearts of Men* (1919), *One Man in a Million* (1921), *The Sign of the Rose* (1922), *The Greatest Love of All* (1924), *The Loves of Ricardo* (1926).

56. George Beban, *Photoplay Characterization; One of a Series of Lectures Especially Prepared for Student Members of the Palmer Plan* (Los Angeles: Palmer Photoplay Corp., 1921), 19, 15.

57. This, of course, cannot but recall Harriet Beecher Stowe's *Uncle Tom's Cabin* (1852) and its numerous stage and filmic adaptations.

58. Guterl, *Color of Race*, 6. Guterl has argued that the success of Griffith's film "southernized" the American racial discourse; Jacobson places this biracialist emphasis in the 1920s. See Jacobson, *Whiteness of a Different Color*.

59. Michael Rogin partly addressed this development in his *Blackface, White Noise*, particularly in chapters 4 and 5. Yet by limiting his analysis to "four race movies—*Uncle Tom's Cabin* [1902–1903], *The Birth of a Nation* [1915], *The Jazz Singer* [1927], and *Gone With the Wind* [1939]" (73)—relatively distant in time from one another, his nevertheless groundbreaking study paints a rather curtailed account of the range, dynamics, and workings of American cinema's racial representations.

60. Nelli, *Business of Crime*, 100.

61. Compare, e.g., F. M. White's "The Black Hand in Control of Italian New York," *Outlook Magazine*, Aug. 16, 1913, 858–859, with his later articles "The Police and the Black Hand," *Outlook*, June 14, 1916, 347–348; and "The Passing of the Great Hand," *Century Magazine*, Jan. 1918, 331–336. I have not found much information about a film that may have addressed the demise of the Black Hand, *Black Hand Blues* (Pathè Exchange, 1925) directed by Hal E. Roach.

62. Michael Fiaschetti, the successor of Petrosino at the helm of the Italian Police Squad, commented negatively about the impact of Prohibition on Italian criminality. In his 1930 autobiography, *You Gotta Be Rough*, he sarcastically complained, "We broke the Black Hand, kept after the gangs, sent leaders and members to prison and the electric chair. . . . Today the Black Hand is almost gone. Prohibition helped a lot. It took a bad thing and turned into something much worse. . . . The Eighteenth Amendment endowed the Black Hand with fabulous funds and took it from the isolated Italian quarters and bestowed it on the cities at large" (Michael Fiaschetti, as told to Prosper Buranelli, *You Gotta Be Rough: The Adventures of Detective Fiaschetti of the Italian Squad* [Garden City, N.Y.: Doubleday, 1930], 13–15).

63. "Thus immigration restriction, along with the Prohibition, marked the end of the Black Hand era and introduced many who had been involved in crime within the Italian community into the mainstream of American gangsterdom" (Humbert S. Nelli, "Italians and Crime in Chicago: The Formative Years, 1890–1920," *American Journal of Sociology* 74 [Jan. 1969]: 380). See also Tommaso Sassone, "Italy's Criminals in the United States," *Current History* 15 (Oct. 1921): 23–31.

64. Henry Barrett Chamberlain, "Crime as a Business in Chicago," *Bulletin of the Chicago Crime Commission*, no. 6 (Oct. 1, 1919), 1, quoted in Nelli, "Italians and Crime," 386.

65. Consider, e.g., *Little Italy* (Realart Pictures, 1921), *Look Your Best* (Goldwyn Pictures, 1923), *Defying the Law* (William B. Brush Productions, 1924), *The Man in Blue* (Universal, 1925), *Sally in Our Alley* (Columbia Pictures, 1927), *The Secret Hour* (Paramount, 1928), and *Love, Live, and Laugh* (Fox Film Corp., 1929).

66. The most famous include Sonya Levien, Anita Loos, Frances Marion, Jeanie Macpherson, and June Mathis. Levien wrote the script for *Who Will Marry Me?* (1919) and *Salomè of the Tenements* (1925). June Mathis, apart from writing the script for *The Black Hand* (Rolma Films/Metro Pictures, 1917), worked on several films starring actress Mabel Taliaferro, such as *Dawn of Love* (1916), *Purple Lady* (1916), *Magdalene of the Hills* (1917), *Threads of Fate* (1917), and *Lombardi, Ltd.* (1919), and was instrumental in launching the career of Rudolph Valentino. Frances Marion wrote *The Social Highwayman* (1916); *Poor Little Peppina* (1916), starring Mary Pickford; and *The Love Light* (1921), a love story set in Italy during WWI, again starring Mary Pickford.

67. This, of course, could be the subject of an entirely different essay. I have begun to explore the 1920s encounter of racial and gender tensions with regard to American media's representation of such Italians as Mussolini and Valentino in G. Bertellini, "*Duce/Divo*: Masculinity, Racial Identity, and Politics among Italian-Americans in 1920s New York City," *Journal of Urban History* 31 (2005).

68. Consider, e.g., his character's enduring of torture in *The Sheik* (1921), seduction and death in *Blood and Sand* (1922), sentimental self-sacrifice in *Cobra* (1924), deceit and whipping in *The Last of the Sheik* (1926). Quite interestingly, referring to the sadomasochistic fantasy of the "whipping boy," Miriam Hansen refers to Freud's intriguing mentioning of *Uncle Tom's Cabin* as an example. See Miriam Hansen, *Babel and Babylon: Spectatorship in American Silent Film* (Cambridge, Mass.: Harvard University Press, 1991), 287.

69. Nelli nicely summarizes this dynamic: "In this process of 'Americanizing' Italian criminal activities, 'American' Italians established the Italian 'syndicate'" (Nelli, "Italians and Crime," 391).

70. David E. Ruth, *Inventing the Public Enemy: The Gangster in American Culture, 1918–1934* (Chicago: University of Chicago Press, 1996), 2–3.

71. Several gangster films of the 1920s, from *Racing Luck* (Grand-Usher, 1924) to *The Beautiful City* (First National, 1925), instead, told stories in which the heavily racialized Italian criminal operates almost exclusively within the Italian quarters.

T HE PECULIAR AMERICAN MIX of race, class, and gender that in many crucial ways defines native cultures of criminality finds its surest expression in
mob movies with a Chinatown setting. Underworld gang activities of the
tongs and Triads in Chinatown have repeatedly provided the narrative motivation
for action and detective investigations. In *Chinatown* (1974) or *Hammett* (1982)
Chinatown is ultimately the unsolvable mystery; in *Big Trouble in Little China*
(1986) it operates as a home-grown exotic location for Indiana Jones–style antics;
Year of the Dragon (1985) constructs its Chinatown as an explicitly racist commentary on contemporary American identity; and, more recently, Chinatown serves as
authenticating background for American-located star vehicles for Hong Kong mar-
tial arts heroes Jet Li in *Romeo Must Die* (2000), Yun-Fat Chow in *The Replacement
Killers* (1998) and *The Corruptor* (1999), and Jackie Chan in *Rush Hour* (1998). Yet
Chinatown far exceeds its immediate role as dramatic location for the pursuit and
capture of criminal gangs. Rather, the symbolic resonance of the "city within the
city," the alien and mysterious within the quotidian ordinariness of "American" culture, suggests most forcefully that it is the locale itself that is set up for epistemological investigation.

The "alien" and "exotic" location that Chinatown represents inevitably casts its
occupants as "other," yet Chinatown is also an American location. This contradiction produces a potential collapse of the boundaries that separate self from other —
American from Chinese, foreign from native, white from yellow, legitimate from
illegitimate, known from unknown. As this chapter reveals, fictional American
Chinatowns and their underworld habitués have a long and complex history, but it
is one that coheres around questions of racial and ethnic identity. Furthermore, as

my short history shows, American cinema has often deployed images of Chinatown as a way of investing an element of novelty into generic formulas such as the gangster film. The repetitive use of underworld stories with Chinatown settings suggests this is a narrative trope that transcends any particular cycle of crime movies. Although Chinatown may appear peripheral to the concerns of the majority of films within any given cycle, its recurrence within and across cycles conversely suggests its centrality and importance to the production of fictional American ganglands.

Whether located in London's Limehouse or the irregular triangle formed by New York's Doyers, Pell, and Mott streets or the area in San Francisco bound by Stockton, Washington, Dupont, and Pacific streets, which housed the Devil's Kitchen, Ragpicker's Alley, and the Dog Kennel, Chinatown provided an apparently inexhaustible source of inspiration for the workers who produced stories for the new mass media. In the popular culture of the day the Chinatowns situated in the great seaports of Europe and America became imaginative spaces where the fears and desires engendered by the urban instabilities around racial difference were especially pronounced. For the better part of the late nineteenth, and well into the twentieth, century in the popular Western imagination Chinatown was synonymous with organized crime, prostitution, gambling, and narcotics; the exotic mysticism of the Orient turned these otherwise mundane activities into feverishly seductive acts of subterranean debauchery.

In his surrealist novel *Nadja* André Breton recalled watching an American film "in which a Chinese who had found some way to multiply himself invaded New York by means of several million self reproductions. He entered President Wilson's office followed by himself, and by himself, and by himself; the President removed his *pince-nez*. This film, which has affected me more than any other, was called *The Grip of the Octopus*."[1] The multiple images of Chinese characters within the popular cultural products I examine in this chapter are all versions of Breton's self-reproducing man, fearsome white projections of being swallowed whole by an encroaching alien culture. They point, as Sean McCann has suggested of the dead yellow women in Dashiell Hammett's detective fiction, "to the social force of race" while emphasizing the "fictive nature" of race.[2] The images of white slavery, dope dens, and other illicit activities of Chinatown, organized and controlled by the tongs, fall within the remit of the 1930s gangster movie as described by Jonathan Munby: the "talking gangster films had everything to do with an attack on the terms of assimilation and ruling definitions of America and Americanness. Objections to the gangster film were thus not limited to questions of morality but national self-image."[3] If this was true for Irish or Italian Americans, it was doubly the case for Chinese Americans. Despite the prevailing mythology that the tongs are a foreign criminal organization, they are a product of American immigration policies and the popular imagination—a compelling image of an outlawed miscegenated culture, which with ever-vigilant policing could be safely contained within the borders of Chinatown, located within, yet not part of, the United States.

Whatever the reality of America's Chinatowns, their primary function in fiction is to act as a symbolic space where issues of national and international identity can be dramatized; Chinatown represents a miscegenated culture: a mess of European, African, and Chinese elements. In his illustrated guide to the slums of New York, published in 1890, Jacob Riis wrote: "The one thing you shall vainly ask for in the chief city of America is a distinctly American community. There is none."[4] Italian, French, African, Spanish, Bohemian, Russian, Scandinavian, Jewish, Chinese, and even Arab you can find for the asking, but not an American. The films considered in this chapter ultimately recognize the impossibility of securing a conception of an American identity unsullied by racial and ethnic mixing yet nevertheless attempt to maintain the appearance of an essential American identity free from Oriental, African, and low European borrowings. Hellish visions of Chinatown's polyglot communities suggest what will befall America's urban masses if racial, gender, and class boundaries are not rigorously policed. Contained within the borders of Chinatown, America's mongrel hordes can be controlled even as they produce a dramatic tension drawn out of the threatened collapse of the boundaries that separate self from other. Popular fictions, therefore, exploit the moments when the border is envisioned as permeable, producing fables of racial hybridity that are now commonly recognized as representative American narratives.

In films such as *Chinatown Villains* (1916), *The Tong Man* (1919), *Shadows of Chinatown* (1926), *Welcome Danger* (1929), *Chinatown Nights* (1929), *East Is West* (1930), *Law of the Tong* (1931), *Chinatown after Dark* (1931), *The Hatchet Man* (1932), and *Yellow Cargo* (1936), Hollywood's exploitation of Chinatown locales is located within a wider cultural enthrallment with Sino-American crossings. Visible in the 1920s and 1930s vogue for chinoiserie in ceramic, fabric, and furnishing design, the popular motifs of Asiatic decorative culture were part of a fascination with China that informed the themes and narratives of a range of media: fashion illustration, novels, magazine fiction, newspaper comic strips, blood-and-thunder melodramas, theater shows and vaudeville, moving pictures, city tours, and on radio and phonograph records, a number of which are explored here. The rest of this chapter considers how the play with racial crossings and overlap is shaped through the merging of fact and fantasy, authenticity and fabrication; the visible world of the urban streets and an invisible subterranean realm; how the dissembling of identity through disguise is both the object of a detective's inquiry and his means of insinuation into the criminal fraternity of Chinatown; the chapter concludes with an analysis of the Warner Bros. 1932 production *The Hatchet Man*, starring Edward G. Robinson playing a Chinese assassin who belongs to a San Francisco tong. Like most Chinatown stories, the film is a didactic tale about the impossibility of Chinese and American assimilation.

Writing in the mid-1930s, French journalist and avant-garde poet Blaise Cendrars described the nature of the criminal underworld as contemporary fiction factories imagined it:

> The passage between the reality of the street and the blazing artificiality of a bar happens so easily, and so unexpectedly. . . . You feel a sense of vertigo. Suddenly, you are hanging on to your table for dear life, like a wreck tossed about a tidal wave of dancing couples in a hot-jazz club. The first shot of alcohol down, overwhelmed by the abstract décor, nothing can help you figure out where you are, or how you got there.
>
> Are you in Shanghai? In Buenos Aires? In a New York "speak-easy"? Or are you in Paris?
>
> Without being aware of it, you have landed, simply and completely, in *gangsland*—a cynical and triumphant spectacle of neon lights in a miserable little room, where nothing is a mystery, but everything is disturbing.[5]

The fantastical reality of Cendrars's "gangsland" finds its apposite location in Chinatown: a country within a country, a city within a city, a familiar world given a fantastical twist. The setting is defined by customary tropes of Orientalism; the sense of dislocation that accompanies the excited activities of characters lured into the dark alleys and underground warrens of Chinatown is exaggerated by its location within a Western city.[6] The meeting of the Orient and the West in these tales promises a thrilling conflict of cultures that is similar to that produced by stories of Westerners in Shanghai, Macao, Hong Kong, or other colonial seaports in the Orient, but it also has its peculiarities. Historian of American detective fiction Sean McCann suggests the most significant difference is that, "where the border is a 'chasm' in the foreign-adventure story, it is a sieve" in America's urban environment.[7]

The disruptive forces that infuse their presence into the American mainstream, breeching the borders of Chinatown, are the organized criminal gangs known as tongs. In his highly popular informal history of the gangs of New York, Herbert Asbury dedicates a chapter to the disenfranchised riffraff and hoodlums of Chinatown, the tongs, who, like the gangster members of the Plug Uglies, Dead Rabbits, and Whyos, mark time as pawns in the governance of the city, part of the great lumpen mob.[8] According to Asbury the tongs, Chinese equivalents of the book's Irish, Jewish, and Italian mobsters, controlled Chinatown's graft. Despite the period's prevailing belief that the tongs were once venerable associations or guilds with roots in the Old World, they were in fact, as Asbury liked to point out, "American as chop suey—the latter is said to have been invented by an American dishwasher in a San Francisco restaurant, while the first tong was organized in the Western gold fields about 1860."[9] Like other contemporary American gangs, the tongs were a loose confederation that helped organize and exploit the illicit activities of gambling, prostitution, and dope peddling.

241

A product of the popular construction of Chinese Americans, the tongs sat alongside the opium den, white slavery, fan-tan games, and the network of underground galleries and passageways that were said to run beneath Chinatown. Writing in 1948, Jack Lait and Lee Mortimer recognized the importance of Chinatown as a key attraction in tourist guides that promise to take the reader on an unorthodox journey to the less well lit parts of the town: "P-s-s-t—Lait and Mortimer want a word with you—confidential . . . off the record and on the up-and-up." [10] Unlike, for example, Sax Rohmer, author of the Fu Manchu stories and *Dope*, his 1919 novel with a Limehouse setting, Lait and Mortimer's exposé did not pull back the curtain on debauched aristocrats "kicking the gong around" and "hitting the pipe to beat hell" but, in an echo of Asbury, instead revealed Chinatown to be as "counterfeit as chop suey." The "musty gag" about the anatomy of Chinese girls is laughed down; the women are chaste, gambling is confined among Chinese, narcotics only circulate among non-Americanized Chinese sailors, and the many tongs have been reduced to two competitors. The tongs "in their more pugnacious days, might have been compared to the white gangs and mobs that fought each other, with even more ferocious violence, for territorial control of rackets. Now the tongs are business and social groups, boards of trade or chambers of commerce, as it were." [11] Like their contemporaries, the American Mafia, the Chinese racketeers are represented as hiding behind a veneer of respectability. This, however, says less about the actuality of the tongs' activities and rather more about a shift in contemporary discourses on crime and ethnicity.

One of Lait and Mortimer's professed aims was to protect the innocent from being "taken" by the big city's shysters, grifters, and flimflam men: "The hick who takes in Chinatown from a sightseeing bus is led first to the Rescue Society for bowery bums, which, according to the guide, is located in what was once an opium den. Then he is shown a joss house, in back of the Chinatown post office, and he is told about the maze of secret tunnels which are supposed to connect most of the buildings in the area, for use during the tong wars, opium or prohibition raids." [12] What the tourist wishes to see is no longer there, if, indeed, it ever was. The play between Chinatown as a reality of urban ghetto life and as a site for a white-sponsored fantasy of opium-fueled illicit activities runs throughout the fictional and popular histories. [13] Bum, burglar, highwayman, opium fiend, and leading light in the brotherhood of yeggs, Jack Black, in his 1926 autobiography, writes: "The hypos [drug addicts] I spent the night with in the city prison had aroused my curiosity about Chinatown. I put in many a night prowling through the alleys watching these mysterious people gambling, smoking opium, and trafficking in their women slaves. There were rumors of strange, mysterious underground passages below the streets and under the buildings, but I never saw them and I have since come to doubt whether they ever existed." [14] Sax Rohmer's stories are particularly notable for the manner in which Rohmer calls the reader's attention to the fictive nature of America's Chinatowns: "Unlike its sister colony in New York, there are no show places in

Limehouse. The visitor sees nothing but mean streets and dark doorways. The superficial inquirer comes away convinced that the romance of the Asiatic district has no existence outside the imaginations of writers of fiction. Yet here lies a secret quarter, as secret and as strange, in its smaller way, as its parent in China which is called the Purple Forbidden City."[15] Rohmer's ploy for authenticating London's Chinatown, by revealing the artifice of America's Chinatowns, is a motif repeated in his work. ("The place, which was quite palpably an opium den, must have disappointed anyone familiar with the more ornate houses of Chinese vice in San Francisco and elsewhere.")[16] Rohmer's need to distinguish between the authentic (London's Chinatown) and the inauthentic (San Francisco's Chinatown) was driven by the need to give credence to his imaginative work.

By the 1920s the image of the evil Chinaman was such a cliché that in his "Detective Story Decalogue" (1928), the writer of detective stories Ronald A. Knox warned readers that if a Chinaman figured in a mystery story, it would be no good: "Why this should be so I do not know, unless we can find a reason for it in our western habit of assuming that the Celestial is over-equipped in the matter of brains, and under-equipped in the matter of morals. I only offer it as a fact of observation that, if you are turning over the pages of a book and come across some mention of the 'slit-like eyes of Chin Loo,' you had best put it down at once; it is bad."[17] In the two-reel comedy *The Detectress* (1919) the formula of the sinister Chinese overlord and the crime-infested underworld of Chinatown is parodied as the heroine gives chase, and in turn is chased, along corridors hidden behind walls, falls through trapdoors in the floor, and hides behind concealed doors. The cliché situations are repeated to an absurd degree until the denouement, when it is revealed that the whole escapade has been nothing more than a fantasy, induced by opium smoke the heroine had accidentally inhaled while loitering outside the window of a real dope den.

Chinatown's tentative fix in reality is highlighted in the second of Asbury's series of informal histories of America's underworld, which focused on San Francisco's Barbary Coast. In this book he seemed to confirm all the purported wickedness of America's Chinese: "The seeker after thrills or depravity found in Chinatown no melodeons, no dance-halls, no concert saloons, and only an occasional bar-room, but he did find an abundance of opium-smoking resorts, houses of prostitution, and gambling hells." However, Asbury also reveals that many of the

> places wherein opium was smoked, or was supposed to be smoked, were fakes, tourist-shockers conducted by the professional guides to the quarter, who were licensed by the city and were organized as the Chinatown guides Association. These abodes of synthetic sin were invariably dank and dreary cellars, and the entrances to them were so arranged as to persuade the visitor that he was traversing innumerable and, of course, dangerous underground passages. In many of these dimly lighted ways evil-looking Chinamen, in the employ of the guides, slunk back and forth, carrying knives and hatchets and providing atmosphere and local

color. It was this illusion, together with the tall tales told by tourists of their experiences in San Francisco, which gave rise to the belief that Chinatown was a veritable network of subterranean galleries. This fancy persisted until the district was destroyed in 1906. While it lay in ruins, the whole area was carefully explored and mapped. Not a single underground passage was discovered, and few cellars larger or deeper than are commonly found under dwellings and business houses.[18]

Whether reality or tourist fantasy, following the earthquake, San Francisco's Chinatown, according to Asbury, never returned to sinful ways. He suggests few of the opium resorts or slave cribs for prostitutes were rebuilt: "As an organized center of vice and crime Chinatown virtually came to end on that catastrophic spring day" in 1906.[19] Chinatown's importance to the sellers of pulp fiction did not diminish, however; it continued to hold a grip on the public's imagination. The 1923 Lon Chaney feature *The Shock* ends with the spectacular destruction of San Francisco's Chinatown, which had been described in the intertitles as "a cesspool of poppyland . . . street of crime, of fear, of hate, of mystery . . . a whirlpool of vice and intrigue." Indeed, the earthquake simply appeared in subsequent fictions as an act of God that clears away the corruption, with Chinatown as a place of urban dread and danger now safely buried in the rubble of the past, the veneer of history giving credibility to otherwise formulaic tales.

Paramount, then, in fictions located within the realm of Chinatown was the need to establish an aura of authenticity, or at least a suspension of disbelief, against counterclaims of skepticism and incredulity. To avoid accusations of being overly generic and cliché, Dashiell Hammett's best-known Chinatown story, "Dead Yellow Women" (1925), goes to some lengths to gain a credible fictional verisimilitude. Like other fiction producers Hammett is quick to advance the idea that Chinatown is all artifice, lit up for the tourists: "Grant Avenue, the main street and spine of the strip, is for the most of its length a street of gaudy shops and flashy chop-suey houses catering to the tourist trade, where the racket of American jazz orchestras drowns the occasional squeak of a Chinese flute."[20] The Continental Op is aware that the labyrinth of corridors and stairways that he has to traverse in order to get an interview with the Chinese overlord Chang Li Ching exists because it is what is expected of Chinatown as much as for any practical purpose: "We did a lot more of the winding around, we did some stair climbing and some stair descending, and the rest of the foolishness. I figured I'd been indoors nearly half an hour by now, and I had seen nobody but my guide."[21] When he finally meets Chang they engage in a conversation that lampoons conventional encounters between well-matched adversaries:

"If the Terror of Evildoers will honor one of my deplorable chairs by resting his divine body on it, I can assure him the chair shall be burned afterward, so no lesser being may use it. Or will the Prince of Thief-catchers permit me to send a servant to his palace for a chair worthy of him?"

I went slowly to a chair, trying to arrange words in my mind. This old joker was spoofing me with an exaggeration—a burlesque—of the well-known Chinese politeness. I'm not hard to get along with; I'll play anybody's game up to a certain point.[22]

Despite this tomfoolery, Chinatown's mandarins pose a very real and present threat: "If you leave the main thoroughfares and showplaces and start poking around in alleys and dark corners, and nothing happens to you, the chances are you'll find some interesting things—though you won't like some of them."[23] By the end of the story the twists and turns of the mystery have unraveled, revealing only a very prosaic smuggling of coolies, but as the Continental Op confesses, he has "stopped eating in Chinese restaurants, and that if I never have to visit Chinatown again it'll be soon enough."[24]

Chinatown Nights (Paramount, 1929), William Wellman's first sound film, makes the fictive nature of Chinatown the film's subject. The "rapturous revelry" that occurs when East meets West is the promise that lures tourists into Chinatown after dark, but are the seductive entreaties of Chinatown real or illusions designed for vacationing pleasure-seekers? Joan Fry (Florence Vidor), a society lady touring Chinatown, witnesses the killing of a Chinaman who crossed the boundary separating the warring tongs, but was the murder real or a piece of theater? She leaves the security of the tour bus, curiosity leading her to Chuck Riley (Wallace Beery), who has been loitering in the shadows—is he a key to the truth? She follows Riley through a labyrinth of corridors and passageways, which eventually lead to a room; the door is locked behind her, and she is held captive—an amusing distraction for Riley. The room is small, though well furnished; she can hear classical music through the walls, and the library of books contains the plays of Shakespeare, which prompts Fry and Riley to trade quotes: she *Julius Caesar,* he *The Taming of the Shrew.* Fry's curiosity about this savage, yet apparently cultivated, man grows into a sexual attraction. Her desire for the educated brute appears tangible, but it is not so readily reciprocated. Riley considers her just another bored uptown woman who comes down to Chinatown for thrills. But for Fry, Riley is the "only real man I have ever known." She is willing to risk all to experience "once" in her life what it is to be a "real woman." The following morning she is shown dressed in silk pajamas, and Riley describes her as "having her head uptown and her body in the Barbary Coast."

By making love with Riley she experiences a sexual thrill enhanced by the crossing of class boundaries, which is given an added dimension through evoking the fear and pleasure in crossing racial borders. The seduction of Chinatown that drew her to Riley in the first instance, the miscegenational impulse, is only implicit, but kidnapped by Boston Charley (Warner Oland), Riley's Chinese rival for the control of Chinatown, it is made explicit—a once "decent" woman now belongs to Chinatown. The film's coda returns to the tour bus with the guide repeating his appeal to holiday makers, but this time a young working-class girl is not persuaded to join the tour; turning to her boyfriend, she declaims that it is all baloney—a fake. But is it all a fake? For the slumming society woman the desire to experience the real creates out of Chinatown a plausible eroticized space, but for the working-class girl who already experiences the "real," Chinatown is simply and transparently phony. In fictions such as this, chinoiserie or Chinatown's appeal was the thrill of crossing into the "unknown" of an alien culture—moving out of the certainties of white middle-class values into a space defined as liminal in terms of the racial, class, gender, and sexual crossings that occur.

Moving through the liminality of Chinatown is the symbolic figure of the detective, who, through the use of disguise, is able to travel anonymously between cultures.[25] Like Sherlock Holmes, Paul Harley in Sax Rohmer's Chinatown tales is a gentleman detective.[26] Harley rents a small apartment in London's East End that he visits only after dark, where he transforms himself into a seaman: "There was nothing in its appointments, as revealed in the light of an oil lamp burning on the solitary table, to distinguish it from a thousand other such apartments which may be leased for a few shillings a week in the neighborhood. That adjoining might have told a different story, for it more closely resembled an actor's dressing room than a seaman's."[27] Harley is the consummate actor—"'Where 'ave you been, old son?' growled Harley, in that wonderful dialect of his which I had so often and so vainly sought to cultivate."[28] His skill in the art of disguise is such that not even his closest companions could recognize him if he so wished: "I struck a match. It revealed my ruffianly looking companion—in whom his nearest friends must have failed to recognize Mr. Paul Harley of Chancery Lane."[29]

This is not a uniquely British conception of character. The mid-1930s syndicated newspaper strip, *Red Barry*, for example, featured an American equivalent of Paul Harley. In the 1935/1936 newspaper strip *The Bells of Pell Street*, Red Barry, an "undercover" agent, roams the streets of Chinatown disguised, so as not to attract attention to himself, as a hoodlum.[30] Erle Stanley Gardner's series character Ed Jenkins, who was first introduced in a 1927 edition of *The Black Mask* magazine, is another example:

I was cold. My limbs were cramped from a night on the bare floor. My bones ached. My nostrils rebelled at the stench of the place, at the smell of my own clothing.

For I was disguised as a Chinaman of the lower class, and the building was an abandoned, condemned community house, given over to rats, cockroaches, cobwebs, smells.

I was wanted for first-degree murder. As far as the police knew, Ed Jenkins, the Phantom Crook, arrested for murder, had escaped after being arrested. They didn't know of a confidential conversation I had had with the district attorney in which that official had told me he knew I was innocent, but that he had important work for me. Because he had found corruption in his own force and knew not whom to trust, he asked me to escape from the police and undertake a dangerous mission.[31]

Jenkins not only crosses between classes and races, but he also subverts comfortable notions of innocence and legitimacy. He is a middle-class white man working for the district attorney, who, as the Phantom Crook, is wanted for murder and is presently masquerading as a lower-class Chinaman. Corruption in the police force is rife — the police are criminals, and, in Jenkins's case, the criminals are the police. Nothing appears fixed. In these stories the urban world is defined in terms of the instabilities of institutions and identities.[32] The disguise practiced by detectives, then, only adds to the sense of Chinatown as a place of deception and unreality.[33]

If the easy crossing between classes (at least from above to below) partly defines the fictional appeal of Chinatown, then the racial crossings are more significant still. In these popular fictions Chinatown symbolizes the racial and ethnic diversity and cultural hybridity that defines the modern city: "He descended three stairs, and entered a room laden with a sickly perfume, compounded of stale beer and spirits, of greasy humanity, European, Asiatic and African, of cheap tobacco and cheaper scents, and, vaguely, of opium. . . . [A]n unsavory den was Malay Jack's, where flotsam of the river might be found. Yellow men there were, and black men and brown men. But all the women were white."[34] The introduction to Limehouse in D. W. Griffith's *Broken Blossoms* (1918) offers a complimentary image: inside a dope den, called in the intertitles a "Scarlet House of Sin . . . where the Orient squats at the portals of the West," is a motley collection of men, "Chinese, Malays, Lascars," and, as in Rohmer's story, an exclusive clientele of white women. Similarly, The "Shanghai Lil" sequence in *Footlight Parade* (Warner Bros., 1933) is set in a polyglot space — the International Saloon, where men and women of all races mix; the dope den at the rear of the saloon, however, is used exclusively by blonde white women. In the Lon Chaney feature *The Blackbird* (MGM, 1925) the initial scenes are set in a working-class musical hall in the Limehouse district, where a party of slumming toffs plan a late-night visit to Plum Street to watch the "Chinkies smoking." The male and female upper-class dalliance with the pleasures of Chinatown is contrasted with the working-class prohibition against a young white woman dating a Chinese man.[35] In stories such as these the fear and dread of Chinatown are conceived as a threat to the sanctity of white women.

In his fascinating history of the birth of the British drug underground, Marek Kohn cites a report from a San Francisco physician whose trip to a Chinatown dope den had left him appalled: "the sickening sight of young white girls from sixteen to twenty years of age lying half-undressed on the floor or couches, smoking with their 'lovers.' Men and women, Chinese and white people, mix in Chinatown smoking houses." The "ultimate menace of drugs," concludes Kohn, was that they "facilitated the seduction of young white women by men of other races."[36] The purity of white British women is threatened by drugs and, therefore, by Chinatown (through which it is presumed the drugs are peddled), putting the very health of the nation under threat. As Kohn notes, the first of the British drug panics developed in the months following the end of the Great War. It drew from the stories of the white slave trade and took its form from the xenophobic spy stories that the war had made so popular, but its most striking feature was its emphasis on women:

> Actresses, chorus girls, "night club girls," "bachelor girls," "flappers," "women of the unfortunate class"; whether they played the part of victim or harpy, the women of the drug underworld were of uncontainable class. Theirs was not a political radicalism, but they all laid claim to an independence that was highly disturbing to orthodox commentators. No form of journalism, popular literature or film is more didactic than the drug story, and contemporary narratives were indefatigable in their efforts to impress the folly of drug taking upon the public. In continually retelling the story of the downfall of young women, these narratives also asserted that, without protection and dependence, women were in deadly danger.[37]

The inevitable campaign to control the distribution of drugs was partly fueled by scare stories of a moral vacuum in the United States that had led, so it was claimed, to an "absence of order in America's own house." This in turn led to claims being made by some British campaigners that cocaine not only "triggered outbursts of violence in black men" but made them apt to rape white women: "there was talk of Southern police officers acquiring larger caliber guns to counter this individualized version of the specter of black rebellion."[38] According to Kohn the subtext of this campaign rhetoric was based on America's emergence as a postwar world power and of Britain's decline. Symptomatic of this new dominance was the novel vogue for jazz music in London in the years immediately after the end of the war: "Jazz was the sound of the Aftermath; a revivifying breath from America — and, radically, from Africa — after Europe's bout of self-destruction. It threatened an inversion of the cultural order, with its paradoxical combination of the modern and the 'primitive.'"[39] Concomitant with the fear of losing power was the British fear of losing identity — drugs, America, and jazz, with Chinatown as an alien host, became overriding symbols of this anxiety. In *Dope: A Story of Chinatown and the Drug Traffic* Rohmer wrote: "From the rooms below arose the strains of an American melody. Dancing was in progress, or, rather, one of those orgiastic ceremonies which passed for dancing during this pagan period."[40] London appeared to be under siege. Toward the end of another story with a Chinatown setting, Rohmer noted that it was "the one district of London which possesses the property of swallowing people up."[41] In Chinatown identity dissolves. In British stories that feature America's Chinatowns the border between white and yellow cultures is dramatized as all too porous (confirming the transatlantic image of Americans as racial hybrids), whereas America's own Chinatown fictions emphasize the maintenance of the borders.

As cultural historian Jennifer DeVere Brody argues in *Impossible Purities*, Britain had a long-standing tradition of casting American culture, in contrast to itself, as hybrid and impure. In this, the figure of the female mulatto is America's ultimate symbol, precisely the image that so much American cultural activity seeks to counter.[42] Hammett's "Dead Yellow Women" begins with just such a portrait of racial and cultural hybridity:

> She was sitting straight and stiff in one of the Old Man's chairs when he called me into his office—a tall girl of perhaps twenty-four, broad-shouldered, deep-bosomed, in mannish gray clothes. That she was an Oriental showed only in the black shine of her bobbed hair, in the pale yellow of her unpowdered skin, and in the fold of her upper lids at the outer eye-corners, half-hidden by the dark rims of her spectacles. But there was no slant to her eyes, her nose was aquiline, and she had more chin than Mongolians usually have. She was modern Chinese-American from the flat heels of her tan shoes to the crown of her untrimmed felt hat.[43]

This mannish, hyphenated Chinese American woman represents an unstable identity that accompanies images of racial and gender hybridity. She is the daughter of a wealthy Chinese merchant who lives on the coast some distance, but not too far, from Chinatown. Educated at an eastern university, she has a number of degrees, won a tennis championship, Anglicized her name to Lillian, and "published a book on the nature and significance of fetishes, whatever all that is or are."[44] However, her ties to the Old World remain strong, and toward the end of the story she makes a surprise appearance transformed into an Oriental beauty: "The queen of something stood there! She was a tall woman, straight-bodied and proud. A butterfly-shaped headdress decked with the loot of a dozen jewelry stores exaggerated her height. Her gown was amethyst filigreed with gold above, a living rainbow below. The clothes were nothing!"[45] The amethyst, gold and rainbow coloring of her dress contrast sharply with the gray suit, flat heels, and felt hat she had worn earlier. Her appearance as an Oriental queen posits the idea that this is her true identity; her cross-racial and gender identity is revealed as a facade. At the conclusion of the story, Hammett has imposed a racial order on things, a momentary stability at this level, sufficient, at least, to allow for a satisfactory resolution.[46]

As with Hammett, maintaining a racial divide is characteristic of Jacob Riis's work. In his chapter on Chinatown, Riis authenticates his account by dismissing the notion that Chinatown is a site of attraction: "as a spectacle it is disappointing."[47] Emphasizing the sordid and despoiled nature of the ghetto, Riis maintains the border between white and yellow worlds by highlighting the commonly held idea that what makes the Chinaman unique among the alien horde of New York's tenement dwellers is his lack of willingness to assimilate—to become an American. All "attempts to make an effective Christian of John Chinaman will remain abortive in this generation; of the next I have, if anything, less hope. Ages of senseless idolatry, a mere-grub worship, have left him without the essential qualities for appreciating the gentle teachings of a faith whose motive and unselfish spirit are beyond his grasp."[48] Chinatown is a closed society, at least to authority, and it is not because "all Chinamen look alike, but rather to their acting 'alike,' in a body, to defeat discovery at any cost."[49] But the Chinaman's desire "to be let alone" needs to be balanced by the one group he is willing to let into his world—young white women. Although Riis offers the then liberal view that this traffic in souls can be stemmed by allowing the Chinese to bring their wives to America so they will no longer be "homeless strangers among us," his image of the innocent young white girl lured into the warrens of Chinatown, and then to be held there in the viselike grip of opium addiction, is wholly in keeping with the period's dominant conception of the white slave trade: "the women, all white, girls hardly yet grown to womanhood, worshipping nothing save the pipe that has enslaved them body and soul. Easily tempted from homes that have no claim upon the name, they rarely or never return."[50] Although the Chinese resistance to absorption into the American body is explained by their inability to admit Christian ideals, the register of their desire for white women encourages a policing of the Chinese ghetto to doubly insure against miscegenation and assimilation.

Riis's conception of Chinese Americans as barely human sits neatly alongside the period's racial belief system as outlined by labor historian Alexander Saxton:

> The outstanding characteristic of all those disparate elements which composed the non-Chinese labor force was that they were not Chinese. Aspirant leaders engaged in a search for facts or fictions to express the values of non-Chineseness. Christianity would be stressed in contrast to earlier (and eastern) focus on the Catholic-Protestant cleavage. Assimilability was on the point of being discovered—that mysterious substance which resided in the circulatory systems of persons having certain ancestries and which rendered them desirable as neighbors, sons-in-law, fellow workers, even as voters. The words *assimilable, white,* and the pseudo-scientific term *Caucasian,* just then coming into fashion, would be taken as equivalents. Before the decade of the seventies was out, there would be California workingmen, styling themselves brothers in the Order of Caucasians, who would undertake the systematic killing of Chinese in order to preserve their assimilable fellow toilers from total ruin.[51]

During the studio period, American films that dramatized either foundational events in the nation's becoming or an emerging modern urban culture tended to use Chinese characters in a manner similar to that described by Saxton. The exclusion/inclusion trope is particularly marked in films like *Barbary Coast* (Goldwyn, 1933), which transposed the gangster genre to California at the height of the gold rush. Louis Chamalis (Edward G. Robinson) runs San Francisco and the Bella Donna saloon, where he tricks miners out of their new wealth. Mary Rutledge (Miriam Hopkins), who is absolutely broke, has traveled by ship from New York to marry a man she has never met. On her arrival she discovers her betrothed has been killed after losing his money to Chamalis. Virtually destitute, the only thing of value that she possesses is her whiteness. Disembarking from the ship, Mary is met by gasps of surprise and desire: "Suffering snakes, a white woman," says Old Atrocity (Walter Brennan), who ferries her to shore. His observation is repeated again and then reinforced by a call from a group of men waiting at the quayside: "What you got there?" They shout to him, "A white woman." "You're lying!" They respond. "No, I'm not. A New York white woman—whiter than a hen's egg."

The scene introduces the main musical themes, a medley of Stephen Foster's minstrel songs, interspersed with other nineteenth-century signature tunes, such as "Molly Malone." The men, making a great fuss, carry Mary across the muddy streets and walk her past a line of bars, out of which piano renditions of more minstrel tunes are heard; as they pass a group of Chinese men the music changes to an Oriental theme. An American specificity returns to this image of a godless alien hellhole when an offscreen female is heard singing a few lines of "Frankie and Johnny." Mary's presence (her whiteness) ends a performance of "De Camptown Races" at the Bella Donna saloon, and, like all the men, Louis Chamalis is instantly smitten. Mary begins working for him at a crooked roulette wheel, and he changes her name to Swan.

Although the dialogue denies any physical relationship between Chamalis and Mary, her self-loathing and easy manner when drinking hard liquor suggest she is a kept woman. When Chamalis demands that she love him, her reply is that he should be content with what he has: "Do you still think I'm Mary Rutledge?" she asks him. "Do you think I'm still a white woman?" Eventually, she finds redemption through the love of the poet and prospector James Carmichael (Joel McCrea), who takes her away from the saloon, Chamalis, and minstrel songs and gives her instead marriage, self-respect, a book of poems by Shelley, and the symbolic restitution of her whiteness. Like Mary Rutledge, Old Atrocity, who has conned James Carmichael out of his gold, reforms midway through the film. He wishes to cleanse his "black soul" by returning some of Carmichael's gold; "the only decent thing I've done in my whole black life, sort of overwhelms me," he tells Carmichael. "I feel like a little white kitten—reborn." Both moral and material progress is measured by the characters' distance from negritude.

In *Barbary Coast* blackness is equated with the deep mud the characters are endlessly shown trudging through—it is the primal element out of which America is formed, but like the mud it is destined to be cleaned away: "Rome wasn't built in a day," says the town's first newspaperman. "The paths of empire have always started in mud and ended in glory." The mud neatly represents the idea of racial hybridity; neither solid nor liquid it is simply in a permanent state of process, moving between the two extremes. Early in the film a group of white men chase an unfortunate

Chinaman through the muddy streets of the Barbary Coast. A commentator explains that the white men are out to cut off his pigtail, but it is all in good sport, and anyway, he says to Mary Rutledge, "Opium and Chinamen sure perfume up a stink." The Chinese are what the white characters construct their sense of self against and thus begin the process of racial refinement and purification that will run throughout the course of the film, which ends in the death of the dark-skinned ethnic character Chamalis, and the marriage of Carmichael and Rutledge.

"My mother may have given birth in Rumania, but I was born the day I set foot on American soil," wrote Emanuel Goldenberg, a.k.a. Edward G. Robinson, who, since arriving in Hollywood with considerable theatrical experience, had begun to build a reputation as an actor capable of playing with a deal of credibility tough guy characters with an ethnic urban identity.[52] His star billing was confirmed following his success as the Italian American gangster in *Little Caesar*, which was preceded by hoodlum roles in two Universal pictures produced in 1930: *Night Ride* and *Outside the Law*. His ethnic persona was developed in films such as *Tiger Shark* (First National, 1932), in which he played a Portuguese American, and in *Barbary Coast*. Portraying a construction worker in *Two Seconds* (First National, 1932), he built on his urban persona as established in, for example, *Five Star Final* (First National, 1931), where he played a newspaperman. In *Smart Money* (Warner Bros., 1931) Robinson plays a small-town gambler who is first taken in by city hustlers but then gets his own back. The specifically urban quality of Robinson's persona and his ability to represent "off-white" ethnicities was further enhanced by the racial masquerade presented in *East Is West* (Universal, 1930), in which he impersonated a Chinese character. He was, therefore, ably qualified for the role of a Chinese American assassin who worked for one of the Chinatown tongs.

Executive vice president of the Studio Relations Committee—the body responsible for administrating Hollywood's production code—Fred W. Beetson wrote to Warner Bros. producer Daryl Zanuck, in a letter dated October 28, 1931, to recommend that references to "racketeering," "gang," and "gang rule" in Warners' proposed production *The Honorable Mr. Wong* be played down so as to placate the New York censor board, which was showing a very "unreasonable" attitude toward the "portrayal of crime in pictures." Furthermore, official representatives of the Chinese government had communicated a "decided objection to any pictures portraying Tong activities." The negative reaction from the Chinese to Harold Lloyd's *Welcome Danger* (1929) and Universal's *East Is West* (1930) "convinces us that it is not economically sound to make a picture of this kind without first securing official Chinese approval."[53] Beetson's comments were responses to two distinct but linked production cycles: first, the previous season's high-profile gangster movies (*Beast of the City, City Streets, Quick Millions, The Public Enemy*, and *Little Caesar*) and, second, the recurrent production of films with a Chinatown setting that focused on the activities of Chinese racketeers (tongs). In the timing of its production *The Honorable Mr. Wong* drew specific attention because it suggested that the two cycles had convergent concerns. Seeking to emulate the success of *Little Caesar*, Warner Bros./First National cast its star, Edward G. Robinson, as a tong member in *The Honorable Mr. Wong*. The novelty of combining the gangster and Chinatown cycles was the obvious angle of exploitation to be played in studio-controlled publicity; distributed under its new title *The Hatchet Man*, the film was released in the early months of 1932.

What makes *The Hatchet Man* unique when compared to the films mentioned above is that the drama is concerned with Chinese characters' experience of living in Chinatown rather than with a white character's tourist views. Along with a focus on white characters the film forgoes self-reflexivity on its fictive nature. Nevertheless, because white actors play the lead characters, there is still an air of deception, the racial masquerade suggesting this is simply a variation on the white tourist's point of view. The setting of *The Hatchet Man* is San Francisco, but in this version there are no white bosses; indeed, with one exception, individuated white characters are absent from the diegesis. Wong Low Get (Robinson) works as an assassin for one of the tongs, and his skill with a hatchet is without equal.[54] His loyalty to his masters is put to the test, however, when he is told to assassinate his best friend. The friend, though, understands that Wong is bound by his code of honor and consents to his own death with the understanding that Wong will care for and raise his six-year-old daughter, Toya, and, when she is of age, become her husband.

Wong belongs to a community that is insular, bound by tradition, and virtually untouched by the wider world of American culture. However, with the passing of years — Toya (Loretta Young) is now twenty-one and has married Wong — modern American values and business practices have begun to take effect both on the couple and the wider culture of Chinatown. Wong Low Get now wears his hair short and dresses in Western suits; although still an honorable hatchet man, his center of operations is a legitimate import/export concern that brings him into daily contact with the outside world. The waning of tradition is further felt when the tongs' power base is threatened by external criminal gangs, which necessitates the use of Americanized Chinese "bodyguards" from New York — who have forsaken traditional clothes and customs and adopted the dress and manners of the Jazz Age and Chicago gangsters. The hold that tradition has over the community is increasingly weakened — an idea that is dramatized through the trials and tribulations of Wong and Toya's marriage.

Modernity's corrupting influence is particularly marked by its effects on Toya, who readily exchanges tradition and forsakes her marriage vows for the sensual attractions of urban America. Sent to protect Chinatown, Harry (Leslie Fenton), one of the New York bodyguards, instead inadvertently helps to further diminish the role of tradition within the community. Young and handsome, he captivates and seduces Toya, introducing her to the delights of whiskey and the wild abandonment of dancing to jazz music. More than anything else, it is jazz music that symbolizes the corrosive effect of modern American culture on the traditional Chinese way of life.

1. Wong Low Get (Edward G. Robinson) is the honorable hatchet man in the 1932 Warner Bros. film *The Hatchet Man*. Photo courtesy of the British Film Institute.

Compared to the modern urban world in which it is situated, Chinatown is depicted as primitive, but it is, nevertheless, a cultured primitivism. However alien and decadent Chinese culture may appear to white Americans, it is still considered to be a culture born from a centuries-old civilization.

"American" characters are limited to the mounted police who lead a funeral procession, an Irish-American gangster, and, significantly, a black railroad porter and a black jazz band. Although white Americans police the borders of Chinatown, a sense of a wider America is carried almost exclusively by reference to a low, non-white American culture. "Big Jim" Malone is the leader of Irish American mobsters who are angling to take over the rackets in Chinatown. Wong first tries to broker a deal that will avoid violence, but when the mobster kills a member of his tong, he takes bloody vengeance. His excursion to Sacramento to assassinate Malone brings him into a brief encounter with a black porter who chauffeurs him from platform to train. It is the only view we have of Wong in America outside of Chinatown. This symbolic encounter with a wider (black) American culture is echoed in the lone scene in which his wife is shown in the city outside of Chinatown; Toya's encounter with American culture is similarly cast in racial terms, occurring at an afternoon jazz dance. In isolation, the inhabitants of Chinatown will continue to practice their "primitive" and centuries-old customs, untouched by the surrounding sounds

2. The business suit and short hair represent Wong Low Get's American-ization. Edward G. Robinson in *The Hatchet Man* (Warner Bros., 1932). Photo courtesy of the British Film Institute.

and sensations of an American modernity. But when corrupting agents (symbolized by the Irish American gangster and the black primitivism of jazz) breach their borders, the forces of modernity undermine Chinese culture—a black American primitivism repositions the discursive valence of an Oriental primitivism.

In their adoption of jazz age culture the young couple reveals a modern sensibility that is also, paradoxically, a regression to a primitive state of physical sensuality. This paradox is coded as American or, rather more complexly, as black *and* American.[55] Jazz represents both an ultra modernity in its headlong rush into a future devoid of tradition, collapsing the bridges that link the present with the past, *and* an attachment to a premodern world signaled in the idea of jungle rhythms with roots in the slave music of the southern United States and, still further back, to Africa. The threat to Chinatown, then, is not directly posed by white American culture; rather it comes from two cultures—Irish proletarian culture and black American culture—that are complementary in their outsider status to the white mainstream but that have been given a symbolic cultural centrality under the aegis of modernity. The brutish nature of the Irish mobster underscores the downside of consumer culture's promise of inclusivity, while the instinctual primitivism of black culture returns an authenticity lost within the mass-produced artifice of modernity. The white mainstream secures its distinctiveness by maintaining the borders between itself and outsider cultures because, as it is dramatized in *The Hatchet Man*, the adoption of black culture leads inevitably to the destruction of the host culture.

The explicit subject of Hoagy Carmichael's "Hong Kong Blues," published in 1939, is the troubles caused when racial borders are breached and black and yellow cultures merge. Carmichael had been working on the song for the best part of a decade; written originally under the title "San Francisco Blues," the tune and lyrics were Carmichael's late contribution to the 1920s vogue for mixing jazz and the fad for chinoiserie.[56] The titles of these Chinese jazz songs partly tell the story: "China Boy," "Chinatown, My Chinatown," "Broken Idol," "Original Chinese Blues," "Chinese Rhythm," "Street of Dreams," "Singapore Sorrows," "Chong (He Come from Hong Kong)," "Limehouse Blues," and so on. Like these tunes, "Hong Kong Blues" utilizes a faux-Chinese musical motif carried by a standard Western melody line, which the performer then jazzes. The lyrics complement the apparent mismatch of Eastern and Western musical modes with the singer, as happens in so many of Carmichael's songs, assuming the persona of a black man from the southern States. The colored man's drug habit has left him stranded, either literally or (most likely) figuratively, in "old Hong Kong," where he was caught "kicking the gong" — a commonplace euphemism for opium smoking. The journey the black piano player makes from Tennessee to the Orient, by way of San Francisco, presented a familiar set of locales.

As an exemplar of American cultural identity, the blues provided an American specificity to that with which it is conjoined, in this instance Hong Kong. The blues are also coded as southern and black, however, and thus are considered separate and distinct from the white American mainstream. In Hong Kong, or the narcoticized state of being that could be called "Hong Kong," the black man is cast outside of the United States. His claim on America as his home is mitigated first by the presence of Chinatown in his favored port of call, San Francisco, where presumably he nourished his habit, and then by the counterclaim that really his home is in Tennessee — doubly exiled from the United States, he is, indeed, a very unfortunate colored man; for him, a ticket to the land of the free is nothing more than a pipe dream.

Opium had first appeared on the American scene with the arrival of the Chinese who had immigrated to the United States to work, first, in California's gold fields and, later, as laborers on the railroad. During the late nineteenth century both the temporary Chinatowns of the mining and railroad camps and the permanent Chinatowns situated in urban centers (both in the States and Europe) were renowned for the relatively easy access they provided for users of the drug, which, by and large, was consumed in a social setting known as a "den" — the back room or cellar of a restaurant or laundry equipped with cots and bunks. Initially, according to David Courtwright, a historian of drug addiction in America before 1940, opium smoking by non-Chinese was confined to a demimonde of prostitutes and their pimps; precisely the kind of characters alluded to in "Hong Kong Blues."[57] By the turn of the century, however, the exotic attraction of opium and Chinatown had begun to appeal to the fast set of sensation-seeking American blue bloods, and in the popular imagination, at least, the seductions of Chinatown appealed particularly to wealthy white women. The image of the slumming aristocrat feasting on the illicit pleasures offered by Chinatown corresponded, and by the 1920s coexisted, with white slumming trips to Harlem.

One of Harlem's biggest attractions was Cab Calloway, star of the Cotton Club, who found fame and fortune through rewriting the urban folk tunes "Willie the Weeper" and "Cocaine Lil" as "Minnie the Moocher" (1931), in which the heroine is introduced to Chinatown and the pleasure of kicking the gong around— *hi-de-hi-de-ho!* This song, and his other songs that sought to exploit its notoriety and popularity—"Minnie the Moocher's Wedding Day," "Kickin' the Gong Around," and "Reefer Man"—made vocally explicit what some of the other Chinese jazz tunes only implied: the call of the opium den and the white fascination with Harlem nightlife were one and the same.[58] For Duke Ellington on his recording of "Drop Me Off in Harlem," the relocation of a black American specificity into the Orient was equally unproblematic: "If Harlem moved to China/There'd be nothing finer/Than to stow away on a plane."[59] Jazz and chinoiserie were of a piece, or so it would appear. In America's racially polyglot cities, Harlem, like Chinatown, functioned as an imaginary space, an exoticized domestic locale, where racial and ethnic overlap could be contained and policed—if not from within, then, at least, from without.

That jazz tunes should use the Orient as figurations of exoticness indicates some complex cultural transactions: with its origin in the *black* experience of urban modernity, jazz was a popular form already highly ambiguous and contested for its capacity to blur the racialized distinctions holding black and white performers and audiences apart. As a musical form that focused anxieties around racial difference organized across binaries of black/white, primitive/civilized, sexual/repressed, body/mind, and vulgar/refined, the appearance of Chinese-themed tunes in jazz music of the 1920s and early 1930s indicates cultural discourses still yet more complex in their operations to stabilize multiple racial, class, sexual, and political boundaries. The proliferation of such cross-media narratives is symptomatic of the construction of "Chinatown" as a *symbolic* space: in America's racially polyglot cities "Chinatown" functioned as an imaginary place in which dominant cultural definitions of racial and ethnic difference could be produced, contained, and policed. Thus the location of "Chinatown" needs to be examined more fully to understand it as a *fabrication*, which will then enable an appreciation of why the figure of the gangster is a common occurrence in this setting.

Although limited in *The Hatchet Man*, encounters between Chinese American culture and black American culture are endemic to American film of the studio era. In the Paramount musical short *Singapore Sue* (1931), starring Anna Chang, with support from Joe Wang and Pickard's Chinese Syncopators, the setting is a cafe in Singapore. Amusement for the mostly European clientele is provided by a traditional Chinese dancing troupe. However, when a group of American sailors appear, the entertainment changes and assumes a distinct American accent. Propositioning an attractive Chinese waitress, an American sailor is momentarily struck dumb when she responds in fluent English—she was brought up near the Brooklyn navy yards and has an accent to prove it. Following Joe Wang's sentimental romantic number, she removes her kimono to reveal a silver dancing costume like those worn on Broadway's musical stages and a fine pair of gams. She sings and shimmies along to the band of Chinese syncopators, finishing her turn by squirting water from a joke flower into the eye of the most forward of the American sailors (Cary Grant). The absurd idea of Chinese Brooklynite jazz hounds is sure to have provided laughs galore; at least it might have if the idea was not already a much-overworked cliché.

In *Chinatown Nights* one of the first disorientating experiences felt by Joan Fry during her excursion into Chinatown's labyrinth is to stumble into a bar packed with American sailors and their partners dancing to a black jazz band. Here the meeting of Chinatown, black jazz, American sailors, and a slumming American blue blood suggest racial and class liminality—Chinatown as a polyglot world. In *Painted Faces* (1929) a customer in a Chinese restaurant asks a white jazz band for his favorite song: "Can't you play something with a little lift in it? You know what I mean. Something hot. You know, one of those old blues numbers—'St. Louis Blues.'" The jazz played in the setting of a Chinese restaurant and the coarse interruption of the performance to demand a particular tune is suggestive of a vital, lively, sensational culture, but it also signifies a lowbrow, vulgar, and unrestrained mixed-race culture. In cases such as these the mixing of racial and ethnic signifiers enhances an understanding of American culture as hybrid and impure. The narrative logic of Chinatown gangster films, therefore, is to drive out the corrupting and contaminating elements, to police stable class, gender, racial, and ethnic boundaries.

Discussing black and white cultural interactions, cultural historian W. T. Lhamon Jr. notes the links between the races can just as easily account for white and yellow cultures:

> Music, sculpture and dance, speech and writing and lore, religion and food and costume—black life had touched every corner of American life, had long been a part of white life. The paradox that had propped up the shabby house of American racism, however, was the pre-fifties tenet that such ethnic cultures were somehow separable. This fiction was one of the most victimizing beliefs for Americans of all races. Belief in separability kept the two largest American racial cultures touching while allowing whites the fantasy of distance. It inhibited the powerful even from contemplating any aspect of the black ethic, because by definition they were not allowed to recognize it.[60]

In its use of black and Chinese culture Hollywood conformed to the paradigm of racial separation and togetherness articulated by Lhamon: it evoked the possibility of racial mixing in order to show just how far apart the races were. When characters, of whatever race, allow the touch of the other to linger too long or to take too firm a hold on their bodies and souls, then they are condemned, ostracized, punished, and destroyed. There is no middle ground. *The Hatchet Man* concludes with the three principal characters back in China with no possibility of a return to the United States: Toya has ended up as a prostitute, Harry has taken to kicking the gong around, and Wong, although he kills Harry and "saves" Toya, is a broken man.

The Hatchet Man plays out an exclusionary logic that is repeated across media representations of the Chinese in America. The exclusion of Chinese people from the body politic of American life was so compounded within the popular imagination that it moved beyond mere formulaic plot device to absolute cliché. Like many of the stories detailed above, the low-budget thriller *Yellow Cargo* (1936), produced by poverty row studio Grand National, is overtly self-conscious in dealing with a mechanistic plot device. In this instance the narrative of "Asiatics" being smuggled into the West Coast is framed by an excessive self-reflexivity on the processes involved in telling stories of Chinamen and Chinatown. The gangsters involved in the smuggling of coolies operate behind a phony business front, a low-budget independent Hollywood film company called Globe Productions. Using the ruse of shooting a Chinese pirate movie, the gangsters ferry film extras in yellow face to an island just off the Hollywood coastline. They pretend to shoot the movie and then send the extras back to the mainland on the regular ferry. Dressing the Chinese workers in the extras' costumes they are then smuggled into the country under the noses of unsuspecting immigration officials, who, beneath the cover of darkness, don't notice that these Chinese are not wearing makeup! This neat but ludicrous ploy is foiled by the sharp-witted undercover agent from the Immigration and Nationalization Service, Alan O'Connor (Conrad Nagel). Masquerading as an actor looking for work in the movies, O'Connor teams up with a female cub reporter, Bobbie Reynolds (Eleanor Hunt), who, unbeknown to him, is also a federal agent working for the Justice Department. However, what expedites the film's conclusion is a letter to the gangsters from the Motion Pictures and Producers Association stating that Globe Productions is under investigation for not providing scripts for approval by the PCA—"you don't write those guys off," says one of the heavies. With the threat of the industry's censors ringing in their ears the mobsters hope to pull one last smuggling trip under the ruse of switching the film extras for the Chinese workers, but, unfortunately for them, O'Connor has wised up and, dressed as a Chinese coolie, insinuates himself into the group of illegal immigrants. The game is up—after a long car chase, the mobsters are finally apprehended.

Chinese characters enable narratives of criminal intrigue to deal overtly with questions of national identity. Positioned as a threat to the always tentative racial boundaries of urban life, American identity as a stable racial caste is repeatedly tested. Yet because the Chinese are so self-evidently unable to pass as "Americans" in a manner available to European immigrant groups, the threat and fear of assimilation can be readily contained and policed. Films like *The Hatchet Man* and

PETER STANFIELD

Yellow Cargo rehearse and confirm norms of racial difference and identity using Chinatown—the alien culture within the host—and the Chinese—the alien outside the borders of the United States—to define that which constitutes received notions of a legitimate American culture. Gangster film narratives that use Chinatown as a setting for narcotics trafficking, gambling, people smuggling, and organized crime simultaneously invoke images of the Chinese and Chinatown as symptoms of an illegitimate culture.

Notes

1. André Breton, *Nadja* (London: Penguin, 1999), 32, 37.
2. Sean McCann, *Gumshoe America: Hard-Boiled Crime Fiction and the Fall of New Deal Liberalism* (Durham, N.C.: Duke University Press, 2000), 83.
3. Jonathan Munby, *Public Enemies, Public Heroes: Screening the Gangster from "Little Caesar" to "Touch of Evil"* (Chicago: University of Chicago Press, 1999), 107.
4. Jacob A. Riis, *How the Other Half Lives* (New York: Penguin, 1997), 21.
5. Blaise Cendrars, *Panorama de la Pegre* (1935), quoted and translated by Robin Walz, *Pulp Surrealism* (Berkeley: University California Press, 2000), 153.
6. On Hollywood and Orientalism see Matthew Bernstein and Gaylyn Studlar, eds., *Visions of the East: Orientalism in Film* (London: I. B. Tauris, 1997); and Gina Marchetti, *Romance and the "Yellow Peril": Race, Sex, and Discursive Strategies in Hollywood Fiction* (Berkeley: University of California Press, 1993).
7. McCann, *Gumshoe America*, 69.
8. Herbert Asbury, *The Gangs of New York: An Informal History of the Underworld* (New York: Garden City, 1927), 299–324.
9. Ibid., 301. Asbury repeats the chop suey simile in *The Barbary Coast*, although he gives a different account of the invention of America's favorite Chinese dish. See Herbert Asbury, *The Barbary Coast: An Informal History of the San Francisco Underworld* (New York: Knopf, 1933), 184.
10. Jack Lait and Lee Mortimer, *New York Confidential: The Lowdown on the Big Town* (Chicago: Ziff-Davis, 1948), ix.
11. Ibid., 80.
12. Ibid.
13. For analysis of early cinema's actualities of Chinatown and popular journalism's contemporaneous coverage of tourism see Sabine Haenni, "Filming 'Chinatown': Fake Visions, Bodily Transformations," in *Screening Asian Americans*, ed. Peter X. Feng (New Brunswick: N.J.: Rutgers University press, 2002), 21–52.
14. Jack Black, *You Can't Win* (1926; repr. London: AK Press/Nabat, 2000), 125.
15. Sax Rohmer, *Tales of Chinatown* (London: Cassell, 1920), 13.
16. Ibid., 138.
17. Ronald A. Knox, "A Detective Story Decalogue" (1928), in *Detective Fiction: A Collection of Critical Essays*, ed. Robin Winks (Englewood Cliffs, N.J.: Prentice-Hall, 1980), 201.
18. Asbury, *The Barbary Coast*, 166–167.
19. Ibid., 280.
20. Dashiell Hammett, "Dead Yellow Women," in *The Big Knockover and Other Stories* (Harmondsworth: Penguin, 1969), 198.
21. Ibid., 201.
22. Ibid., 203.
23. Ibid., 198.
24. Ibid., 234.
25. For a broad contextual placing and a history of the bourgeois journey into the underworld see Rosalind Williams, *Notes on the Underground: An Essay on Technology, Society, and the Imagination* (Cambridge, Mass.: MIT Press, 1990). For a more specific account of "slumming" see Ann Douglas, *Terrible Honesty: Mongrel Manhattan in the 1920s* (London: Picador, 1996), 74.

26. For example, the Sherlock Holmes tale, "The Man with the Twisted Lip" offers many similarities with Rohmer's Chinatown stories.

27. Rohmer, *Tales of Chinatown*, 130.

28. Ibid., 129.

29. Ibid., 128.

30. Will Gould, *Red Barry* (Seattle: Fantagraphic Books, 1989).

31. Erle Stanley Gardner, "Hell's Kettle," in *The Black Mask Boys: Masters in the Hard-Boiled School of Detective Fiction*, ed. William Nolan (New York: William Morrow, 1985), 103–104.

32. For the best analysis on the role of disguise in popular fictions see Michael Denning, *Mechanic Accents: Dime Novels and Working Class Culture in America* (London: Verso, 1987); and Marcus Klein, *Easterns, Westerns, and Private Eyes: American Matters, 1870–1900* (Madison: University of Wisconsin Press, 1994). See also my work on disguise and masks in the 1930s singing western, Peter Stanfield, *Horse Opera: The Strange History of the Singing Western* (Urbana: University of Illinois Press, 2002). For an analysis of Erle Stanley Gardner's *Black Mask* Chinatown stories see Erin A. Smith, *Hard-Boiled: Working-Class Readers and Pulp Magazines* (Philadelphia: Temple University Press, 2000), 120–125.

33. The movement between classes facilitated by Jenkins's disguise lays open the arbitrary basis of wealth allocation and social power, exposes the political complicity of institutions in maintaining the economic and social gulf between wealthy and poor, and offers a tacit social criticism that appealed to disenfranchised working-class readers. For a class analysis of turn-of-the-century magazine stories see Richard Ohmann, *Selling Culture: Magazines, Markets, and Class at the Turn of the Century* (London: Verso, 1997).

34. Rohmer, *Tales of Chinatown*, 63.

35. Apart from *The Blackbird* and *The Shock*, the Lon Chaney feature *The Penalty* also had a Chinatown background, and in *Bits of Life* (1921), *Flesh and Blood* (1922), *Shadows* (1922), and *Mr. Wu* (1927) Chaney impersonated Oriental characters. For more on Chaney see Gaylyn Studlar's fascinating study in *This Mad Masquerade: Stardom and Masculinity in the Jazz Age* (New York: Columbia University Press, 1996), 199–258.

36. Marek Kohn, *Dope Girls: The Birth of the British Drug Underground* (London: Granta, 2001), 2. The key American history of drug use is David T. Courtwright, *Dark Paradise: Opiate Addiction in America before 1940* (Cambridge, Mass.: Harvard University Press, 1982).

37. Kohn, *Dope Girls*, 5.

38. Ibid., 3.

39. Ibid., 6.

40. Sax Rohmer, *Dope: A Story of Chinatown and the Drug Traffic* (London: Cassell, 1919), 120.

41. Rohmer, *Tales of Chinatown*, 140.

42. Jennifer DeVere Brody, *Impossible Purities: Blackness, Femininity, and Victorian Culture* (Durham, N.C.: Duke University Press, 1998).

43. Hammett, "Dead Yellow Women," 185.

44. Ibid., 186.

45. Ibid., 227.

46. This reading of the racial politics in Hammett's work is at odds with Sean McCann, who reads the racial "category confusion" as "a fact of political economy, not a feature of racial identity" that undermines the absolutist position of racist propaganda. His position is well argued but does not, I suggest, fully confront the fact that the stories are narrated from a white point of view that seeks to establish order in all things, including racial identity, even if this proves an impossible task. The inevitability of failure that marks the shift to the hard-boiled detective fiction from its earlier incarnation is, of course, something that racist fictions never contemplate, which is McCann's point, but it does not, I think, in any way subvert a white-centric view of an urban reality. See McCann, *Gumshoe America*, 69–72.

47. Riis, *How the Other Half Lives*, 73.

48. Ibid.

49. Ibid., 80.

50. Ibid., 76.

51. Alexander Saxton, *The Indispensable Enemy: Labor and the Anti-Chinese Movement in California* (Berkeley: University of California Press, 1995), 18.

52. Alan L. Gansberg, *Little Caesar: A Biography of Edward G. Robinson* (Kent: New English Library, 1985), 13. For an analysis of Robinson's ethnicity see Munby, *Public Enemies, Public Heroes*, 107.

53. Fred W. Beetson to Daryl Zanuck, Oct. 28, 1931, *The Hatchet Man* PCA file, Margaret Herrick Library, Academy of Motion Picture Arts and Sciences). See also Ruth Vasey, *The World According to Hollywood, 1918–1939* (Exeter: University of Exeter Press, 1997), 140–144.

54. A racist "explanation" for such primitive skill with a hatchet is proffered by Asbury in *Gangs of New York*, where he suggests that the Chinese are incapable of using guns because they involuntarily close their eyes when squeezing the trigger.

55. For a broader discussion of the cultural impact of jazz on the American imagination see Kathy J. Ogren, *The Jazz Revolution: Twenties America and the Meaning of Jazz* (Oxford: Oxford University Press, 1989).

56. Richard M. Sudhalter, *Stardust Melody: The Life and Music of Hoagy Carmichael* (New York: Oxford University Press, 2002), 132.

57. See Courtwright, *Dark Paradise*, 36–42.

58. The best collection of early recordings by Cab Calloway and His Orchestra is the four-CD set *The Early Years: 1930–1934* (JSP Records, JSPCD908, 2001).

59. Duke Ellington, *Masterpieces: 1926–1949* (Proper Box 25, 2001) (4 compact discs).

60. W. T. Lhamon Jr., *Deliberate Speed: The Origins of a Cultural Style in the American 1950s* (Cambridge, Mass.: Harvard University Press, 2002), 39.

The Underworld Films of Oscar Micheaux and Ralph Cooper

Toward a Genealogy of the Black Screen Gangster

Jonathan Munby

O TALK OF BLACK AMERICAN COMMERCIAL CINEMA is to talk about a highly truncated legacy of false dawns in the struggle against white racist representation on the big screen. Moreover, the few moments where a discernibly "black" commercial cinema has appeared seem to have depended on the manufacture and perpetuation of criminal stereotypes for their economic viability. The furor surrounding the 1990s cycle of "'hood" films starring members of the gangsta rap fraternity highlighted an apparent contradiction at the heart of any attempt on the part of black popular culture producers to gain entry and access to the mass market.[1] However much participants in this kind of cinema defended it as a candid indictment of white racism ("keeping it real," in gangsta argot), the films remained open to accusations of being complicit with white racist visions of black male youth as both indolent and violent. In the process stewards of both black and white morality placed a peculiar burden on "black" film — as a form of entertainment with a particular mission: racial uplift.

Yet the previous moments in which a discernibly black commercial cinema appeared have also been marked as "criminal." The so-called blaxploitation cycle of the late 1960s and 1970s indulged self-consciously in exaggerated criminal self-representations — telling stories of gangster "Caesars" and pimping "Macks" who, although they occasionally had the chance to "kick whitey's ass," bore a highly ambivalent relationship to the mission of racial uplift. Continuity between these cycles has drawn a degree of critical attention recently, most notably in the work of Michael Eric Dyson, Robin D. G. Kelley, and Eithne Quinn.[2] The moment, however, that such criminal self-representation first appeared on the big screen — in the form of the 1930s talking "race film" as shaped by two of its key proponents, Oscar Micheaux and Ralph Cooper — has gone relatively unnoticed.[3]

263

The silent cinema of Oscar Micheaux has received extensive scholastic treatment in recent years. Micheaux pioneered the making and exhibition of films made for segregated black audiences — and his career more or less spanned the entirety of the history of the race film, 1919–1948.[4] The indubitable influence of Micheaux has encouraged a vision of race film as a separate cinema (and has certainly encouraged an "auteurist" approach to his own career). The tendency to treat the race film as a cinema apart has been fueled by mutually reinforcing forces: the status of the business as something conducted outside the major studios, the fact that these films were dedicated to a segregated audience, and the desire on the part of scholars to define this cinema's significance against the dominant white cinema.

Although the race film was not a one-man show, its conditions of production, distribution, and exhibition necessarily involved "independent" economic behavior. Like other filmmaking concerns operating outside the major studios, the race-film business did not enjoy control of distribution and exhibition of its wares.[5] A filmmaker like Micheaux was forced to make his films on the cheap and try to recover investments through "road showing" his films (a practice that bypassed the distributor either by taking a film directly to an exhibitor and booking the picture on a percentage basis, or leasing the theater for a temporary period). Road showing came to exist alongside the more pervasive practice of selling films on the states' rights market — a system responsible for distribution of products in various territories for a fee or a percentage of box office income — and for a limited time.[6]

Race films were even more clearly separate from most other parts of the movie industry to the extent that they were "all-Negro"/"all-Colored" cast films directed at a segregated movie audience. Race films put black actors into roles mainstream cinema denied them and dramatized aspects of the black experience that were given no representation on the white screen. Yet, race films *were* bound up with Hollywood to the extent that they adopted many of the generic frameworks (especially once sound arrived) that defined the dominant cinema. The prime reason for the race film's apparent acquiescence to the dominant cinematic style was the advent of sound and the consequences of the Wall Street crash in 1929. Sound brought with it additional costs that could only be relieved through standardization. Much like Hollywood's product, race films were "presold" on the basis of generic categories that were familiar and popular with black audiences in order to help guarantee investors a financial return. Such consolidation was only exacerbated by the onset of the Great Depression, which placed additional pressures on the business of getting audiences to spend their decreasing dollars on recreational pursuits.

Race-film criticism has given less attention to the more "standardized" talking products of the business than to its more idiosyncratic silent era products. Perhaps this is because these more generic efforts hold out less interest for those seeking to uncover a distinctively black cinema aesthetic. For these talking race films are categorically less easy to separate from the mainstream and thus less easy to accord a (positive) value when it comes to discussions of the relationship underlying race,

racism, and commercial American cinema. The particular story of Micheaux's declining ability to remain truly independent once sound arrived (which forced him
into league with white financiers) has also reinforced an impression that the silent
era held out more possibilities for the development of a distinctive black cinematic
aesthetic and politics.[7] Equally, such a pejorative view of generic similitude has
led to the "forgetting" of key race-film figures who excelled in more standardized
products — especially Ralph Cooper, the original black screen gangster.

Although the transition to sound certainly exacerbated the race film's generic
streamlining (contemporaneous African American press reviews often lamented
that talking race films constituted a poor man's version of the Hollywood experience), what should interest us, instead, is what forms became favored *within* this
process of apparent standardization during the 1930s. These putatively impoverished emulations of the dominant cinema proved to be significant venues for the
showcasing of black revue talent in an age of decline for live black entertainment.
Sound synchronization may have been expensive, but it opened up cinema's possibilities for African Americans, especially in terms of music and dance. And any attempt to evaluate the significance of the talking race film needs to acknowledge
that, in this kind of cinema, investment in the delivery of performance and spectacle
took priority over obligations to narrative continuity. In this context I will argue that
it made particular sense for race-film producers to adopt the tropes and conventions
of the Hollywood gangster film — and that a proper reading of why should lead us to
different conclusions about the aesthetic and political consequences of the talking
race film's apparent standardization.[8]

The mass-screen projection of black experience was framed by the problem of
working within a visual and narrative economy that from its very birth depended on
the consolidation of "either/or" conceptions of race and identity dating back to the
first minstrel shows.[9] Economic interests helped shape the character of the white
racist tropes and conventions that came to dominate Hollywood as it consolidated
its business infrastructure during the 1920s. As Ruth Vasey has pointed out, in an
age where the industry had become increasingly dependent on foreign markets for
profit, it did not make business sense to indulge in openly defamatory visions of
"other" races. And on the domestic front, in the context of antimiscegenation legislation, censorship laws dictated that filmmakers should avoid depicting the races
in conflict (or in sexual liaison) with each other.[10] Such forces fueled a tendency to
keep the races apart onscreen and helped consolidate a very particular cinematic
understanding of what "all-Negro" or "all-Colored" cast entertainment should provide and connote. White cinema staged blackness predominantly in a subordinate
position within its diegesis — black actors assuming servant roles or appearing as
song-and-dance entertainers in "sideshow" scenes that offered temporary "time
out" from the center of dramatic attention, which was the white world. Such a tan-
gential relationship to narrative meaning also enabled editors to cut scenes featuring black performers from reels destined for exhibition to white audiences south of

the Mason-Dixon Line without damage to continuity. In this way Hollywood guaranteed that its products would not offend Jim Crow sensibilities with southern audiences and thus maximized chances of making a profit.

On the rare occasions that Hollywood did make a commitment to a fuller portrayal of black experience this, too, was screened to preserve an ontological distinction between white and black. Hollywood's more benign vision of African American experience came in the form of a "plantation cycle." Classic examples such as *Hallelujah!* (1929), *Show Boat* (1936), and *Green Pastures* (1936) situated the scene of blackness in a "premodern" (often Civil War era) Old South, replete with a spiritual-singing, God-fearing, "natural" and innocent cotton-picking country folk. Here blackness signified most powerfully a lost prelapsarian America set to the nostalgic sound of lamentation songs.[11] Thus, even where Hollywood put a black world center stage, this was inevitably encoded as something that had passed before the time and space of the modern (of cinema itself). Although such sounds and visions may have serviced white America's negotiation of modernity's costs, they made it all but impossible for blacks to find representation as a modernizing and urbanizing people. And understanding why race-film makers gravitated to the underworld milieu as the preferred setting for their films can only be fully understood in this context. As a contemporaneous reporter for the African American newspaper *New York Age* complained:

> There are twelve million colored Americans who desire to see members of the race depicted in life on screen other than hewers of wood and drawers of water. Negro life has its tragedy, comedy, romance, running the gamut of emotions in moving, ever-changing and diverse settings. But either due to ignorance, prejudice or "cold feet," the big producer so far has failed to recognize these great potentialities of our native every day existence, and has confined himself very largely to primitive scenes on plantation and on the levee. There is more intense, vibrant gripping drama packed in our congested northern cities than in the rural South or on "Ol' Man River."[12]

For those making race films it made sense to stage black experience in terms of the underworld for a host of mutually reinforcing reasons. Not only did the underworld milieu offer a chance to contest white visions, but, more significant, it also allowed the "sideshow" to become the main event.

The early talking pictures of Oscar Micheaux offer a fascinating insight into the development of a talking race-film style that would come to be dominated by underworld-nightclub settings. In the sound era, of the seventeen films we know he made, at least nine were set in the underworld milieu: *The Exile* (1931), *Ten Minutes to Live* (1932), *The Girl from Chicago* (1932), *Harlem after Midnight* (1934), *Murder in Harlem* (1935), *Temptation* (1936), *Underworld* (1937), *Swing!* (1938), and *Lying Lips* (1939).[13] Micheaux had always believed that film could be a

266

powerful agent of racial uplift and moral edification. His talking films revealed, however, that a narrative continuity designed to service the delivery of moral lessons was often at odds with other representational opportunities sound afforded the black community. Micheaux's early sound efforts are marked by a distinct attenuation of their narrative and diegetic logic. This can be partly attributed to the economic problems brought on by sound for African American filmmakers, who operated on extremely small budgets without access to the same resources as their white counterparts.

A prime case in point is *Ten Minutes to Live*. Much of the film was shot silent and included intertitles. The sound scenes are primarily devoted to revue talent performing at the Lybia Club, a Harlem cabaret. The tortuously convoluted narrative is taken from short stories that purportedly made up a volume entitled "Harlem after Midnight." Of the film's sixty-three minutes, over half are given over to members of the Primetime Revue in scenes filmed from a fixed camera position and which interrupt and further attenuate an already disjointed story line (partly told in flashback) about a philanderer, faked marriage, vengeful ex-lovers, mistaken identity, and attempted and successful murder.

The *Kansas City Call* reported that filming of the "red hot stage show scenes" was directed not by Micheaux but Donald Heywood, the film's musical score arranger.[14] The consequently "seamed" montage undermines narrative continuity and its attendant moral endgame. As if to compound matters, African American comedy duo "Gallie and George" (Gallie DeGaston and George Williams) perform an extended blackface routine in which they pastiche the very ideals of continuity and moral mission by misremembering key moments and figures in U.S. history, as well as parodying "racial uplift" and its most revered agents (such as Frederick Douglass, Booker T. Washington, and Marcus Garvey). All of this constitutes an ironic metacommentary on the burden of the race film itself. In the end *Ten Minutes to Live*'s entertainment value comes to rest mainly on the way it showcases black revue talent. The obvious convenience of a nightclub setting for a story of moral lassitude and criminal intrigue afforded the display of urban black America's most creative and conspicuous resource. In the process dancers, singers, jazz musicians, and stand-up comedians come to assume a status more center stage than background.

What characterized *Ten Minutes to Live* so drastically can still be detected in Micheaux's less "seamed" efforts in the mid to late 1930s. He was able to construct a more coherent narrative reason to showcase song-and-dance routines in *The Girl from Chicago*. The film weaves a story of adultery (focused on a philandering and criminal town boss, Jeff Ballinger [played by John Everett], and his morally loose lover, Liza [Grace Smith]), into another story of moral virtue (featuring the growing love between a righteous U.S. Secret Service agent, Alonso [Carl Mahon], and a modest schoolteacher, Norma [Starr Calloway]). The plot moves its protagonists from Batesburg, in "dear Old Virginia," and Mississippi, to the sin city of Harlem (understood initially as moving "home to Harlem")—where Liza has turned herself into an exotic dancer at the Radium Club and married the Cuban gangster and boss of the numbers racket, Gomez (Juano Hernandez). Both Liza and Gomez are subjected to the law of moral compensation at the end — Liza shoots Gomez and is then caught by the police. Additionally, Norma's friend Mary (Eunice Brooks) is rescued from her addiction to numbers playing so that she can return to the sanctity of the South. The film ends with Alonso and Norma embarking on a honeymoon in Bermuda, disabused of their naive notions of Harlem as home. To this extent the film typified Micheaux's reforming view of the costs of so-called progress and the role of the city as a breeding ground for vice and moral turpitude.

At the same time, however, the film's engagement with the underworld-nightclub milieu was more than a matter of moral necessity. Incorporation of revue talent was a prime means to sell a race film's entertainment value to investors and audiences alike. The need to keep costs down also increased dependency on more predictable "generic" frameworks and topical settings. Not accidentally, then, even Micheaux, the most independent of race-film producer-directors found himself adopting the conventions and tropes of the underworld-nightclub milieu as the optimal way to secure a return on his investments. By the mid-1930s Micheaux further sacrificed his autonomy by going into business with a race-film distribution company, Sack Amusement Enterprises, in order to guarantee the economic viability of his films.

By 1937, in *Underworld*, we see the consolidation of a talking underworld race-film formula to the cost of Micheaux's morally reforming interests. Although Micheaux continued to envision the underworld-nightclub milieu as the dangerous scene of moral lassitude for the race, his favored South-North/city-country comparative framework had now been reduced to a bookend convention, with the vast majority of the screen action being devoted to dramatizing urban nightlife. *Underworld*'s plot focuses on the fate of Paul Bronson (played by Sol Johnson), a greenhorn graduate from a black college in the South who gets conned and fleeced by an unscrupulous gambler, LeRoy Giles ("Slick" Chester) in Chicago's underworld-nightclub environment. Paul is framed for the murder of the gangster boss of the Red Lilly nightclub, Sam Brown (Oscar Polk), by LeRoy and his numbers-running singer-lover, Dinah Jackson (Bee Freeman), the adulterous wife of the deceased. The film concludes with Paul and loyal lover, Evelyn (Ethel Moses), leaving for Oklahoma.

Underworld's moral frame narrative tried to suggest that the best chance for black advancement lay outside the city limits and under the guidance of an enlightened middle class. Yet a contradictory message is relayed about the excitement and potential of city nightlife and the revue stage as a primary site of black expression and ambition. The Red Lilly nightclub features scene-stealing barmen who provide constant comic relief and background singing, an extended tap routine by "Stringbeans," "The Pope Sisters," a protracted blues number, "The Six Sizzlers," "Harlem's Apache Chorus," and "The Bobby Hargreaves Orchestra."[15]

No matter how much Micheaux may have tried to tailor and control its meaning in the name of his reforming agenda, the nightclub underworld came across as a space of vital black expression and creative energy. His talking race films provided images of a feisty class-divided urban people located not on the periphery of modern America but right at its heart. Black audiences used to watching both Hollywood and race films would have been entertained by this richer vision of themselves. And black actors would have found roles that testified to a reality so systematically excluded by Hollywood. Most conspicuous in this regard was the appearance of Oscar Polk as a gangster, Sam Brown, in *Underworld*. He had just enjoyed Hollywood acclaim playing the Angel Gabriel in MGM's "all-Colored" cast plantation musical *Green Pastures* the previous year.[16]

If Micheaux struggled to make the talking race film fit his prescriptive "uplift" agenda, Ralph Cooper seemed free of such problems. Born in 1918 (the year before Micheaux released his first film), Cooper emerged as one of the most significant talking race-film talents (as producer, director, star, and screenwriter) in the late 1930s. Billed variously as the "Bronze Bogart" or "Dark Gable," he based all his race films (except for *The Duke Is Tops* [1938] — a musical revue film) on the gangster formula. Collectively, *Dark Manhattan* (1937), *Bargain with Bullets* (1937; re-released as *Gangsters on the Loose* [1945]), *Gang War* (1940), and *Am I Guilty?* (1940; rereleased as *Racket Doctor* [1945]) communicated the meaning of the gangster from a distinctively metropolitan and necessarily theatrical black perspective.[17] Cooper's viewpoint would not reinforce binary moral distinctions between city and country. For unlike Micheaux, who was of rural working-class, mid-American stock, Cooper was a proud Harlemite. Moreover, he was a song-and-dance man brought up on the revue stage.

Before embarking on his brief film career, Cooper had already established a reputation not only as a song-and-dance man but also as the emcee of one of Harlem's most famous revue palaces, the Apollo Theatre. As a Harlemite showman and talent spotter Cooper was ideally positioned to use the talking race film as a vehicle to promote black revue talent. Moreover, as someone sensitive to the dominance of white overlords in Harlem's entertainment industry Cooper would also find a vicarious pleasure in making movies in which black gangsters were the main players.

Throughout the period of Prohibition, gangsters financed 125th Street, Harlem's Broadway, for black revue theaters were primary outlets for the sale of illegal alcohol as glorified speakeasies.[18] Typically, Harlem's most famous nightclub, the Cotton Club, was operated by white gangsters and had a whites-only audience policy. Yet the club had a 100 percent black employee policy, and its reputation depended on hiring the best African American revue talent, including Duke Ellington as the club's main act and bandleader. Like all the other major Harlem theaters, the Cotton Club brought wealthy white trade into the black community to spend money on Harlem's primary legal industry: revue entertainment.

Cooper was to fight successfully against Harlem's theatrical apartheid by helping turn the Apollo Theatre into 125th Street's first desegregated house of entertainment in January 1934. This success, however, was somewhat Pyrrhic and presaged his flight to Hollywood, for breaking the color barrier was only made possible by the disintegration of white gangster interest in Harlem that had come with Prohibition. As Cooper highlights in his autobiography, with the repeal of Prohibition in 1933 "the bottom fell out of the market for illegal booze, and the white warlords who depended on it began to loosen their bloody grip on Harlem. In February 1936, the mob closed its flagship and moved the Cotton Club downtown." [19] Most of the little clubs that Prohibition had spawned in Harlem went to the wall, followed gradually by the failure of larger vaudeville palaces to sustain live black entertainment. The Alhambra, the Lincoln, the Renaissance, and the Lafayette had all become exclusively movie theaters by mid-1934. [20] Furthermore, white finance traditionally directed toward the revue circuit was redirected into making "all-Colored"-cast race films.

By 1936, although Cooper had assumed the role of the Apollo's main emcee (introducing the world to figures such as Billie Holiday), he continued to labor for one of the most unscrupulous and powerful of Harlem's white overseers, Frank Schiffman. According to Cooper, "Schiffman was a smart businessman. But he was also a ruthless competitor who would do anything, including taking advantage of his black employees and exploit the great black artists who worked for him, in order to increase profits and beat down opposition. . . . He was one of the many self-ordained great white fathers of Harlem. Schiffman and other theatrical managers ran their theatres like small plantations where they were masters of all they surveyed." [21] Under Schiffman the contingencies of black revue employment in the modern metropolis continued to resemble those of the plantation under a regime described by Cooper as "showbusiness sharecropping." [22] And when Twentieth Century Fox talent scouts invited Cooper to Hollywood, he found more to attract him to California than to hold him in Harlem.

Cooper's move to Hollywood was to produce a supremely ironic moment in black commercial arts. In 1937 *Dark Manhattan*, his first race film, premiered at the Apollo Theatre — the vaudeville space from which he had flown. Shown after a live act and in a community where revue houses now concentrated on exhibition of movies, this black gangster film performed over the palimpsest of Harlem's lost gangster-sponsored vaudeville past. It brought Cooper (playing the main gangster protagonist) back in the image of the white warlords who had once bossed 125th Street — and it constituted a brief avenging moment against the power of the white Harlem overseers. For Cooper, then, the opportunity to make race films constituted a way to sustain revue talent in more ways than one. For as entertainment still in need of an exhibition house, the race film helped sustain the viability of the theaters themselves. As he put it: "I got a big kick out of hearing that when the movie was screened at the Apollo, it broke all attendance records at my home theatre." [23]

The release of a Cooper gangster vehicle was to be valued for something more significant, perhaps, than the content of the film itself. It was grounds for a first-night black urban gala featuring a live revue program in which the screening was the main event. In a climate where, as one reporter put it, "the nightclub field has dwindled to a joke" and the "big chain of moving picture houses equipped with stages have already sounded the death-knell of vaudeville,"[24] a premiere screening of a black film was no small thing. *Dark Manhattan*'s world premiere at the Apollo was anticipated effusively in the black press, a *Philadelphia Tribune* correspondent commenting that "Harlem is expected to turn out in all its gaudy finery for the first grand opening since Nina Mae McKinney made her personal appearance with *Hallelujah* some years ago."[25] The release of *Bargain with Bullets* in Los Angeles later that year became an excuse for a "dazzling first nite session" in which black Hollywood luminaries such as Louise Beavers and Hattie McDaniel turned out: "Living up to the predictions made by daily papers that Central Avenue and the Negro district would stage a stylish formal premiere equal to the regular first nights in Hollywood, the debut of *Bargain with Bullets* at the Lincoln Theatre last Friday was just that." Appropriately, "luxurious limousines and foreign roadsters" delivered stars of the black screen firmament "under blazing lights" in "formal dress" to be greeted by emcee Clarence Muse (broadcasting the event for KMTR radio) and a host of photographers and autograph seekers.[26]

These gala premieres were major social and symbolic spectacles in which the black community stepped out, strolled, and showed off in a manner that defied the rationale that subordinated them in the mainstream industry. Such expressions of community pride brought the rich mix of black urbanites together under a media glare — and around films that placed black folk very much at the heart of modern America and exhibited, in spite of disadvantaged production conditions, African American ability to master modern representational technology. Furthermore, these gangster vehicles produced an afterlife for a primary form of black expression, revue talent, whose viability had been threatened by the repeal of Prohibition and the onset of the Great Depression in the early 1930s.

In 1936 Cooper was called in by Twentieth Century Fox to replace the incapacitated Bill "Bojangles" Robinson as choreographer to *Poor Little Rich Girl* (1936), arguably Shirley Temple's best dance film. The success of Cooper's choreography led to his being given a five-year contract:

> Later I was nicknamed "Dark Gable," but Hollywood wasn't really interested in a black leading man. When *Poor Little Rich Girl* wrapped, I hoped for acting work, but all they offered me were Uncle Tom parts. "Yassuh" and "nosuh" dummy parts were all that was available for a young black actor in those days, even one with a studio contract. The stereotypes seem so offensive today; but in the 1930s, it was heresy to think that a black actor could do anything but play the devil or the dummy. . . . If you didn't want to mug wide-eyed and scared and act the fool, there was no room for you in the big studios.[27]

271

1–2. "Making it," race-film style—from cloth-capped numbers runner, to policy collector, controller, and ultimately organization "king" (Curly Thorpe [Ralph Cooper] in *Dark Manhattan*). Courtesy of the Library of Congress Motion Picture, Broadcasting, and Recorded Sound Division.

Cooper "decided that instead of appearing in pictures that demeaned blacks," he "would try to *make* pictures that glorified blacks."[28] Ironically, even though the studio itself had no use for African Americans as filmmakers, Fox trained Cooper (as a contractual obligation) at their studio school in all the skills required to make movies (directing, scriptwriting, lighting, set designing). This provenance might

272

3–4. Continued.

explain why Cooper's own race-film efforts exhibit a style that's closer to Hollywood than Micheaux, who was self-trained.

Ever the entrepreneur, in 1937 Cooper set up an independent production company, Randol-Cooper Productions, with his dance partner George Randol to make films destined for a segregated black audience. Randol-Cooper Productions' first film was *Dark Manhattan*, starring Cooper as a small-time Harlem hoodlum who makes it to the top of the Harlem numbers racket only to be killed off at the film's conclusion. *Dark Manhattan* rehashed many of the conventions associated with

Hollywood's gangster film (rise-and-fall narrative pattern, topical urban criminal milieu), but it also marked itself as a film grounded in concerns unique to the black community. Most important in this regard, *Dark Manhattan* countered the negative view of the numbers racket exemplified in Micheaux's *The Girl from Chicago* and *Underworld.*

As a "numbers racket gangster film," *Dark Manhattan* linked the unique significance of the black underworld economy to the conventions of the Hollywood gangster film. Much like his Hollywood counterpart, *Dark Manhattan*'s gangster, Curly Thorpe, has his journey from ghetto tough to organization boss measured through improvements in sartorial display and the accruing of cultural capital and good taste associated with the higher classes. He starts out as a cloth-capped brawler who, on receiving employment from the numbers banker, is asked to invest in better clothing. He first buys a white suit (which is noted as being too gaudy). He then learns to dress in something more suave and appropriate—a three-piece black suit. His upward mobility also brings with it expensive cigars, a desk job (replete with a name sign, "Mr. James A. Thorpe"), and a beautiful secretary. Thus far, *Dark Manhattan* can be understood as an emulation of a well-established film formula that fed desires for class mobility shared by disadvantaged social groups across the race line. Yet *Dark Manhattan*'s meanings are both more local and more extensive than this.

As a *black* gangster, Curly rises to the top, his ascent signified through his journeying from numbers "runner" to "banker/king" via the stages of "collector" and "controller." Throughout the 1920s and 1930s, numbers was an integral part of the urban black experience and was understood more as "business" than racket. As one of the scions of the Harlem Renaissance, Claude McKay, highlighted, the "business of numbers" was a vital part of black urban life that defied the understanding of white onlookers:

> Playing numbers is the most flourishing clandestine industry in Harlem. It is the first and foremost of the rackets and the oldest. . . . [I]n its halcyon period . . . the operators ("kings" and "queens" as they were called) each had a turnover of a quarter of a million dollars yearly. . . . Numbers is a people's game, a community pastime in which old and young, literate and illiterate, the neediest folk and the well-to-do all participate. Harlemites seem altogether lacking in comprehension of the moral attitude of the white world towards its beloved racket.[29]

The numbers or policy kings and queens held special significance for the urban black community. Far from being figures of fear and hatred, they were revered as proficient operators of a black-owned business in which all citizens had a stake. And in their battles to stop the attempts of white gangsters (especially Dutch Schultz) muscling in on the action, numbers operators only enhanced their status as examples of assertive defiance in the face of segregation and subordination. Moreover, playing and operating the numbers game provided metropolitan black folk with a vicarious experience of participating in a modern exchange economy from which they were otherwise excluded. Numbers results were computed from Wall Street Clearing House reports, and the policy organization also emulated the world of corporate banking and its management structure (with "runners," "collectors," "controllers," and "bankers").[30] As such, the policy racket "signified" on the world of corporate capitalist relations to which black folk had limited access. To African American audiences of the 1930s and 1940s, then, a black screen gangster would have brought with him (or her) these particular connotations.

In words redolent of Claude McKay, Larry B. Lee (played by Clarence Brooks), the numbers banker whom Curly later usurps in *Dark Manhattan*, asserts that he runs his bank like a legitimate business: "Hard work, underhand methods are never used—it's love not war, it's business." The whole operation is run behind the legitimate front of a real estate company. All the employees are given white-collar roles (secretaries, accountants, telephonists) and adhere to the prudent protocols associated with white-collar behavior. Numbers per se, is not, therefore, the problem in *Dark Manhattan*. For numbers sustains and nurtures small-scale black entrepreneurship and enables its participants to work within a sanctioned corporate structure. The line between legitimate and illegitimate business practices is violated only when Curly breaks Larry B. Lee's rules and resorts to "underhand" methods to bully and intimidate the competition in trying to monopolize control of the numbers game. In this sense what turns the numbers business into a racket evolves from the unfettered desire for ever greater profits—a counterproductive desire that rides roughshod over the more civic-minded interests of the small business community.

In the highly limited context of African American entrepreneurship, numbers constituted a valid business framework. And in many ways this relationship bears some resemblance to the white lower-class urban ethnic's relationship to bootlegging in the context of Prohibition. Like Larry B. Lee, Al Capone insisted that he was just a businessman supplying a legitimate public demand in a discriminatory context. And any analysis of the African American gangster film of the 1930s and 1940s must be sensitive to such parallels if it is to understand how and why the talking race-underworld film is more than a simplistic rehashing of tired Hollywood tropes.

The success of *Dark Manhattan* led to Cooper's setting up a joint venture with white investors to found one of the most successful race-film companies, Million Dollar Productions—in which Cooper as the self-styled "Bronze Bogart" or "Dark Gable" became the major saleable commodity and front man. Cooper's next two Million Dollar gangster films, *Bargain with Bullets* (which he also cowrote) and *Gang War*, capitalized on his gangster image while also refining the underworld race-film formula as a vehicle to showcase revue talent. *Bargain with Bullets* (with Cooper in the lead gangster role as fur thief "Mugsy") contrived that the main female romantic interest was a radio singer, enabling Theresa Harris to demonstrate her vocal powers with the backing of Les Hite and his Cotton Club Orchestra,

Eddie Barfield's Trio, and the Covan Studio Dancers. *Gang War* featured, conveniently, a battle between two gangs for the control of Harlem's jukebox trade (with Cooper in the lead as gangster Bob "Killer" Mead). This contrivance highlighted the importance of the roadhouse/juke-joint to black life and business and gave ample time to airing a hit ballad, "Remember the Moon," by Lew Porter and Johnny Lange.

Cooper's film career swan song was *Am I Guilty?* (1940). Having left Million Dollar Productions earlier in the year, his final film was produced by Supreme Pictures, a company in which he had no stake. The question raised by the film's title invited reflection on Cooper's own indulgence in the underworld-film form. The main doctor protagonist, James Dunbar (Cooper), is an idealist who runs a clinic in the deprived inner city. He becomes involved, however, with a ruthless gangster, "Trigger" Bennett (Lawrence Criner), who covertly finances the clinic after Dunbar treats him for an injury incurred during a payroll heist. The ambivalent relationship between the underworld economy and basic institutional care needs produces a moral impasse for the good doctor (who ends up with a prison sentence for his association with gangsters). Dunbar's impasse was in many ways Cooper's as he reached a point of exhaustion with the limits of the race film.

In 1941 he took back the job of sustaining the only venue left for live black revue talent in Harlem. As emcee for "Amateur Night at the Apollo" (for almost fifty years), Cooper went on to introduce the world to a massive range of black talent, including Gladys Knight, the Ronettes, the Shirelles, Patti LaBelle, the Isley Brothers, Wilson Pickett, Jackie Wilson, Dionne Warwick, Ben E. King, Luther Vandross, James Brown, The Jackson 5, and Big Daddy Kane. In the process Cooper nurtured the sound track that bridged the years between the race film and the early years of hip-hop.[31]

The patterning of Micheaux's and Cooper's films around criminal melodrama that could showcase revue talent became increasingly definitive of the talking race film from the late 1930s onward.[32] Collectively, these movies inverted the way Hollywood diegesis, with its commitment to narrative continuity, subordinated the space, time, and relevance of black expression onscreen. The ease of affiliation and identification across the racial divide with the gangster story and type provided a conventional, yet opportune, framework (with uniquely African American resonance in the case of films featuring the numbers racket) for a montage that could be set to the rhythm of revue performance and programming.

Significantly, blaxploitation and 'hood film cycles have shared the talking race film's investment in the gangster story as germane to the experiences and desires of blacks. And like the talking underworld race film, blaxploitation and 'hood cycles have operated as venues to showcase black musical talent. The challenge remains to refine the connections between these different eras and their films, but we can see obvious structures of resemblance that point to the centrality of the gangster to an enduring tactics of counterhegemonic and antiessentialist black self-representation. Echoing *Dark Manhattan*'s relationship to Hollywood gangster fare in the 1930s, for example, blaxploitation's *Black Caesar* (1973) "signified" on *The Godfather* (1972). Tommy Gibbs (Fred Williamson) infiltrates and destroys the Italian American Cardoza family to become Manhattan's first black godfather—all to the rhythm of a James Brown sound track. *Superfly's* (1972) story of a Harlem pusher trying to get out of "the game" through "the game" was sold as much on the basis of Curtis Mayfield's streetwise funk sound track as anything else—and indeed this film's montage and meaning is directly dependent on its sound track. The 'hood films of the 1990s took this logic a step further—gangsta rappers becoming stars of vehicles that not only sold their hardcore raps but that depended on these raps and rappers for their street credibility with audiences.

The gangster/gangsta relationship has brought attention to a black view on American possibility through cross-racial identification with white gangster icons who strove to "make it" in America. Black male youth have identified with the irony of the gangster's position: as someone seeking legitimacy but who can only do so through illegitimate means. But as gangstas—as black popular culture producers—they have recognized that being a gangster is at once "the American way"—albeit from the dark side. As such, they have muscled in and appropriated cross-racial signs of subordination that can be used against the grain. Gangsta rap monikers such as "Capone" and "Scarface" underscore a legacy of cinematic crossing-over embodied most notably in Tupac Shakur's obsession with James Cagney (as Cody Jarrett in *White Heat*) in *Juice* (1992).

However, we should not let the interrelationship between Hollywood's gangster and African American gangstas blind us to other fields of reference for the black gangster film. Recently, *Hoodlum* (1997), directed by Bill Duke, became the first attempt since the late 1930s to dramatize the high point of the Harlem numbers business—an initial step in the quest to connect the era of gangsta to that of the race film. In this spirit I have suggested that we look at the films of Ralph Cooper and Oscar Micheaux as a revised point of origin for any discussion on the meaning of criminal self-representation in African American cinema.

Notes

1. *Boyz N the Hood* (1991), *New Jack City* (1991), and *Juice* (1992) drew media attention as films that provided tough and controversial views of inner-city black experience. Deploying the talents of gangsta rap stars Ice Cube, Ice T, and Tupac Shakur, respectively, these films consolidated the 'hood cycle's style—blending contemporaneous explicit street "realism" with long-established conventions and tropes associated with the Hollywood gangster.

2. Dyson, Kelley, and Quinn have identified this kind of self-representation as part of the enduring and misunderstood lore of the badman in black culture. For their various investigations of how criminal self-construction has serviced the needs of black folk, particularly in contexts of diminished access to political power, see Michael Eric Dyson, *Reflecting Black: African American Cultural Criticism* (Minneapolis: University of Minnesota Press, 1993); Michael Eric Dyson, *Between God and Gangsta Rap* (Oxford: Oxford University Press, 1996); Robin D. G. Kelley, *Race Rebels: Culture, Politics, and the Black Working Class* (New York: Free Press, 1994); Robin D. G. Kelley, *Yo' Mama's Disfunktional: Fighting the*

Culture Wars in Urban America (Boston: Beacon Press, 1997); Eithne Quinn, "'Who's the Mack?' The Performativity and Politics of the Pimp Figure in Gangsta Rap," *Journal of American Studies* 34, no. 1 (2000): 115–136; and Eithne Quinn, "'Pimpin' Ain't Easy': Work, Play, and 'Lifestylization' of the Black Pimp Figure in Early 1970s America," in *Media, Culture, and the Modern African American Freedom Struggle*, ed. Brian Ward (Gainesville: University Press of Florida, 2001), 211–232.

3. Other terms for these films existed—such as "all-Negro" and "all-Colored"—but "race film" best captures the burden these films bore as agents of racial uplift or improvement. For a fine exploration of the term's origins, appropriateness, and problems see Jane M. Gaines, *Fire and Desire: Mixed-Race Movies in the Silent Era* (Chicago: University of Chicago Press, 2001). In the early 1990s Mark A. Reid raised some initial speculations about the connections between the 1960s/1970s black gangster types (in both film and literature) and the 1930s/1940s black-cast gangster film—see Mark A. Reid, "The Black Gangster Film," *Journal of Social Philosophy* 24, no. 3 (winter 1993): 143–154.

4. J. Ronald Green, *Straight Lick: The Cinema of Oscar Micheaux* (Bloomington: Indiana University Press, 2000) offers the most exhaustive coverage of Micheaux's films—and sets these as the dates that bookend his moviemaking career, from *The Homesteader* to *The Betrayal* (see 239–242). See also Gaines, *Fire and Desire*; and the entry on Micheaux in Michael R. Pitts, *Poverty Row Studios, 1929–1940* (Jefferson, N.C.: McFarland, 1997), 261–263.

5. Through the ownership of theaters and the practice of block booking major studios maintained monopolistic control of distribution and exhibition of their products. For more on the antitrust features of this system and the challenge to its legitimacy see Ernest Borneman, "United States versus Hollywood: The Case Study of an Anti-Trust Suit," in *The American Film Industry*, ed. Tino Balio (Madison: University of Wisconsin Press, 1976), 342–345.

6. For more on the contingencies of independent film production and distribution see Balio, *American Film Industry*, 107–109; and Pitts, *Poverty Row Studios*, vii–viii, 261–263.

7. For example, Henry T. Sampson asserts that these talking race films, "although technically superior in many respects to earlier black film productions, followed the typical Hollywood movie genre so popular in the late 1930s. Westerns, gangster, and comedy films were made using all-black casts. Unlike the black features of the previous decades, they made no serious attempt to treat the unique aspects of the black experience in America" (Henry T. Sampson, *Blacks in Black and White: A Source Book on Black Films*, 2nd ed. (Metuchen, N.J.: Scarecrow Press, 1995), 12.

8. I question the reductive understanding of standardization on two counts. First, the valorization of the freedom of silent film against the straw man of standardization/commercialization is part of an essentialist project in search of an ontologically "black" cinema. I agree with Stuart Hall ("What Is This 'Black' in Black Popular Culture?" in *Black Popular Culture*, ed. Gina Dent [Seattle: Bay Press, 1992], 21–33), James Snead (*White Screens/Black Images: Hollywood from the Dark Side* [London: Routledge, 1994], esp. 121–129), and Gaines (*Fire and Desire*), who argue that looking for an essentially black cinema blinds us to the value of black cultural production that takes place *within* the limits of a white racist political and visual economy—blinds us to that which seeks to transform things from *within* the field of cultural relations.

9. Film criticism often equates the birth of American narrative cinema with D. W. Griffith's *Birth of a Nation* (1915). And those concentrating on race and cinema have highlighted how this film consolidated many of the stereotypes associated with blackness on the white screen. See Donald Bogle, *Toms, Coons, Mulattoes, Mammies, and Bucks: An Interpretative History of Blacks in American Films* (New York: Viking, 1973); Thomas Cripps, *Slow Fade to Black: The Negro in American Film, 1900–1942*, 2nd ed. (New York: Oxford University Press, 1993); Ed Guerrero, *Framing Blackness: The African American Image in Film* (Philadelphia: Temple University Press, 1993); James Snead, *White Screens/Black Images*; and Michael Rogin, *Blackface, White Noise: Jewish Immigrants in the Hollywood Melting Pot* (Berkeley: University of California Press, 1996) for further elaboration on the development of Hollywood's Old South black typology and racial masquerade in the wake of *Birth of a Nation*.

10. The film industry's internal monitoring agency, the Production Code Administration (PCA), for a host of reasons outlined by Ruth Vasey in *The World according to Hollywood, 1918–1939* (Exeter: University of Exeter Press, 1997), made miscegenation inadmissible and outlawed interracial affairs for fear of offending the domestic and foreign markets. My own research bears this out. The PCA file on Ralph Cooper's black gangster film *Dark Manhattan* (1937), for example, states that there should be no "indication that the gangsters who muscle in on the racket are white gangsters"—and emphasizes that

the film's producers should "eliminate any suggestion of conflict between whites and negroes [*sic*]" (*Dark Manhattan* PCA file, Martha Herrick Library, Academy of Motion Picture Arts and Sciences [hereafter cited as MHL-AMPAS]). In the case of another gangster race film, *Moon over Harlem* (1939), censors objected to "inference of sex suggestion" between the major black gangster protagonist, Dollar Bill, and a seemingly white woman (*Moon over Harlem* PCA file, MHL-AMPAS).

11. Snead, *White Screens/Black Images* (esp. chaps. 4 and 6), provides a fine discussion of the coding of blackness in terms of white lack in plantation films.

12. "The Negro on the Screen," *New York Age*, July 23, 1932, unpaginated clipping from the New York Public Library's Schomburg Center for Research in Black Culture (hereafter cited as Schomburg Center).

13. *The Exile*, *Ten Minutes to Live*, *The Girl from Chicago*, *Underworld*, *Swing!*, and *Lying Lips* were all viewed at Library of Congress Motion Picture and Television Reading Room, Washington, D.C.—Black Films: Paper Print Collection. *Murder in Harlem* viewed on VHS.

14. *Kansas City Call*, July 15, 1932; article reprinted in Sampson, *Blacks in Black and White*, 432.

15. The same can also be said of two subsequent Micheaux efforts, *Swing!* and *Lying Lips*. *Swing!* again features a South-North conceit in which morally loose and righteous southerners venture north to Harlem and its vaudeville world to be embroiled in the criminal deceits perpetuated by nightclub owners. *Lying Lips* abandons the South-North/city-country comparative frame altogether and focuses exclusively on the traumas of a nightclub showgirl caught up in murder and insurance fraud. Both give ample space for staging a diverse range of revue talent.

16. The race film often provided the few African American actors who had found a Hollywood calling a chance to break with mainstream stereotypes. In *Life Goes On* (1938) the urban criminal setting offered Louise Beavers the chance to be something other than a Hollywood southern "mammy" or northern "maid" whose duties are tied to (pre-)serving the white family. Although cast in a "motherly" role, she is now fighting (in Harlem as a single mother) to save her crime-oriented son and the structure of her own family. *Gang Smashers* (1939) turned Nina Mae McKinney from plantation sweetheart into a gun-toting detective who assumes the guise of a cabaret star to infiltrate a ruthless Harlem gangster protection racket. Both films were products of Million Dollar Productions—cofounded by Ralph Cooper and one of the few companies in which African Americans had a stake.

17. Sadly, of these films only *Dark Manhattan* (Library of Congress Black Film Collection), *The Duke Is Tops* (on DVD), and *Gang War* (on VHS) seem to be extant. Synopses and other information on the other films are drawn from press clippings and *The American Film Institute Catalog of Motion Pictures Produced in the United States*, Kenneth W. Munden, exec. ed. (New York: Bowker, 1971–).

18. In his autobiography Cooper details how the Cotton Club, Harlem's most famous revue venue, functioned also as a "gangland flagship." Under the proprietorship of Owney Madden ("a former Hell's Kitchen street-gang leader" and bootlegger) the Cotton Club became "the New York underworld's favorite hangout" (most notably for Dutch Schultz, Legs Diamond, and Lucky Luciano). As a result, "[h]oods were an attraction almost as powerful as the Cotton Club's music" (Ralph Cooper with Steve Dougherty, *Amateur Night at the Apollo: Ralph Cooper Presents Five Decades of Great Entertainment* [HarperCollins: New York, 1990], 53).

19. Ibid., 55.

20. Ibid., 103.

21. Ibid., 44.

22. Ibid., 120.

23. Ibid., 128.

24. Dan Burley, *New York Amsterdam News*, Aug. 19, 1939, unpaginated clipping, Schomburg Center.

25. *Philadelphia Tribune*, Feb. 25, 1937, unpaginated clipping, Schomburg Center.

26. *Philadelphia Tribune*, Sep. 30, 1937, unpaginated clipping on microfilm, Schomburg Center.

27. Cooper, *Amateur Night at the Apollo*, 124.

28. Ibid., 125.

29. Claude McKay, *Harlem: A Negro Metropolis* (New York: Dutton, 1940), 101.

30. Ibid., 109.

31. Cooper also persuaded New York radio station WMCA to air "Amateur Night at the Apollo" as a live broadcast—which was subsequently syndicated to over twenty affiliated radio stations nation-

wide. In the 1950s Cooper promoted the Apollo's variety talent on his own television show, "Harlem Spotlite," which aired on Saturday nights on New York's Channel 13. See Cooper, *Amateur Night at the Apollo*.

32. This formula is typified in films such as *Mystery in Swing* (1940), *Murder with Music* (1941), *Dirty Gertie from Harlem USA* (1946), and *Tall, Tan, and Terrific* (1946)—whose titles betray the fact that these are as much revue vehicles as crime melodramas. Viewed at Library of Congress, Motion Picture Division.

Walking the Streets

Black Gangsters and the "Abandoned City" in the 1970s Blaxploitation Cycle

Peter Stanfield

But Dante's hell is heaven. Look at things in another light.

        –LEROI JONES, *The System of Dante's Hell*

"FOR 20 YEARS GANG WARFARE HAS RAGED on the streets of Los Angeles, claiming more than 10,000 lives," runs a newspaper headline in 2003. "So can the city's new police chief repeat what he did in New York and reduce the murder rate?" Chief of police Bill Bratton underscored the enormity of the task facing him and his department when he compared the old and new order of street crime: "[A]s insidious as the Mafia was, in no one year did they kill 300 people. This is a form of urban terrorism. I make no apologies for saying that."[1] Bratton's comparison between the old folk devil of organized crime and the new terror represented by black street gangs may seem strangely familiar, yet the origin of this comparison lies not in academic studies or even popular journalism concerned with America's inner cities but, most visibly, in the popular fictions produced in America's film factories during the first half of the 1970s.

The trope of blacks having wrested control of the inner-city streets away from the Mafia is used tirelessly in the cycle of films produced in the first five years of the 1970s that came to be known as blaxploitation: *Shaft* (1971), *Black Gunn* (1971), *Come Back Charleston Blue* (1972), *Slaughter* (1972), *Across 110th Street* (1972), *Black Caesar* (1973), *Run Nigger Run* (1973), *The Slams* (1973), *Trick Baby* (1973), *Hell Up in Harlem* (1973), *The Mack* (1973), *Slaughter's Big Rip-Off* (1973), *Coffy* (1973), *Foxy Brown* (1973), *Black Samson* (1974), *Black Belt Jones* (1974), *Mean Johnny Barrows* (1976), *No Way Back* (1976), *J. D.'s Revenge* (1976), and many others.

A formative and representative film from this cycle begins with a bird's-eye view of Times Square; then, following a cut, the camera tracks past a line of 42nd Street

281

1–4. The opening seven shots from *Shaft* (1971).

5–7. Continued.

cinema marquees. The first advertises a Western double bill of Burt Lancaster in *The Scalphunters* and George Peppard and Dean Martin in *Rough Night in Jericho*; the second is showing *Little Fauss and Big Halsey*, starring Robert Redford and Michael J. Pollard, along with a rerun of *Barbarella*. The third and fourth cinemas are show-ing double bills of sex films, and the camera tracks past *He and She* and *The Animal*, *School for Sex*, and *The Wild Females*, at which point the title appears on the screen —*Shaft*.[2] The camera descends to street level to meet John Shaft (Richard

Roundtree) rising from the subway. Summarized within this opening sequence is the idea of the decline and rebirth of urban cinema: old Hollywood (Westerns) by-passed by young Hollywood represented by Jane Fonda and Robert Redford (the latter film's tagline: "Little Fauss and Big Halsey are not your father's heroes"), who in turn are outstripped by X-rated sex films. Surpassing all these forms of cinematic entertainment is John Shaft—a new-old hero: "new" because he is a black star of this MGM feature—a "new expression of black in film"[3]—and "old" because he is a re-play of the venerable genre stalwart—the private detective.

The opening of *Shaft* neatly and economically encapsulates two interlocked themes in 1970s cinema: it announces mainstream American cinema's concern to exploit a hitherto marginal target audience—young black inner-city filmgoers—and it documents a growing public awareness of the black population's dominance of America's inner-city landscape. With its concentration on crime and gangster narratives the cycle of blaxploitation films played to the newly constituted black urban filmgoer and represented a version of the new black urban experience. Rising into consciousness, like John Shaft from the underworld of New York's subways, came a compellingly new set of images of America's urban landscape, yet these images were made utterly familiar by their borrowings from earlier urban crime genres. Like Los Angeles chief of police Bill Bratton's "natural" linking of the Mafia with L.A.'s gangsta culture, Hollywood thirty-odd years earlier had figured it could best sell the new by garbing it in the costumes of old.

Shaft is hired by Bumpy, a Harlem gangster, to retrieve his daughter, who has been kidnapped by the Mafia. Bumpy is going head-to-head with the Italian mobsters for control of the rackets, while Shaft is walking the line between the police and the racketeers. As he rises from the 42nd Street subway, he shows a mastery of the streets, dodging traffic, moving with and through the crowd. In his brown leather trench coat he sweeps down the bustling streets as if he owns them. A young black guy blocks his path and offers him a watch, then darts back into the crowd when Shaft flashes a police badge. He picks up information from a blind newspaper seller, which is confirmed by a bootblack at a shoeshine parlor. A police detective corners him; he wants to know what's happening on the street. The streets of Harlem belong to John Shaft.

Blaxploitation's urban crime films work with the assumption that crime syndicates, such as the Mafia, control America's inner cities. The drift and flow of these films' narratives, then, is toward a confrontation between black residents of the ghetto and their absentee comptrollers. Simultaneously, gaining dominion over the urban space of the street holds out the promise of escape from the confinement of ghetto life. As he moves effortlessly through the urban space of Harlem, Shaft is the perfect embodiment of this idea—individuated, self-possessed, and self-empowered. However, rising from the underside of the ghetto, he is doubly limited: there is no alternative image proffered to a world made on the city's streets, and the images of black empowerment are further circumscribed by concealment of the real economic, social, and racial policies that determine much of black life in the ghetto behind a familiar formulaic crime fiction.

As urban-located and contemporary-set films that were aimed initially and primarily at the black inner-city filmgoer, the blaxploitation cycle drew its understanding of crime and urban disorder not from news stories or from authoritative accounts of life in the black inner cities but from the fictions and myths about cities first propagated in the late 1940s and early 1950s. These stories suggested that America's inner cities were run by highly organized crime syndicates, chiefly the Mafia, who were responsible for turning once healthy, productive, and thriving metropolises into squalid and brutal worlds of vice and crime. In his exemplary study of the 1950s cycle of mob films—*The Phenix City Story* (1955), *New Orleans Uncensored* (1955), *Kansas City Confidential* (1955), *Las Vegas Shakedown* (1955), *Portland Expose* (1957)—Will Straw notes the narratives were "secondary to their cataloguing of vice, and to the formal organization of these films as sequences of scenes in night-clubs, gambling dens and along neon-lit streets."[4] Simultaneously with their representation in film, these urban spaces were being explored in exposé books and magazines, as well as in congressional investigations, but what marks this intertextual space, according to Straw, is the proliferation of urban sites: "New York, Chicago and other prominent cities will figure in many of these texts, but as the cycle unfolds there is a dispersion of attention outwards, towards medium-sized cities, regional capitals, and, in a variety of films, fictionalized versions of the mythically corruption-ridden 'wide open' town." The abundance of city locations is explained, in part, in order "that the production of differentiated texts may continue."[5] The proliferation of urban spaces placed under the camera's investigative eye leads to a displacement of a recognizable metropolitan center, whether represented by New York, San Francisco, Chicago, or Los Angeles, a displacement that is rhymed in the development of the suburbs and the consequent middle-class evacuation of city spaces. Straw draws a provocative comparison between the dissolution and dispersion of fixed urban centers in popular American crime fictions of the 1950s and the breakup of the Hollywood studio system across the same time period. The decline of centralized film-production culture is measurable in the shift from Hollywood to "regionalist" independent production companies and in the ascendancy of sensational "exploitative filmmaking practices" that diminished mainstream Hollywood production values.

The primary audiences for the cycle of two hundred–plus blaxploitation films of the first half of the 1970s were the unwitting beneficiaries, then, of an established representation of America's city centers — a space abandoned by the middle classes and controlled by crime syndicates —*and* the changing patterns of ownership and control of the film industry. Between 1971 and 1975 the high watermark for the production of blaxploitation films, the film industry, according to Richard Maltby, retrenched after a period of escalating production costs and overproduction of films that saturated an unresponsive theatrical market. The mainstream industry had shown a marked reluctance to abandon the concept of the universal, undifferentiated audience that had characterized production, marketing, and exhibition under the studio system. However, the dwindling urban audience for the studios' core product, the effect of the ratings system, and the new sites of film exhibition located in suburban shopping malls, contributed to the organization of production based on a projection of differentiated audiences.[6]

The new suburban film theaters attracted a young audience whose tastes were catered to by the rising stars of Hollywood's "renaissance" such as Steven Spielberg, Brian De Palma, George Lucas, Francis Ford Coppola, William Friedkin, and others, whose sensationalist fare, *The Godfather* (1972), *The Exorcist* (1973), *American Graffiti* (1973), *Jaws* (1975), and *Carrie* (1976) were big-budget reworkings of the kind of juvenile material that had previously been the exclusive concern of independent film companies that served the drive-in market. "The shift in content to exploitation genres was, like the use of saturation booking and the relocation of the site of moviegoing," argues Maltby, "part of what Thomas Doherty has called the 'juvenilization' of American cinema, and ultimately a consequence of the juvenilization of its primary audience."[7]

While the movie brats played to the new youthful suburban audience, what of the inner-city filmgoer and the long-established theaters? One consequence of the 1948 Paramount decrees (which broke the major studios' grip over all aspects of the industry) was that the major exhibition chains "were not permitted to acquire theaters without court permission, which was regularly refused when they proposed closing a downtown movie theater and replacing it with one in the suburbs."[8] Unable to shift their sites of exhibition, the major chains needed film product that would appeal to its principal inner-city audience of young black consumers, furthering Hollywood's differentiation of films along generational *and* racial lines. The blaxploitation film cycle recognized and played to this newly targeted constituency.

Countering the "ironic" retrieval of blaxploitation as depthless and ahistorical "camp," Professor of Black Studies Cedric Robinson refuses the easy assimilation of blaxploitation into the lexicon of postmodern style by which cinema is cut loose from meaningful social, economic, or political determination. Instead, Robinson returns the film cycle to the actuality of the context of black consciousness in the 1970s. He does not, however, find a progressive political agenda and describes the cycle of films instead as a "degraded cinema." It "degraded the industry which prostituted itself to political and market exigencies and constructed the genre of a[n] urban jungle; it degraded the Black actors, writers, and directors who proved more affectionate to money than to the Black lower classes they caricatured; it degraded its audiences who were subjected to a mockery of the aspirations of Black liberationists."[9] Robinson's position is a necessary rejoinder to the facile absorption of the cycle into "camp," yet it may be precipitous to dismiss blaxploitation films as "degraded" because of their failure to meet a responsibility for articulating explicit political platforms. Although Robinson is justified in finding them wanting in respect to their contribution to the progressive ideals of black American identity he espouses, there is enough evidence to suggest that, however speculatively, blaxploitation films *do* express "political" concerns. Uncovering these concerns, however, requires a more oblique approach to the ways in which the historical specificity of black social experience registers in these films. Black social experience prompts consideration of blaxploitation film not as direct social documentary or transparent record of current political realities but as a cinematic type in which political and social meanings are overdetermined by the dominance of *fictional* structures that displace them. The question of how the social experience of the cinema audience is addressed by the films is a properly political one, even though the nature of blaxploitation films makes appeal to direct political intervention ultimately unproductive. Although the overtly politicized agendas of the black liberation movement do appear under specific conditions in some of the films, the wider political import of the cycle, it can be argued, lies instead in its *particular representation of street life* in black inner cities. The films work to construct a specific city experience, one that is grounded in the physical geography of urban centers yet also transformed by the narratives inspired by formulaic urban crime fictions. Blaxploitation film of the 1970s narrates stories in which the representation of street life simultaneously invokes and dramatizes the experience of everyday life.

The duality of melodrama and the everyday clearly structures a film like *Mean Johnny Barrows*, the story of a black Vietnam veteran's return to civilian life and his search for gainful and honest employment. The film signals a political line with end titles that dedicate it to the "Veteran who traded his place on the front line for a place on the unemployment line — Peace in Hell." This idea is represented most fully in the film's first twenty-five minutes. Johnny Barrows (Fred Williamson) is a highly decorated Vietnam veteran and ex-college football star given a dishonorable discharge for hitting a racist officer who called him "boy," and Barrows encounters an equally unjust United States on his first night back in Los Angeles. He is mugged and, while still reeling from the muggers' blows, is arrested for being drunk and disorderly. To exacerbate matters, the arresting officer also calls him "boy." Following his release from jail, Johnny walks the streets of Hollywood, a place with no soul, no opportunities for a penniless black man, and no meaningful and legitimate employment. Forced to ask for food in restaurant kitchens, Johnny is recognized from his old football days by one of the heads of an Italian crime family. Offered a plate of spaghetti and meatballs and a job in the organization, Johnny accepts the former but rejects the latter. He wants honest work. More scenes follow of Johnny walking the streets before he meets a debonair bum, played by Elliott Gould, who introduces him to the world of the flaneur and the street hassle. After Barrows takes a demeaning and exploitative job cleaning lavatories in a garage, circumstances conspire to ensure he has no other option but to work for the Italians as a hit man. The streets are black and honest but without opportunity. Opportunity exists only in crime, and crime is run by the Italians.

Until Johnny is given no other option but to pick up his guns, the film has held closely to conventions of social realism in cinema, with its emphasis on the search for work undertaken by a proletarian male. Yet when Johnny strikes out at his oppressors, the whole ethos of the film changes: the slow walks along city streets tramping for work are exchanged for fast car chases, being mugged gives way to hitting hoodlums, pumping gas into automobiles segues into pumping bullets into mobsters, cleaning toilets is swapped for cleaning the city streets of the scum of organized crime. The world of inaction gives way to a world of action. The everyday gives way to the melodramatic, as in *Shaft* when the hero swings through a hotel window like a caped crusader, as black liberationists disguised as hotel workers kick down the mobsters' doors from inside the hotel. These are worlds turned upside down, where the powerless become suddenly and meaningfully powerful.

The combination of contemporary social concerns and formulaic fictions portrayed in a film such as *Mean Johnny Barrows* originates in the formative body of popular fictions for a mass audience — dime novels — that were produced around the turn of the twentieth century. Cultural historian Michael Denning argues that the dime novel story was a fantastical resetting of the "everyday": "a story to be a story had to be set in a contemporary time and knowable landscape, but its plot had to be out of the ordinary; 'everyday happenings,' according to this . . . aesthetic, did not make a story. The story was an interruption in the present, a magical, fairy tale transformation of familiar landscapes and characters, a death and rebirth that turned the world upside down."[10] The heroes and heroines of blaxploitation may be fantastical or, as Robinson contends, "degraded" versions of contemporary black liberationists — Huey Newton or Angela Davis perhaps — but they *are* linked to the quotidian realities of their contemporary audiences. Popular fictional tales of the city are not a kind of documentary on the social realities of the time; rather, they are melodramatic excursions into a world that offers an extended play on escape and confinement.

Blaxploitation films never promised to mirror faithfully their audiences' own social circumstances but, with the purchase of a cinema ticket, did offer the promise of wish fulfillment. Surrealist René Crevel's 1927 critique of this contract between cinema and its patrons, between the street and the screen, is still germane: "In spite of all the gazes met with, the street had already proved a disappointment. In the absence of all those glances that might have done something for us, our indolence has expected a lot of those black-and-white creatures with whom most adult males would like to fall in love. . . . At pavement level you used to tell yourself the marvelous bliss could never end, since the marquee announced *nonstop entertainment*."[11] Cinema, though, never fulfills its part of the contract. Desire is never satisfied; the *jouissance* of "marvelous bliss" is always deferred, held over for the next screening. Escape into the cinema from the ennui of the streets outside does not represent a mirroring of social realities but a mirroring of the confinement of the city's streets and strangers' ill-met glances.

The strangers on the cinema screen—who promise to meet the audiences' glances—are always predetermined and thus never representative of the aleatory flow of chance encounters of the real city streets. Although the police represent "society's and the state's emblem of order," Robinson notes that rarely is their presence felt in these films. "Other erasures from this imagined community are less obvious but nevertheless telling: the absence of children and oldsters, of families, churches, legitimate businesses, recreational sites, schools and ordinary family dwellings." "How," he asks, "might the manufacturers of such a fantastically unrealistic portrayal expect that their creation would achieve the ring of authenticity?" The short answer is that they did not. Why should an adolescent audience, the primary consumer of blaxploitation, care for such an "authentic" representation? And if this was not its primary appeal, are not the structures of narrative fiction and spectatorial pleasure as important in accounting for their appeal? The cycles' notion of verisimilitude, or authenticity, then, is linked not only to the social reality of the black ghetto but also to a Manichean understanding of the world copped wholesale from blood and thunder melodrama and, more directly, its cinematic offspring—the urban crime film. The streets of the ghetto are "authenticated" through reference to canonical gangster movies and to the postwar cycle of crime films that held out the image of the abandoned city and the mob's control of urban centers.

Systemic civic corruption and the barren city were tropes that defined the 1950s urban crime film. In the popular imaginary located in the mismatched collection of films commonly called films noirs, the post–Second World War urban landscape is conceived as a space of eternal night, a nocturnal subterranean urban world populated by the criminal fraternity of syndicate operatives, grifters, gamblers, punch-drunk pugilists, strippers, B-girls, junkies, drunks, gimps, and pimps. Citizens of good character have deserted the inner city for the safer suburban realm, leaving behind an "abandoned city." The cinematic cityscape of the 1940s and early 1950s has been examined by film scholars David Reid and Jayne Walker. In their revisionist attack on the dominant conception of film noir as located within, and produced by, a "post-war depression and the reorganization of the American economy," they undermine the conventional explanation for the feelings of "loss and alienation" felt by noir characters. Instead, the authors argue there was no postwar depression, that images of a bankrupt economy were produced out of fear, not in response to an immediate reality: "The midnight streets, furnished rooms, low bars, dance halls, precinct offices, rain, heat, shadows, whiskey fumes and cigarette smoke—all the familiar elements of New York *noir's misé en scène*—are the sometimes overstrained vehicles for an imagination fundamentally melodramatic and Manichean. . . . They are very much rooted in the experience of the Depression, when the fear (or, in other quarters, hope) arose that capitalism and its incarnation in the modern metropolis had entered some permanent crisis."[12] Furthermore, and more pertinent, the inner cities were not simply being "abandoned" in the years following the close of the Second World War but were, in counterpoint to the images propagated in the films and stories Reid and Walker discuss, being filled to overflow.

The moneyed and middle classes may have been leaving the city centers for the suburbs, but between 1940 and 1970 five million Americans migrated from the rural South of the country, relocating in the industrial cities of the North and West. Social historian Nicholas Lemann writes: "In 1940, 77 per cent of black Americans still lived in the South — 49 per cent in the rural South. . . . Between 1910 and 1970, six and a half million black Americans moved from the South to the North; five million moved after 1940. . . . In 1970, when migration ended, black America was only half Southern, and less than a quarter rural; 'urban' had become a euphemism for 'black.'" [13] The real story of postwar urban America is not the city's abandonment, however representative that may be of middle-class fears and anxieties, but its re-population by black American migrants and the subsequent making of a new underclass of disenfranchised, undereducated, and underemployed urban citizens. If the mainstream crime film of the 1940s and 1950s failed to represent the enormity of this demographic shift—which it did—it nevertheless laid the groundwork for the cycle of films produced in the early to mid-1970s that did represent a black urban milieu. In *New Centurions* (1972) an experienced police officer describes to a rookie the kind of situation they will meet on the streets: "This division is mostly black, some Mexicans, some whites, mostly crime." The rookie responds: "Well, considering the intensity of living conditions — poverty — I'm surprised there's not more crime." This short exchange is capped when the older cop sums it all up: "Ah, it's just a city." Just a city: black and criminal.

In just about all of the films in the cycle with an urban setting there is at least one lengthy scene of the hero tramping the city's sidewalks. These are sequences that attempt to enunciate poetically everyday black street life. Shaft's street walks are particularly pronounced in the film's opening and in a later scene, cut to Isaac Hayes's slow-moving ballad of social commentary "Early Sunday Morning" — "crime rate is rising too, if you were hungry what would you do?" His long leather coat buttoned up to keep out the cold of winter, Shaft walks the streets, following faint traces of an illusive figure who may supply him with clues to the whereabouts of Bumpy's kidnapped daughter. The search seems fruitless: down long dark tenement streets, into the tenements themselves, asking questions, loitering in doorways, watching faces, people on the streets moving by oblivious to his presence. Inside a restaurant, walking past the Apollo Theater, drifting past a long line of street stores, their goods flowing out on the sidewalk, street peddlers with their shoddy wares compete for the stores' customers. The city: bleak, winter cold, hopeless. The contrast with the double-speed ending, as Shaft, like Batman, swings from outside through a hotel window to meet the Mafia's guns and free Bumpy's daughter, could not be stronger. The reality and passivity of the city streets give way to the fantasy and activity of the resolution — order restored. The city streets are back in Shaft's (black) control; the cause of distress and actionable unrest, the Mafia, is defeated.

Released in 1972, the year following *Shaft, Across 110th Street* walks the same New York streets, which are also controlled by the Mafia. Opening with a helicopter shot of Manhattan, the camera moves down toward the streets following a black Cadillac as it moves uptown across 110th Street, past the ubiquitous Apollo Theater and deeper into Harlem. White Mafia bagmen are collecting money from black Harlem numbers' bankers, when two black men, disguised as cops, stick them up. By the time the phony cops have left the scene with their getaway driver, seven men are dead, including two policemen. Downtown in an apartment overlooking Central Park, the head of the Italian crime family explains that the park is a no-man's-land, a small green strip that separates them from black Harlem. "Harlem is ours," explains another Italian mobster. "We found it, we made it and we're gonna keep it." To insure there is no loss of "prestige" on the part of the family, Nick D'Salvio (Anthony Franciosa) is sent to Harlem to make certain the thieves pay for their deeds.

Intercut with D'Salvio crossing into Harlem is police captain Mattelli, an Italian American. On the scene of the killings he learns, for political reasons, that he is to play a subordinate role to the black Lt. Pope (Yaphet Kotto). Like the Mafia, the Italian police officer has to face the possibility of losing control of Harlem's streets to its black racketeers and to black policemen. Mattelli (Anthony Quinn) is a blunt, foul-mouthed, violent officer, a throwback to the 1940s, who for years has been taking money from the black racketeers. Pope speaks quietly and uses stealth and intelligence as his main tools of investigation; he cannot be bought. Mattelli and the Mafia are a matched pair, corrupt old forces whose time has passed, or is in the process of passing. Pope and the black racketeers are also matched — they are the future. The racketeers, whose base in a subterranean garage is decorated with posters of Malcolm X, Angela Davis, and Mohammed Ali, eventually control the basements, the streets, and the upper worlds of Harlem: a perverse image of black empowerment.

The three thieves who knocked over the bankers, bagmen, and police officers are nobodies, three figures that momentarily rise from the subterranean world of the black underclass: an epileptic ex-con with no future and a girlfriend with "white woman's dreams" on her mind, a young street punk who has abandoned his wife and child, and a guy who scratches out a living working in a laundry. Their shot at holding on to something does not last long. The ex-con's home is a basement room in a tenement building owned by an absentee landlord, and nothing in the building works. When he takes it on the lam to avoid the police and the mobsters, his knowledge of the world is so circumscribed his hideout is less than a couple of blocks from where he lived and worked — a derelict building on Lenox Avenue. The junk between the buildings is so deep he has to wade knee high in places to get through it.

When the ex-con dies, it is on the building's roof. He has gone nowhere, his only redeeming act is a small drama of wealth distribution — throwing the booty down from on high into a children's play area. Before the police arrived, the ex-con had machine-gunned the Italian mobsters who had sought him out for his part in the robbery of the numbers' bank. Up on the roof he takes numerous hits from police bullets, but it is the black police officer Pope who finally kills him. The ex-con's two partners in crime fare no better: one is caught trying to cross 110th Street, and the other is caught in a Harlem whorehouse. The streets nor the basements nor the rooftops afford security for these thieves; their world is completely circumscribed by the ghetto's borders. When Mattelli is killed, the victim of a sniper who works for the black racketeers, the last Italian holdout in Harlem had ended. The city, Harlem, is now all black.

Sociologist William Julius Wilson writes:

> Blacks in Harlem and in other ghetto neighborhoods did not hesitate to sleep in parks, on fire escapes, and on rooftops during hot summer nights in the 1940s and 1950s, and whites frequently visited inner-city taverns and nightclubs. There was crime, to be sure, but it had not reached the point where people were fearful of walking the streets at night, despite the overwhelming poverty in the area. There was joblessness, but it was nowhere near the proportions of unemployment and labor-force nonparticipation that have gripped ghetto communities since 1970. There were single-parent families, but they were a small minority of all black families and tended to be incorporated within extended family networks and to be headed not by unwed teenagers and young adult women but by middle-aged women who were usually widowed, separated, or divorced. There were welfare recipients, but only a very small percentage of the families could be said to be welfare-dependent. In short, unlike the present period, inner-city communities prior to 1960 exhibited the features of social organization — including a sense of community, positive neighborhood identification, and explicit norms and sanctions against aberrant behavior.[14]

The rise in unemployment and single-parent families, and the concomitant fracturing of community values and organization, was exacerbated by an exodus of skilled black workers and members of the black middle-classes from the inner city.[15] Discussing the impact of these demographic and economic shifts on the city of Chicago, Wilson records the creation of an underclass and consequent social pathologies, not the least of which was a staggering rise in violent street crime:

> The 1970s was a violent decade in the history of Chicago. The number of violent crimes in the city began to rise in the mid-1960s and reached record levels in the 1970s. The number of homicides jumped from 195 in 1965 to 810 in 1970. During the severe recession year of 1974, the city experienced a record 970 murders (30.8 per 100,000 population) and 4,071 shooting assaults. Despite the record number of homicides in Chicago in 1974, Chicago's murder rate was actually lower than those in Detroit, Cleveland, Washington, D.C., and Baltimore. In 1981, another recession year, 877 murders were committed in Chicago, the

second highest number ever; yet its rate placed Chicago only fifth among the ten largest urban areas in the country.[16]

The steep rise in violent assaults and murders in America's inner cities during the 1970s had been preceded by summer after summer of black riots. Following an incident in Watts in August 1965 between a black motorist and a white policeman that escalated into a riot lasting five days and leaving a thousand injured and thirty-four dead, the idea of a "severe crisis" in the black slums moved from "being an issue only among a small coterie to being a national obsession."[17] And things seemed only to get worse. There were 164 race riots in the first nine months of 1967. Forty-seven hundred federal troops had been deployed in July in Detroit, and forty-three deaths had been recorded before order was restored. The following spring, in response to the assassination of Martin Luther King, riots broke out in Chicago, Baltimore, Washington, and many other cities. Lemann writes that "it seemed at least possible that a full-scale national race war might break out."[18] Yet American films barely paused directly to represent this state of affairs, turning instead to the familiar ground of generic archetypes to carry messages of social import for black audiences.

Many of the films produced by the movie brats of Hollywood's renaissance pandered to their principal white suburban audience by playing on their fears and prejudices of American inner cities aroused by news stories of race riots, rising crime rates, the ranking of cities according to the number of murders committed within their borders, an escalating drug problem, and endemic poverty.[19] Hollywood's images of America's inner cities in the early years of the 1970s hardly matched the reality, but Hollywood did finally register the racial composition of urban centers, and it specifically played on the white fear of street crime. In different but allied ways Friedkin's two box office hits *The Exorcist* and *The French Connection* (1971) convey the idea and image of the contemporary American city as completely inhospitable, a nightmare world peopled by supernatural devils in the former and by more corporeal spooks in the latter.[20] Following the lead of *Rosemary's Baby* (1968), *The Exorcist* located the source of horror in America's cities, an idea that was subsequently exploited by other horror films.[21] Although *The French Connection's* opening sequence is set in France, the story quickly relocates to Brooklyn, where two hard-boiled policemen, one dressed as Santa Claus, are the only white men in a world of blackness. A chase on foot between the two policemen and a black junkie takes the viewer on a short tour of the black inner city — a dingy bar, with a blaring jukebox, crowded with underemployed men, garbage-covered sidewalks, abandoned automobiles, burning tires, derelict buildings, and vacant lots. The coppers want the junkie's connection, his dealer. Their search will eventually connect Brooklyn with Marseilles, and the black underclass with organized crime. As one of the heads of the five Mafia families in *The Godfather* expostulates, he wants to run the drug trade like a business but keep the stuff away from schools and children: "In my city we will keep the traffic with the dark people — they're animals anyway, so let them lose their souls." This is the world of lost souls that Travis Bickle (Robert De Niro) traverses in *Taxi Driver* (1976).

Filtered through Bickle's subjectivity, New York appears as a Dantesque inferno of vice and crime, overwhelmingly imagined as black. Paul Schrader's screenplay lays it out: "We see the city as TRAVIS sees it. . . . Our eyes scan the long line of pedestrians. The regulars — bums, junkies, tourists, hookers, homosexuals, hippies — they mean nothing now. They only blend into the sidewalks and lighted storefronts. . . . It's a long wait — a black streetwalker crosses in front of the cab." [22] He calls his black passengers "spooks," and through him we bear witness to the black street trash, the whores and their johns. And we hear the voice and see the eyes of a cuckolded passenger (Martin Scorsese): "Ya see that woman there? . . . That's my wife. . . . But it ain't my apartment. (Pause.) A nigger lives there." [23] Four scenes later Bickle shoots and kills a young black punk sticking up an all-night delicatessen in Spanish Harlem. Unlike many of his fellow taxi drivers, Bickle takes and picks up passengers from all over, even 122nd Street — "fucking Mau Mau land," says one of his colleagues, an image of black savagery visually underscored by cutting to a group of black men dressed in pimp style. Bickle's inferno is colored black, and his fall into complete psychosis, into the "darker shadows," is visually confirmed when he shaves the sides of his head. His Mohican haircut complements his deranged senses and violent impulses. New York is no longer simply "Mau Mau land"; it is now another version of the city as the Wild West.

Introducing his thesis on the "gutting" of industrial production in the great American and European cities and the consequent reorganization of urban spaces around massive international airports, cultural theorist Paul Virilio cites the mayor of Philadelphia's announcement, following a summer of race riots in the early 1960s, that "from here on in, the frontiers of the State pass to the interior of the cities." [24] This was not a new conception of America's cities; the conflation of the Wild West and new industrial cities, such as Chicago, had been common currency since the turn of the nineteenth century, and the savage Indian was a ubiquitous metonym for the hordes of immigrant laborers. [25] Even in Europe the metonymic Indian had a role to play in defining the city's inhabitants. Discussing Walter Benjamin's conception of the flaneur (streetwalker), Rob Shields writes:

> The figure of the flaneur appropriates the figure (and ventriloquizes the point of view) of the savage "Mohican," a figure whose unreadability represented the null-point of physiognomy, the implosive moment of reversal to any attempt at "reading" the character of this foreign Other no matter how hard the flaneur may squint. The figure of the impassive and deceptive (because un-self-revealing) "Mohican" [who covers his tracks] is thus the perfect persona for the flaneur. The "Mohican" of Paris is a foil to the distracted and thus un-self-guarded gregariousness of the other inhabitants of the streetscape. Those others lose their individuality and sink into the chthonic mass. . . . In this act of transportation and appropriation,

metropolitan Paris (a center of European empire) is transmogrified not only into a foreign landscape but a virgin forest inhabited by primitive savages.[26]

The mayor of Philadelphia is clearly not referring to the fanciful figures of the European literati, nor to the undifferentiated alien ethnic horde of urban immigrants, but has instead consciously confused the black urban dweller with the savage Indian. Hollywood, in a manner, configures both the mayor's view and Benjamin's. *Taxi Driver* is particularly overt in its representation of the city as another version of the Wild West. Initially and subsequently referred to as a cowboy ("He wears rider jeans, cowboy boots, a plaid western shirt."—"Hey cowboy! Gimme the rod, cowboy. This ain't Dodge City, cowboy. You don't need no piece."), Bickle's transformation into a savage Indian is in keeping with his image as an unseen presence that moves invisibly through the landscape: "TRAVIS is now drifting in out of the New York City night life, a dark shadow among darker shadows. Not noticed, with no reason to be noticed, TRAVIS is one with his surroundings."[27] *Taxi Driver* is notorious for the manner in which its filmmakers referenced John Ford's *The Searchers* (1956), with Travis Bickle in the part of Ethan Edwards (John Wayne), the psychotic searcher; Iris (Jodie Foster) in the part of Debbie (Natalie Wood), his object of desire; and Sport (Harvey Keitel), Iris's pimp, in the part of the American Indian chief, Scar. However, unlike Ford's film, *Taxi Driver's* filmmakers deny their own racial logic by making the figure of the pimp a white man.[28] Nevertheless, the film marked the racial nature of demographic change in the city—change that was also being recorded and commented on in the cycle of blaxploitation films.

If the city had to be reconfigured by America's filmmakers, albeit on borrowed terrain of earlier crime films, what better way to display and remap this space than through the "savages" of the modern city—detectives, drug dealers, pimps, and gangsters—tour guides drawn from the streets and underworld? Inhabiting the city, as Walter Benjamin noted, takes place not in houses but on its streets: "for it is they that are on the move, the being that experiences, learns, knows, and imagines as much between the houses as the individual between his four walls."[29] For the streetwalker the city is "a landscape made up of living people," and landscape, according to Benjamin, "is what the city becomes for the flaneur. Or, more precisely, the city splits into dialectical poles. It becomes a landscape that opens up to him and a parlor that encloses him."[30] In the new black ghettos imagined by Hollywood, the detective, drug dealer, pimp, and gangster pit their knowledge and experience of the city's streets against an old order for whom the city is no longer readable. The wresting of the control of the streets from the Mafia represents empowerment for the black hero, but as Benjamin suggests of his flaneur, it is a power limited only to the streets. Still, for those young urban black male audiences, the streetwalker's entitlement to his natural environment must have presented itself as a pleasurable and satisfying commercial spectacle.

In *The Mack* (1973) the pimp is the film's nominal hero and also its victim; in *Superfly* (1972) the drug dealer is similarly hero and victim. In the former, Goldie (Max Julien), an ex-con, looks for an opening that will allow him to crawl out from under the mob and claim his space on the streets. In a pool hall a blind old pimp promises Goldie that if he joins the game and becomes a player (pimp) he will have a "bank roll so big that when you walk down the street it's gonna look like your pockets got mumps." Dreams of being a doctor or a big shot lawyer "or something heavy like that" are for the whites, according to Goldie. For the black man pimping or hustling is the only way he can save himself from being owned and sold like Goldie's stable of whores. Caught between corrupt white cops and the mobsters led by the Fat Man, Goldie tries to exploit a little piece of the street for himself. As a pimp he is an entrepreneur building an independent business. The success of his business, however, makes him a target of the cops, who are looking for kickbacks, and the mobsters, who want their cut. Goldie's ambitions reveal the limitations of an illegitimate ghetto-centric black economy. Priest dreams of one last job that will get him out of the "life" and off the streets, but buying thirty kilos of cocaine only puts him more firmly in the grasp of the Man.

In *Superfly* the Priest (Ron O'Neal) has already made enough at the game of hustling drugs to claim his street space. At the end of the film the possibility is held out that Priest may escape from the streets and into the arms of the woman who loves him, but given the story's thematic concern with entrapment, escape is illusory. At midpoint in the film Priest is seen with his girlfriend looking over railings into Central Park at white kids playing in the snow—an image of freedom, innocence, and whiteness denied to those on Priest's side of the iron bars. Desire and its denial are reinforced as the couple walk the city's streets talking of their dreams and hopes, but, as Priest's dope-dealing partner has already explained, what else can he do apart from hustle drugs and pimp? "It's a rotten game, but it's the only one the Man left us to play."

In *The Mack* the trappings of success accompany Goldie's initial achievement as a pimp: much money, fine clothes, and beautiful automobiles. The outsized hats, crushed velvet suits with coat tails sweeping the floor, ostentatious jewelry, bouffant hairstyles, suede capes, and gold-handled walking canes support his affectation as a man of leisure, a streetwise dandy. He is not a worker; he is a "player." He does not produce; he only consumes. As a pimp selling women's bodies, Goldie can claim autonomy, but his success at this "game," signified by his clothes and Cadillac, makes him visible and vulnerable. The Fat Man threatens to take him and his business—to make the pimp Goldie into the Fat Man's whore.

In one particularly noteworthy scene Goldie has gathered together his stable of whores in a planetarium. His voice is broadcast into the auditorium as the whores gaze in wonder at the stars projected onto the roof and with adoration for Goldie. He explains that they are all part of his family, and the family is like a large corporation with him at its head, as well as holding all stock and all positions of authority.

With the universe as his backdrop Goldie thinks he is God. Goldie's fantasy of omnipotence is short-lived; the movement from the street to more starry realms, symbolized in the planetarium and his winning of the "Pimp of the Year" award (conferred on him at The Players' Ball, a gutter-puddle reflection of the Academy Awards), also figures his estrangement from family, friends, and community.

The image of alienation worked in conjunction with streetwalking is a recurring trope within the films discussed here. *Superfly*, like *The Mack*, has only a slender narrative. Much screen time is taken with shots of the hero moving through city spaces. Like *Across 110th Street* and *Shaft*, *Superfly* begins with a bird's-eye view of the streets. In this case the camera follows two junkies looking for a fix — junk and trash claim most of the space on the sidewalks — a tour of the black ghetto has been set in motion. One scene later the two junkies have mugged Priest and taken his coke. Priest fights back and pursues the junkie that has his drugs. As in *The French Connection*, the chase takes pursued and pursuer deeper into a derelict city, to the rear of tenement buildings, ending in the impoverished home of a black mother and children, where Priest kicks the junkie in the head and watches him vomit on the family's floor. In his fine clothes and fancy Rolls Royce convertible Priest has left this world of destitution behind, but although he might dream of entering the white world, he cannot leave the streets. This image of entrapment differs little from that which defined the social horizons of the gangster in the canonical films of the 1930s.

Borrowing its structure of social commentary from *Angels with Dirty Faces*, Goldie's Cagney-like street gangster is matched with his brother Olinga (Roger E. Mosley), a black liberationist — updating Pat O'Brien's streetwise priest and lifetime buddy of Cagney's hoodlum. The film suggests a choice can be made between crime and meaningful social engagement. Adored by the local kids, Goldie gives them money to attend school and makes them promise to work hard so they can become a doctor or lawyer but not a pimp. The Cagney/Warner Bros. borrowings are further developed in Goldie's cloying love for his mother (he buys her a swank apartment overlooking a marina). However, following Goldie's fall from grace, the ending of the film pulls back from completely emulating its model. Legitimate representatives of law and order, who are anyway entirely absent from the film, do not punish Goldie. He is made to suffer through the murder of his mother, and then, finally having exacted revenge for her death, he is exiled from the community. Penniless, he is last seen riding a Greyhound bus to an unknown destination. His departure is witnessed by his brother, the black power liberationist, who, like Pat O'Brien's priest, assumes an unassailable position of moral authority.

The title of the Fred Williamson vehicle *Black Caesar* makes clear its link with the canonical gangster film *Little Caesar*. Williamson plays Tommy Gibbs, the gimp with a limp, who connives his way from bootblack to becoming king of Harlem by working as a hit man for the mob. The film begins in 1955, when Tommy is a young adolescent earning chump change running errands for a Mafia hit man. When he is caught skimming $50 from a kickback paid to a crooked copper, he is given a severe beating that leaves him crippled in one leg. Having spent time in jail, Tommy reemerges in 1965 and inveigles his way into the Mafia family that runs Harlem's rackets. Sometime later he makes a bid for control of the rackets when he gains ownership of the syndicate's ledgers that detail their transactions with corrupt city officials. Using a white lawyer as his front, his rise from the underworld to success in the world of organized crime is marked when he announces, "Instead of just shaking down the white man, we're going into business with him." Invited to his lawyer's penthouse apartment that overlooks the East Side of New York, he stays beyond the dinner engagement when he buys the apartment and everything in it, clothes, furnishings, paintings, everything. This symbolic appropriation of the white man's property marks the limits of Tommy's success and marks the point of his subsequent decline.

Tommy has acquired the apartment in order to gain approval from his mother, who worked as a maid for his lawyer. She rejects his gift — even Tommy Gibbs's mother would not be welcome in such a place. As she explains to Tommy, "Jewish folk ain't even allowed in here." His mother's rejection coincides with the return of his father, who left his mother when he was called into the services during the Second World War. Since then, Gibbs Sr. has been traveling the South, selling cosmetics; his return justifies a visit to the tenement block where Tommy was raised. All that is left of his old home is rubble surrounded by crumbling derelict buildings. Gibbs Sr. tries to explain his absence, looking back to the effect of the Great Depression, his enlistment, and then taking a chance to get away and make something of himself: "You've never been trapped or not known where to run, or what to hate — twenty years old when I enlisted." What does he do now? His answer: "I travel a lot." The price Gibbs Sr. paid for not returning to his wife and child was to have no home; when Tommy's mother dies, the son, too, has no home.

Although Tommy had cleaned out the Mafia from Harlem, he still has to deal with the corrupt chief of police, the man who broke his leg. While shopping for a gift, Tommy is shot by an assassin. Bleeding profusely he drags himself along the city streets he once walked as if he owned them. His death pangs draw the eyes of passing strangers; in his suffering he becomes an even greater spectacle than when he was at the height of his powers, a point ironically underscored when he passes a cinema playing *The Godfather*. His final act before dying on the rubble of his old home is to first humiliate the chief of police by covering his face with bootblack; filled with hate, Tommy calls him Al Jolson, an Alabamy minstrel, before promising to make him die "like a field nigger." With a cry of "I wanna go home," Tommy staggers toward his death. On the debris of his old tenement home he is beset on by a gang of young black street punks who beat him mercilessly, before robbing him. Like Rico in *Little Caesar* he dies a pathetic death, devoid of glamour or glory. His passing is marked only by the film's final title: "August 20th 1972" — Tommy, like Rico, is now a figure of the past.

The image of the black gangster as a figure from history is worked more fully in two films that offered a supernatural twist on the formula. *Come Back Charleston*

Blue, based on a novel by Chester Himes, is concerned with a police investigation into a series of murders apparently carried out by a deceased 1930s black mobster, Charleston Blue. Charleston's trademark is to leave a blue-steel cutthroat razor beside the body of his victims. In *J. D.'s Revenge* the spirit of a murdered 1940s black hoodlum, J. D. Walker, enters the soul of a young black man studying to pass his law examinations. Like Charleston, J. D.'s preferred form of attack is with a razor. Murdered in a New Orleans slaughterhouse, J. D. erupts into the present like a malignant spirit of a bygone black masculinity. Ike (Glynn Turman) is a likable, well-intentioned, and mildly ambitious young man with dreams of becoming a lawyer. He is in a loving and mutually supportive relationship, yet when J. D. enters his soul, he turns into a mean-spirited, violent man who sexually abuses his girlfriend. Unique among the films discussed here, *J. D.'s Revenge* offers a contrasting world of values to those of the black gangster, one based on middle-class aspirations of a career in one of the professions, of relationships between men and women based on love and trust rather than on commercial exploitation and abuse, and of friendships between men based on notions of comradeship and loyalty rather than on fear and self survival. Nevertheless, the film still clings to the image of the city as a despoiled and corrupt space where no one is safe, not even from the past's gangster ghosts.

Like all the films discussed in this chapter, *J. D.'s Revenge* has a long scene of the characters walking the streets. For approximately eight minutes Ike and his entourage tour the sidewalks and bars of the area around New Orleans's Bourbon Street; the street famous around the world as the cradle of jazz is a neon-lit nightmare of strip joints, sex clubs, and gin mills. It is in one of these clubs that the spirit of J. D. enters Ike during a hypnotist's act. Even with middle-class aspirations to professional status, the street is still the terrain where characters' destinies are fashioned.

As described in the blaxploitation cycle, the urban space of the street initially holds out the promise of escape from the limitations placed on the black underclass, but there is no image of a world that will not ultimately be reclaimed by the city streets. In the final reckoning, ousting the Mafia, or whoever is deemed to control the city streets, is no victory at all because, according to the terms laid down by the films, the street itself cannot be transcended by its black habitués. The fictional city streets of American film in the first half of the 1970s register black experiences and values while utterly limiting those experiences and values to a world exclusively defined and confined by them.

Notes

1. Duncan Campbell, "Gangs of LA," *Guardian supplement,* April 21, 2003, 6–7.
2. Late 1960s and early to mid-1970s auteurist films are often emphatic in their display of sites of cinema exhibition. See, e.g., Peter Bogdanovich's use of the drive-in theater in *Targets* (1967) and of the rural cinema in *The Last Picture Show* (1971); Martin Scorsese's use of John Ford's *The Searchers* and Roger Corman's *The Tomb of Ligeia* (1964) in *Mean Streets* and Travis Bickle's haunting of porn theaters in *Taxi Driver* (1976).

3. *Soul in Cinema: Filming "Shaft" on Location*, documentary accompanying the DVD release of *Shaft* (Warner Home Video, 2000).

4. Will Straw, "Urban Confidential: The Lurid City of the 1950s," in *The Cinematic City*, ed. David B. Clarke (London: Routledge, 1997), 111.

5. Ibid., 113.

6. Richard Maltby, "'Nobody Knows Everything': Post-Classical Historiographies and Consolidated Entertainment," in *Contemporary Hollywood Cinema*, ed. Steve Neale and Murray Smith (London: Routledge, 1998), 21–44.

7. Ibid., 34.

8. Ibid., 43.

9. Cedric J. Robinson, "Blaxploitation and the Misrepresentation of Liberation," *Race and Class* 40, no. 1 (1998): 1–12.

10. Michael Denning, *Mechanic Accents: Dime Novels and Working-Class Culture in America* (London: Verso, 1997), 200.

11. René Crevel, "Battlegrounds and Commonplaces," in *The Shadow and Its Shadow: Surrealist Writings on the Cinema*, ed. Paul Hammond (San Francisco: City Lights, 2000), 57.

12. David Reid and Jayne L. Walker, "Strange Pursuit: Cornell Woolrich and the Abandoned City of the Forties," in *Shades of Noir*, ed. Joan Copjec (London: Verso, 1993), 74.

13. Nicholas Lemann, *The Promised Land: The Great Black Migration and How It Changed America* (London: Macmillan, 1991), 6.

14. William Julius Wilson, *The Truly Disadvantaged: The Inner-City, the Underclass, and Public Policy* (Chicago: University of Chicago Press, 1990), 3.

15. Ibid., 20–63; and Lemann, *Promised Land*, 199.

16. Wilson, *Truly Disadvantaged*, 22–23.

17. Lemann, *Promised Land*, 172.

18. Ibid., 190.

19. Elliott Currie, *Reckoning: Drugs, the Cities, and the American Future* (New York: Hill and Wang, 1994).

20. *Spooks* as a derogatory term for blacks is used in *Taxi Driver*: "Some won't take spooks — Hell, don't make no difference to me."

21. *It's Alive* (1974) is a particularly notable example of this horror trend. Key science fiction films of the period also represented the American city through a dystopian filter. Charlton Heston's two starring vehicles *The Omega Man* (1971) and *Soylent Green* (1973) spring readily to mind, along with the reductio ad absurdum of the picture of inner-city deprivation in John Carpenter's *Escape from New York* (1981).

22. Paul Schrader, *Taxi Driver* (London: Faber and Faber, 2000), 26.

23. Ibid., 36–37.

24. "Basically, the American mayor's statement revealed a general phenomenon that was just beginning to hit the capital cities as well as the provincial towns and hamlets, the phenomenon of obligatory introversion in which the City sustained the first effects of a multinational economy modeled along the lines of industrial enterprises, a real urban redeployment which soon contributed to the gutting of certain worker cities such as Liverpool and Sheffield in England, Detroit and Saint Louis in the United States, Dortmund in West Germany, and all at the very moment in which other areas were being built up, around tremendous international airports, a METROPLEX, a metropolitan complex such as Dallas/Fort Worth" (Paul Virilio, "The Overexposed City," in *The Blackwell City Reader*, ed. Gary Bridge and Sophie Watson [Oxford: Blackwell, 2002], 440).

25. Richard Slotkin writes that the "reversible analogy between workers and savages is the most significant new term in the language of American mythology after the [Civil] war" (Richard Slotkin, *The Fatal Environment: The Myth of the Frontier in the Age of Industrialization, 1800–1890* (New York: Atheneum, 1985), 311. See also Marcus Klein, *Easterns, Westerns, and Private Eyes: American Matters, 1870–1900* (Madison: University of Wisconsin Press, 1994), 105–108.

26. Rob Shields, "Fancy Footwork: Walter Benjamin's Notes on Flanerie," in *The Flaneur*, ed. Keith Tester (London: Routledge, 1994), 69, 71.

27. Schrader, *Taxi Driver*, 1.

28. Edward Buscombe, *The Searchers* (London: British Film Institute, 2000), 68.

29. Walter Benjamin, "The Return of the Flaneur," in *Selected Writings: Volume 2, 1927–1934* (Cambridge, Mass.: Harvard University Press, 1999), 264.

30. Ibid., 263.

Notes on Contributors

GIORGIO BERTELLINI is an assistant professor in the Film and Video Studies Program and in the Department of Romance Languages and Literatures at the University of Michigan. Author of *Emir Kusturica* (Il Castoro, 1996) and editor of *The Cinema of Italy* (Wallflower Press, 2004), he has published extensively on silent cinema and race. He is completing a book on southern Italians' film experience and representation in Italy and New York City at the turn of the twentieth century.

LEE GRIEVESON is the director of the Graduate Program in Film Studies at University College London. He is author of *Policing Cinema: Movies and Censorship in Early-Twentieth-Century America* (University of California Press, 2004) and coeditor, with Peter Kramer, of *The Silent Cinema Reader* (Routledge, 2004). He is currently working on a coedited collection on the history of film studies.

RICHARD MALTBY is a professor of Screen Studies and head of the School of Humanities at Flinders University, South Australia. Before moving to Australia in 1997, he was the founding director of the Bill Douglas Centre for the History of Cinema and Popular Culture at the University of Exeter and then research professor of Film Studies at Sheffield Hallam University. His publications include *Hollywood Cinema*, 2nd ed. (Blackwell's, 2003), *Dreams for Sale: Popular Culture in the Twentieth Century* (Harrap and Oxford University Press, 1989), and a series of books on Hollywoods audiences coedited with Melvyn Stokes. He is the series editor of Exeter Studies in Film History. With Ruth Vasey he is currently writing *Reforming the Movies: Politics, Censorship, and the Institutions of the American Cinema, 1908–1939*.

JONATHAN MUNBY is director and senior lecturer in American Studies, Institute for Cultural Research, Lancaster University, U.K. Research areas include the cultural history of American cinema, African American popular culture, transatlantic exile, and theories of popular culture. His publications include *Public Enemies, Public*

Heroes: Screening the Gangster from "Little Caesar" to "Touch of Evil" (University of Chicago Press, 1999) and "The 'No' to the Great American 'Yes': Hollywood's Criminal Representation of Organised Crime, 1929–1951," in *Crime and Hollywood Incorporated*, ed. Françoise Clary and John Dean (Publications de l'Universite de Rouen, 2003). He is currently completing a new book, *Stagger Lee to Gangsta* (on African American criminal self-representation in American popular culture since 1890), for the University of Chicago Press.

MARTHA P. NOCHIMSON is the creator and current director of the Mercy College Film Studies Program. She is the author of *No End to Her: Soap Opera and the Female Subject* (University of California Press, 1993); *The Passion of David Lynch: Wild at Heart in Hollywood* (University of Texas Press, 1997); and *Screen Couple Chemistry: The Power of 2* (University of Texas Press, 2002). She is a frequent contributor to *Cineaste* and *Film Quarterly* and a member of the Advisory Board of the Columbia Film Seminar. She is now working on a book about gangster films in Hollywood and Hong Kong.

ESTHER SONNET is head of media at the University of Portsmouth. She has considerable experience teaching in undergraduate, postgraduate, and doctoral programs in film, television, media, and cultural studies. Her doctoral thesis examined the histories and practice of European and American film avant-gardes of the twentieth century in relation to modern and postmodern philosophies of visual epistemology. Her research is underpinned by analysis of the gender politics of cinema: she has an extensive range of publications in journals, edited collections, and encyclopedias in the areas of cinema, popular fiction, feminism, postfeminism, and sexuality. She is currently extending research into women, crime, and (hetero-)sexual transgression in a study of Hollywood production cycles of the 1930s.

PETER STANFIELD is a senior lecturer in Film Studies at the University of Kent at Canterbury. His primary area of interest is film genres and cycles in American cinema. He has published two books on the western: *Hollywood, Westerns, and the 1930s: The Lost Trail* (University of Exeter Press, 2001) and *Horse Opera: The Strange History of the Singing Cowboy* (University of Illinois Press, 2002). His latest book is *Body and Soul: Jazz, Blues, and Race in American Film, 1927–63* (University of Illinois Press, 2005). He is currently writing a book on the films of Anthony Mann.

MARY ELIZABETH STRUNK defended her dissertation, "'The Girl behind the Man behind the Gun': Women Outlaws, Public Memory, and the Rise and Fall of Hoover's FBI," at the University of Minnesota in 2003. She is now a part-time faculty member in Syracuse University's English Department, where she teaches classes in popular culture and film.

GAYLYN STUDLAR is Rudolf Arnheim Collegiate Professor of Film Studies at the University of Michigan, Ann Arbor, where she has directed the Program in Film and Video Studies since 1995. She is the author of *This Mad Masquerade: Stardom and Masculinity in the Jazz Age* (Columbia University Press, 1996) and *In the Realm of Pleasure: Von Sternberg, Dietrich, and the Masochistic Aesthetic* (Columbia University Press, 1992), as well as the coeditor of four anthologies, most recently, with Matthew Bernstein, *John Ford Made Westerns: Filming the Legend in the Sound Era* (Indiana University Press, 2001). She is currently working on a book dealing with female transition in classical Hollywood cinema.

RONALD W. WILSON is an independent scholar residing in Lawrence, Kansas. He has written essays and reviews for *Film History, Film and History, Film Quarterly, Literature/Film Quarterly, Journal of Popular Film and Television, Film International,* and *Scope: An Online Journal of Film Studies.* His primary interest in film is genres and motion picture exhibition history. He has contributed essays to *Film Genre 2000* (SUNY Press, 2000), *The Encyclopedia of Stage Plays into Film* (Facts on File, 2001), and *The Columbia Companion to American History on Film* (Columbia University Press, 2004). He also served as coeditor and contributor to *The Encyclopedia of Filmmakers* (Facts on File, 2002). He is currently researching the heist film genre and is also working on a book concerning the history of the Interstate Theatre Circuit of Texas.

Index